Conflict, Order & Action

Second Edition

edited by
Ed Ksenych and David Liu

Canadian Scholars' Press   Toronto   1996

Conflict, Order and Action
Readings in Sociology, Second Edition
Edited by Ed Ksenych and David Liu

First Published in 1996 by
Canadian Scholars' Press Inc.
180 Bloor Street West, Ste. 402
Toronto, Ontario
M5S 2V6

Original material copyright © 1996 Canadian Scholars' Press
and the editors. All rights reserved. No reproduction, copy or
transmission of this publication may be made without written permission.

Canadian Cataloguing in Publication Data

Main entry under title:
Conflict, order and action: readings in sociology

2nd ed.
Includes bibliographical references.
ISBN 1-55130-096-6

1. Sociology. I. Ksenych, Edward, 1950– .
II. Liu, David, 1957– .

HM51.C5947   1996   301   C96-931392-6

Page layout and cover design by Brad Horning

Table of Contents

Acknowledgements vii

Introduction ix

Section One: Sociological Perspectives

1. Social Interaction in Times Square
   Vernon Boggs and William Kornblum 2

2. The Promise
   C. Wright Mills 5

3. Science and the Disenchantment of the World
   Max Weber 13

4. Precontractual Solidarity
   Emile Durkheim 21

5. Alienated Labour
   Karl Marx 25

6. Sex and Destiny
   Germaine Greer 29

Section Two: Culture

7. Sharing the Continent
   Northrop Frye 40

8. Body Ritual Among the Nacirema
   Horace Miner 51

9. Anti-Semite and Jew
   Jean Paul Sartre 56

10. Television: The Shared Arena
    Joshua Meyrowitz 64

Section Three: Action and Interaction

11 Society as Symbolic Interaction
    Herbert Blumer 82

12 Tacit Coordination
    Thomas C. Schelling 92

13 Laughter in the Clinic: Humor as Social Organization
    William C. Yoels and Jeffrey Michael Clair 101

14 The Black Male in Public
    Elijah Anderson 113

Section Four: Socialization

15 Historical Emergence of Children and Child's Play
    Gregory P. Stone 126

16 Behavioural Study of Obedience
    Stanley Milgram 130

17 Equality to Benefit from Schooling: The Issue of Educational Opportunity
    Stephen Richer 146

18 The Professionalization of Medical Students: Developing Competence and a Cloak of Competence
    Jack Haas and William Shaffir 157

Section Five: Work and Organizations

19 The Educational Implications of Our Technological Society
    James Turk 170

20 Life in a Fast-Food Factory
    Ester Reiter 178

21 Is There a Future for the Canadian Labour Movement?
    Mary Lou Coates 185

Section Six: Social Inequality

22 Poverty in Canada
    National Council of Welfare 196

23 Who Owns Canada?
    Edward G. Grabb 208

24 And So They Were Wed
   Lillian Breslow Rubin 221

25 Ideology and Social Organization
   M. Patricia Marchak 238

Section Seven: Gender

26 Sex, Lies and Conversation: Why Is It so Hard for Men and Women to Talk to Each Other?
   Deborah Tannen 250

27 Woman's Place in Man's Life Cycle
   Carol Gilligan 255

28 Men as Success Objects and Women as Sex Objects
   Simon Davis 267

29 The Language of Sex: The Heterosexual Questionnaire
   M. Rochlin 276

Section Eight: Family

30 Old Order Mennonites Provide Support While at the Same Time Preserving the Independence of Their Elderly
   John B. Bond, Jr. 280

31 Thinking About the Future
   Meg Luxton 285

32 The Family
   Claude Levi-Strauss 305

Section Nine: Deviance and Social Control

33 The Criminal Justice System
   Laureen Snider 322

34 Subterranean Processes in the Maintenance of Power: An Examination of the Mechanisms Coordinating Police Action
   Clifford D. Shearing 337

35 Wife Battering in Canada
   Linda MacLeod 350

36 The Body of the Condemned
   Michel Foucault 359

Section Ten: Social Change

37 English Society Before and After the Coming of Industry
    Peter Laslett 372

38 Quebec and the Canadian Question
    Hubert Guindon 378

39 The Dissolution of the Self
    Kenneth Gergen 394

40 Jihad vs. McWorld
    Benjamin R. Barber 403

Appendix: Field Projects

1 Observation
   Jacqueline Aaron and Marcia Wiseman 416

2 Participant Observation
   Jacqueline Aaron and Marcia Wiseman 422

3 The Depth Interview
   Jacqueline Aaron and Marcia Wiseman 428

4 Role Analysis
   Jacqueline Aaron and Marcia Wiseman 434

5 Content Analysis
   Jacqueline Aaron and Marcia Wiseman 442

Acknowledgements

We would like to thank Jack Wayne and Brad Lambertus of Canadian Scholars' Press for their ongoing support and guidance in this project, and to commend them for maintaining their commitment to the value of liberal education and scholarship. We would also like to thank the following for their helpful comments and suggestions: Brenda Bennett, Patricia Cormack, Jim Cosgrave, Sherri Kimmel, Cathy Boyd-Withers, Ed Hooven, Alja Pirosok, James Moore and Joan Allen.

Introduction

While introductory sociology texts generally provide a useful overview of research, concepts and theories within sociology, they tend to describe sociology rather than exemplify the activity of doing sociological inquiry. This reader is intended to complement introductory texts, and aims to offer students a clearer and livelier sense of the practice of sociology.

The first edition of this book of readings grew out of our experience teaching community college students on the fast track to jobs, primarily in the field of health care. In addition to the very positive responses we received from students, we were delighted to find that several instructors chose to adopt it for a variety of courses at other community colleges and universities. In revising the text we have tried to keep in mind the initial educational interest of deepening students' understanding of sociology in the context of preparing to undertake professional responsibilities, while continuing to encourage an appreciation of the discipline in its own terms.

Pedagogically, the collection of articles reflects a particular approach to teaching that has successfully managed to integrate the practical needs and interests of our students with a desire to expose them to sociology as a form of inquiry. At the centre of this pedagogy is the presentation of familiar topic areas as a series of questions or problems, and sociology as a practice that both generates questions and is brought to bear on the questions it poses.

While some of the articles are particularly relevant to the health care profession, our intention has been to invite students, regardless of their post-secondary program, to examine a broad range of areas and issues in contemporary society. It is our conviction that students need to understand and contend with the dynamics of society at large and its implications for their private and public lives as a whole, rather than just the application of the discipline to a specialized vocational area.

More than half of the following selections are new to this edition. This reflects our ongoing attention to the evolving need of students, teachers and the ever-changing curricular landscape of post-secondary educational institutions.

The readings represent a variety of topic areas, human interests, theoretic approaches and research methods. We have included examples of conflict theory, the structural-functionalist tradition, and the symbolic interactionist perspective as well as contributions of the sociological perspective to cultural studies, black studies and feminist scholarship. In addition we have selected contributions from classical theorists to understanding central problems of modern life, which they have helped to formulate.

The selections vary in complexity. We have continued to find that students enjoy and benefit from diverse and challenging material if they have been appropriately prepared, and are assisted with providing a context for, and connection to, the problem that the author is exploring. Some of the selections have been edited to promote accessibility and conceptual continuity. As a guide, each selection has been prefaced by remarks that serve to highlight important concerns, identify basic questions or suggest an approach to discussing the reading. The reader also includes a section on field projects, which may be done individually or in groups, and several articles have been selected that represent or relate to each project.

Overall, our aim has been to have sociological concepts, theories and research methods come to life through addressing enduring questions surrounding the formation and development of human society. Topic areas, research methods and theoretical orientations are organized here as salient examples, and stepping-off points, for the exploration of social phenomena such as domination and group conflict, social order and change, and human action and the construction of shared meaning.

This reader does not claim to comprehensively cover the field of sociology. It is intended to stand as a resource for introducing students to sociological inquiry and, as such, to serve as an opportunity for both students and teachers to undertake a shared re-examination of their own experiences, conduct and embeddedness in the distinctive web of social relations and meanings we call modern society.

Ed Ksenych and David Liu
Toronto
1996

Section One

Sociological Perspectives

The problems that will interest the sociologist are not necessarily what other people may call "problems".... People comonly speak of a "social problem" when something in society does not work the way it is supposed to work according to official interpretations.... It is important...to understand that a sociological problem is something quite different from a "social problem" in this sense.... The sociological problem is always the understanding of what goes on here in terms of social interaction. Thus the sociological problem is not so much why some things "go wrong" from the viewpoint of the authorities and the management of the social scene, but how the whole system works in the first place, what are its presuppositions and by what means is it held together.

Peter Berger, *Invitation to Sociology*,
Anchor Books/Doubleday, 1963: 36-7.

1
Social Interaction in Times Square

Vernon Boggs and William Kornblum

In this article, Boggs and Kornblum's observations of New York City's Times Square give us a glimpse of sociology's subject matter—the orderly nature of everyday life. Amid the apparently unrelated and disorganized activities of people going about their daily business, the authors show us a clearly defined social structure with demarcated roles and statuses.

A warm summer night on "the Deuce," West Forty-second Street, the southern boundary of Manhattan's theatre district. It is past midnight, and the Broadway audiences are long gone. Dope dealers muttering, "Smoke, smoke," stand in the glare of movie marquees touting *Dirty Radio Sex* and other films. Some alcoholic derelicts—a "bottle gang"—weave along the broad sidewalk, on their way to a darker side street where they can sit and pass a pint. Men in business suits wander in and out of store-fronts whose flashing lights promise pornographic thrills. At the corner of Eighth Avenue, a prostitute begins arguing with her pimp, then tears away and heads east on Forty-second toward the intersection where Seventh Avenue crosses Broadway—the Great White Way—and forms Times Square.

To European and Asian tourists, and to many American out-of-towners as well, such sights are to be expected in any major city. But if the outsider sees Forty-second Street as a place where violent and exotic creatures tear at one another and at a victimized public in a fierce struggle to survive, those who make their homes there experience a way of life that is ordered, predictable, and controlled. There is a human ecology in Times Square that is at least as elaborate and as fascinating as the ecology of the tropical jungle to which the area has often been compared. What appears to be chaos and confusion is actually a complex interaction of social groups, each with its codes and rituals.

Vernon Boggs and William Kornblum, "Social Interaction in Times Square" adapted from "Symbiosis in the City" *The Sciences*, January/February, 1985: 25-30. [As reprinted in Peter Morrill (ed), *Societies: A Cultural Reader*, HarperCollins, 1991.]

The literature of social science has long recognized that great urban centres create "natural areas" like Times Square where very different kinds of people come in contact. Robert Park observed in his seminal 1921 essay "The City," that people come together in cities "not because they are alike, but because they are useful to one another. This is particularly true in great cities, where social distances are maintained in spite of geographical proximity, and where every community is likely to be composed of people who live together in relationships that can best be described as symbiotic rather than social."

Street people are all around Manhattan, but the Times Square area is among the few places where they have staked out territories. Prostitutes, drug dealers, and bottle gangs all have their "strolls," or regularly travelled routes, each with its "stations," or oases of rest. Liquor stores, dark corners, and doorways serve as stations for the alcoholic derelicts who haunt the narrower, less populous side streets. Corners where a waiting woman can pick up a trick are the stations along the prostitutes' stroll on the west side of Eight Avenue, north of Forty-second Street. For the drug peddlers, whose stroll is the Deuce itself, the stations are recesses and courtyards where their transactions can be made out of sight.

Another type of turf is the hustling spot, set up, like a nomad's camp, only when conditions are right. People with a hustle to pull off, such as three-card monte or the con known as the Murphy (an elaborate scheme to persuade the mark to turn over his savings), will not stage such shows along the strolls of those selling drugs or sex. Working in small teams, hustlers ply their trade with an eye always out for "the man," in both his uniformed and plainclothes guises. Periods of stepped-up police work, like times of bad weather, are viewed as natural obstacles to be overcome with cunning and luck.

Different territories in Times Square mark not only different occupations but different levels of status as well. Through the city, street people rank themselves according to a hierarchy. Alcoholics and the mentally ill occupy the bottom rungs. The young men who hustle for their living are further up. And the pimps who set up shop in bars, safe from arrest and other dangers outside, are at the top—in the street world, an admired elite. The members of each of these status groups share rituals and norms learned in prisons and on the mean streets of the city's ghetto neighbourhoods. A prostitute who has chosen a pimp knows she must "give up choosing cake"—turn over a lump sum that the pimp accepts as a kind of dowry. An older man wise in the ways of straight society will be respectfully consulted as a "wisdom brother." Even the gangs of drinkers at the bottom of the hierarchy have rituals to determine who buys a bottle and who drinks from it last. Before anyone takes a swig, a few drops are poured on the pavement, in memory of those who have died or gone to jail.

By far the largest and most complex of these status groups is the hustlers. Hustling in Times Square involves running con games, selling phony jewellery, shoplifting, and a host of other activities requiring good street sense and an aptitude for calculating the risks of arrest, injury, or being taken in by somebody else's "game." Large numbers of passers-by offer a ready market for a wide variety of goods and services that the hustler can provide.

Hustling zones often overlap, and the various players sometimes try to hustle one another. But not all the relationships of hustlers are exploitative. Regulars on the street know and depend on one another. Some drug dealers are related by family ties, others are acquaintances from prison; a number live in the same buildings nearby. Though at a glance it may seem that every hustler on the stroll is fiercely competing with every other, hustlers actually belong to identifiable cliques, whose members can be seen sharing drugs, loaning one another money, and calling out one another's names. They often arrive at a station on their stroll the same time every morning, as if they were going to an entirely routine job.

Though prostitutes, drug dealers, and con men are well dispersed throughout Manhattan, their concentration in Times Square creates a permanent marketplace, the likes of which exists nowhere else in the city. Times Square is more than a home for groups of street people; it is also visited by thousands from the mainstream of society—office workers, garment-district employees, tourists, theatre-goers, retail merchants, restaurateurs, entertainers, and the middle-class and working-class people of Clinton, the residential neighbourhood to the west. Some 113,000 people use the subway stations every day, and another 100,000 arrive at and depart from the bus terminal. Most of these trips occur during the morning and late-afternoon rush hours, but in the evening, too, the area is crowded with people seeking entertainment, from Broadway plays and first-run movies to live sex shows and twenty-five-cent glimpses at silent pornographic shorts. As theatre-goers and seekers of sexual thrills head home and most of the city descends into the dark quiet of the early-morning hours, West Forty-second Street remains one of New York's liveliest streets.

2

The Promise

C. Wright Mills

Mills's introduction to the sociological imagination is an essay to be studied rather than skimmed for information. In it, Mills highlights significant characteristics of the sociological imagination and exercises this imagination in a study of the central issues of contemporary North American society. Some guiding questions for the reader are: What is the sociological imagination? What is the difference between a personal trouble and a public issue? What is the key issue of our times according to Mills? And what are the societal and historical roots of this issue?

Nowadays men often feel that their private lives are a series of traps. They sense that within their everyday worlds, they cannot overcome their troubles, and in this feeling, they are often quite correct: What ordinary men are directly aware of and what they try to do are bounded by the private orbits in which they live; their visions and their powers are limited to the close-up scenes of job, family, neighbourhood; in other milieux, they move vicariously and remain spectators. And the more aware they become, however vaguely, of ambitions and of threats which transcend their immediate locales, the more trapped they seem to feel.

Underlying this sense of being trapped are seemingly impersonal changes in the very structure of continent-wide societies. The facts of contemporary history are also facts about the success and the failure of individual men and women. When a society is industrialized, a peasant becomes a worker; a feudal lord is liquidated or becomes a businessman. When classes rise or fall, a man is employed or unemployed; when the rate of investment goes up or down, a man takes new heart or goes broke. When wars happen, an insurance salesman becomes a rocket launcher; a store clerk, a radar man; a wife lives alone; a child grows up without a father. Neither the life of an individual nor the history of a society can be understood without understanding both.

From *The Sociological Imagination* by C. Wright Mills. Copyright © 1959, 1987 by Oxford University Press, Inc. Renewed 1987 by Yaraslava Mills. Reprinted by permission of the publisher.

Yet men do not usually define the troubles they endure in terms of historical change and institutional contradiction. The well-being they enjoy, they do not usually impute to the big ups and downs of the societies in which they live. Seldom aware of the intricate connection between the patterns of their own lives and the course of world history, ordinary men do not usually know what this connection means for the kinds of men they are becoming and for the kinds of history-making in which they might take part. They do not possess the quality of mind essential to grasp the interplay of man and society, of biography and history, of self and world. They cannot cope with their personal troubles in such ways as to control the structural transformations that usually lie behind them.

Surely it is no wonder. In what period have so many men been so totally exposed at so fast a pace to such earthquakes of change? That Americans have not known such catastrophic changes as have the men and women of other societies is due to historical facts that are now quickly becoming "merely history." The history that now affects every man is world history. Within this scene and this period, in the course of a single generation, one sixth of mankind is transformed from all that is feudal and backward into all that is modern, advanced, and fearful. Political colonies are freed; new and less visible forms of imperialism installed. Revolutions occur; men feel the intimate grip of new kinds of authority. Totalitarian societies rise, and are smashed to bits—or succeed fabulously. After two centuries of ascendancy, capitalism is shown up as only one way to make society into an industrial apparatus. After two centuries of hope, even formal democracy is restricted to a quite small portion of mankind. Everywhere in the underdeveloped world, ancient ways of life are broken up and vague expectations become urgent demands. Everywhere in the overdeveloped world, the means of authority and of violence become total in scope and bureaucratic in form. Humanity itself now lies before us, the super-nation at either pole concentrating its most coordinated and massive efforts upon the preparation of World War Three.

The very shaping of history now outpaces the ability of men to orient themselves in accordance with cherished values. And which values? Even when they do not panic, men often sense that older ways of feeling and thinking have collapsed and that newer beginnings are ambiguous to the point of moral stasis. Is it any wonder that ordinary men feel they cannot cope with the larger worlds with which they are so suddenly confronted? That they cannot understand the meaning of their epoch for their own lives? That—in defence of selfhood—they become morally insensible, trying to remain altogether private men? Is it any wonder that they come to be possessed by a sense of the trap?

It is not only information that they need—in this Age of Fact, information often dominates their attention and overwhelms their capacities to assimilate it. It is not only the skills of reason that they need—although their struggles to acquire these often exhaust their limited moral energy.

What they need, and what they feel they need, is a quality of mind that will help them to use information and to develop reason in order to achieve lucid summations of what is going on in the world and of what may be happening within themselves. It is this quality, I am going to contend, that journalists and scholars, artists and publics, scientists and editors are coming to expect of what may be called the sociological imagination.

I

The sociological imagination enables its possessor to understand the larger historical scene in terms of its meaning for the inner life and the external career of a variety of individuals. It enables him to take into account how individuals, in the welter of their daily experience, often become falsely conscious of their social positions. Within that welter, the framework of modern society is sought, and within that framework the psychologies of a variety of men and women are formulated. By such means the personal uneasiness of individuals is focused upon explicit troubles and the indifference of publics is transformed into involvement with public issues.

The first fruit of this imagination—and the first lesson of the social science that embodies it—is the idea that the individual can understand his own experience and gauge his own fate only by locating himself within his period, that he can know his own chances in life only by becoming aware of those of all individuals in his circumstances. In many ways it is a terrible lesson; in many ways a magnificent one. We do not know the limits of man's capacities for supreme effort or willing degradation, for agony or glee, for pleasurable brutality or the sweetness of reason. But in our time we have come to know that the limits of "human nature" are frighteningly broad. We have come to know that every individual lives, from one generation to the next, in some society; that he lives out a biography, and that he lives it out within some historical sequence. By the fact of his living he contributes, however minutely, to the shaping of this society and to the course of its history, even as he is made by society and by its historical push and shove.

The sociological imagination enables us to grasp history and biography and the relations between the two within society. That is its task and its promise. To recognize this task and this promise is the mark of the classic social analyst. It is characteristic of Herbert Spencer—turgid, polysyllabic, comprehensive; of E.A. Ross—graceful, muckraking, upright; of August Compte and Emile Durkheim; of the intricate and subtle Karl Mannheim. It is the quality of all that is intellectually excellent in Karl Marx; it is the clue to Thorstein Veblen's brilliant and ironic insight, to Joseph Schumpeter's many-sided constructions of reality; it is the basis of the psychological sweep of W.E.H. Lecky no less than of the profundity and clarity of Max Weber. And it is the signal of what is best in contemporary studies of man and society.

No social study that does not come back to the problems of biography, of history and of their intersections within a society has completed its intellectual journey. Whatever the specific problems of the classic social analysts, however limited or however broad the features of social reality they have examined, those who have been imaginatively aware of the promise of their work have consistently asked three sorts of questions:

1) What is the structure of this particular society as a whole? What are the essential components, and how are they related to one another? How does it differ from other varieties of social order? Within it, what is the meaning of any particular feature for its continuance and for its change?

2) Where does this society stand in human history? What are the mechanics by which it is changing? What is its place within and its meaning for the development of humanity as a whole? How does any particular feature we are examining affect, and how is it affected by, the historical period in which it moves? And this period—what are its essential features? How does it differ from other periods? What are its characteristic ways of history-making?

3) What varieties of men and women now prevail in this society and in this period? And what varieties are coming to prevail? In what ways are they selected and formed, liberated and repressed, made sensitive and blunted? What kinds of "human nature" are revealed in the conduct and character we observe in this society in this period? And what is the meaning for "human nature" of each and every feature of the society we are examining?

Whether the point of interest is a great power state or a minor literary mood, a family, a prison, a creed—these are the kinds of questions the best social analysts have asked. They are the intellectual pivots of classic studies of man in society— and they are the questions inevitably raised by any mind possessing the sociological imagination. For that imagination is the capacity to shift from one perspective to another—from the political to the psychological; from examination of a single family to comparative assessment of the national budgets of the world; from the theological school to the military establishment; from considerations of an oil industry to studies of contemporary poetry. It is the capacity to range from the most impersonal and remote transformations to the most intimate features of the human self—and to see the relations between the two. Back of its use there is always the urge to know the social and historical meaning of the individual in the society and in the period in which he has his quality and his being.

That, in brief, is why it is by means of the sociological imagination that men now hope to grasp what is going on in the world, and to understand what is happening in themselves as minute points of the intersections of biography and history within society. In large part, contemporary man's self-conscious view of himself as at least an outsider, if not a permanent stranger, rests upon an absorbed realization of social relativity and of the transformative power of history. The sociological imagination is the most fruitful form of self-consciousness. By its use men whose mentalities have swept only a series of limited orbits often come to feel as if suddenly awakened in a house with which they had only supposed themselves to be familiar. Correctly or incorrectly, they often come to feel that they can now provide themselves orientations. Older decisions that once appeared sound now seem to them products of a mind unaccountably dense. Their capacity for astonishment is made lively again. They acquire a new way of thinking, they experience a transvaluation of values; in a word, by their reflection and by their sensibility, they realize the cultural meaning of the social sciences.

II

Perhaps the most fruitful distinction with which the sociological imagination works is between "the personal troubles of milieu" and "the public issues of social structure." This distinction is an essential tool of the sociological imagination and a feature of all classic work in social science.

Troubles occur within the character of the individual and within the range of his immediate relations with others; they have to do with his self and with those limited areas of social life of which he is directly and personally aware. Accordingly, the statement and the resolution of troubles properly lie within the individual as a biographical entity and within the scope of his immediate milieu—the social setting that is directly open to his personal experience and to some extent his wilful activity. A trouble is a private matter: values cherished by an individual are felt by him to be threatened.

Issues have to do with matters that transcend these local environments of the individual and the range of his inner life. They have to do with the organization of many such milieux into the institutions of an historical society as a whole, with the ways in which various milieux overlap and interpenetrate to form the larger structure of social and historical life. An issue is a public matter: some value cherished by publics is felt to be threatened. Often there is a debate about what that value really is and about what it is that really threatens it. This debate is often without focus if only because it is the very nature of an issue, unlike even widespread trouble, that it cannot very well be defined in terms of the immediate and everyday environments of ordinary men. An issue, in fact, often involves a crisis in institutional arrangements, and often too it involves what Marxists call "contradictions" or "antagonisms."

In these terms, consider unemployment. When, in a city of 100,000, only one man is unemployed, that is his personal trouble, and for its relief we properly look to the character of the man, his skills, and his immediate opportunities. But when in a nation of 50 million employees, 15 million men are unemployed, that is an issue and we may not hope to find its solution within the range of opportunities open to any one individual. The very structure of opportunities has collapsed. Both the correct statement of the problem and the range of possible solutions require us to consider the economic and political institutions of the society, and not merely the personal situation and character of a scatter of individuals.

Consider war. The personal problem of war, when it occurs, may be how to survive it or how to die in it with honour; how to make money out of it; how to climb into the higher safety of the military apparatus; or how to contribute to the war's termination. In short, according to one's values, to find a set of milieux and within it to survive the war or make one's death in it meaningful. But the structural issues of war have to do with its causes; with what types of men it throws up into command; with its effects upon economic and political, family and religious institutions, with the unorganized irresponsibility of a world of nation-states.

Consider marriage. In a marriage a man and a woman may experience personal troubles, but when the divorce rate during the first four years of marriage is 250 out of every 1,000 attempts, this is an indication of a structural issue having to do with the institutions of marriage and the family and other institutions that bear upon them.

Or consider the metropolis—the horrible, beautiful, ugly, magnificent sprawl of the great city. For many upper-class people, the personal solution to "the problem of the city" is to have an apartment with private garage under it in the heart of the city, and forty miles out, a house by Henry Hill, garden by Garrett Eckbo, on a hundred acres of private land. In these two controlled environments—with a small staff at each end and a private helicopter connection—most people could solve many of the problems of personal milieux caused by the facts of the city. But all this, however splendid, does not solve the public issues that the structural fact of the city poses. What should be done with this wonderful monstrosity? Break it all up into scattered units, combining residence and work? Refurbish it as it stands? Or, after evacuation, dynamite it and build new cities according to new plans in new places? What should those plans be? And who is to decide and to accomplish whatever choice is made? These are structural issues; to confront them and to solve them requires us to consider political and economic issues that affect innumerable milieux.

In so far as an economy is arranged that slumps occur, the problem of unemployment becomes incapable of personal solution. In so far as war is inherent in the nation-state system and in the uneven industrialization of the world, the ordinary individual in his restricted milieu will be powerless—with or without psychiatric aid—to solve the troubles this system or lack of system imposes upon him. In so far as the family as an institution turns women into darling little slaves and men into their chief providers and unweaned dependants, the problem of a satisfactory marriage remains incapable of purely private solution. In so far as the overdeveloped megalopolis and the overdeveloped automobile are built-in features of the overdeveloped society, the issues of urban living will not be solved by personal ingenuity and private wealth.

What we experience in various and specific milieux, I have noted, is often caused by structural changes. Accordingly, to understand the changes of many personal milieu we are required to look beyond them. And the number and variety of such structural changes increase as the institutions within which we live become more embracing and more intricately connected with one another. To be aware of the idea of social structure and to use it with sensibility is to be capable of tracing such linkages among a great variety of milieux. To be able to do that is to possess the sociological imagination.

III

What are the major issues for publics and the key troubles of private individuals in our time? To formulate issues and troubles, we must ask what values are cherished yet threatened, and what values are cherished and supported, by the characterizing trends of our period. In the case both of threat and of support we must ask what salient contradictions of structure may be involved.

When people cherish some set of values and do not feel any threat to them, they experience well-being. When they cherish values but do feel them to be threatened, they experience a crisis—either as personal trouble or as public issue. And if all their values seem involved, they feel the total threat of panic.

But suppose people are neither aware of any cherished values nor experience any threat? That is the experience of indifference, which, if it seems to involve all their values, becomes apathy. Suppose, finally, they are unaware of any cherished values, but still are very much aware of a threat? That is the experience of uneasiness, of anxiety, which, if it is total enough, becomes a deadly unspecified malaise.

Ours is a time of uneasiness and indifference—not yet formulated in such ways as to permit the work of reason and the play of sensibility. Instead of troubles—defined in terms of values and threats—there is often the misery of vague uneasiness; instead of explicit issues there is often merely the beat feeling that all is somehow not right. Neither the values threatened nor whatever threatens them has been stated; in short, they have not been carried to the point of decision. Much less have they been formulated as problems of social science.

In the 'thirties there was little doubt—except among certain deluded business circles that there was an economic issue which was also a pack of personal troubles. In these arguments about "the crisis of capitalism," the formulations of Marx and the many unacknowledged re-formulations of his work probably set the leading terms of the issue, and some men came to understand their personal troubles in these terms. The values threatened were plain to see and cherished by all; the structural contradictions that threatened them also seemed plain. Both were widely and deeply experienced. It was a political age.

But the values threatened in the era after World War Two are often neither widely acknowledged as values nor widely felt to be threatened. Much private uneasiness goes unformulated; much public malaise and many decisions of enormous structural relevance never become public issues. For those who accept such inherited values as reason and freedom, it is the uneasiness itself that is the trouble; it is the indifference itself that is the issue. And it is this condition, of uneasiness and indifference, that is the signal feature of our period.

All this is so striking that it is often interpreted by observers as a shift in the very kinds of problems that need now to be formulated. We are frequently told that the problems of our decade, or even the crises of our period, have shifted from the external realm of economics and now have to do with the quality of individual life—in fact with the question of whether there is soon going to be anything that can properly be called individual life. Not child labour but comic books, not poverty but mass leisure, are at the centre of concern. Many great public issues as well as many private troubles are described in terms of "the psychiatric"—often, it seems, in a pathetic attempt to avoid the large issues and problems of modern society. Often this statement seems to rest upon a provincial narrowing of interest to the Western societies, or even to the United States—thus ignoring two-thirds of mankind; often, too, it arbitrarily divorces the individual life from the larger institutions within which that life is enacted, and which on occasion bear upon it more grievously than do the intimate environments of childhood.

Problems of leisure, for example, cannot even be stated without considering problems of work. Family troubles over comic books cannot be formulated as problems without considering the plight of the contemporary family in its new relations with the newer institutions of the social structure. Neither leisure nor its debilitating uses can be understood as problems without recognition of the extent to which malaise and indifference now form the social and personal climate of contemporary American society. In this climate, no problems of "the private life" can be stated and solved without recognition of the crisis of ambition that is part of the very career of men at work in the incorporated economy.

It is true, as psychoanalysts continually point out, that people do often have "the increasing sense of being moved by obscure forces within themselves which they are unable to define." But it is not true, as Ernest Jones asserted, that "man's chief enemy and danger is his own unruly nature and the dark forces pent up within him." On the contrary: "Man's chief danger" today lies in the unruly forces of contemporary society itself, with its alienating methods of production, its enveloping techniques of political domination, its international anarchy—in a word, its pervasive transformations of the very "nature" of man and the conditions and aims of his life.

It is now the social scientist's foremost political and intellectual task—for here the two coincide—to make clear the elements of contemporary uneasiness and indifference. It is the central demand made upon him by other cultural workmen—by physical scientists and artists, by the intellectual community in general. It is because of this task and these demands, I believe, that the social sciences are becoming the common denominator of our cultural period, and the sociological imagination our most needed quality of mind.

3

Science and the Disenchantment of the World

Max Weber

Classical social theorists, such as Weber, continue to be read, not only because they elucidated some of the central principles and problems of the discipline of sociology, but also because they did so through examining major social issues. In this excerpt from "Science as a Vocation" (1918), Weber formulates one of the enduring problems of modern society—the disenchantment of the world that accompanies the rise of science, technology and rationalization. What exactly does Weber mean by the "disenchantment of the world?" How does this disenchantment reflect what is both valuable and problematic about science? In what ways does his analysis continue to be applicable today?

...[S]cience has a fate that profoundly distinguishes it from artistic work. Scientific work is chained to the course of progress; whereas in the realm of art there is no progress in the same sense. It is not true that the work of art of a period that has worked out new technical means, or, for instance, the laws of perspective, stands therefore artistically higher than a work of art devoid of all knowledge of those means and laws....

In science, each of us knows that what he has accomplished will be antiquated in ten, twenty, fifty years. That is the fate to which science is subjected; it is the very *meaning* of scientific work, to which it is devoted in a quite specific sense, as compared with other spheres of culture for which in general the same holds. Every scientific 'fulfilment' raises new 'questions'; it *asks* to be 'surpassed' and outdated.... In principle, this progress goes on *ad infinitum*. And with this we come to inquire into the *meaning* of science. For, after all, it is not self-evident that something subordinate to such a law is sensible and meaningful to itself. Why does one engage in doing something that in reality never comes, and never can come, to an end?...

From *From Max Weber: Essays in Sociology* edited and translated by H.H. Gerth and C. Wright Mills. Copyright © Oxford University Press, Inc.; renewed 1973 by Hans H. Gerth. Reprinted by permission of the publisher.

This questions raises a few general considerations.

Scientific progress is a fraction, the most important fraction, of the process of intellectualization which we have been undergoing for thousands of years and which nowadays is usually judged in such an extremely negative way. Let us first clarify what this intellectualist rationalization, created by science and by scientifically oriented technology, means practically.

Does it mean that we, today, for instance, everyone sitting in this hall, have a greater knowledge of the conditions of life under which we exist than has an American Indian or a Hottentot? Hardly. Unless he is a physicist, one who rides on the streetcar has no idea how the car happened to get into motion. And he does not need to know. He is satisfied that he may 'count' on the behavior of the streetcar, and he orients his conduct according to this expectation; but he knows nothing about what it takes to produce such a car so that it can move. The savage knows incomparably more about his tools. When we spend money today I bet that even if there are colleagues of political economy here in the hall, almost every one of them will hold a different answer in readiness to the question: How does it happen that one can buy something for money—sometimes more and sometimes less? The savage knows what he does in order to get his daily food and which institutions serve him in this pursuit. The increasing intellectualization and rationalization do *not*, therefore, indicate an increased and general knowledge of the conditions under which one lives.

It means something else, namely, the knowledge or belief that if one but wished one *could* learn it at any time. Hence, it means that principally there are no mysterious incalculable forces that come into play, but rather that one can, in principle, master all things by calculation. This means that the world is disenchanted. One need no longer have recourse to magical means in order to master or implore the spirits, as did the savage, for whom such mysterious powers existed. Technical means and calculations perform the service. This above all is what intellectualization means.

Now, this process of disenchantment, which has continued to exist in Occidental culture for millenia, and, in general, this 'progress,' to which science belongs as a link and motive force, do they have any meanings that go beyond the purely practical and technical?...

What is the value of science?

Here the contrast between the past and the present is tremendous. You will recall the wonderful image at the beginning of the seventh book of Plato's *Republic*: those enchained cavemen whose faces are turned toward the stone wall before them. Behind them lies the source of the light which they cannot see. They are concerned only with the shadowy images that this light throws upon the wall, and they seek to fathom their interrelations. Finally one of them succeeds in shattering his fetters, turns around, and sees the sun. Blinded, he gropes about and stammers of what he saw. The others say he is raving. But gradually he learns to behold the light, and then his task is to descend to the cavemen and to lead them to the light. He is the philosopher; the sun, however, is the truth of science, which alone seizes not upon illusions and shadows but upon the true being.

Well, who today views science in such a manner? Today youth feels rather the reverse: the intellectual constructions of science constitute an unreal realm of artificial abstractions, which with their bony hands seek to grasp the blood-and-the-sap of true life without ever catching up with it. But here in life, in what for Plato was the play of shadows on the walls of the cave, genuine reality is pulsating; and the rest are derivatives of life, lifeless ghosts, and nothing else. How did this change come about?

Plato's passionate enthusiasm in *The Republic* must, in the last analysis, be explained by the fact that for the first time the *concept*, one of the great tools of all scientific knowledge, had been consciously discovered. Socrates had discovered it in its bearing. He was not the only man in the world to discover it. In India one finds the beginnings of a logic that is quite similar to that of Aristotle's. But nowhere else do we find this realization of the significance of the concept. In Greece, for the first time, appeared a handy means by which one could put the logical screws upon somebody so that he could not come out without admitting either that he knew nothing or that this and nothing else was truth, the *eternal* truth that never would vanish as the doings of the blind men vanish. That was the tremendous experience which dawned upon the disciples of Socrates. And from this it seemed to follow that if one only found the right concept of the beautiful, the good, or, for instance, of bravery, of the soul—or whatever—that then one could also grasp its true being. And this, in turn, seemed to open the way for knowing and for teaching how to act rightly in life and, above all, how to act as a citizen of the state; for this question was everything to the Hellenic man, whose thinking was political throughout. And for these reasons one engaged in science.

The second great tool of scientific work, the rational experiment, made its appearance at the side of this discovery of the Hellenic spirit during the Renaissance period. The experiment is a means of reliably controlling experience. Without it, present-day empirical science would be impossible. There were experiments earlier; for instance, in India physiological experiments were made in the service of ascetic yoga technique; in Hellenic antiquity, mathematical experiments were made for purposes of war technology; and in the Middle Ages, for purposes of mining. But to raise the experiment to a principle of research was the achievement of the Renaissance. They were the great innovators in *art*, who were the pioneers of experiment. Leonardo and his like and, above all, the sixteenth-century experimenters in music with their experimental pianos were characteristic. From these circles the experiment entered science, especially through Galileo, and it entered theory through Bacon; and then it was taken over by the various exact disciplines of the continental universities, first of all those of Italy and then those of the Netherlands.

What did science mean to these men who stood at the threshold of modern times? To artistic experimenters of the type of Leonardo and the musical innovators, science meant the path to *true* art, and that meant for them the path to true *nature*. Art was said to be raised to the rank of a science, and this meant at the same time and above all to raise the artist to the rank of the doctor, socially and with reference to the meaning of his life. This is the ambition on which, for instance, Leonardo's sketch book was based. And today? 'Science as the way to nature' would sound like blasphemy to youth. Today, youth proclaims the opposite: redemption from the intellectualism of science in order to return to one's own nature and therewith to nature in general. Science as a way to art? Here no criticism is even needed.

But during the period of the rise of the exact sciences one expected a great deal more. If you recall Swammerdam's statement, 'Here I bring you the proof of God's providence in the anatomy of a louse,' you will see what the scientific worker, influenced (indirectly) by Protestantism and Puritanism, conceived to be his task: to show the path to God. People no longer found this path among the philosophers, with their concepts and deductions. All pietist theology of the time, above all Spener, knew that God was not to be found along the road by which the Middle Ages had sought him. God is hidden, His ways are not our ways, His thoughts are not our thoughts. In the exact sciences, however, where one could physically grasp His works, one hoped to come upon the traces of what He planned for the world. And today? Who—aside from certain big children who are indeed found in the natural sciences—still believes that the findings of astronomy, biology, physics, or chemistry could teach us anything about the *meaning* of the world? If there is any such 'meaning,' along what road could one come upon its tracks? If these natural sciences lead to anything in this way, they are apt to make the belief that there is such a thing as the 'meaning' of the universe die out at its very roots.

And finally, science as a way 'to God'? Science, this specifically irreligious power? That science today is irreligious no one will doubt in his innermost being, even if he will not admit it to himself. Redemption from the rationalism and intellectualism of science is the fundamental presupposition of living in union with the divine.... The only thing that is strange is the method that is now followed: the spheres of the irrational, the only spheres that intellectualism has not yet touched, are now raised into consciousness and put under its lens. For in practice this is where the modern intellectualist form of romantic irrationalism leads. This method of emancipation from intellectualism may well bring about the very opposite of what those who take to it conceive as its goal.

After Nietzsche's devastating criticism of those 'last men' who 'invented happiness,' I may leave aside altogether the naive optimism in which science—that is, the technique of mastering life which rests upon science—has been celebrated as the way to happiness. Who believes in this?—aside from a few big children in university chairs or editorial offices. Let us resume our argument.

Under these internal presuppositions, what is the meaning of science as a vocation, now after all these former illusions, the 'way to true being,' the 'way to true art,' the 'way to true nature,' the 'way to true God,' the 'way to true happiness,' have been dispelled? Tolstoi has given the simplest answer, with the words: 'Science is meaningless because it gives no answer to our question, the only question important for us: "What shall we do and how shall we live?"' That science does not give an answer to this is indisputable. The only question that remains is the sense in which science gives 'no' answer, and whether or not science might yet be of some use to the one who puts the question correctly.

Today one usually speaks of science as 'free from presuppositions.' Is there such a thing? It depends upon what one understands thereby. All scientific work presupposes that the rules of logic and method are valid; that these are the general foundations of our orientation in the world; and, at least for our special question, these presuppositions are the least problematic aspect of science. Science further presupposes that what is yielded by scientific work is important in the sense that it is 'worth being known.' In this, obviously, are contained all our problems. For this presupposition cannot be proved by scientific means. It can only be *interpreted* with reference to its ultimate meaning, which we must reject or accept according to our ultimate position towards life.

Furthermore, the nature of the relationship of scientific work and its presuppositions varies widely according to their structure. The natural sciences, for instance, physics, chemistry, and astronomy, presuppose as self-evident that it is worth while to know the ultimate laws of cosmic events as far as science can construe them. This is the case not only because with such knowledge one can attain technical results but for its own sake, if the quest for such knowledge is to be a 'vocation.' Yet this presupposition can by no means be proved. And still less can it be proved that the existence of the world which these sciences describe is worth while, that it has any 'meaning,' or that it makes sense to live in such a world. Science does not ask for the answers to such questions.

...Natural science gives us an answer to the question of what we must do if we wish to master life technically. It leaves quite aside, or assumes for its purposes, whether we should and do wish to master life technically and whether it ultimately makes sense to do so....

Finally, you will put the question: 'If this is so, what then does science actually and positively contribute to practical and personal "life"?' Therewith we are back again at the problem of science as a 'vocation.'

First, of course, science contributes to the technology of controlling life by calculating external objects as well as man's activities....

Second, science can contribute...methods of thinking, the tools and the training for thought....

Fortunately, however, the contribution of science does not reach its limit with this. We are in a position to help you to a third objective: to gain *clarity*. Of course, it is presupposed that we ourselves possess clarity. As far as this is the case, we can make clear to you the following:

In practice, you can take this or that position when concerned with a problem of value—from simplicity's sake, please think of social phenomena as examples. *If* you take such and such a stand, then, according to scientific experience, you have to use such and such a *means* in order to carry out your conviction practically. Now, these means are perhaps such that you believe you must reject them. Then you simply must choose between the end and the inevitable means. Does the end 'justify' the means? Or does it not? The teacher can confront you with the necessity of this choice. He cannot do more, so long as he wishes to remain a teacher and not to become a demagogue. He can, of course, also tell you that if you want such and such an end, then you must take into the bargain the subsidiary consequences which according to all experience will occur. Again we find ourselves in the same situation as before. These are still problems that can also emerge for the technician, who in numerous instances has to make decisions according to the principle of the lesser evil or of the relatively best. Only to him one thing, the main thing, is usually given, namely, the end. But as soon as truly 'ultimate' problems are at stake for us this is not the case. With this, at long last, we come to the final service that science as such can render to the aim of clarity, and at the same time we come to the limits of science.

Besides we can and we should state: In terms of its meaning, such and such a practical stand can be derived with inner consistency, and hence integrity, from this or that ultimate *weltanschauliche* position. Perhaps it can only be derived from one such fundamental position, or maybe from several, but it cannot be derived from these or those other positions. Figuratively speaking, you serve this god and offend the other god when you decide to adhere to this position. And if you remain faithful to yourself, you will necessarily come to certain final conclusions that subjectively make sense. This much, in principle at least, can be accomplished. Philosophy, as a special discipline, and the essentially philosophical discussions of principles in the other sciences attempt to achieve this. Thus, if we are competent in our pursuit (which must be presupposed here) we can force the individual, or at least we can help him, to give himself an *account of the ultimate meaning of his own conduct*. This appears to me as not so trifling a thing to do, even for one's own personal life. Again, I am tempted to say of a teacher who succeeds in this: he stands in the service of 'moral' forces; he fulfils the duty of bringing about self-clarification and a sense of responsibility. And I believe he will be the more able to accomplish this, the more conscientiously he avoids the desire personally to impose upon or suggest to his audience his own stand.

This proposition, which I present here, always takes its point of departure from the one fundamental fact, that so long as life remains immanent and is interpreted in its own terms, it knows only of an unceasing struggle of gods with one another. Or speaking directly, the ultimately possible attitudes toward life are irreconcilable, and hence their struggle can never be brought to a final conclusion. Thus it is necessary to make a decisive choice. Whether, under such conditions, science is a worth while 'vocation' for somebody, and whether science itself has an objectively valuable 'vocation' are again value judgments about which nothing can be said in the lecture-room. To affirm the value of science is a presupposition for teaching there. I personally by my very work answer in the affirmative, and I also do so from precisely the standpoint that hates intellectualism as the worst devil, as youth does today, or usually only fancies it does. In that case the word holds for these youths: 'Mind you, the devil is old; grow old to understand him.' This does not mean age in the sense of the birth certificate. It means that if one wishes to settle with this devil, one must not take to flight before him as so many like to do nowadays. First of all, one has to see the devil's ways to the end in order to realize his power and his limitations.

Science today is a 'vocation' organized in special disciplines in the service of self-clarification and knowledge of interrelated facts. It is not the gift of grace of seers and prophets dispensing sacred values and revelations, nor does it partake of the contemplation of sages and philosophers about the meaning of the universe. This, to be sure, is the inescapable condition of our historical situation. We cannot evade it so long as we remain true to ourselves. And if Tolstoi's question recurs to you: as science does not, who is to answer the question: 'What shall we do, and, how shall we arrange our lives?' or, in the words used here tonight: 'Which of the warring gods should we serve? Or should we serve perhaps an entirely different god, and who is he?' then one can say that only a prophet or a savior can give the answers. If there is no such man, or if his message is no longer believed in, then you will certainly not compel him to appear on this earth by having thousands of professors, as privileged hirelings of the state, attempt as petty prophets in their lecture-rooms to take over his role. All they will accomplish is to show that they are unaware of the decisive state of affairs; the prophet for whom so many of our younger generation yearn simply does no exist. But this knowledge in its forceful significance has never become vital for them. The inward interest of a truly religious 'musical' man can never be served by veiling to him and to others the fundamental fact that he is destined to live in a godless and prophetless time by giving him the *ersatz* of the armchair prophecy. The integrity of his religious organ, it seems to me, must rebel against this....

The fate of our times is characterized by rationalization and intellectualization and, above all, by the 'disenchantment of the world.' Precisely the ultimate and most sublime values have retreated from public life either into the transcendental realm of mystic life or into the brotherliness of direct and personal human relations. It is not accidental that our greatest art is intimate and not monumental, nor is it accidental that today only within the smallest and intimate circles, in personal human situations, in *pianissimo*, that something is pulsating that corresponds to the prophetic *pneuma*, which in former times swept through the great communities like a firebrand, welding them together. If we attempt to force and to 'invent' a monumental style in art, such miserable monstrosities are produced as the many monuments of the last twenty years. If one tries intellectually to construe new religions without a new and genuine prophecy, then, in an inner sense, something similar will result, but with still worse effects. And academic prophecy, finally, will create only fanatical sects but never a genuine community.

To the person who cannot bear the fate of the times like a man, one must say: may he rather return silently, without the usual publicity build-up of renegades, but simply and plainly. The arms of the old churches are opened widely and compassionately for him. After all, they do not make it hard for him. One way or another he has to bring his 'intellectual sacrifice'—that is inevitable. If he can really do it, we shall not rebuke him. For such an intellectual sacrifice in favor of an unconditional religious devotion is ethically quite a different matter than the evasion of the plain duty of intellectual integrity, which sets in if one lacks the courage to clarify one's own ultimate standpoint and rather facilitates this duty by feeble relative judgments. In my eyes, such religious return stands higher that the academic prophecy, which does not clearly realize that in the lecture-rooms of the university no other virtue holds but plain intellectual integrity. Integrity, however, compels us to state that for the many who today tarry for new prophets and saviors, the situation is the same as resounds in the beautiful Edomite watchman's song of the period of exile that has been included among Isaiah's oracles:

> He calleth to me out of Seir, Watchman, what of the night?
> The watchman said, The morning cometh, and also the night:
> if ye will enquire, enquire ye: return, come.

The people to whom this was said has enquired and tarried for more than two millenia, and we are shaken when we realize its fate. From this we want to draw the lesson that nothing is gained by yearning and tarrying alone, and we shall act differently. We shall set to work and meet the 'demands of the day,' in human relations as well as in our vocation. This, however, is plain and simple, if each finds and obeys the demon who holds the fibers of his very life.

4

Precontractual Solidarity

Emile Durkheim

In this excerpt from The Division of Labour *(1893), Durkheim examines the fundamental question of sociological inquiry: What makes society possible? Durkheim challenges the prevailing view that self-interested humans create society by rationally entering into exchanges, or "social contracts," which they believe will be mutually beneficial. This "utilitarian" view, which continues to be popular in North America today, fails to express a simple question: If every exchange is an implied or expressed contract, why would anyone trust another to live up to his or her commitment to the contract, given the primacy of individual self-interest? Durkheim claims this utilitarian view does not actually explain human society but already assumes it. If this is so, what is the basis of human sociality and human society, according to Durkheim's systematic theoretical analysis?*

It is true that in the industrial societies...social harmony comes essentially from the division of labor.[1] It is characterized by a co-operation which is automatically produced through the pursuit by each individual of his own interests. It suffices that each individual consecrate himself to a special function in order, by the force of events, to make himself solidary with others....

But if...[we have] justly noted what the principal cause of social solidarity in higher societies is...[we have] misunderstood the manner in which this cause produces its effect....

[How does this social solidarity actually occur? Herbert Spencer and others argue it is the result of contractual relations.]

As Spencer says, all industrial affairs take place through the medium of free exchange, and this relation becomes predominant in society in so far as individual society becomes dominant.[3] But the normal form of exchange is the contract....

Reprinted with permission of The Free Press, a division of Simon & Schuster from *The Division of Labour in Society* by Emile Durkheim, translated by George Simpson. Copyright © 1933 the Macmillan Company; 1964 by The Free Press.

The hypothesis of a social contract is irreconcilable with the notion of the division of labor. The greater the part taken by the latter, the more completely must Rousseau's postulate be renounced. For in order for such a contract to be possible, it is necessary that, at a given moment, all individual wills direct themselves toward the common bases of the social organization, and, consequently, that each particular conscience pose the political problem for itself in all its generality. But that would make it necessary for each individual to leave his special sphere, so that all might equally play the same role, that of statesman and constituents. Thus, this is the situation when society makes a contract: if adhesion is unanimous, the content of all consciences is identical. Then, in the measure that social solidarity proceeds from such a cause, it has no relation with the division of labor.

Nothing, however, less resembles the spontaneous automatic solidarity which, according to Spencer, distinguishes industrial societies....

Thus, the conception of a social contract is today difficult to defend, for it has no relation to the facts. The observer does not meet it along his road, so to speak. Not only are there no societies which have such an origin, but there is none whose structure presents the least trace of a contractual organization. It is neither a fact acquired through history nor a tendency which grows out of historical development....

[If solidarity were based solely on social contract] social solidarity would then be nothing else than the spontaneous accord of individual interests, an accord of which contracts are the natural expression. The typical social relation would be the economic, stripped of all regulation and resulting from the entirely free initiative of the parties. In short, society would be solely the stage where individuals exchanged the products of their labor, without any action properly social coming to regulate this exchange.

Is this the character of societies whose unity is produced by the division of labor? If this were so, we could with justice doubt their stability. For if interest relates men, it is never for more than some few moments. It can create only an external link between them. In the fact of exchange the various agents remain outside of each other, and when the business has been completed, each one retires and is left entirely on his own. Consciences are only superficially in contact; they neither penetrate each other, not do they adhere. If we look further into the matter, we shall see that this total harmony of interests conceals a latent or deferred conflict. For where interest is the only ruling force each individual finds himself in a state of war with every other since nothing comes to mollify the egos, and any truce in this eternal antagonism would not be of long duration. There is nothing less constant than interest. Today, it unites me to you; tomorrow, it will make me your enemy. Such a cause can only give rise to transient relations and passing associations. We now understand how necessary it is to see if this is really the nature of organic solidarity....

To be sure, when men unite in a contract, it is because, through the division of labor, either simple or complex, they need each other. But in order for them to co-operate harmoniously, it is not enough that they enter into a relationship, nor even that they feel the state of mutual dependence in which they find themselves. It is still necessary that the conditions of this co-operation be fixed for the duration of their relations. The rights and duties of each must be denied, not only in view of the situation such as it presents itself at the moment when the contract is made, but with foresight for the circumstances which may arise to modify it. Otherwise, at every instant, there would be conflicts and endless difficulties. We must not forget that, if the division of labor makes interests solidary, it does not confound them; it keeps them distinct and opposite. Even as in the internal workings of the individual organism each organ is in conflict with others while co-operating with them, each of the contractants, while needing the other, seeks to obtain what he needs at the least expense; that is to say, to acquire as many rights as possible in exchange for the smallest possible obligations.

It is necessary therefore to pre-determine the share of each, but this cannot be done according to a preconceived plan. There is nothing in the nature of things from which one can deduce what the obligations of one or the other ought to be until a certain limit is reached. Every determination of this kind can only result in compromise. It is a compromise between the rivalry of interests present and their solidarity. It is a position of equilibrium which can be found only after more or less laborious experiments. But it is quite evident that we can neither begin these experiments over again nor restore this equilibrium at fresh expense every time that we engage in some contractual relation. We lack all ability to do that. It is not at the moment when difficulties surge upon us that we must resolve them, and, moreover, we can neither foresee the variety of possible circumstances in which our contract will involve itself, nor fix in advance with the aid of simple mental calculus what will be in each case the rights and duties of each, save in matters in which we have a very definite experience. Moreover, the material conditions of life oppose themselves to the repetition of such operations. For, at each instant, and often at the most inopportune, we find ourselves contracting, either for something we have bought, or sold, somewhere we are traveling, our hiring or one's services, some acceptance of hostelry, etc. The greater part of our relations with others is of a contractual nature. If, then, it were necessary each time to begin the struggles anew, to again go through the conferences necessary to establish firmly all the conditions of agreement for the present and the future, we would be put to rout. For all these reasons, if we were linked only by their terms of our contracts, as they are agreed upon, only a precarious solidarity would result.

But contract-law is that which determines the juridical consequences of our acts that we have not determined. It expresses the normal conditions of equilibrium, as they arise from themselves or from the average. A résumé of numerous, varied experiences, what we cannot foresee individually is there provided for, what we cannot regulate is there regulated, and this regulation imposes itself upon us, although it may not be our handiwork, but that of society and tradition. It forces us to assume obligations that we have not contracted for, in the exact sense of the word, since we have not deliberated upon them, not even, occasionally, had any knowledge about them in advance. Of course, the initial act is always contractual, but there are consequences, sometimes immediate, which run over the limits of the contract. We co-operate because we wish to, but our voluntary co-operation creates duties for us that we did not desire....

Endnotes

[1] *Principles of Sociology*, III, pp. 332 ff....
[2] *Principles of Sociology*, II, p. 160....

5

Alienated Labour

Karl Marx

There are few statements that capture the lived experience of a problem with such analytic force as Karl Marx's characterization of alienated labour, published in 1844. Marx's formulation of this ongoing problem of modern life centres on how work is generally organized and conducted in the world that emerged in the wake of industrialization and the rise of capitalism. What are the major features of alienated labour to which Marx directs our attention? Why is understanding the activity and structure of work so important for comprehending how men and women experience human society more generally?

We have proceeded from the presuppositions of political economy. We have accepted its language and its laws. We presupposed private property, the separation of labor, capital and land, hence of wages, profit of capital and rent, likewise the division of labor, competition, the concept of exchange value, etc. From political economy itself, in its own words, we have shown that the worker sinks to the level of commodity, the most miserable commodity; that the misery of the worker is inversely proportional to the power and volume of his production; that the necessary result of competition is the accumulation of capital in a few hands and thus the revival of monopoly in a more frightful form; and finally that the distinction between capitalist and landowner, between agricultural laborer and industrial worker, disappears and the whole society must divide into the two classes of *proprietors* and *propertyless* workers.

Political economy proceeds from the fact of private property. It does not explain private property. It grasps the actual, *material* process of private property in abstract and general formulae which it then takes as *laws*. It does not *comprehend* these laws, that is, does not prove them as proceeding from the nature of private property. Political economy does not disclose the reason for

From *Writings of the Young Marx on Philosophy and Society*, ed. and trans. Loyd D. Easton and Kurt H. Guddat (Garden City, NY: Doubleday, 1967), pp. 287-296. Reprinted with permission of Loyd D. Easton and Mrs. Kurt H. Guddat.

the division between capital and labor, between capital and land. When, for example, the relation of wages to profits is determined, the ultimate basis is taken to be the interest of the capitalists; that is, political economy assumes what it should develop. Similarly, competition is referred to at every point and explained from external circumstances. Political economy teaches us nothing about the extent to which these external, apparently accidental circumstances are simply the expression of a necessary development. We have seen how political economy regards exchange itself as an accidental fact. The only wheels which political economy puts in motion are *greed* and the *war among the greedy, competition*....

We now have to grasp the essential connection among private property, greed, division of labor, capital and land ownership, and the connection of exchange with competition, of value with the devaluation of men, of monopoly with competition, etc., and of this whole alienation with the *money*-system....

We proceed from a *present* fact of political economy.

The worker becomes poorer the more wealth he produces, the more his production increases in power and extent. The worker becomes a cheaper commodity the more commodities he produces. The *increase in value* of the world of things is directly proportional to the *decrease in value* of the human world. Labor not only produces commodities. It also produces itself and the worker as a *commodity*, and indeed in the same proportion as it produces commodities in general.

This fact simply indicates that the object which labor produces, its product, stands opposed to it as an *alien thing*, as a *power independent* of the producer. The product of labor is labor embodied and made objective in a thing. It is the *objectification* of labor. The realization of labor is its objectification. In the viewpoint of political economy this realization of labor appears as the *diminution* of the worker, the objectification as the *loss of and subservience to the object*, and the appropriation as *alienation [Entfremdung]*, as externalization *[Entäusserung]*.

So much does the realization of labor appear as diminution that the worker is diminished to the point of starvation. So much does objectification appear as loss of the object that the worker is robbed of the most essential objects not only of life but also of work. Indeed, work itself becomes a thing of which he can take possession only with the greatest effort and with the most unpredictable interruptions. So much does the appropriation of the object appear as alienation that the more objects the worker produces, the fewer he can own and the more he falls under the domination of his product, of capital.

All these consequences follow from the fact that the worker is related to the *product of his labor* as to an *alien* object. For it is clear according to this premise: The more the worker exerts himself, the more powerful becomes the alien objective world which he fashions against himself, the poorer he and his inner world become, the less there is that belongs to him. It is the same in religion. The more man attributes to God, the less he retains in himself. The worker puts his life into the object; then it no longer belongs to him but to the object. The greater this activity, the poorer is the worker. What the product of his work is, he is not. The greater this product is, the smaller he is himself. The *externalization* of the worker in his product means not only that his work becomes an object, an *external* existence, but also that it exists *outside him* independently, alien, an autonomous power, opposed to him. The life he has given to the object confronts him as hostile and alien....

Up to now we have considered the alienation, the externalization of the worker only from one side: his *relationship to the products of his labor*. But alienation is shown not only in the result but also in the *process of production*, in the *producing activity* itself. How could the worker stand in an alien relationship to the product of his activity if he did not alienate himself from himself in the very act of production? After all, the product is only the résumé of activity, of production. If the product of work is externalization, production itself must be active externalization, externalization of activity, activity of externalization. Only alienation—and externalization in the activity of labor itself—is summarized in the alienation of the object of labor.

What constitutes the externalization of labor?

First is the fact that labor is *external* to the laborer—that is, it is not part of his nature—and that the worker does not affirm himself in his work but denies himself, feels miserable and unhappy, develops no free physical and mental energy but mortifies his flesh and ruins his mind. The worker, therefore feels at ease only outside work, and during work he is outside himself. He is at home when he is not working and when he is working he is not at home. His work, therefore, is not voluntary, but coerced, *forced labor*. It is not the satisfaction of a need but only a *means* to satisfy other needs. Its alien character is obvious from the fact that as soon as no physical or other pressure exists, labor is avoided like the plague. External labor, labor in which man is externalized, is labor of self-sacrifice, of penance. Finally, the external nature of work for the worker appears in the fact that it is not his own but another person's, that in work he does not belong to himself but to someone else. In religion the spontaneity of human imagination, the spontaneity of the human brain and heart, acts independently of the individual as an alien, divine or devilish act. Similarly, the activity of the worker is not his own spontaneous activity. It belongs to another. It is the loss of his own self.

The result, therefore, is that man (the worker) feels that he is acting freely only in his animal functions—eating, drinking, and procreating, or at most in his shelter and finery—while in his human functions he feels only like an animal. The animalistic becomes the human and the human the animalistic.

To be sure, eating, drinking, and procreation are genuine human functions. In abstraction, however, and separated from the remaining sphere of human activities and turned into final and sole ends, they are animal functions....

We have now to derive the third aspect of *alienated labor* from the two previous ones.

Man is a species-being [*Gattungswesen*] not only in that he practically and theoretically makes his own species as well as that of other things his object, but also—and this is only another expression for the same thing—in that as present and living species he considers himself to be a *universal* and consequently free being....

In alienating (1) nature from man, and (2) man from himself, his own active function, his life activity, alienated labor also alienates the *species* from him; it makes *species-life* the means of individual life. In the first place it alienates species-life and the individual life, and secondly it turns the latter in its abstraction into the purpose of the former, also in its abstract and alienated form.

For labor, *life activity*, and *productive life* appear to man at first only as a *means* to satisfy a need, the need to maintain physical existence. Productive life, however, is species-life. It is life begetting life. In the mode of life activity lies the entire character of a species, its species-character; and free conscious activity is the species-character of man. Life itself appears only as a *means of life*.

The animal is immediately one with its life activity, not distinct from it. The animal is its life activity. Man makes his life activity itself into an object of will and consciousness. He has conscious life activity. It is not determination with which he immediately identifies. Conscious life activity distinguishes man immediately from the life activity of the animal. Only thereby is he a species-being. Or rather, he is only a conscious being — that is, his own life is an object for him—since he is a species-being. Only on that account is his activity free activity. Alienated labor reverses the relationship in that man, since he is a conscious being, makes his life activity, his *essence*, only a means for his *existence*....

By degrading free spontaneous activity to the level of a means, alienated labor make the species-life of man a means of physical existence.

The consciousness which man has from his species is altered through alienation, so that species-life becomes a means for him.

(3) Alienated labor hence turns the *species-existence of man*, and also nature as his mental species-capacity, into an existence *alien* to him, into the *means* of his *individual existence*. It alienates his spiritual nature, his human essence, from his own body and likewise from nature outside him.

(4) A direct consequence of man's alienation from the product of his work, from his life activity, and from his species-existence, is the *alienation of man from man*. When man confronts himself, he confronts *other* men. What holds true of man's relationship to his work, to the product of his work, and to himself, also holds true of man's relationship to other men, to their labor, and the object of their labor.

In general, the statement that man is alienated from his species-existence means that one man is alienated from another just as each man is alienated from human nature.

The alienation of man, the relation of man to himself, is realized and expressed in the relation between man and other men.

Thus in the relation of alienated labor every man sees the other according to the standard and the relation in which he finds himself as a worker....

6

Sex and Destiny

Germaine Greer

This excerpt from Greer's larger study resonates with many of the themes that have characterized the feminist contribution to sociological inquiry—a re-examination of the interplay of nature and culture; the body and the dynamics of reproduction; the issues of power and ideology; the place of language in generating a meaningful, human reality; care for others; and the legitimacy of subjective experience, all from a feminine standpoint. Here, Greer's rigorous argument provokes us to examine the decadence of consumer society and the effect our views and practices have, not only on ourselves, but also on those upon whom we foist our culture and economic development.

"A Child is Born"

In World Population Year, the location chosen for the international conference was Bucharest. The choice was perhaps unfortunate, for the *raison d'être* behind the whole jamboree was fear of the population explosion and the promotion of birth-control programmes. Just the year before the Rumanian government had outlawed abortion and banned the sale of contraceptives, because the decline in population growth and the increasing senility of the population have been construed as a threat to the country's economic future....

The Rumanian example is just one of many which could be cited to show that even the government of totalitarian countries cannot counteract the profound lack of desire for children which prevails in Western society, especially among upwardly mobile social groups.... Historically, babies have been welcome additions to society; their parents derived prestige and joy and satisfaction from their proximity and suffered little or no deterioration in the quality of their lives, which could even have been positively enhanced by the arrival of children.

Germaine Greer. From *Sex and Destiny: The Politics of Human Fertility*, Picador/Martin Secker and Warburg, 1984.

Parents, themselves still relatively junior in the social hierarchy, had no need to cudgel their brains to decide if they were ready for the experience, for they were surrounded by people who watched their reproductive career with passionate interest, who would guide them through the fears and anguish of childbirth and take on a measure of responsibility for child-rearing. Historically, human societies have been pro-child; modern society is unique in that it is profoundly hostile to children. We in the West do not refrain from childbirth because we are concerned about the population explosion or because we feel we cannot afford children, but because we do not like children.

Conventional piety is still such that to say such a thing is shocking. Parents will point angrily to the fact that they do not beat or starve or terrorise their children but struggle to feed, house, clothe and educate them to the best of their ability. Our wish that people who cannot feed, house, clothe and educate their children adequately should not have them is born of our concern for the children themselves, or so most of us would claim. At the heart of our insistence upon the child's parasitic role in the family lurks the conviction that children must be banished from adult society. Babies ought not to be born before they have rooms of their own: when they are born they must adhere to an anti-social time-table. Access to the adult world is severely rationed in terms of time, and in any case what the child enters is not the adult's reality but a sort of no-man's land of phatic communication. Mothers who are deeply involved in exploring and developing infant intelligence and personality are entitled to feel that such a generalisation is unjust, but even they must reflect that they share the infant's ostracised status. No one wants to hear the fascinating things that baby said or did today, especially at a party. Mother realises she is becoming as big a bore as her child, and can be shaken by the realisation. The heinousness of taking an infant or a toddler to an adult social gathering is practically unimaginable; as usual the discomfort and uneasiness are manifested as concern. A baby may be produced and brandished momentarily but then it must disappear, otherwise well-meaners begin cooing about it being time for bed: the more baby chirps and chatters and reaches for necklaces and earrings, the more likely it is to be told that it is a poor little thing....

Adults cannot have fun while kids are around; kids must be "put down" first. Drinking and flirting, the principal expressions of adult festivity, are both inhibited by the presence of children. Eventually our raucousness wakes them and they watch our activities through the stair-rails and learn to despise us. In lieu of our real world we offer them a fake one, the toy world. Parents shocked by some family crisis try to mend the cracks in the nuclear family by dating their children, abjectly courting them. The scale and speed of our world is all anti-child; children cannot be allowed to roam the streets, but must run a terrifying gauntlet to get to the prime locus of their segregation, school. They cannot open doors or windows, cannot see on top of counters, are stifled and trampled in crowds, hushed when they speak or cry before strangers, apologised for by harassed mothers condemned to share their ostracised condition....

If the truth is, we of the industrialised West do not like children, the corollary is equally true, our children do not like us. It is blasphemy to deny that parents love their children (whatever that may mean) but it is nevertheless true that adults do not like children. People of different generations do not consort together as a matter of preference: where a child and an old person develop any closeness, we are apt to suspect the motives of the older person. Most social groupings tend to be formed of individuals in the same age set and social circumstances, and even within the family, parents and children spend very little time in each other's company....

The gulf that yawns between adult society and the world of children in the "Anglo-Saxon" West is by no means universal. There are societies where adults and children laugh at the same jokes, where adults would not dream of eating their evening meal without their children about them and would not inhibit discussion of serious matters because children were present. In fact such societies are still more populous than our own. There are huge cities which are practically run by children, children who support their parents and their brethren by their skills and initiative, where children and adults inhabit the same cruel world and survive by clinging to each other. But these are the societies whose children, we think, should not be born....

Sophisticated Caucasians are a shrinking proportion of all human beings, for reasons which should be becoming obvious. People for whom pregnancy is not a strange and disorienting condition already outnumber us and threaten to do so by an ever-increasing margin. In their societies a woman's body is not the more admired the less of it there is. Even in comparatively sophisticated Tuscany, a woman with a gap between her thighs is called *secca*, dry; the word is the same as is used for dead plants.[1] Only in consumer society is the famished female type admired, partly because it is so rare....

The ways of managing childbirth in traditional societies are many and varied; their usefulness stems directly from the fact that they are accepted culturally and collectively so that the mother does not have the psychic burden of re-inventing the procedure.[2] Even though the potential catastrophes are alive in the memory of her community and the index of anxiety high, a ritual approach to pregnancy which hems the pregnant woman about with taboos and prohibitions helps to make the anxiety manageable. A woman who observes all the prohibitions and carries out all the rites will be actively involved in holding the unknown at bay. She will have other reinforcements, for many of the ritual observances of pregnancy involve the participation of others who should support her, primarily her husband, then her kinfolk and then the other members of her community....

It would be clearly absurd to maintain that traditional childbirth is more efficient than modern obstetric techniques in keeping perinatal mortality to a minimum. Some of the procedures appear instead to be calculated to cull the newborn, such as cutting the umbilical cord with a dirty sickle or branding the infant with a hot iron. People living at subsistence level or below know that there are worse fates than death; slow starvation is a more painful end than extinction on the threshold of life. Traditional societies are aware of a wider range of anguish than we of the cushioned West. At the same time that the child confronts artificial hazards at birth, care is taken to see that nothing threatens the establishment of suckling and lactation. Thus the newborn is not separated from its mother, not "monitored" for twenty-four hours to see that all its systems are functioning and no intervention is required. If such intervention is in fact required, the infant will die....

Childbirth has been transformed from an awesome personal and social event into a medical phenomenon, from a heroic ordeal into a meaningless and chaotic one; physical pain which we can bear has been transformed into mental stress, which we are less well geared for. The management of pregnancy, childbed and child raising was the principal expression of the familial and societal network of women, itself one of the essential cohesive elements in any society and a necessary leaven to the competitive hierarchies of men. The institutionalisation of child production has destroyed this alternative structure. It is largely as an unconscious reaction to this diminution of women's role that women are now exerting such pressure to be allowed into the competitive male hierarchy. It is probably inevitable that such women, who have the considerable advantages of literacy and articulacy, should see in the lives of women sill living in the web of fertility and continuity the meaninglessness and bewilderment that they themselves would experience in such roles in a society that sets no store by them. The women who are active in international organisations are likely to assume that no one who had a choice would go through childbirth more than once or twice and at a relatively advanced age; the women who compile the Knowledge-Attitude-Practice studies, beloved of family planning organisations, noting the correlation between education level and decline in fertility, may be convinced that their "own-society" values are valid for all times and places. The women they are seeking to help might feel sorrier for them than they can well imagine. The majority of the world's women have not simply been entrapped into motherhood: in societies which have not undergone demographic transition, where children are a priceless resource, the role of mother is not a marginal one but central to social life and organisation....

This discussion of the difference in the role of mother in highly industrialised bureaucratic communities and in traditional agricultural communities is not meant as a panegyric for the disappearing world, but simply to indicate something of the context in which the birthrate in the developed world has fallen. There is little point in feeling sorry for Western mothers who are most often as anxious to be freed of their children as their children are to be freed of them. The inhabitants of old people's homes and retirement villages do not sit sobbing and railing against destiny, although they do compete with each other in displaying the rather exiguous proofs of their children's affection. As the recession bites deeper and unemployment rises, more and more adult children are having to remain dependent on their parents, who are lamenting loudly and wondering more vociferously than usual why they let themselves in for such a thankless task as parenting. The point of the contrast is simply to caution the people of the highly industrialised countries which wield such massive economic and cultural sway over the developing world against assuming that one of the things they must rescue the rest of the world from is parenting. That motherhood is virtually meaningless in our society is no ground for supposing that the fact that women are still defined by their mothering function in other societies is simply an index of their oppression. We have at least to consider the possibility that a successful matriarch might well pity Western feminists for having been duped into futile competition with men in exchange for the companionship and love of children and other women.

There is no possibility of return to the family-centred world. Groups of individuals may attempt to live in the electronic age by the values of an earlier time: they may go back to the land, live in artificial extended families, and give birth at home according to rituals they have learned from anthropology books or from Lamaze or Leboyer, but their freedom to do so is itself dependent upon the wealth created by the workers who live in the mobile nuclear families which the communards despise. If they fail in their chosen lifestyle, the safety net of consumer society will catch them: if their home birth goes wrong, they can load the suffering woman into a car and speed down the tarmac road to the nearest hospital. The women giving birth in African or Asian villages cannot telephone for emergency squads to speed to their aid, supposing there existed a road suitable for travelling on at speed. Yet the chances are that women in traditional societies will cling to their own methods, for such methods are among the ways that peoples define themselves. Humane and intelligent planning could devise ways of decreasing perinatal morbidity without destroying the character and significance of the experience, but international aid does not come in such forms. There are too many indications that the impact of our medical technology on traditional mothering has been disastrous, to the point of raising the question of whether it has not been our subconscious intention to discourage parenting among foreigners even more effectively than we have discouraged it among ourselves....

If we turn birth from a climatic personal experience into a personal disaster, it matters little that the result is more likely to be a live child. Women will not long continue to offer up their bodies and minds to such brutality, especially if there is no one at home to welcome the child, to praise the mother for her courage and to help her raise it. In fact peasant communities are more level-headed and sceptical of us and our methods than we realise and they have resisted the intrusion of our chromium-plated technology more successfully than we like to think. They know that death attends too frequently in the traditional birthplace, but they also know that there are worse fates than death. Nevertheless, all that stops our technology from reaching into every hut and hovel is poverty: the cultural hegemony of Western technology is total.

The voices of a few women raised in warning cannot be heard over the humming and throbbing of our machines, which is probably just as well, for if we succeed in crushing all pride and dignity out of child bearing, the population explosion will take care of itself.

The Myth of Overpopulation

...Is the world overpopulated? If I must adopt some position on this pint, it will be a highly compromised one. I have been to old Delhi, as Paul Ehrlich has, but somehow, as usual, I saw the wrong thing. Here follows the apocalyptic vision of Paul Ehrlich, set out on page one of his bestseller, under the heading "The Problem."

> I have understood the population problem intellectually for a long time. I came to understand it emotionally one stinking hot night in Delhi a few years ago. My wife and daughter and I were returning to our hotel in an ancient taxi. The seats were hopping with fleas. The only functional gear was third. As we crawled through the city, we entered a crowded slum area. The temperature was well over 100°F; the air was a haze of dust and smoke. The streets seemed alive with people. People eating, people washing, people sleeping. People visiting, arguing and screaming. People thrusting their hands through the taxi window begging. People defecating and urinating. People clinging to buses. People herding animals. People, people, people, people. As we moved slowly through the mob, hand horn squawking, the dust, noise, heat and cooking fires gave the scene a hellish aspect. Would we ever get to our hotel? All three of us were, frankly, frightened. It seemed that anything could happen—but, of course, nothing did. Old India hands will laugh at our reaction. We were just some over-privileged tourists, unaccustomed to the sights and sounds of India. Perhaps, but since that night I've known the feel of over-population.[3]

This then is the problem that Ehrlich and his paymasters and the gullible public are setting out to solve....

If we exclude the carping about the taxi and the temperature, we are left with people, people, people, people. This slum is rather odd in that there are buses and people herding animals in it, so we might guess that Ehrlich did not get himself inside a real slum, where there is no room for buses, taxis or herds, just huts. What he seems to have seen were settlements. The area was certainly not more crowded that Manhattan at three o'clock on a weekday afternoon: the difference is that in Delhi the people were all at pavement level. If they had been nicely shut up in high-rises Ehrlich would not have troubled his head about them, even if he had heard that most of them were drugging themselves with heroin or alcohol or doctors' substitutes. He saw no drunks, no crazy people, no obese people, either, I'll be bound. If he did, he does not say. He does not say that he saw anyone laughing, or men and women playing with their babies. Some of the smells around those tiny fires, made by burning the tips of scrap wood, were spicy and good. Those people had not come there as a couple, years ago, and multiplied until they filled up the area. If he had been less of a ninny and got out of the taxi to talk to the people (who are better at speaking his language than he is at speaking theirs) he might have found out how they got there.

But no. Intellectual understanding precludes investigation. If he had gone to the shanties, he would have been surprised to find that the earthen floors were swept smooth, that the family possessions, most of the wife's dowry, were neatly hung on poles or standing on a narrow shelf, the brass bowls polished till they shine in the darkness, reflecting every sliver of available light, polished with earth. He did not notice that the people doing their washing-up were not using detergents. Cow dung smoke and dust are hard on the sinuses but they are less deadly than industrial effluent and exhaust fumes, which Dr Ehrlich seems to prefer. He did not notice the complete absence of the United States' principal product, trash. The greatest insult about all these people living shoulder to shoulder, the visible counterpart of the population planner's nightmare, is that they make do with so little. Such low purchasing power is anathema to men of Ehrlich's kidney. He does not tell us how he treated the beggars, whose presence seems to indicate that he did not get very far off the beaten track. If he had gone to some parts of Delhi in 1970 he would have found American teenagers begging to support their drug habit, much as they do in America. Still, one can sympathise, for the good doctor has had himself sterilised after the birth of one daughter; this matter has been made public presumably in order to show the utter sincerity of his preaching of Zero Population Growth, only to have to contemplate the ghastly vision of the world being taken over by thin brown people who eat, wash, defecate and cling to buses in defiance of him.

In order to feel in his bowels the reality of overpopulation Ehrlich had to go to India; others feel it more strongly when they come across discarded aluminium beer cans in the wilderness. If we agree that the world is over-populated we have still to decide what we mean by the term and what the phenomenon consists in. An Indian Paul Ehrlich might see the sudden exponential increase in the global human population as the result of an ecological disaster which happened about five hundred years ago, namely the explosion of Europe. This was not caused by population pressure, although population pressure there was and always will be, but by the demands of the European trade economy....

Whether we believe that the world is over-populated or not depends to some extent on how we think people should live. If we in the West think that only our kind of life is worth living, then clearly the numbers that the earth supports will have to be substantially reduced. The world could become a vast luxury hotel, complete with recreational space for us to hunt and ski and mountaineer in, but it must not be forgotten that our luxurious lifestyle demands the services of a huge number of helots, who cannot be paid so much that they can afford rooms in the hotel for themselves. Like Ricardo, we would like to see the supply of helots kept constant, neither falling so low that we have to take out the trash ourselves or becoming so high that we shake in our shoes fearing insurrection in the compound. The official ideology is that the guests in the hotel create all the wealth; only by the extraordinary efficiency of their wealth-creation are all the rest able to survive by merely drudging in the kitchens and the lavatories and the market gardens. At very little cost to himself the guest creates the wealth which is apportioned to them for these worthless but indispensable and time-consuming activities. If this is so, if the capitalist system is actually the best system for creating wealth ever devised, perhaps it could be made less spectacularly unjust; for example, perhaps the cultivation of inessentials which are regarded as essentials, but for which we will not pay a price commensurate with the human labour that they absorb, should be made illegal. Perhaps we should impose the same penalties on the consumption of sugar, tobacco and tea as we do on heroin, so that people brutalised by this kind of cultivation could go back to farming food crops. Perhaps we should outlaw speculation on commodities, which, if it is a way to maintain a "fair" market price, seems to have got a very odd idea of fairness. When primary producers try to do a little speculation on their own behalf, we quickly decide that speculative buying of commodities is not at all fair, as when the London Metal Exchange closed trading in tin, when it was suspected that the government of Malaysia was bidding to force up the price of a ship-load of tin already on the water.

I don't know how many people the earth can support, and I don't believe that anybody else does either; it can certainly support more people on a low calorie intake than it can on a high calorie intake, but as the world is not a huge soup-kitchen the fact is irrelevant. It is quite probable that the world is overpopulated and has been so for some time but getting into a tizzy about it will not prove helpful. Nothing good can come of fear eating the soul. We cannot take right decisions if we are in a funk. We do not have access to our imagination, if we are convinced that catastrophe lurks just around the corner. We may be living in catastrophe now; perhaps we shall have to adapt to it, or go under. Perhaps catastrophe is the natural human environment, and even though we spend a good deal of energy trying to get away from it, we are programmed for survival amid catastrophe. It is an odd thing that people living precariously have more commitment to the continuity of their line than people safely ensconced in plenty. If this is the case, there is not much we can do about it, for we cannot design a political system which will supply the right proportions of potential catastrophe. If we are to deal with the problem of people at all gracefully, we will have to stop rushing into situations we do not understand encumbered with all kinds of non-solutions. In the past we have tried to avoid this by undertaking all kinds of research, which cost many times what practical help would have cost, and came up with conclusions that were no use to anyone. What does it help to know that when all the statistical correctives are applied to the reproductive histories of a small number of Egyptian women that the death of a child made no difference to overall reproductive performance, did not lead to shorter birth intervals, etc. etc? As we have no plan to kill Egyptian babies, or keep them alive, there is no way we can use this information....

Let us therefore abandon the rhetoric of crisis, for we *are* the crisis. Let us stop wasting energy in worrying about a world crammed with people standing shoulder to shoulder and counting the babies born every minute (one in every five of them a Chinese and just about all of them foreign) and begin to use our imagination to understand how it is that poverty is created and maintained. Let us get to know Lady Poverty up close, so that we lose our phobia about the poor. If we must be afraid, let us rather be afraid that man, the ecological disaster, now has no enemy but his own kind. Rather than being afraid of the powerless, let us be afraid of the powerful, the rich sterile nations, who, whether they be of the Eastern or the Western variety, have no stake in the future. The birth of every unwanted child is a tragedy, for itself and for the unwilling parents, but in spite of all the attention we have given to the matter, more unwanted children are born to us, the rich, than to them, the poor. This may seem a paradox, but the time gives it proof.

Notes

[1] Among the Sande women of Sierra Leone, "The opposite of fat is not thin, but dry, connoting among other things, a dry and barren uterus." C. P. McCormick, "Health, Fertility and Birth in Moyamba District, Sierra Leone" *Ethnography of Fertility and Birth* ed. C. P. McCormick (London, 1982), p. 122.

[2] Although there is very much less literature on pregnancy and childbirth management in other cultures than there would have been if more anthropologists had been women, and women interested in female society, some context for these remarks can be got from H. H. Ploss and M. and P. Bartels, *Woman* trans. E. Dingwall (London, 1935) Vol. 2, *passim*; K. E. Mershon, *Seven plus Seven: Mysterious Life-Rituals in Bali* (New York, 1971); Richard Hessney, "Birth Rites—a Comparative Study", *Eastern Archaeologist*, XXIV, 2, May-August, 1971; Jean Lois Davitz, "Childbirth Nigerian Style", *R.N. Magazine*, IV, March 1972; F. Landa Jocano, "Maternal and Child Care Among the Tagalos in Bay, Laguna, Philippines", *Asian Studies*, VIII, 3 December 1970; Joel Simmons Kahn, "Some Aspects of Vietnamese Domestic and Communal Ritual", unpublished M.Phil. thesis, London School of Economics, 1969; Joyce S. Mitchell, "Life and Birth in New Guinea" *Ms*, I, May, 1973, pp. 21-3; "Rites de la Naissance", *France-Asie* XII, March-May 1956; Helen Gideon, "A Baby is Born in the Punjab", *American Anthropology*, LXIV, pp. 1220-1234.

[3] Paul Ehrlich, *The Population Bomb* (London, 1971).

Section Two

Culture

Culture is a blank space, a highly respected, empty pigeonhole. Economists call it "tastes" and leave it severely alone. Most philosophers ignore it—to their own loss. Marxists treat it obliquely as ideology or superstructure, psychologists avoid it by concentrating on child subjects. Historians bend it any way they like. Most believe it matters, especially travel agents.

Mary Douglas

7

Sharing the Continent

Northrop Frye

The underlying premise of this article is that a culture is the consequence of a people's history and an encounter with their geography. Canadians are curiously indifferent to their own history and, as such, their culture remains continually invisible to them. In this essay Northrop Frye develops the idea of "Canadian identity" and some of the artistic, economic, political and geographic forces which have shaped and continue to shape it. Part of the particular character of Canada is the result of having to "share the continent" with the United States. Canada's continual comparison with, and increasing resemblance to, the U.S. raises the question of what is worth preserving and whether we have the means or collective will to do it.

Practically all Canadians have friends or relatives in the United States, and have spent a good deal of time there. Hence it is generally assumed, in both countries, that English-speaking Canadians, at least, cannot be told apart from Americans. This was a view that I held myself until I spent a couple of years in England as a student. Then I realized that there was a difference, but I found it hard to put the difference into words, and because our civilization is tied up in words, we are apt to think that whatever we can't verbalize is unreal. After that, I began an academic career, and have taught briefly at several American universities. My American students often ask me if I notice much difference between teaching them and teaching Canadians in Toronto. They usually expect the answer to be no, but my answer is yes. Here is, perhaps, something that it is possible to put into words. American students have been conditioned from infancy to think of themselves as citizens of one of the world's great powers. Canadians are conditioned from infancy to think of themselves as citizens of a country of uncertain identity, a confusing past, and a hazardous future. Nine-tenths of the

---

"Sharing the Continent" from *Divisions of a Ground* by Northrop Frye. Copyright © Stoddart Publishing Co. Limited, in association with the House of Anansi Press, 1982: 57-70.

time the responses of my American students are identical with those of Canadian students, but the tenth time I know that I'm in a foreign country and have no idea what the next move is. The sensation must be rather similar to that of a Dane in Germany or a Finn in Russia; or, on a smaller scale, of a Welshman in England. What I should like to try to do here is to define the areas of likeness and of difference a little more precisely. The history and the geography of the two countries have been so different that the cultural response to them has to be different too.

I begin with the geographical differences. Some years ago I first saw Herbert Marcuse's *One Dimensional Man* in a bookshop, and what came into my mind was a quite irrelevant reflection: "I wonder what he'd say if he had to live in a one-dimensional country?" For Canada, through most of its history, has been a strip of territory as narrow as Chile, besides being longer and more broken up. In the United States, the general historical pattern has been based on a north-south axis with a western frontier that moved gradually across mountains and rivers and prairies to the Pacific. In Canada there is a single gigantic east-west thrust down the St. Lawrence, up the Great Lakes, and across the prairies, then through whatever holes a surveyor could find in the Rockies to the west coast. Consider the emotional difference between coming to the United States by ship from England and coming to Canada. The United States presents a fairly symmetrical coastline, with relatively few islands, apart from a minor group in the mouth of the Hudson, and one is reminded of the old remark about Columbus' discovering America: "How could he have missed it?" One enters Canada through the Strait of Belle Isle in the Gulf of St. Lawrence, where five Canadian provinces surround us, with enormous islands and glimpses of a mysterious mainland in the distance, but in the foreground only sea and sky. Then we go down to waterway of the St. Lawrence, which in itself is only the end of a chain of rivers and lakes that starts in the Rockies. The United States confronts the European visitor; Canada surrounds and engulfs him, or did until the coming of the airplane.

In the United States, the frontier has been, imaginatively; an open-ended horizon in the west; in Canada, wherever one is, the frontier is a circumference. Every part of Canada is shut off by its geography, British Columbia from the prairies by the Rockies, the prairies from the Canadas by the immense hinterland of northern Ontario, Quebec from the Maritimes by the upthrust of Maine, the Maritimes from Newfoundland by the sea. A generation ago, Hugh MacLennan took a phrase from Rilke, "two solitudes," as the title for a novel about the mutual isolation of English and French in Montreal. But everywhere in Canada we find solitudes touching other solitudes: every part of Canada has strong separatist feelings, because every part of it is in fact a separation. And behind all these separations lies the silent north, full of vast rivers, lakes and islands that, even yet, very few Canadians have ever seen. The Mississippi, running north to south through the middle of the country, is a symbol of the American frontier and its steady advance into the sunset. The largest river in Canada, the Mackenzie, pouring slightly into the Arctic Ocean at what seems the end of the earth, is a symbol of the terra incognita in Canadian consciousness, or what Rupert Brooke called the "unseizable virginity" of the Canadian landscape. Or, as another British visitor, Wyndham Lewis, remarked: "This monstrous, empty habitat must continue to dominate this nation psychologically, and so culturally."

In looking at two countries as closely related as Canada and the United States, no difference is unique or exclusive: we can point to nothing in Canada that does not have a counterpart, or many counterparts, south of its border. What is different is a matter of emphasis and of degree. In the United States exploration and the building of railways have naturally been of central importance in the imagination of the country. In Canada they have been obsessive. The Confederation of 1867 depended on the building of a railway from one ocean to the other: the political necessity to keep the CPR entirely within Canada meant that the railway had to be built in the face of almost unimaginable natural obstacles. The CPR remained a private corporation, but the great difficulty of establishing communication in Canada meant that Canada became accustomed very soon to nationalized railways, broadcasting corporations, film boards, air lines, and similar efforts of deficit financing. Canadian culture has reflected the same preoccupations. The first wave of exploration was mainly religious and economic, carried on by missionaries and voyageurs and fur-traders, along with the explorers who worked in their interests. The second wave was technological and scientific, an age of railway building and geological surveys. The third wave was cultural, and was spearheaded by painters, from the earliest travelling and military artists of the nineteenth century, Krieghoff, Paul Kane, Thomas Davies, to the Group of Seven and their contemporaries a generation ago.

A strong documentary interest in painting, in films, even in literature, is an obvious and distinctive feature of Canadian culture, and it follows the tradition of the early explorers and missionaries, of the Jesuit Relations and the reports of the Hudson's Bay Company. But it is painting in particular that expresses this interest: painting, the art that began in the deep caves of palaeolithic times, has always had something of an unborn world about it, the projecting on nature of colours in the dark, this last phrase being the title of a Canadian play by James Reaney. Painting is in the front line of imaginative efforts to humanize a non-human world, to fight back, in a sparsely-settled country, against a silent otherness that refuses to assimilate to anything human.

A fascination with landscape is the dominant feature of Canadian painting down to about 1930. Even in later and more abstract painters, Riopelle, for example, it seems to me that there is a strong basis of landscape in the underlying vision. The exploring and pioneering aspect of this is clearest in Tom Thomson, Emily Carr, and the Group of Seven, where we are still very largely in the Canada of the blazed trail and the canoe. The painter keeps shifting our eye from the foreground into the opening in the woods, the bend of the river, the break through the distant hills. The use of expressionist and fauve techniques, with powerful colour-contrasts exploding against one another, suggests a natural world that is unconscious of man and is absorbed in an internecine battle of titans. In historical perspective another element emerges which is much more sinister than simply the unblinking stare of a stark "solemn land," as H.E.H MacDonald called one of his best known paintings. Just as, in a crowded country like Great Britain, the practice of archaeology is a matter of keeping one jump ahead of the bulldozer, so these precious records of nature in her "unspoiled" loveliness of snow and rock and red sumach and maple seem to be hastily jotted notes of a hunted refugee, set down before civilization arrives and turns the scene into one more garbage dump.

Literature during this period did not fare so well as painting, because this long-range perspective in literature is very apt to turn rhetorical, in a rather bad sense. Thus Charles G.D. Roberts:

> Awake, my country, the hour is great with change!
> Under this gloom which yet obscures the land,
> From ice-blue strait and stern Laurentian range
> To where giant peaks our western bounds command,
> A deep voice stirs...
> ("An Ode for the Canadian Confederacy")

I quote this because it is typical of what made so much Canadian poetry of a century ago immature and colonial. The poet is not expressing his feelings but talking about the feelings he thinks he ought to have, and the clue to his poetic insincerity is the remote surveying vision that is really focused on nothing but a map. In other contexts this kind of rhetoric turns didactic, as in Bliss Carman's rather forced praises of the strenuous life. No poets of this period gave us the sense of an inward struggling nature that Thomson and Emily Carr do, except for some brilliant flashes in one writer, Isabella Crawford, who died unknown at 37. English-Canadian poetry had to wait for E.J. Pratt to convey the real sense of this centrifugal and linear rhythm in Canadian life. His themes are those that are most closely connected with this rhythm; the martyrdom of the Jesuit missionaries, the building of the CPR, the stories of whale hunts and shipwrecks that bring out the sense of a beleaguered and surrounded garrison.

I have been speaking of one direction in the Canadian imagination; the direction that followed the east-west Laurentian movement and responded emotionally to the national motto *a mari usque ad mare*. This was both a romantic and a conservative movement: romantic because it sought the new and the unknown, conservative because its original impetus was in Europe. The Confederation that took shape around a transcontinental railway was part of a global chain of communication that started in London and linked together all the pieces of an empire on which the sun never set. But as settlement to the country advanced, a more longitudinal and north-south consciousness developed. This perspective focused on the American connection rather than the British Empire, and tended to see the country as a series of northern spurs of the United States. When I was growing up in the Maritime provinces during the nineteen-twenties, there was a strong political loyalty to Confederation, but an even stronger sense that Boston was our real capital, and that the Maritimes formed the periphery of New England, or what was often called "the Boston states." In the nineteenth century, at least, the Liberal party reflected the north-south North American outlook, as the Conservative party reflected the Laurentian one.

Once again it is painting that gives us the clearest sense of the contrast. If we turn from the Group of Seven to the Quebec landscape painters, to Maurice Cullen, Suzor-Côté, Clarence Gagnon and the very little of Morrice that was done in Canada, we are in a world of softer and gentler outlines where the sense of being lived in shows through. The painter's eye is more restricted and at the same time more precise. The landscape is receding from a human eye, not absorbed in itself. Quebec is the only part of Canada which has been settled long enough for a sense of imaginative digestion, so to speak, to emerge. When E.J. Pratt spoke of a kind of poetry he disapproved of, a poetry that avoided social issues and cultivated an easy self-indulgence, he described it in the pictorial metaphor of "still life." In his use of this phrase there is, perhaps, something of that odd fear of catching nature's eye that is very characteristic of that stage in Canadian development. It is significant, first, that the best still-life painter in the earlier period, Ozias Leduc, lived and died in Quebec, and, second, that the still-life perspective, where the imagination has completely surrounded the subject, begins to emerge rather later than the Group of Seven, with David Milne, and further west, Lemoine Fitzgerald.

What has been gradually revealed in this development is the fact that cultural movements are different in direction and rhythm from political and economic ones. Politically and economically, the current of history is toward greater unity, and unity in this context includes uniformity. Technology is the most dramatic aspect of this development: one cannot take off in a jet plane and expect a radically different way of life in the place where the plane lands. But culture has something vegetable about it, something that increasingly needs to grow from roots, something that demands a small region and a restricted locale. The fifty states of the Union are not, in themselves, a cultural entity: they are a political and economic entity that provides a social background for a great variety of cultural developments. We speak for convenience of American literature, but its real cultural context usually turns out to be something more like Mississippi or New England or Chicago or an expatriate group in Paris. Even in the much smaller Great Britain we have Thomas Hardy largely confined to "Wessex," Dylan Thomas to South Wales, D.H. Lawrence to the Midlands. Similarly in Canada: as the country has matured, more and more of its local areas have come to life imaginatively.

This fact has given French Canadian writers, in particular, one considerable advantage. The French Canadian poet or novelist knows that he is contributing to the articulateness of a beleaguered language, hence he need have no doubt about his social function or the importance of being a writer in such a situation. He has no competitors closer than European France, and they live in a very different social context. The English Canadian writer has not had this advantage, and the tedium of a permanent identity crisis has afflicted English Canada for a century. Soon after the Second World War, French Canada entered what has been called the quiet revolution, an awareness of belonging both to itself and to the modern world, which shook off most of the isolating features that had been previously restricting its cultural life. I think it was partly a response to the French act of self-definition that made for a sudden and dramatic emergence of English Canadian culture after about 1960. Since then there has been a tremendous cultural explosion, in literature and painting particularly, which has produced a mood that is often called cultural nationalism.

This is a most misleading phrase, and for two reasons. First nationalism suggests something aggressive, like a nineteenth-century jingoist waiting for the next war to start, or a twentieth-century third-world revolutionary. But culture in itself seeks only its own identity, not an enemy: hostility only confuses it. Second, contemporary Canadian culture, being a culture, is not a national development but a series of regional ones, what is happening in British Columbia being very different from what is happening in New Brunswick or Ontario. Even there we find an increasing decentralization: one reason why Montreal has been so lively a cultural centre is that there are a good many Montreals, each one with its own complexities and inner conflicts. Then again, while a certain amount of protection may be needed for Canadian writers and artists, cultural products are export products. If we look at, say, the literature that has come out of Ireland during the last century, we can see that culture, like a grain or wine crop, is produced in a local area but is not necessarily consumed there.

Politically, economically and technologically, the world is uniting; Canada is in the American orbit and will remain so for the foreseeable future. Canadians could not resist that even if they wanted to, and not many of them do want to. Culturally, both nations should run their own show, and the way to run a cultural show is to let a thousand flowers bloom, in Mao's phrase. Things go wrong when cultural developments are hitched on to economic or technological ones. That gives us, on this continent, a sub-culture dominated by advertising and distributed through the mass media. The influence of this in our lives is often spoken of, both inside and outside the United States, as an Americanizing influence. Ten years ago, during the centenary of Confederation, a sour little joke was circulating in Canada to the effect that what had been aimed at in Canada was a combination of British political institutions, American economic buoyancy and French culture, and that what we had, after a century, was French politics, British economic buoyancy, and American culture. However, the growth of an anonymous, mass-produced, mindless sub-culture is American only to the extent that the United States is the world's most highly industrialized society. Its effect on genuine American culture is quite as lethal as its effect everywhere else, and its main features are as Japanese or German or Russian as they are American.

Things go wrong in the opposite direction when economic or political developments are hitched on to cultural ones, as has happened in the Quebec separatist movement. It is a part of M. Levesque's sales pitch to speak of separation as inevitable, and to compare it with the American Revolution. It seems to me a retrograde and counter-historical movement, both in its neocolonial attitude to France and in its arrogant attitude to French Canadians outside Quebec. As for the American analogy, what was of permanent importance there was not the separation from Britain but the principle of *e pluribus unum*: politically and economically, the colonies had to unite, though culturally there was no reason why Massachusetts and Virginia should not be quite different. Separatism in Quebec is an intellectuals' movement, a *trahison des clercs*: it has dominated the communications media for some years, and by-passes economic issues with a simple emotional construct in which Confederation equals bondage and separation freedom. As an intellectuals' movement, even a revolutionary one, it may settle for a purely symbolic separation: if it goes beyond that, whatever is distinctive in the culture of Quebec will be its first casualty.

My reasons for thinking so take me into the second group of conditioning differences from the United States, the historical ones. The pattern of Canadian history has been almost the opposite of the pattern of American history. The United States had a War of Independence against a European power in the eighteenth century, and a civil war on its own soil a century later. Canada had a civil war of European powers on its own soil in the eighteenth century, and a movement of independence against its American partner in the nineteenth. This started with the invasion of 1775 and continued in the war of 1812, which had very little point as a war with Britain, but was in many respects a war of independence for Canada. I discover that Americans, while they know about the bombardment of Washington and the battle of New Orleans, are often hardly aware that this war involved Canada at all, much less that the bombardment of Washington was a reprisal for the burning of what is now Toronto. All through the nineteenth century, up to and beyond Confederation, there continued to be a certain edginess about the aggressive expansion of America, as it came through in Fenian raids and boundary disputes, and Confederation itself completed what the American invasions had begun, the sense that there was an identity on the north side of the border that could be brought into being only by some kind of political unity.

Another historical contrast is even more important. The United States reached its peak of articulateness in the latter part of the eighteenth century, the age when it became a nation, the age of Washington, Adams, Jefferson, and Franklin.

The United States is today the oldest country in the world: that is, no other nation has lasted so long with so relatively little social change. The party now in power is the world's oldest political party, and the American flag is one of the world's oldest flags. Canada, by contrast, had no eighteenth century. It started with the expansion of French Canada in the seventeenth century, and started again with the influx of defeated Tories into Ontario and the Maritimes after the Revolution, going directly from Baroque to Romantic expansion, but never achieving the moment of self-definition that the United States achieved.

It would be a great mistake to exaggerate the strength of the British connexion in Canada, even in the nineteenth century. There was a great deal of superficial loyalty, or at least a good many expressions of it, but there was also much resentment, and a feeling that colonials would have been treated with more respect in London if, like Americans, they had represented an independent nation. Some years ago a book appeared in Quebec called *White Niggers of America*, meaning the French Canadians, an expression of strong separatist feelings in Quebec, but the same metaphor had been used over a century earlier by the deeply conservative Haliburton of Nova Scotia, who makes his Sam Slick remark that a colonial and a freed black slave differed in nothing but colour: they had theoretical rights but no power to enforce them.

It would, I think, make for a clearer sense of Canada if we thought of it, not as British North America, but as a country that grew out of a Tory opposition to the Whig victory in the American Revolution, thus forming, in a sense, something complementary to the United States itself. This may sound like a very English-based view of Canadian history, but I am not sure that it is. Not long after the British conquest came the French Revolution with its strongly anti-clerical bias. The clergy remained the ideologically dominant group in Quebec down to a generation ago, and the clergy wanted no part of the French Revolution or anything it stood for. Quebec still flies the pre-revolutionary flag of lilies. Nor, from that clergy's point of view, was the American Revolution really so different from the French one. But apart from the clerical influence, French Canada had excellent and foresighted reasons for accepting a conservative modus vivendi which, from the Quebec Act in the eighteenth century to Confederation in the nineteenth, had as its central idea the uniting of a French and an English community on a basis that guaranteed some cultural integrity for both.

Historically, the Tories stood for the supremacy of the crown and the established church, and for a society closely connected with the land. Conservatives in both Britain and Canada are called Tories, but the real Tories were pre-Conservative: they revolved around a domestic economy and a personal relationship to the working class that was destroyed by the Industrial Revolution. Expressions of Canadian opposition to American ideology, all through the nineteenth century, attack from the left quite as often as from the right. One writer, in 1841, spoke of "the United States, where from the great mixture of races, British feelings and British connexion have given way before a flood of undefinable notions about liberty and equality, mixed with aristocratic wealth, slavery, and bigotry in religion." I quote this not because it is profound but because it is commonplace; and we notice that what the writer dislikes is not only American democracy but American oligarchy, the inequalities of wealth and opportunity. It is not surprising, then, that so many of Canada's intellectuals, both English and French, should be one form or another of Tory radical. One of these, and also one of the ablest commentators on the Canadian scene, George Grant, writes near the end of his *Lament for a Nation*:

> The impossibility of conservatism in our era is the impossibility of Canada. As Canadians we attempted a ridiculous task in trying to build a conservative nation in the age of progress, on a continent we share with the most dynamic nation on earth. The current of modern history was against us.

Yet before we write off Canada as an abortive and quixotic culture that has failed to break through the heavy snow-crust of a technological world, it might be worth asking what there is, in this Tory devotion to crown and church and land, that can be translated into terms of the nineteen-seventies. Human ideas have an extraordinary power of metamorphosis, and many things that are outdated or absurd in their original context may reappear later in a very different aspect. For instance, no church has ever been established in Canada, but there has been a much closer connexion between church and state, especially in education, which has given Canadian culture a distinctive colouring. Again, there may be advantages in having the personal symbol of the Queen instead of the impersonal one of the flag, which Canada did not have until recently, and would hardly miss if it still did not. But I think something rather different is involved here, which I shall illustrate by an example. When I first came to Toronto, in 1929, it was a homogeneous Scotch-Irish town, dominated by the Orange Order, and greatly derided by the rest of Canada for its smugness, its snobbery, and its sterility. The public food in restaurants and hotels was of very indifferent quality, as it is in all right-thinking Anglo-Saxon communities. After the war, Toronto took in immigrants to the extent of nearly a quarter of its population, and large Greek, Italian, Portuguese, Central European, West Indian communities grew up within it. The public food improved dramatically. More important, these communities all seemed to find their own place in the larger community with a minimum of violence and tension, preserving much of their own cultures and yet taking part in the total one. It has always seemed to me that this very relaxed absorption of minorities, where there is no concerted effort at a "melting pot," has something to do with what the Queen symbolizes, the separation of the head of state from the head of government. Because Canada was founded by two peoples, nobody could ever know what a hundred percent Canadian was, and hence the decentralizing rhythm that is so essential to culture had room to expand.

Still more important is the Canadian sense of the close relation of the people to the land. Everywhere we turn in Canadian literature and painting, we are haunted by the natural world, and even the most sophisticated Canadian artists can hardly keep something very primitive and archaic out of their imaginations. This sense is not that of the possession of the land, but precisely the absence of possession, a feeling that here is a nature that man has polluted and imprisoned and violated but has never really lived with.

Canada does not have quite so heavy a burden of guilt toward red and black peoples as the United States, and the French record with the Indians was rather better than the British or Spanish record. Even so there is little to be proud of: in Newfoundland, for instance, a gentle and inoffensive people, the Beothuks, were exterminated as casually as though they were mosquitoes. But still the main focus of guilt in Canada seems to fall on the rape of nature. The deaths of animals seems to have an extraordinary resonance in Canadian literature, as though the screams of all the trapped and tortured creatures who built up the Canadian fur trade were still echoing in our minds. One of the silliest of Tory fetishes, the preserving of game, seems to be taking a very different role in the Canadian imagination.

The seventeenth-century invaders of both countries brought with them the Cartesian ego, the sense of man as a perceiving subject, totally different from everything else in nature by virtue of his consciousness. It was a long time before the philosophers got around to realizing that egocentric consciousness is primarily a consciousness of death, but the poets had always known that: even the nineteenth-century rhetorical poets I spoke of wrote their best poetry in elegiac or nostalgic or other moods that were close to the sense of death. The narrative poets gave us stories of death in log jams, on glaciers, in hunting expeditions where the hunter seems to identify with his victim. This was not of course confined to Canada: one thinks of Whitman, who also wrote his best poetry about death and his worst rhetoric about democracy. But it was so strong in Canada as to give most of its serious literature, especially its poetry, a very sombre cast.

In 1948 a group of Quebec artists, headed by Paul-Emile Borduas, produced a surrealist manifesto called *Refus Global*, which seems to me a most important break-through in Canadian culture, not because of what it said, which was naive and confused enough, but because it was a sign that the old antithesis between a conscious mind and an unconscious nature was breaking down. For Borduas, the human mind contained an It as well as an I or ego, and this It was what he felt needed expression. In more recent painting, in the quasi-realism of Alex Colville and Christopher Pratt, in the ghostly figures of Jean-Paul Lemieux, there is often a feeling of loneliness and emptiness, as though the conscious mind were deliberately draining itself of its contents, and waiting for something else to move in. Meanwhile an interest in Indian and Eskimo art, with all their nature-spirits, has grown into a fascination, and many of our younger poets—Susan Musgrave, John Newlove, Gwendolyn MacEwen—write as though Indians and

Eskimos were our direct cultural ancestors whose traditions continue in them and in us. In fiction, there are some curious stories, such as Margaret Atwood's *Surfacing* and Marian Engel's *Bear*, of heroines turning away from their civilized heritage toward an identity with nature. It seems clear that for Canadian culture the old imperialist phrase "going native" has come home to roost. We are no longer an army of occupation, and the natives are ourselves.

The first half of the twentieth century saw a bitter dispute between democratic and Marxist conceptions of the best way to minimize the exploitation of man by man. Nobody seemed to notice that both sides were exploiting nature with equal recklessness. It seems to me that the capitalist-socialist controversy is out of date, and that a detente with an outraged nature is what is important now. Canada is still a place of considerable natural resources, but it is no longer simply a place to be looted, either by Canadians or by non-Canadians. It is of immense importance to the United States itself that there should be other views of the human occupation of this continent, rooted in different ideologies and different historical traditions. And it is of immense importance to the world that a country which used to be at the edge of the earth and is now a kind of global Switzerland, surrounded by all the world's great powers, should have achieved the repatriating of its culture. For this is essentially what has happened in the last twenty years, in all parts of Canada: and what was an inarticulate space on a map is now responding to the world with the tongues and eyes of a matured and disciplined imagination.

8

Body Ritual Among the Nacirema

Horace Miner

In this article Miner takes a satirical look at the 'Nacirema,' a people whose culture is riddled with magic, and whose everyday lives are based in superstition and the supernatural. Miner subtly sensitizes the reader to his or her own ethnocentricity, and presses the reader to recognize that the primitive and the magical are less a matter of specific practices than the assumptions that we draw upon to interpret those practices.

The anthropologist has become so familiar with the diversity of ways in which different peoples behave in similar situations that he is not apt to be surprised by even the most exotic customs. In fact, if all of the logically possible combinations of behaviour have not been found somewhere in the world, he is apt to suspect that they must be present in some yet undescribed tribe. This point has, in fact, been expressed with respect to clan organization by Murdock (1949: 71). In this light, the magical beliefs and practices of the Nacirema present such unusual aspects that it seems desirable to describe them as an example of the extremes to which human behaviour can go.

Professor Linton first brought the ritual of the Nacirema to the attention of anthropologists twenty years ago (1936: 326), but the culture of this people is still very poorly understood. They are a North American group living in the territory between the Canadian Cree, the Yaqui and Tarahumare of Mexico, and the Carib and Arawak of the Antilles. Little is known of their origin, although tradition states that they came from the east. According to Nacirema mythology, their nation was originated by a culture hero, Notgnihsaw, who is otherwise known for two great feats of strength—the throwing of a piece of wampum across the river Pa-To-Mac and the chopping down of a cherry tree in which the Spirit of Truth resided.

Nacirema culture is characterized by a highly developed market economy which has evolved in a rich natural habitat. While much of the people's time is

---

Horace Miner, "Body Ritual Among the Nacirema," *American Anthropologist* 50(3):503-7.

devoted to economic pursuits, a large part of the fruits of these labours and a considerable portion of the day are spent in ritual activity. The focus of this activity is the human body, the appearance and health of which loom as a dominant concern in the ethos of the people. While such a concern is certainly not unusual, its ceremonial aspects and associated philosophy are unique.

The fundamental belief underlying the whole system appears to be that the human body is ugly and that its natural tendency is to debility and disease. Incarcerated in such a body, man's only hope is to avert these characteristics through the use of the powerful influences of ritual and ceremony. Every household has one or more shrines devoted to this purpose. The more powerful individuals in the society have several shrines in their houses and, in fact, the opulence of a house is often referred to in terms of the number of such ritual centres it possesses. Most houses are of wattle and daub construction, but the shrine rooms of the more wealthy are walled with stone. Poorer families imitate the rich by applying pottery plaques to their shrine walls.

While each family has at least one such shrine, the rituals associated with it are not family ceremonies but are private and secret. The rites are normally only discussed with children, and then only during the period when they are being initiated into these mysteries. I was able, however, to establish sufficient rapport with the natives to examine these shrines and to have the rituals described to me.

The focal point of the shrine is a box or chest which is built into the wall. In this chest are kept the many charms and magical potions without which no native believes he could live. These preparations are secured from a variety of specialized practitioners. The most powerful of these are the medicine men, whose assistance must be rewarded with substantial gifts. However, the medicine men do not provide the curative potions for their clients, but decide what the ingredients should be and then write them down in an ancient and secret language. This writing is understood only by the medicine men and by the herbalists who, for another gift, provide the required charm.

The charm is not disposed of after it has served its purpose, but is placed in the charm-box of the household shrine. As these magical materials are specific for certain ills, and the real or imagined maladies of the people are many, the charm-box is usually full to overflowing. The magical packets are so numerous that people forget what their purposes were and fear to use them again. While the natives are very vague on this point, we can only assume that the idea in retaining all the old magical materials is that their presence in the charm-box, before which the body rituals are conducted, will in some way protect the worshipper.

Beneath the charm-box is a small font. Each day every member of the family, in succession, enters the shrine room, bows his head before the charm-box, mingles different sorts of holy water in the font, and proceeds with a brief rite of ablution. The holy waters are secured from the Water Temple of the community, where the priests conduct elaborate ceremonies to make the liquid ritually pure.

In the hierarchy of magical practitioners, and below the medicine men in prestige, are specialists whose designation is best translated "holy-mouth-men." The Nacirema have an almost pathological horror of and fascination with the mouth, the condition of which is believed to have a supernatural influence on all social relationships. Were it not for the rituals of the mouth, they believe that their teeth would fall out, their gums bleed, their jaws shrink, their friends desert them, and their lovers reject them. They also believe that a strong relationship exists between oral and moral characteristics. For example, there is a ritual ablution of the mouth for children which is supposed to improve their moral fibre.

The daily body ritual performed by everyone includes a mouth-rite. Despite the fact that these people are so punctilious about care of the mouth, this rite involves a practice which strikes the uninitiated stranger as revolting. It was reported to me that the ritual consists of inserting a small bundle of hog hairs into the mouth, along with certain magical powders, and them moving the bundle in a highly formalized series of gestures.

In addition to the private mouth-rite, the people seek out a holy-mouth-man once or twice a year. These practitioners have an impressive set of paraphernalia, consisting of a variety of augers, awls, probes, and prods. The use of these objects in the exorcism of the evils of the mouth involves almost unbelievable ritual torture of the client. The holy-mouth-man opens the client's mouth and, using the above mentioned tools, enlarges any holes which decay may have created in the teeth. Magical materials are put into these holes. If there are no naturally occurring holes in the teeth, large sections of one or more teeth are gouged out so that the supernatural substance can be applied. In the client's view, the purpose of these ministrations is to arrest decay and to draw new friends. The extremely sacred and traditional character of the rite is evident in the fact that the natives return to the holy-mouth-men year after year, despite the fact that their teeth continue to decay.

It is to be hoped that, when a thorough study of the Nacirema is made, there will be careful inquiry into the personality structure of these people. One has but to watch the gleam in the eye of a holy-mouth-man, as he jabs an awl into an exposed nerve, to suspect that a certain amount of sadism is involved. If this can be established, a very interesting pattern emerges, for most of the population shows definite masochistic tendencies. It was to these that Professor Linton referred in discussing a distinctive part of the daily body ritual which is performed only by men. This part of the rite involves scraping and lacerating the surface of the face with a sharp instrument. Special women's rites are performed only four times during each lunar month, but what they lack in frequency is made up in barbarity. As part of this ceremony, women bake their heads in small ovens for about an hour. The theoretically interesting point is that what seems to be a preponderantly masochistic people have developed sadistic specialties.

The medicine men have an imposing temple, or *latipso*, in every community of any size. The more elaborate ceremonies required to treat very sick patients can only be performed at this temple. These ceremonies involve not only the thaumaturge but a permanent group of vestal maidens who move sedately about the temple chambers in distinctive costume and headdress.

The *latipso* ceremonies are so harsh that it is phenomenal that a fair proportion of the really sick natives who enter the temple ever recover. Small children whose indoctrination is still incomplete have been known to resist attempts to take them to the temple because "that is where you go to die." Despite this fact, sick adults are not only willing but eager to undergo the protracted ritual purification, if they can afford to do so. No matter how ill the supplicant or how grave the emergency, the guardians of many temples will not admit a client if he cannot give a rich gift to the custodian. Even after one has gained admission and survived the ceremonies, the guardians will not permit the neophyte to leave until he makes another gift.

The supplicant entering the temple is first stripped of all his or her clothes. In every-day life the Nacirema avoids exposure of his body and its natural functions. Bathing and excretory acts are performed only in the secrecy of the household shrine, where they are ritualized as part of the body-rites. Psychological shock results from the fact that body secrecy is suddenly lost upon entry into the *latipso*. A man, whose own wife has never seen him in an excretory act, suddenly finds himself naked and assisted by a vestal maiden while he performs his natural functions into a sacred vessel. This sort of ceremonial treatment is necessitated by the fact that the excreta are used by a diviner to ascertain the course and nature of the client's sickness. Female clients, on the other hand, find their naked bodies are subjected to the scrutiny, manipulation and prodding of the medicine men.

Few supplicants in the temple are well enough to do anything but lie on their hard beds. The daily ceremonies, like the rites of the holy-mouth-men, involve discomfort and torture. With ritual precision, the vestals awaken their miserable charges each dawn and roll them about on their beds of pain while performing ablutions, in the formal movements of which the maidens are highly trained. At other times they insert magic wands in the supplicant's mouth or force him to eat substances which are supposed to be healing. From time to time the medicine men come to their clients and jab magically treated needles into their flesh. The fact that these temple ceremonies may not cure, and may even kill the neophyte, in no way decreases the people's faith in the medicine men.

There remains one other kind of practitioner, known as a "listener." This witch-doctor has the power to exorcise the devils that lodge in the heads of people who have been bewitched. The Nacirema believe that parents bewitch their own children. Mothers are particularly suspected of putting a curse on children while teaching them the secret body rituals. The counter-magic of the witch-doctor is unusual in its lack of ritual. The patient simply tells the "listener" all his troubles and fears, beginning with the earliest difficulties he can remember. The memory displayed by the Nacirema in these exorcism sessions is truly remarkable. It is not uncommon for the patient to bemoan the rejection he felt upon being weaned as a babe, and a few individuals even see their troubles as going back to the traumatic effects of their own birth.

In conclusion, mention must be made of certain practices which have their base in native aesthetics but which depend upon the pervasive aversion to the natural body and its functions. There are ritual fasts to make fat people thin and ceremonial feasts to make thin people fat. Still other rites are used to make women's breasts larger if they are small, and smaller if they are large. General dissatisfaction with breast shape is symbolized in the fact that the ideal form is virtually outside the range of human variation. A few women afflicted with almost inhuman hypermammary development are so idolized that they make a handsome living simply going from village to village and permitting the natives to stare at them for a fee.

Reference has already been made to the fact that excretory functions are ritualized, routinized, and relegated to secrecy. Natural reproductive functions are similarly distorted. Intercourse is a taboo as a topic and scheduled as an act. Efforts are made to avoid pregnancy by the use of magical materials or by limiting intercourse to certain phases of the moon. Conception is actually very infrequent. When pregnant, women dress so as to hide their condition. Parturition takes place in secret, without friends or relatives to assist, and the majority of women do not nurse their infants.

Our review of the ritual life of the Nacirema has certainly shown them to be a magic-ridden people. It is hard to understand how they have managed to exist so long under the burdens which they have imposed upon themselves. But even such exotic customs as these take on real meaning when they are viewed with the insight provided by Malinowski when he wrote (1948: 70):

> Looking from far and above, from our high places of safety in the developed civilization, it is easy to see all the crudity and irrelevance of magic. But without its power and guidance early man could not have mastered his practical difficulties as he has done, nor could man have advanced to the higher stages of civilization.

References

Linton, Ralph. (1936). *The Study of Man*. New York, D. Appleton-Century Co.
Malinowski, Bronislaw. (1948). *Magic, Science, and Religion*. Glencoe, The Free Press.
Murdock, George P. (1949). *Social Structure*. New York, The Macmillan Co.

9

Anti-Semite and Jew

Jean Paul Sartre

What is racism? How does it develop and what sustains it? In this excerpt, Sartre attempts to answer these questions by examining the anti-Semite as one particular expression of racism.

If a man attributes all or part of his own misfortunes and those of his country to the presence of Jewish elements in the community, if he proposes to remedy this state of affairs by depriving the Jews of certain of their rights, by keeping them out of certain economic and social activities, by expelling them from the country, by exterminating all of them, we say that he has anti-Semitic *opinions*.

This word *opinion* makes us stop and think. It is the word a hostess uses to bring to an end a discussion that threatens to become acrimonious. It suggests that all points of view are equal; it reassures us, for it gives an inoffensive appearance to ideas by reducing them to the level of tastes. All tastes are natural; all opinions are permitted. Tastes, colours, and opinions are not open to discussion. In the name of democratic institutions, in the name of freedom of opinion, the anti-Semite asserts the right to preach the anti-Jewish crusade everywhere.

But I refuse to characterize as opinion a doctrine that is aimed directly at particular persons and that seeks to suppress their rights or to exterminate them. The Jew whom the anti-Semite wishes to lay hands upon is not a schematic being defined solely by his function, as under administrative law; or by his status or his acts, as under the Code. He is a Jew, the son of Jews, recognizable by his physique, by the colour of his hair, by his clothing perhaps, and, so they say, by his character. Anti-Semitism does not fall within the category of ideas protected by the right of free opinion.

Indeed, it is something quite other than an idea. It is first of all a *passion*. No doubt it can be set forth in the form of a theoretical proposition. The "moderate" anti-Semite is a courteous man who will tell you quietly: "Personally, I do not

---

From *Anti-Semite and Jew* by Jean Paul Sartre, trans. by George Becker. Copyright 1948 and renewed 1976 by Schocken Books, Inc. Reprinted by permission of Schocken Books, published by Pantheon Books, a division of Random House, Inc.

detest the Jews. I simply find it preferable, for various reasons, that they should play a lesser part in the activity of the nation." But a moment later, if you have gained his confidence, he will add with more abandon: "You see, there must be *something* about the Jews; they upset me physically."

This argument, which I have heard a hundred times, is worth examining. First of all, it derives from the logic of passion. For, really now, can we imagine anyone saying seriously: "There must be something about tomatoes, for I have a horror of eating them?"

Some men are suddenly struck with impotence if they learn from the woman with whom they are making love that she is a Jewess. There is a disgust for the Jew, just as there is a disgust for the Chinese or the Negro among certain people. Thus it is not from the body that the sense of repulsion arises, since one may love a Jewess very well if one does not know what her race is; rather it is something that enters the body from the mind. It is an involvement of the mind, but one so deep-seated and complete that it extends to the physiological realm, as happens in cases of hysteria.

This involvement is not caused by experience. I have questioned a hundred people on the reasons for their anti-Semitism. Most of them have confined themselves to enumerating the defects with which tradition has endowed the Jews. "I detest them because they are selfish, intriguing, persistent, oily, tactless, etc."—"But, at any rate, you associate with some of them?"—"Not if I can help it!" A painter said to me: "I am hostile to the Jews because, with their critical habits, they encourage our servants to insubordination." Here are examples a little more precise. A young actor without talent insisted that the Jews had kept him from a successful career in the theatre by confining him to subordinate roles. A young woman said to me: "I have had the most horrible experiences with furriers; they robbed me, they burned the fur I entrusted to them. Well, they were all Jews." But why did she choose to hate Jews rather than furriers? Why Jews or furriers rather than such and such a Jew or such and such a furrier? Because she had in her a predisposition toward anti-Semitism.

People speak to us also of "social facts," but if we look at this more closely we shall find the same vicious circle. There are too many Jewish lawyers, someone says. But is there any complaint that there are too many Norman lawyers? Even if all the Bretons were doctors would we say anything more than that "Brittany provides doctors for the whole of France?" Oh, someone will answer, it is not at all the same thing. No doubt, but that is precisely because we consider Normans as Normans and Jews as *Jews*. Thus wherever we turn it is the *idea of the Jew* which seems to be the essential thing.

It has become evident that no external factor can induce anti-Semitism in the anti-Semite. Anti-Semitism is a free and total choice of oneself, a comprehensive attitude that one adopts not only toward Jews but toward men in general, toward history and society; it is at one and the same time a passion and a conception of the world. No doubt in the case of a given anti-Semite certain characteristics will be more marked than in another. But they are always all present at the same time, and they influence each other. It is this syncretic totality which we must now attempt to describe.

I noted earlier that anti-Semitism is a passion. Everybody understands that emotions of hate or anger are involved. Bur ordinarily hate and anger have a *provocation:* I hate someone who has made me suffer, someone who condemns or insults me. We have just seen that anti-Semitic passion could not have such a character. It precedes the facts that are supposed to call it forth; it seeks them out to nourish itself upon them; it must even interpret them in a special way so that they may become truly offensive. Indeed, if you so much as mention a Jew to an anti-Semite, he will show all the signs of a lively irritation. If we recall that we must always *consent* to anger before it can manifest itself and that, as is indicated so accurately by the French idiom, we "put ourselves" into anger, we shall have to agree that the anti-Semite has *chosen* to live on the plane of passion. It is not unusual for people to elect to live a life of passion rather than one of reason. But ordinarily they love the objects of passion: women, glory, power, money. Since the anti-Semite has chosen hate, we are forced to conclude that it is the state of passion that he loves. Ordinarily this type of emotion is not very pleasant: a man who passionately desires a woman is impassioned because of the woman and in spite of his passion. We are wary of reasoning based on passion, seeking to support by all possible means opinions which love or jealousy or hate have dictated. We are wary of the aberrations of passion and of what is called monoideism. But that is just what the anti-Semite chooses right off.

How can one choose to reason falsely? It is because of a longing for impenetrability. The rational man groans as he gropes for the truth; he knows that his reasoning is no more than tentative, that other considerations may supervene to cast doubt on it. He never sees clearly where he is going; he is "open;" he may even appear to be hesitant. But there are people who are attracted by the durability of a stone. They wish to be massive and impenetrable; they wish not to change. Where, indeed, would change take them? We have here a basic fear of oneself and of truth. What frightens them is not the content of truth, that thing of indefinite approximation. It is as if their own existence were in continual suspension. But they wish to exist all at once and right away. They do not want any acquired opinions; they want them to be innate. Since they are afraid of reasoning, they wish to lead the kind of life wherein reasoning and research play only a subordinate role, wherein one seeks only what he has already found, wherein one becomes only what he already was. This is nothing but passion. Only a strong emotional bias can give a lightning-like certainty; it alone can hold reason in leash; it alone can remain impervious to experience and last for a whole lifetime.

The anti-Semite has chosen hate because hate is a faith; at the outset he has chosen to devaluate words and reasons. How entirely at ease he feels as a result. How futile and frivolous discussions about the rights of the Jew appear to him.

He has placed himself on other ground from the beginning. If out of courtesy he consents for a moment to defend his point of view, he lends himself but does not give himself. He tries simply to project his intuitive certainty onto the plane of discourse. I mentioned awhile back some remarks by anti-Semites, all of them absurd: "I hate Jews because they make servants insubordinate, because a Jewish furrier robbed me, etc." Never believe that anti-Semites are completely unaware of the absurdity of their replies. They know that their remarks are frivolous, open to challenge. But they are amusing themselves, for it is their adversary who is obliged to use words responsibly, since he believes in words. The anti-Semites have the *right* to play. They even like to play with discourse for, by giving ridiculous reasons, they discredit the seriousness of their interlocutors. They delight in acting in bad faith, since they seek not to persuade by sound argument but to intimidate and disconcert. If you press them too closely, they will abruptly fall silent, loftily indicating by some phrase that the time for argument is past. It is not that they are afraid of being convinced. They fear only to appear ridiculous or to prejudice by their embarrassment their hope of winning over some third person to their side.

If then, as we have been able to observe, the anti-Semite is impervious to reason and to experience, it is not because his conviction is strong. Rather his conviction is strong because he has chosen first of all to be impervious.

He has chosen also to be terrifying. People are afraid of irritating him. No one knows to what lengths the aberrations of his passion will carry him—but he knows, for this passion is not provoked by something external. He has it well in hand; it is obedient to his will: now he lets go the reins and now he pulls back on them. He is not afraid of himself, but he sees in the eyes of others a disquieting image—his own—and he makes his words and gestures conform to it. Having this external model, he is under no necessity to look for his personality within himself. He has chosen to find his being entirely outside himself, never to look within, to be nothing save the fear he inspires in others. What he flees even more than Reason is his intimate awareness of himself. But someone will object: What if he is like that only with regard to the Jews? What if he otherwise conducts himself with good sense? I reply that that is impossible. There is the case of a fishmonger who, in 1942, annoyed by the competition of two Jewish fishmongers who were concealing their race, one fine day took pen in hand and denounced them. I have been assured that this fishmonger was in other aspects a mild and jovial man, the best of sons. But I don't believe it. A man who finds it entirely natural to denounce other men cannot have our conception of humanity; he does not see even those whom he aids in the same light as we do. His generosity, his kindness are not like our kindness, our generosity. You cannot confine passion to one sphere.

The anti-Semite readily admits that the Jew is intelligent and hard-working; he will even confess himself inferior in these respects. This concession costs him nothing, for he has, as it were, put those qualities in parentheses. Or rather they derive their value from the one who possesses them: the more virtues the Jew has the more dangerous he will be. The anti-Semite has no illusions about what he is. He considers himself an average man, modestly average, basically mediocre. There is no example of an anti-Semite's claiming individual superiority over the Jews. But you must not think that he is ashamed of his mediocrity; he takes pleasure in it; I will even assert that he has chosen it. This man fears every kind of solitariness, that of the genius as much as that of the murderer; he is the man of the crowd. However small his stature, he takes every precaution to make it smaller, lest he stand out from the herd and find himself face to face with himself. He has made himself an anti-Semite because that is something one cannot be alone. The phrase, "I hate the Jews," is one that is uttered in chorus; in pronouncing it, one attaches himself to a tradition and to a community—the tradition and community of the mediocre.

We must remember that a man is not necessarily humble or even modest because he has consented to mediocrity. On the contrary, there is a passionate pride among the mediocre, and anti-Semitism is an attempt to give value to mediocrity as such, to create an elite of the ordinary. To the anti-Semite, intelligence is Jewish; he can thus disdain it in all tranquillity, like all the other virtues which the Jew possesses. They are so many ersatz attributes that the Jew cultivates in place of that balanced mediocrity which he will never have. The true Frenchman, rooted in his province, in his country, borne along by a tradition twenty centuries old, benefiting from ancestral wisdom, guided by tried customs, does not *need* intelligence. His virtue depends upon the assimilation of the qualities which the work of a hundred generations has lent to the objects which surround him; it depends on property. It goes without saying that this is a matter of inherited property, not property one buys. The anti-Semite has a fundamental incomprehension of the various forms of modern property: money, securities, etc. These are abstractions, entities of reason related to the abstract intelligence of the Semite. A security belongs to no one because it can belong to everyone; moreover, it is a sign of wealth, not a concrete possession. The anti-Semite can conceive only of a type of primitive ownership of land based on a veritable magical rapport, in which the thing possessed and its possessor are united by a bond of mystical participation; he is the poet of real property. It transfigures the proprietor and endows him with a special and concrete sensibility. To be sure, this sensibility ignores eternal truths or universal values: the universal is Jewish, since it is an object of intelligence. What his subtle sense seizes upon is precisely that which the intelligence cannot perceive. To put it another way, the principle underlying anti-Semitism is that the concrete possession of a particular object gives as if by magic the meaning of that object. Maurras said the same thing when he declared a Jew to be forever incapable of understanding this line of Racine:

Dans l'Orient desert, quel devint mon ennui.

But the way is open to me, mediocre me, to understand what the most subtle, the most cultivated intelligence has been unable to grasp. Why? Because I possess Racine—Racine and my country and my soil. Perhaps the Jew speaks a purer French than I do, perhaps he knows syntax and grammar better, perhaps he is even a writer. No matter; he has spoken this language for only twenty years, and I for a thousand years. The correctness of his style is abstract, acquired; my faults of French are in conformity with the genius of the language....The only things that count are irrational values, and it is just these things which are denied the Jews forever. Thus the anti-Semite takes his stand from the start on the ground of irrationalism. He is opposed to the Jew, just as sentiment is to intelligence, the particular to the universal, the past to the present, the concrete to the abstract, the owner of real property to the possessor of negotiable securities.

Besides this, many anti-Semites—the majority, perhaps—belong to the lower middle class of the towns; they are functionaries, office workers, small businessmen, who possess nothing. It is in opposing themselves to the Jew that they suddenly become conscious of being proprietors: in representing the Jew as a robber, they put themselves in the enviable position of people who could be robbed. Since the Jew wishes to take France from them, it follows that France must belong to them. Thus they have chosen anti-Semitism as a means of establishing their status as possessors....

We begin to perceive the meaning of the anti-Semite's choice of himself. He chooses the irremediable out of fear of being free; he chooses mediocrity out of fear of being alone, and out of pride he makes of this irremediable mediocrity a rigid aristocracy. To this end he finds the existence of the Jew absolutely necessary. Otherwise to whom would he be superior? Indeed, it is vis-à-vis the Jew and the Jew alone that the anti-Semite realizes that he has rights. If by some miracle all the Jews were exterminated as he wishes, he would find himself nothing but a concierge or a shopkeeper in a strongly hierarchical society in which the quality of "true Frenchman" would be at a low valuation, because everyone would possess it. He would lose his sense of rights over the country because no one would any longer contest them, and that profound equality which brings him close to the nobleman and the man of wealth would disappear all of a sudden, for it is primarily negative. His frustrations, which he has attributed to the disloyal competition of the Jew, would have to be imputed to some other cause, lest he be forced to look within himself. He would run the risk of falling into bitterness, into a melancholy hatred of the privileged classes. Thus the anti-Semite is in the unhappy position of having a vital need for the very enemy he wishes to destroy.

The equalitarianism that the anti-Semite seeks with so much ardour has nothing in common with that equality inscribed in the creed of the democracies.

The latter is to be realized in a society that is economically hierarchical, and is to remain compatible with a diversity of functions. But it is in protest *against* the hierarchy of functions that the anti-Semite asserts the equality of Aryans. He does not understand anything about the division of labour and doesn't care about it. From his point of view each citizen can claim the title of Frenchman, not because he co-operates, in his place or in his occupation, with others in the economic, social, and cultural life of the nation, but because he has, in the same way as everybody else, an imprescriptible and inborn right to the indivisible totality of the country. Thus the society that the anti-Semite conceives of is a society of juxtaposition, as one can very well imagine, since his ideal of property is that of real and basic property. Since, in point of fact, anti-Semites are numerous, each of them does his part in constituting a community based on mechanical solidarity in the heart of organized society.

Any anti-Semite is therefore, in varying degree, the enemy of constituted authority. He wishes to be the disciplined member of an undisciplined group; he adores order, but a social order. We might say that he wishes to provoke political disorder in order to restore social order, the social order in his eyes being a society that, by virtue of juxtaposition, is egalitarian and primitive, one with a heightened temperature, one from which Jews are excluded. These principles enable him to enjoy a strange sort of independence, which I shall call an inverted liberty. Authentic liberty assumes responsibilities, and the liberty of the anti-Semite comes from the fact that he escapes all of his. Floating between an authoritarian society which has not yet come into existence and an official and tolerant society which he disavows, he can do anything he pleases without appearing to be an anarchist, which would horrify him. The profound seriousness of his aims—which no word, no statement, no act can express—permits him a certain frivolity. He is a hooligan, he beats people up, he purges, he robs; it is all in a good cause. If the government is strong, anti-Semitism withers, unless it be a part of the program of the government itself, in which case it changes its nature....

We begin to understand that anti-Semitism is more than a mere "opinion" about the Jews and that it involves the entire personality of the anti-Semite. But we have not yet finished with him, for he does not confine himself to furnishing moral and political directives: he has a method of thought and a conception of the world all his own. In fact, we cannot state what he affirms without implicit reference to certain intellectual principles.

The Jew, he says, is completely bad, completely a Jew. His virtues, if he has any, turn to vices by reason of the fact that they are his; work coming from his hands necessarily bears his stigma. If he builds a bridge, that bridge, being Jewish, is bad from the first to the last span. The same action carried out by a Jew and by a Christian does not have the same meaning in the two cases, for the Jew contaminates all that he touches with an I-know-not-what execrable quality. The first thing the Germans did was to forbid Jews access to swimming pools; it seemed to them that if the body of an Israelite were to plunge into that confined body of water, the water would be completely befouled. Strictly speaking, the Jew contaminates even the air he breathes.

If we attempt to formulate in abstract terms the principles to which the anti-Semite appeals, it would come to this: A whole is more and other than the sum of its parts; a whole determines the meaning and underlying parts; a whole determines the meaning and underlying character of the parts that make it up. There is not one virtue of courage which enters indifferently into a Jewish character or a Christian character in the way that oxygen indifferently combines with nitrogen and argon to form air and with hydrogen to form water. Each person is an indivisible totality that has its own courage, its own generosity, its own way of thinking, laughing, drinking, and eating. What is there to say except that the anti-Semite has chosen to fall back on the spirit of synthesis in order to understand the world. It is the spirit of synthesis which permits him to conceive of himself as forming an indissoluble unity with all France. It is in the name of this spirit that he denounces the purely analytical and critical intelligence of the Jews. But we must be more precise. For some time, on the Right and on the Left, among the traditionalists and among the socialists, it has been the fashion to make appeal to synthetic principles as against the spirit of analysis which presided over the foundation of bourgeois democracy.

We are now in a position to understand the anti-Semite. He is a man who is afraid. Not of the Jews, to be sure, but of himself, of his own consciousness, of his liberty, of his instincts, of his responsibilities, of solitariness, of change, of society, and of the world—of everything except the Jews. He is a coward who does not want to admit his cowardice to himself; a murderer who represses and censures his tendency to murder without being able to hold it back, yet who dares to kill only in effigy or protected by the anonymity of the mob; a malcontent who dares not revolt from fear of the consequences of his rebellion. In espousing anti-Semitism, he does not simply adopt an opinion, he chooses himself as a person. He chooses the permanence and impenetrability of stone, the total irresponsibility of the warrior who obeys his leaders—and he has no leader. He chooses to acquire nothing, to deserve nothing; he assumes that everything is given him as his birthright—and he is not noble. He chooses finally a Good that is fixed once and for all, beyond question, out of reach; he dares not examine it for fear of being led to challenge it and having to seek it in another form. The Jew only serves him as a pretext; elsewhere his counterpart will make use of the negro or the man of yellow skin. The existence of the Jew merely permits the anti-Semite to stifle his anxieties at their inception by persuading himself that his place in the world has been marked out in advance, that it awaits him, and that tradition gives him the right to occupy it. Anti-Semitism, in short, is fear of the human condition. The anti-Semite is a man who wishes to be pitiless stone, a furious torrent, a devastating thunderbolt—anything except a man.

10

Television: The Shared Arena

Joshua Meyrowitz

The media has historically been an important theme within Canadian social theory from Harold Innis's investigations of oral and literate cultures to Marshall McLuhan's probes into electronic media and society. In this article Meyrowitz explores what happens to culture and society when television rather than physical sites such as town halls and even countries become the arena for public life. While television seems to be all around us, its impacts have yet to be seen clearly.

What is our relationship to the medium of television? In what ways are we attached to, and detached from, each other by the shared experience of viewing television? Meyrowitz discusses how we are identified by television even as we use it to identify with each other. What it reveals and conceals, how it binds and separates, and how its ubiquity undermines some of the central distinctions upon which our culture is based, are issues we are called upon to consider in this era of electronic media proliferation.

In 1950, only 9 percent of U.S. homes owned television sets. Little more than 25 years later, only 2 percent of households were without one. In a remarkably short time, television has taken a central place in our living rooms and in our cultural and political lives. On average, a U.S. household can now receive 30 channels; only 7 percent of homes receive six or fewer stations. Some 95 percent of homes own a colour TV, 63 percent own two or more sets, and 64 percent own a video cassette recorder.

Television is the most popular of the popular media. Indeed, if Nielsen research and other studies are correct, there are few things that Americans do more than they watch television. On average, each household has a TV on almost

---

Joshua Meyrowitz is Professor of Communication at the University of New Hampshire and the author of *No Sense of Place: The Impact of Electronic Media on Social Behavior*. This article originally appeared in *The World & I* in July 1990. Copyright © by Joshua Meyrowitz.

50 hours a week. Forty percent of households eat dinner with the set on. Individually, Americans watch an average of 30 hours a week. We begin peering at TV through the bars of cribs and continue looking at it through the cataracts of old age.

Plato saw an important relationship between shared, simultaneous experience and a sense of social and political interconnectedness. Plato thought that his Republic should consist of no more than 5000 citizens because that was the maximum number of people who could fit in an arena and simultaneously hear the voice of one person. Television is now our largest shared arena. During the average minute of a typical evening, nearly a hundred million Americans are tuned in. While a book can usually win a place on the lists of the top 50 fiction or non-fiction bestsellers for the *year* with 115 000 hardcover sales, a prime-time network program with fewer than 15 million viewers for *each episode* is generally considered a failure.

Even the biggest bestsellers reach only a fraction of the audience that will watch a similar program on television. It took 40 years for *Gone with the Wind* to sell 21 million copies; 55 million people watched the first half of the movie on television in a single evening. The television mini-series "Roots" was watched, in part or whole, by approximately 130 million people in only eight days. Even with the help of the television promotion, fewer than 5 million copies of *Roots* sold in eight years.

The television arena, like a street corner or a marketplace, serves as an environment for us to monitor but not necessarily identify with. Reading a newspaper requires an investment of money and reading effort, and at least some minimal identification with its style and editorial policy. We have to reach out for it and embrace it—both literally and metaphorically. But with television, we simply sit back and let the images wash over us. While we usually select reading material that clearly reflects our own self-image, with TV we often feel we are passively observing what other people are like.

Most of us would feel uncomfortable stopping at a local store to pick up the current issue of a publication titled *Transvestite Times* or *Male Strippers' Review*, or a magazine on incest, child abuse, or adultery. But millions of viewers feel quite comfortable sharing their homes with transvestites, male strippers, and victims and perpetrators of incest, or almost anyone else who appears on "Donahue," "Oprah," or "Geraldo." Ironically, our personal dissociation with TV content allows for the most widespread sharing of similar experience in the history of civilization.

In the 1950s, many intellectuals were embarrassed to admit that they owned a television set, let alone that they spent any valuable time watching it. But the massive saturation of television into virtually every U.S. home now imbues the activity of watching television with multiple layers of social significance. One can watch popular programs not merely to see the program but to see what others are watching. To watch television may not be to stare into the eyes of America, but it is to look over its shoulder and see what Americans see. Watching television—with its often distorted versions of reality—does not allow us to keep our finger on the pulse of the nation so much as it allows us to keep our finger on the pulse the nation is keeping its finger on. With television, it somehow makes sense for a viewer to watch the tube avidly while exclaiming, "My God, I can't believe people watch this stuff!"

Even though many people watch it alone, television is capable of giving each isolated viewer a sense of connection with the outside world and with all the other people who are watching. During major television events—whether fictional or non-fictional—such as the final episode of "M*A*S*H" or the explosion of the *Challenger*, one is likely to find that more than one out of every two people one sees on the street the next day has had a similar experience the night before. Regardless of specific content, then, television often serves a social function similar to the weather: No one takes responsibility for it, often it is quite bad, but nearly everyone pays attention to it and sees it as a basis of common experience and conversational topics. Perhaps this is why even pay cable households spend more than half their viewing time watching "regular" network programming and why the most frequent use of VCRs is for time shifting of programs broadcast by network-affiliated stations.

For many people, someone or something that does not appear on television does not fully exist in the social sense. The Watergate scandals became "real" not when the *Washington Post* reported the stories but when network television news reported that the *Washington Post* reported the stories. Similarly, civil rights and anti-Vietnam War protests became social realities not when demonstrators took to the streets but when the protests were viewed on television. And although most of our early presidents were seen by only a few of the voters of their day, it is now impossible to imagine a serious candidate who would not visit us all on TV. And so it is that politicians, salespeople, protestors, and terrorists all design their messages in the hope of capturing the television eye.

Too Close to the Set

Despite its ubiquity, the impact of television is not yet seen very clearly. For one thing, most of us watch television too closely—not in the way that mothers warn their children about, but in the sense of evaluating television primarily on the basis of whether we like or don't like its programs. Even scholars tend to reduce the impact of television to its past and current programming and to the motives of the institutions that control it. The overwhelming majority of television research and criticism has focused on the nature of the programs, their imitative or persuasive power, their aesthetic value or bankruptcy, the range of meanings that viewers can draw from them, or their underlying economic and political purposes.

These are important but insufficient questions. The effects of a new communication technology cannot be understood fully by looking only at the medium's typical content and patterns of control. To see the limits of such an approach, we need only to consider what its use in the fifteenth and sixteenth centuries would have revealed about the impact of the printing press, then spreading through western culture. A content/institutionalized approach to printing probably would have led observers to conclude that books had two major effects: 1. the fostering of religion (most early books were religious in content) and 2. the strengthening of central religious and monarchal authorities (who controlled much of what was printed). The underlying, but ultimately more significant, long-term effects of the printing press—such as the growth of individual thinking and science and the spread of nationalism and constitutional systems—would remain invisible.

This is not to suggest that the short-term, surface effects are inconsequential. Just look at William Carter. He printed a pro-Catholic pamphlet in England in 1584 and was promptly hanged. Similarly, our current information environment is choked and narrowed by the way television is controlled.

The television business is not structured to deliver quality programming to viewers but rather to deliver viewers to advertisers. We are sold to advertisers in lots of a thousand. The real programming on television is the commercial. That is where the time, the money, and the competition are. That is where the most creative television "artists" (if we want to use that term) are working. The TV shows—whether news or entertainment or "infotainment"—are simply the bait.

We are misled when we are told that program ratings are part of an audience-centred, "democratic" process that allows us to "vote" for shows. In fact, we are usually offered choices among advertiser-friendly programs. This is why TV ratings systems rarely ask whether or why we like or dislike a show or what we would like to see instead. Most ratings simply measure how many of what type of people are there for the ads.

Even if networks can draw millions of viewers to a program, the last thing they want to do is put the audience in a mood that does not mix well with consumption of the advertised products. One of the most-watched programs in television history, "The Day After," for example, was an ad failure. After all, what companies would want their products associated with nuclear holocaust? In fact, as one vice-president of the network confided to me, the airing of "The Day After"—as bland a treatment of its subject as it was—almost led to a stockholder suit against ABC because the network could have made more money airing a rerun of a program such as "The Harlem Globetrotters Visit Gilligan's Island."

But to reduce television to a cultural nuisance or to a slickly disguised salesperson, as some analysts do, is to miss what is happening in our culture because of television and how it—not merely through its content but also as a certain form of shared experience—reshapes our attitudes and behaviours.

The effects of new media of communication arise not solely from their content but also from the new ways in which the medium packages and transmits information. Writing and print, for example, were able to foster the rise of individual thinking and science because they literally put information in the hands of individuals and because they allowed for the recording and wide-scale distribution of ideas that were too complicated to memorize (even by the people who came up with them). Even as William Carter swung from the gallows by regal decree, printing was quietly working against its apparent masters, ultimately secularizing the culture and encouraging the overthrow of monarchies. Similarly, the impact of television cannot be reduced to programs that come through the tube or to the institutions that control it. There are effects apart from, and even in opposition to, these forces.

The most significant long-term effects of television may also lie in its manner of packaging and transmitting information and in the ways that it undoes some of the systems of communication supported by print. Television has changed "who knows what about whom" and "who knows what compared to whom." As a result, it has changed the way we grow from childhood to adulthood, altered our sense of appropriate gender behaviour, shifted our perceptions of our political and other leaders, and affected our general sense of "them" and "us."

Video Nursery

As printing and literacy spread through western culture, literate adults discovered they could increasingly keep secrets from preliterate and semiliterate children. Adults used books to communicate among themselves without children overhearing. Clerics argued for the development of expurgated versions of the classics, and the notion of the innocence of childhood began to take hold, eventually spreading to the lowest classes with the growth of universal education.

Childhood was to be a time of innocence and isolation. Children were protected from the nasty realities of adult life. Unable to read, very young children had no access to the information available in books. Young children were presented with an idealized version of adult life. Children were slowly walked up the ladder of literacy with a new, somewhat less idealized view of adult life presented to them at each step of reading ability.

Television dilutes the innocence of childhood by undermining the system of information control that supported it. Television bypasses the year-by-year slices of knowledge given to children. It presents the same information to adults and to children of all ages. Children may not understand everything they see on television, but they are exposed to many aspects of adult life that their parents (and traditional children's books) would have once protected them from.

Parents often clamour for more and better children's television. But one could argue that there is no such thing as "children's television," at least not in the sense that there is children's literature. Children's literature is the only literature that children can read, and only children read it. In contrast, studies since the early days of television have found that children often prefer to watch programs aimed at adults. And adults often watch programs aimed at children—about a third of the audience for "Pee Wee Herman's Playhouse" is over eighteen.

At some point during the last decade, each of the following has been among the most popular programs in *all* age groups, including ages two to eleven: "Dallas," "The Muppets," "The Dukes of Hazzard," "Love Boat," "The A-Team," "Cheers," "Roseanne," and "The Golden Girls." Thus, children have been avid viewers of adult soap operas, and adults have found pleasure in a children's puppet show.

In both fictional and non-fictional programs, children learn that adults lie, cheat, drink too much, use drugs, and kill and maim each other. But perhaps the most dramatic revelation that television provides to young children is that parents struggle to control children.

Unlike books, television cannot be used easily by adults as a tool to discuss how to raise children. A parental advice book can be used by adults to communicate among themselves about what to tell and not to tell children. But the same conversation on television is usually overheard by thousands of children, who are thereby exposed to the very topics suggested for secrecy and to the "secret of secrecy" itself—the fact that adults are anxious about their parental roles and conspire to keep secrets from children.

Even seemingly innocent programs reveal significant secrets to children. When the first TV generation watched programs such as "Father Knows Best" and "Leave It to Beaver," for example, they learned that parents behaved one way in front of their children and another way when they were alone. In front of their children, the TV parents were calm, cool, and collected, but away from their kids, they were anxious and concerned about their parental behaviour. Because we often reduce the effects of TV to imitation, we forget that while the children *on* such programs were innocent and sheltered, the children *watching* the shows often saw how adults manipulated their behaviours to make it appear to their children that they knew best. This is a view that undermines traditional parental authority by making children less willing to take adult behaviour at face value. It is no wonder, perhaps, that the children who grew up watching "Father Knows Best" became concerned with the "credibility gap"; that is, the difference between what people proclaim publicly and what they say and feel privately.

Subsequent situation comedies, such as "One Day at a Time," shocked many viewers because the parents in the shows revealed their fears and anxieties about parenting in front of their children and because the child characters on the shows were no longer sheltered or innocent. But in terms of what *child* viewers learned about the concerns of parents, there was relatively little new information. The third phase of family shows, including "The Bill Cosby Show" and "Family Ties," offers a compromise between the two earlier family visions: The line between parents and children has been partly re-established, but the children are more sophisticated than early TV children and the parents are both less surefooted in front of their children and less conspiratorial away from them.

In a book culture, control over the flow of information is literally placed in parents' hands. Parents can easily give some books to children and withhold others. Parents can read one book while their children sit in the same room reading another. Television is not so co-operative. Parents often find it difficult to censor their children's viewing without censoring their own, and parents cannot always anticipate what will happen on TV the way they can flip through a book. A father may think he is giving his daughter a lesson in science as they watch the *Challenger* take off, only to discover that he has exposed her instead to adult hubris and tragedy.

Most television programs are accessible to children in a way that most book content is not. The visual/aural form of television allows children to experience many behaviours and events without the skill of decoding written sentences. And it is much simpler for children to wander off "Sesame Street" and slip beyond "Mr. Rogers' Neighborhood" into grown-up television than it is for children to buy or borrow books from a grown-up library or bookstore. Television takes our children across the globe before we as parents even give them permission to cross the street.

As children's innocence declines, children's literature and children's programming have changed as well. Some children's books now discuss sex and drugs and other once-taboo topics, and war and divorce have recently visited "Mr. Rogers' Neighborhood."

This does not mean that adults should abdicate their authority over children or even give up trying to control children's viewing of television. Adults are more experienced and more knowledgeable. But it does mean that the old support system for unquestioned adult authority has been undermined by television. In a television culture, children are more suspicious of adult authority, and many adults feel somewhat exposed, finding it more difficult to pretend to know everything in front of their children. The result is a partial blurring of traditional child and adult roles. Children seem older and more knowledgeable, and adults now reveal to their children the most childish sides of themselves, such as doubts, fears, and anxieties. Thus, we are seeing more adultlike children and more childlike adults, behaviour styles characteristic of preliterate societies.

Gender Blender

Our society once tried to maintain a clear distinction between the male realm and the female realm. The Victorians spoke of the "two spheres": a public, male world of brutal competitions, rationality, and accomplishments; and a private, female world of home, intuition, and childrearing. Men were to suppress their emotions and women were to suppress their competitiveness. The ideal of separate spheres was quite strong in our society when television became the newest home appliance.

Yet even as television situation comedies and other programs featured very traditional gender roles in the two separate spheres, television, as a shared arena, was beginning to break down the distinction between the male and the female, between the public and private realms. Television close-ups reveal the personal side of public figures and events (we see tears well up in the eyes of the president; we hear male voices crack with emotion) just as most public events have become dramas that are played out in the privacy of our kitchens, living rooms, and bedrooms. Television has exposed even homebound women to most of the parts of the culture that were once considered exclusively male domains—sports, war, business, medicine, law, politics—just as it has made men more aware of the emotional dimensions and consequences of public actions.

When Betty Friedan wrote in *The Feminine Mystique* that women in 1960 felt a "schizophrenic split" between the frilly, carefree image of women in women's magazines and the important events occurring in "the world beyond the home," most of her examples of the latter were unwittingly drawn from the top television news stories of the year. By 1960, television was present in nearly 90 percent of U.S. homes. Similarly, other feminist writers have described changes in the 1960s by writing metaphorically of the "breaking of boundaries" (Gloria Steinem), "a sudden enlargement of our world" (Elizabeth Janeway), and of women having "seen beyond the bucolic peacefulness of the suburbs to the war zone at the perimeter" (Barbara Ehrenreich and Deirdre English). But these writers seem unaware of how closely their metaphors describe the literal experience of adding a television to a suburban household.

The fact that early TV programs generally portrayed active men and passive, obedient women had no more of an imitative effect on women viewers than the innocent child characters on "Father Knows Best" had on child viewers. Television, it is true, suggested to women how society thought they should behave, just as etiquette books had for centuries. But television did something else as well: It allowed women to observe and experience the larger world, including all-male interactions and behaviours. Indeed, there is nothing more frustrating than being exposed constantly to adventures, activities, and places that you are told are reserved for someone else. Television also demystified the male realm, making it and its inhabitant seem neither very special nor very intimidating. No wonder women have since demanded to integrate that realm.

Television's impact has been greatest on women because they have traditionally been more isolated. But men are affected as well, partly because women have demanded changes in their behaviour and partly because television emphasizes those traits traditionally ascribed to women: feelings, appearance, emotion. On television, "glorious victories" and "crushing defeats" are now conveyed through images of blood and limp bodies and the howls of survivors. Television has helped men to become more aware of their emotions and of the fact that emotions cannot be completely buried. Even at televised public hearings, it is hard to ignore the facial expressions, the yawns, the grimaces, the fatigue.

The way men react to public issues is also being subtly feminized. Men used to make fun of women for voting for candidates because of the candidates' appearance rather than their stands on the issues. But recent polls show that millions of men, as well as women, will now vote for a candidate they disagree with on the issues, if they "personally like" the candidate. About a third of Ronald Reagan's votes came from such supporters.

Television is one of the few public arenas in our culture where men routinely wear make-up and are judged as much on their personal appearance and "style" as on their "accomplishments." If it was once thought that women communicated and men accomplished, it is telling that our most successful recent president was dubbed the "Great Communicator" and was admired for his gentle voice and manner and his moist-eyed emotional appeals.

With television, boys and girls and men and women tend to share a great deal of similar information about themselves and the "other." Through TV close-ups, men and women see, in one month, many more members of the opposite sex at "intimate distance" than members of earlier generations saw in a lifetime. Further, unlike face-to-face interactions, in which the holding of a gaze may be construed as insulting or as an invitation to further intimacy, television allows one to stare and carefully examine the face, body, and movements of the other sex. Television fosters an easy and uninvolved intimacy.

Just as women have become more involved in the public realm, men are becoming more involved in the private realm, especially in the role of fathers. Traditional distinctions cannot be erased in a generation, of course. But dramatic changes have taken place in a remarkably short time. In 1950, only 12 percent of married women with children under six worked; by 1987, 57 percent did. Recent studies also show that men are now more likely to turn down overtime pay or travel and relocation offers in order to spend more time with their families.

In spite of its often sexist content, television, as an environment shared by both sexes, has made the membranes around the male and female realms more permeable. As a result, the nature of those two realms has been blurring. We are witnessing more career-oriented women and more family-oriented men; we are developing more work-oriented homes, and there is increasing pressure to make the public realm more family-oriented.

Presidential Pimples

Just as television tends to mute differences between people of different ages and sexes, so does it tend to mute differences between levels of social status. Although television is certainly an important weapon in the arsenal of leaders, it often functions as a double-edged sword. Unlike other media, television not only allows leaders to reach followers, it also allows followers to gain unprecedented access to the close-up appearance and gestures of leaders.

"Leadership" and "authority" are unlike mere power in that they depend on performance and appeal; one cannot lead or be looked up to if one's presence is unknown. Yet, paradoxically, authority is weakened by excess familiarity. Awe survives through "distant visibility" and "mystified presence." One of the peculiar ironies of our age is that most people who step forward into the television limelight and attempt to gain national visibility become too visible, too exposed, and are thereby demystified.

The speaker's platform once lifted politicians up and away from average citizens, both literally and symbolically. In newspaper quotes and reports, the politician—as flesh-and-bones person—was completely absent. And on radio, politicians were disembodied voices. But the television camera now lowers politicians to the level of the common citizen and brings them close for our inspection. In recent years, we have seen our presidents sweat, stammer, and stumble—all in living colour.

Presidential images were once much better protected. Before TV coverage of press conferences, newspapers were not even allowed to quote a president without his explicit permission. As late as the start of the Eisenhower administration, *The New York Times* and other publications had to paraphrase the president's answers to questions. In earlier administrations, journalists had to submit their questions in advance and were forbidden from mentioning which questions the president refused to answer. Presidential advisers frequently corrected presidents' answers during meetings with the press, and such assistance went unreported. In the face of a "crisis," our presidents once had many hours, sometimes even weeks or months, to consult with advisers and to formulate policy statements to be printed in newspapers. Now, standing before the nation, a president is expected to have all relevant information in his mind—without notes and without consultation with advisers. A president must often start a sentence before the end of the sentence is fully formed in his mind. Even a five-second pause for thought can seriously damage a leader's credibility. The apparent inarticulateness of all our recent presidents may be related more to the immediacy of television than to a decline in our leaders' mental abilities.

In language, the titles "president," "governor," and "senator" still call forth respect. But the close-up TV pictures of the persons filling those offices are rarely as impressive. We cannot help but notice the sweat on the brow, the nervous twitch, the bags under the eyes.

Television not only reduces our awe of politicians, it increases politicians' self-doubt and lowers self-esteem. A speaker's nervousness and mistakes usually are politely ignored by live audiences and therefore soon forgotten by the speaker as well. But with videotape, politicians have permanent records of themselves misspeaking or anxiously licking their lips. Television may be a prime cause of the complaints of indecisive leadership and hesitant "followership" that we have heard since the mid-1960s.

In the 1950s, many people were shocked that a genuine hero, Dwight Eisenhower, felt the need to hire a Hollywood actor to help with his television appearances. But now we are much more sophisticated—and more cynical. We know that one cannot simply *be* the president, but that one has to *perform* the role of "president." The new communication arena demands more control on the part of politicians, but it also makes the attempts at control more visible. Many citizens lived through twelve years of FDR's presidency without being aware that his legs were crippled and that he often needed help to stand. But we are now constantly exposed to the ways in which our presidents and presidential candidates attempt to manipulate their images to create certain impressions and effects.

The result is that we no longer experience political performances as naïve audiences. We have the perspective of stage hands who are aware of the constructed nature of the drama. Certainly, we prefer a good show to a bad show, but we are not fully taken in by the performances. Rather than being fooled, we are willingly entertained, charmed, courted, and seduced. Ironically, all the recent discussions of how effectively we are being manipulated may only point out how visible and exposed the machinations now are.

I am not suggesting that television has made us a fully informed and aware electorate. Indeed, relatively few Americans realize how selective an image of the world we receive through television news. When the same sort of occurrences take place in El Salvador and in Nicaragua, or in Poland and in Chile, they are often covered in completely different ways, often in keeping with pre-existing news narratives concerning each country. But regardless of the ways in which the content of television news is often moulded, television is having other effects due to its immediacy and visual nature.

Most of our information about other countries once came through the president and State Department, often after careful planning about how to present the information to the public. This allowed the government to appear to be in control of events and always to have a ready response. In many instances, we now experience events at the same moment as our leaders, sometimes before them. The dramatic images of the fall of the Berlin Wall and other changes in Eastern Europe were watched by the president, the secretary of state, and millions of other Americans at the same moment. The immediacy of television often makes leaders appear to be "standing on the sidelines" rather than taking charge or reacting quickly.

Television's accessible, visual nature also works to level authority. Average citizens gain the feeling that they can form their own impressions of Mikhail Gorbachev, Phillippine "People Power," and other people and events without depending on official interpretations. Once formed, the mass perceptions constrain our leaders' presentation of events. Ronald Reagan found he needed to temper his talk of the "Evil Empire" as the public formed a positive perception of Gorbachev. And the televising of Filipinos facing down Marcos's tanks made it difficult for Americans to accept our president's suggestion that the reported results of that country's election should stand because "there was cheating on both sides." President Reagan might have changed the rhetoric on these topics in any case, but the public's direct access to the television images made it appear that Reagan was following rather than leading the nation.

The speed of television affects authority in relation to domestic events as well. The videotape of the attempted assassination of Ronald Reagan aired on television *before* a coded transmission about the event was received by Vice-President Bush aboard his airplane. Several years later, Reagan had no immediate reaction to the *Challenger* explosion, because millions of Americans saw the *Challenger* explode before he had a chance to watch it on videotape. In both cases, the gap between the experience of the event and a unified administration response made the administration appear temporarily impotent.

As our leaders have lost much control over the flow of information—both about themselves and political events—they have mostly given up trying to behave like the imperial leaders of the past. We now have politicians who strive to act more like the person next door, just as our real neighbours seem more worldly and demand to have a greater say in national and international affairs.

Shared Problems

The recognition of television as a new shared arena solves a number of mysteries surrounding television viewing, including: why people complain so bitterly about TV content but continue to watch so much of it; why many Americans say they turn to television for "most" of their news even through the script for an average evening network news broadcast would fill only two columns of the front page of *The New York Times*; why people who purchase videotape machines often discover that they have little interest in creating "libraries" of their favourite television programs.

The shared nature of the television environment creates many new problems and concerns over media content. Content that would be appropriate and uncontroversial in books directed at select audiences often becomes the subject of criticism when presented on television. When television portrays the dominant and "normal" white, middle-class culture, minorities and subcultures protest their exclusion. Yet when television portrays minorities, many members of the majority begin to fear that their insular world is being "invaded." The nature of the portrayal of some groups becomes a catch-22. If homosexuals are portrayed in a negative and stereotypical manner, for example, gay rights groups protest. If homosexuals are portrayed as normal people who simply have a different sexual orientation, however, other viewers object to television "legitimizing" or "idealizing" homosexual life.

Similarly, television cannot exclusively present content deemed suitable only for young children because adult viewers demand more mature entertainment and news. Yet, when truly mature content is placed on television, many parents complain that the minds of child viewers are being defiled.

Without the segregation of audiences, a program designed for one purpose may have quite different effects. An informational program for parents on teenage suicide may not only help some parents prevent a death, it may also encourage a previously non-suicidal teenager to consider the option. Similarly, a program on how to outwit a burglar may make some home owners more sophisticated about protecting their homes against professional criminals at the same time that it makes unsophisticated burglars more professional.

Even a choice between happy endings and realistic endings becomes controversial on television. When programs end happily, critics argue that serious issues are trivialized through 30- or 60-minute formulas for solving major problems. Yet when realistic endings are presented—a criminal escapes or good people suffer needlessly—critics attack television for not presenting young children with the ideals and values of our culture.

When looked at as a whole, then, it becomes clear that much of the controversy surrounding television programming is not rooted in television content per se but in the problems inherent in a system that communicates everything to all types of people at the same time.

As a shared environment, television tends to include some aspect of every facet of our culture. Fairy tales are followed by gritty portrayals of crime and corruption. Television preachers share the airwaves with female wrestlers. Poets and prostitutes appear on the same talk shows. Actors and journalists compete for Nielsen ratings. But there is little that is new about any of the information that is presented on television; what is new is that formerly segregated social arenas are blurred together. Information once shared only among people of a certain age, class, race, religion, sex, profession, or other subgroup of the culture has now been thrown into a shared, public forum—and few are wholly satisfied with the mishmash.

A substantial part of the social significance of television, therefore, may lie less in what is on television than in the very existence of television as a shared arena. Television provides the largest simultaneous perception of a message that humanity has ever experienced. Through television, Americans often gain a strange sort of communion with each other. In times of crisis—whether an assassination or a disaster—millions of Americans sit in the glow of their TV sets and watch the same material over and over again in an effort, perhaps, to find comfort, see meaning, and feel united with the other faceless viewers.

Even when video cassettes and other activities pull people away from broadcast and cable television, the shared arena is not destroyed. The knowledge of its existence functions in many ways like the knowledge of the "family home" where relatives can spontaneously gather at times of crisis or celebration. The shared arena does not have to be used every day to have a constant psychological presence.

Majority Consciousness

The shared arena of television does not lead to instant physical integration or to social harmony. Indeed, the initial effect is increased social tension. Informational integration heightens the perception of physical, economic, and legal segregation. Television enhances our awareness of all the people we cannot be, the places we cannot go, the things we cannot possess. Through exposure to a wider world, many viewers gain a sense of being unfairly isolated in some pocket of it.

Shared experiences through television encourage members of formerly isolated and distinct groups to demand equal rights and treatment. Today's "minority consciousness," then, is something of a paradox. Many people take renewed pride in their special identity, yet the heightened consciousness develops from the ability to view one's group from the outside; that is, it is the result of no longer being fully in the group. The demand for full equality in roles and rights dramatizes the development of a mass "majority," a single large group whose members do not want to accept any arbitrarily imposed distinctions in roles and privileges. The diminutive connotation of the term *minority* does not seem to refer to the small number of people in the group, but rather to the limited degree of access the members feel they have to the larger society. The concept of minority as it is sometimes applied to women—the majority of the population—is meaningless in any other sense.

Ironically, many minority group members express their special desires to dissolve into the mainstream, to know what everyone else knows, to experience what everyone else experiences. When gays, blacks, Hispanics, women, the disabled, and others publicly protest for equal treatment under the law, they are not only saying: "I'm different and I'm proud of it," they are also saying, "I should be treated as if I'm the same as everyone else." As gay politician Harry Britt of San Francisco has said: "We want the same rights to happiness and success as the nongay." In this sense, many minorities proclaim their special identity in the hope of losing at least part of it.

Television makes it seem possible to have integration, but the social mechanisms are not always in place. The potential for gaining access to the male realm, for example, is much greater for some women than for others. The feminist movement has primarily advanced upper- and middle-class women—often through the hiring of lower-class women to clean house and mind children. For many segments of our society, television has raised expectations but provided few new opportunities.

The shared information environment fostered by television also does not lead to the identical behaviour or attitudes among all individuals. Far from it. What is increasingly shared is a similar set of options. The choice of dress, hairstyle, speech pattern, profession, and general style of life is no longer as strongly linked as it once was to traditionally defined groups.

Michel Foucault argued convincingly that the membranes around prisons, hospitals, military barracks, factories, and schools thickened over several hundred years leading up to the twentieth century. Foucault described how people were increasingly separated into distant spheres in order to homogenize them into groups with single identities ("students," "workers," "prisoners," "mentally ill," etc.). The individuals within these groups were, in a sense, interchangeable parts. And even the distinct identities of the groups were subsumed under the larger social system of internally consistent, linearly connected, and hierarchically arranged units. While Foucault, observed that modern society segregated people in their "special spheres" in order to homogenize individuals into components of a larger social machine, he did not observe the current, post-modern counter-process. As the membranes around spatially segregated institutions become more informationally permeable, through television and other electronic media, the current trend is toward integration of all groups into a relatively common experiential sphere—with a new recognition of the special needs and idiosyncrasies of individuals. Just as there is now greater sharing of behaviours among people of different ages, different sexes, and different levels of authority, there is also greater variation in the behaviours of people of the same age, same sex, and same level of authority.

A Global Matrix

In many instances, the television arena is now international in scope. Over 400 million people in 73 countries watch the Academy Awards; "Live Aid" reach 1.5 billion people in 160 countries; Eastern European countries monitor western television; westerners watched Romanian television as capturing the TV station became the first goal of a revolution; the world watched as Chinese students in Tiananmen Square held English protest signs in front of western TV cameras. The shared arena of television is reinforced through worldwide phone systems, satellites, fax machines, and other electronic media.

But this larger sense of sharing with "everybody" is too wide and diffuse, too quickly changing, too insubstantial. Metaphors aside, it is not possible to experience the whole world as one's neighbourhood or village. Even discounting the numerous political, economic, and cultural barriers that remain, there is a limit to the number of people with whom one can feel truly connected. Electronic sharing leads to a broader, but also a shallower, sense of "us."

The effect of this is both unifying and fractionating. Members of the whole society (and world) are growing more alike, but members of particular families, neighbourhoods, and traditional groups are growing more diverse. On the macro level, the world is becoming more homogeneous, but on the micro level, individuals experience more choice, variety, and idiosyncrasy. We share more experiences with people who are thousands of miles away, even as there is a dilution of the commonality of experience with the people who are in our own houses and neighbourhoods. So the wider sense of connection fostered by electronic media is, ironically, accompanied by a greater retreat to the core of the isolated self. More than ever before, the post-modern era is one in which *everyone* else seems somewhat familiar—and somewhat strange.

As traditional boundaries blur—between regions, between nations, between east and west—there is a rise in factional and ethnic violence within areas that formerly seemed relatively homogeneous. Along with increased hope for world peace, the shared arena may stimulate new types of unrest. As the threat of world war recedes, we are faced with an increase in skirmishes, riots, and terrorism. Whether the era we are now entering will ultimately be viewed as a time of unprecedented unity or a period of unprecedented chaos remains to be seen.

Section Three

Action and Interaction

In "action" is included all human behaviour when and in so far as the acting individual attaches a subjective meaning to it.... Action is social in so far as, by virtue of the subjective meaning attached to it by the acting individual (or individuals), it takes account of others and is thereby oriented in its course.

Max Weber, *The Theory of Social and Economic Organization* (Trans. by A.M. Henderson and T. Parsons) New York: Free Press, 1947:88.

11

Society as Symbolic Interaction

Herbert Blumer

Symbolic interactionism is one of the basic theoretical approaches to the study of social life. In contrast to functionalism's emphasis on group cohesion and stability, or conflict theory's image of society as a dynamic negotiation among competing interest groups, symbolic interactionism investigates how individuals are continually creating and recreating society from the ground up as they go about their everyday affairs. Drawing on Max Weber's definition of action as "behaviour that is subjectively meaningful to the acting individual," Blumer discusses the meaning of "symbolic interaction" and some of the premises of this approach to studying human society.

A view of human society as symbolic interaction has been followed more than it has been formulated Partial, usually fragmentary, statements of it are to be found in the writings of a number of eminent scholars, some inside the field of sociology and some outside. Among the former we may note such scholars as Charles Horton Cooley, W. I. Thomas, Robert E. Park, E. W. Burgess, Florian Znaniecki, Ellsworth Faris, and James Mickel Williams. Among those outside the discipline we may note William James, John Dewey, and George Herbert Mead. None of these scholars, in my judgment, has presented a systematic statement of the nature of human group life from the standpoint of symbolic interaction. Mead stands out among all of them in laying bare the fundamental premises of the approach, yet he did little to develop its methodological implications for sociological study. Students who seek to depict the position of symbolic interaction may easily give different pictures of it. What I have to present should be regarded as my personal version. My aim is to present the basic premises of the point of view and to develop their methodological consequences for the study of human group life.

Herbert Blumer, "Society as Symbolic Interaction," from *Symbolic Interactionism*, Prentice-Hall, 1969: 179-192. Reprinted by permission of Prentice-Hall.

The term "symbolic interaction" refers, of course, to the peculiar and distinctive character of interaction as it takes place between human beings. The peculiarity consists in the fact that human beings interpret or "define" each other's actions instead of merely reacting to each other's actions. Their "response" is not made directly to the actions of one another but instead is based on the meaning which they attach to such actions. Thus, human interaction is mediated by the use of symbols, by interpretation, or by ascertaining the meaning of one another's actions. This mediation is equivalent to inserting a process of interpretation between stimulus and response in the case of human behavior.

The simple recognition that human beings interpret each other's actions as the means of acting toward one another has permeated the thought and writings of many scholars of human conduct and of human group life. Yet few of them have endeavored to analyze what such interpretation implies about the nature of the human being or about the nature of human association. They are usually content with a mere recognition that "interpretation" should be caught by the student, or with a simple realization that symbols, such as cultural norms or values, must be introduced into their analyses. Only G. H. Mead, in my judgment, has sought to think what the act of interpretation implies for an understanding of the human being, human action, and human association. The essentials of his analysis are so penetrating and profound and so important for an understanding of human group life that I wish to spell them out, even though briefly.

The key feature in Mead's analysis is that the human being has a self. This idea should not be cast aside as esoteric or glossed over as something that is obvious and hence not worthy of attention. In declaring that the human being has a self, Mead had in mind chiefly that the human being can be the object of his own actions. He can act toward himself as he might act toward others. Each of us is familiar with actions of this sort in which the human being gets angry with himself, rebuffs himself, takes pride in himself, argues with himself, tries to bolster his own courage, tells himself that he should "do this" or not "do that," sets goals for himself, makes compromises with himself, and plans what he is going to do. That the human being acts toward himself in these and countless other ways is a matter of easy empirical observation. To recognize that the human being can act toward himself is no mystical conjuration.

Mead regards this ability of the human being to act toward himself as the central mechanism with which the human being faces and deals with his world. This mechanism enables the human being to make indication to himself of things in his surroundings and thus to guide his actions by what he notes. Anything of which a human being is conscious is something which he is indicating to himself—the ticking of a clock, a knock at the door, the appearance of a friend, the remark made by a companion, a recognition that he has a task to perform, or the realization that he has a cold. Conversely, anything of which he is not conscious is, *ipso facto*, something which he is not indicating to himself. The conscious life of the human being, from the time that he awakens until he falls asleep, is a continual flow of self-indications—notations of the things with which he deals and takes into account. We are given, then, a picture of the human being as an organism which confronts its world with a mechanism for making indications to itself. This is the mechanism that is involved in interpreting the actions of others. To interpret the actions of another is to point out to oneself that the action has this or that meaning of character.

Now, according to Mead, the significance of making indications to oneself is of paramount importance. The importance lies along two lines. First, to indicate something is to extricate it from its setting, to hold it apart, to give it meaning or, in Mead's language, to make it into an object. An object—that is to say, anything that an individual indicates to himself—is different form a stimulus; instead of having an intrinsic character which acts on the individual and which can be identified apart from the individual, its character or meaning is conferred on it by the individual. The object is the product of the individual's disposition to act instead of being an antecedent stimulus which evokes the act. Instead of the individual being surrounded by an environment of pre-existing objects which play upon him and call forth his behavior, the proper picture is that he constructs his objects on the basis of his on-going activity. In any of his countless acts—whether minor, like dressing himself, or major, like organizing himself for a professional career—the individual is designating different objects to himself, giving them meaning, judging their suitability to his actions, and making decisions on the basis of the judgment. This is what is meant by interpretation or acting on the basis of symbols.

The second important implication of the fact that the human being makes indications to himself is that his action is constructed or built up instead of being a mere release. Whatever the action in which he is engaged, the human individual proceeds by pointing out to himself the divergent things which have to be taken into account in the course of his action. He has to note what he wants to do and how he is to do it; he has to point out to himself the various conditions which may be instrumental to his action and those which may obstruct his action; he has to take account of the demands, the expectations, the prohibitions, and the threats as they may arise in the situation in which he is acting. His action is built up step by step through a process of such self-indication. The human individual pieces together and guides his action by taking account of different things and interpreting their significance for his prospective action. There is no instance of conscious action of which this is not true.

The process of constructing action through making indications to oneself cannot be swallowed up in any of the conventional psychological categories. This process is distinct from and different from what is spoken of as the "ego"—just as it is different from any other conception which conceives of the self in terms of composition or organization. Self-indication is a moving communicative process in which the individual notes things, assesses them, gives them a meaning, and decides to act on the basis of the meaning. The human being stands over against the world, or against "alters," with such a process and not with a mere ego. Further, the process of self-indication cannot be subsumed under the forces, whether from the outside or inside, which are presumed to play upon the individual to produce his behavior. Environmental pressures, external stimuli, organic drives, wishes, attitudes, feelings, ideas, and their like do not cover or explain the process of self-indication. The process of self-indication stands over against them in that the individual points out to himself and interprets the appearance or expression of such things, noting a given social demand that is made on him, recognizing a command, observing that he is hungry, realizing that he wishes to buy something, aware that he has a given feeling, conscious that he dislikes eating with someone he despises, or aware that he is thinking of doing some given thing. By virtue of indicating such things to himself, he places over against them and is able to act back against them, accepting them, rejecting them, or transforming them in accordance with how he defines or interprets them. His behavior, accordingly, is not a result of such things as environmental pressures, stimuli, motives, attitudes, and ideas but arises instead from how he interprets and handles these things in the action which he is constructing. The process of self-indication by means of which human action is formed cannot be accounted for by factors which precede the act. The process of self-indication exists in its own right and must be accepted and studied as such. It is through this process that the human being constructs his conscious action.

Now Mead recognizes that the formation of action by the individual through a process of self-indication always takes place in a social context. Since this matter is so vital to an understanding of symbolic interaction it needs to be explained carefully. Fundamentally, group action takes the form of a fitting together of individual lines of action. Each individual aligns his action to the action of others by ascertaining what they are doing or what the intend to do—that is, by getting the meaning of their acts. For Mead, this is done by the individual "taking the role" of others—either the role of a specific person of the role of a group (Mean's "generalized other"). In taking such roles the individual seeks to ascertain the intention or direction of the acts of others. He forms and aligns his own action on the basis of such interpretation of the acts of others. This is the fundamental way in which group action takes place in human society.

The foregoing are the essential features, as I see them, in Mead's analysis of the bases of symbolic interaction. They presuppose the following: that human society is made up of individuals who have selves (that is, make indications to themselves); that individual action is a construction and not a release, being built up by the individual through noting and interpreting features of the situations in which he acts; that group or collective action consists of the aligning of individual actions, brought about by the individual's interpreting or taking into account each other's actions. Since my purpose is to present and not to defend the position of symbolic interaction I shall not endeavor in this essay to advance support for the three premises which I have just indicated. I wish merely to say that the three premises can be easily verified empirically. I know of no instance of human group action to which the three premises do not apply. The reader is challenged to find or think of a single instance which they do not fit.

I wish now to point out that sociological views of human society are, in general, markedly at variance with the promises which I have indicated as underlying symbolic interaction. Indeed, the predominant number of such views, especially those in vogue at the present time, do not see or treat human society as symbolic interaction. Wedded, as they tend to be, to some form of sociological determinism, they adopt images of human society, of individuals in it, and of group action which do not square with the premises of symbolic interaction. I wish to say a few words about the major lines of variance.

Sociological thought rarely recognizes or treats human societies as composed of individuals who have selves. Instead, they assume human beings to be merely organisms with some kind of organization, responding to forces which play upon them. Generally, although not exclusively, these forces are lodged in the make-up of the society, as in the case of the "social system," "social structure," "culture," "status position," "social role," "custom," "institution," "collective representation," "social situation," "social norm," and "values." The assumption is that the behavior of people as members *of a society* is an expression of the play on them of these kinds of factors or forces. This, of course, is the logical position which is necessarily taken when the scholar explains their behavior or phases of their behavior in terms of one or other of such social factors. The individuals who compose a human society are treated as the media through which such factors operate, and the social action of such individuals is regarded as an expression of such factors. This approach or point of view denies, or at least ignores, that human beings have selves—that they act by making indications to themselves. Incidentally, the "self" is not brought into the picture by introducing such items as organic drives, motives, attitudes, feelings, internalized social factors, or psychological components. Such psychological factors have the same status as the social factors mentioned: they are regarded as factors which play on the individual to produce his action. They do not constitute the process of self-indication. The process of self-indication stands over against them, just as it stands over against the social factors which play on the human being. Practically all sociological conceptions of human society fail to recognize that the individuals who compose it have selves in the sense spoken of.

Correspondingly, such sociological conceptions do not regard the social actions of individuals in human society as being constructed by them through a process of interpretation. Instead, action is treated as a product of factors which play on and through individuals. The social behavior of people is not seen as built up by them through interpretation of objects, situations, or by the actions of others. If a place is given to "interpretation," the interpretation is regarded as merely an expression of other factors (such as motives) which precede the act, and accordingly disappears as a factor in its own right. Hence, the social action of people is treated as an outward flow or expression of forces playing on them rather than as acts which are built up by people through their interpretation of the situations in which they are placed.

These remarks suggest another significant line of difference between general sociological views and the position of symbolic interaction. These two sets of views differ in where they lodge social action. Under the perspective of symbolic interaction, social action is lodged in acting individuals who fit their respective lines of action to one another through a process of interpretation; group action is the collective action of such individuals. As opposed to this view, sociological conceptions generally lodge social action in the action of society or in some unit of society. Examples of this are legion. Let me cite a few. Some conceptions, in treating societies or human groups as "social systems," regard group action as an expression of a system, either in a state of balance or seeking to achieve balance. Or group action is conceived as an expression of the "functions" of a society or of a group. Or group action is regarded as the outward expression of elements lodged in society or the group, such as cultural demands, societal purposes, social values, or institutional stresses. These typical conceptions ignore or blot out a view of group life or of group action as consisting of the collective or concerted actions of individuals seeking to meet their life situations. If recognized at all, the efforts of people to develop collective acts to meet their situations are subsumed under the play of underlying or transcending forces which are lodged in society or its parts. The individuals composing the society or the group become "carriers," or media for the expression of such forces; and the interpretative behavior by means of which people form their actions is merely a coerced link in the play of such forces.

The indication of the foregoing lines of variance should help to put the position of symbolic interaction in better perspective. In the remaining discussion I wish to sketch somewhat more fully how human society appears in terms of symbolic interaction and to point out some methodological implications.

Human society is to be seen as consisting of acting people, and the life of the society is to be seen as consisting of their actions. The acting units may be separate individuals, collectivities whose members are acting together on a common quest, or organizations acting on behalf of a constituency. Respective examples are individual purchases in a market, a play group or missionary band, and a business corporation or a national professional association. There is no empirically observable activity in a human society that does not spring from some acting unit. This banal statement needs to be stressed in light of the common practice of sociologists of reducing human society to social units that do not act—for example, social classes in modern society. Obviously, there are ways of viewing human society other than in terms of the acting units that compose it. I merely wish to point out that in respect to concrete or empirical activity human society must necessarily be seen in terms of the acting units that form it. I would add that any scheme of human society claiming to be a realistic analysis has to respect and be congruent with the empirical recognition that a human society consists of acting units.

Corresponding respect must be shown to the conditions under which such units act. One primary condition is that action takes place in and with regard to a situation. Whatever be the acting unit—an individual, a family, a school, a church, a business firm, a labor union, a legislature, and so on—any particular action is formed in the light of the situation in which it takes place. This leads to the recognition of a second major condition, namely, that the action is formed or constructed by interpreting the situation. The acting unit necessarily has to identify the things which it has to take into account—tasks, opportunities, obstacles, means, demands, discomforts, dangers, and the like; it has to asses them in some fashion and it has to make decisions on the basis of the assessment. Such interpretative behavior may take place in the individual guiding his own action, in a collectivity of individuals acting in concert, or in "agents" acting on behalf of a group or organization. Group life consists of acting units developing acts to meet the situations in which they are placed.

Usually, most of the situations encountered by people in a given society are defined or "structured" by them in the same way. Through previous interaction they develop and acquire common understandings or definitions of how to act in this or that situation. These common definitions enable people to act alike. The common repetitive behavior of people in such situations should not mislead the student into believing that no process of interpretation is in play; on the contrary, even though fixed, the actions of the participating people are constructed by them through a process of interpretation. Since ready-made and commonly accepted definitions are at hand, little strain is placed on people in guiding and organizing their acts. However, many other situations may not be defined in a single way by the participating people. In this event, their lines of action do not fit together readily and collective action is blocked. Interpretations have to be developed and effective accommodation of the participants to one another has to be worked out. In the case of such "'undefined" situations, it is necessary to trace and study the emerging process of definition which is brought into play.

Insofar as sociologists or students of human society are concerned with the behavior of acting units, the position of symbolic interaction requires the student to catch the process of interpretation through which they construct their actions. This process is not to be caught merely by turning to conditions which are antecedent to the process. Such antecedent conditions are helpful in understanding the process insofar as they enter into it, but as mentioned previously they do not constitute the process. Nor can one catch the process merely by inferring its nature from the overt action which is its product. To catch the process, the student must take the role of the acting unit whose behavior he is studying. Since the interpretation is being made by the acting unit in terms of objects designated and appraised, meanings are acquired, and decisions made, the process has to be seen from the standpoint of the acting unit. It is the recognition of this fact that makes the research work of such scholars as R. E. Park and W. I. Thomas so notable. To try to catch the interpretative process by remaining aloof as a so-called "objective" observer and refusing to take the role of the acting unit is to risk the worst kind of subjectivism—the objective observer is likely to fill in the process of interpretation with his own surmises in place of catching the process as it occurs in the experience of the acting unit which uses it.

By and large, of course, sociologists do not study human society in terms of its acting units. Instead, they are disposed to view human society in terms of structure or organization and to treat social action as an expression of such structure or organization. Thus, reliance is placed on such structural categories as social system, culture, norms, values, social stratification, status positions, social roles and institutional organization. These are used both to analyze human society and to account for social action within it. Other major interests of sociological scholars center around this focal theme of organization. One line of interest is to view organization in terms of the functions it is supposed to perform. Another line of interest is to study societal organization as a system seeking equilibrium; here the scholar endeavors to detect mechanisms which are indigenous to the system. Another line of interest is to identify forces which play upon organization to bring about changes in it; here the scholar endeavors, especially through comparative study, to isolate a relation between causative factors and structural results. These various lines of sociological perspective and interest, which are so strongly entrenched today, leap over the acting units of a society and bypass the interpretative process by which such acting units build up their actions.

These respective concerns with organization on one hand and with acting units on the other hand set the essential difference between conventional views of human society and the view of it implied in symbolic interaction. The latter view recognizes the presence of organization in human society and respects its importance. However, it sees and treats organization differently. The difference is along two major lines. First, from the standpoint of symbolic interaction the organization of a human society is the framework inside of which social action takes place and is not the determinant of that action. Second, such organization and changes in it are the product of the activity of acting units and not of "forces" which leave such acting units out of account. Each of these two major lines of difference should be explained briefly in order to obtain a better understanding of how human society appears in terms of symbolic interaction.

From the standpoint of symbolic interaction, social organization is a framework inside of which acting units develop their actions. General features, such as "culture," "social systems," "social interaction," or "social roles," set conditions for their action but do not determine their action. People—that is, acting units—do not act toward culture, social structure or the like; they act toward situations. Social organization enters into action only to the extent to which it shapes situations in which people act, and to the extent to which it supplies fixed sets of symbols which people use in interpreting their situations. These two forms of influence of social organization are important. In the case of settled and stabilized societies, such as isolated primitive tribes and peasant communities, the influence is certain to be profound. In the case of human societies, particularly modern societies, in which streams of new situations arise and old situations become unstable, the influence of organization decreases. One should bear in mind that the most important element confronting an acting unit in situations is the actions of other acting units. In modern society, with its increasing criss-crossing of lines of action, it is common for situations to arise in which the actions of participants are not previously regularized and standardized. To this extent, existing social organization does not shape the situations. Correspondingly, the symbols or tools of interpretation used by acting units in such situations may vary and shift considerably. For these reasons, social action may go beyond, or depart from, existing organization in any of its structural dimensions. The organization of a human society is not to be identified with the process of interpretation used by its acting units; even though it affects that process, it does not embrace or cover the process.

Perhaps the most outstanding consequence of viewing human society as organization is to overlook the part played by acting units in social change. The conventional procedure of sociologists is (*a*) to identify human society (or some part of it) in terms of an established or organized form, (*b*) to identify some factor or condition of change laying upon the human society or the given part of it, and (*c*) to identify the new form assumed by the society following upon the play of the factor of change. Such observations permit the student to couch propositions to the effect that a given factor of change playing upon a given organized form results in a given new organized form. Examples ranging from crude to refined statements are legion, such as that an economic depression increases solidarity in the families of workingmen or that industrialization replaces extended families by nuclear families. My concern here is not with the validity of such propositions but with the methodological position which they presuppose. Essentially, such propositions either ignore the role of the interpretative behavior of acting units in the given instance of change, or else regard the interpretative behavior as coerced by the factor of change. I wish to point out that any line of social change, since it involves change in human action, is necessarily mediated by interpretation on the part of the people caught up in the change—the change appears in the form of new situations in which people have to construct new forms of action. Also, in line with what has been said previously, interpretations of new situations are not predetermined by conditions antecedent to the situations but depend on what is taken into account and assessed in the actual situations in which behavior is formed. Variations in interpretation may readily occur as different acting units cut out different objects in the situation, or give different weight to the objects which they note, or piece object together in different patterns. In formulating propositions of social change, it would be wise to recognize that any given line of such change is mediated by acting units interpreting the situations with which they are confronted.

Students of human society will have to face the question of whether their preoccupation with categories of structure and organization can be squared with the interpretative process by means of which human beings, individually and collectively, act in human society. It is the discrepancy between the two which plagues such students in their efforts to attain scientific propositions of the sort achieved in the physical and biological sciences. It is this discrepancy, further, which is chiefly responsible for their difficulty in fitting hypothetical propositions to new arrays of empirical data. Efforts are made, of course, to overcome these shortcomings by devising new structural categories, by formulating new structural hypotheses, by developing more refined techniques of research, and even by formulating new methodological schemes of a structural character. These efforts continue to ignore or to explain away the interpretative process by which people act, individually and collectively, in society. The question remains whether human society or social action can be successfully analyzed by schemes which refuse to recognize human beings as they are, namely, as persons constructing individual and collective action through an interpretation of the situations which confront them.

12

Tacit Coordination*

Thomas C. Schelling

Schelling's article is a study of decision-making in the context of game theory. Schelling's particular research interest is investigating situations in which parties who cannot communicate directly with each other will nevertheless gain if they arrive at the same decision. From the standpoint of social action Schelling's study illustrates how we take others into account as we make decisions about our own conduct in everyday life. What does his study tell us about the rules and strategies we may use when acting in concert with others?

When a man loses his wife in a department store without any prior understanding where to meet if they get separated, the chances are good that they will find each other. It is likely that each will think of some obvious place to meet, so obvious that each will be sure that the other is sure that it is "obvious" to both of them. One does not simply predict where the other will go, since the other will go where he predicts the first will go, which is wherever the first predicts the second to predict the first to go, and so ad infinitum. Not "What would I do if I were she?" but "What would I do if I were she wondering what she would do if she were wondering what I would do if I were she...?" What is necessary is to coordinate predictions, to read the same message in the common situation, to identify the one course of action that their expectations of each other can converge on. They must "mutually recognize" some unique signal that coordinates their expectations of each other. We cannot be sure they will meet, nor would all couples read the same signal; but the chances are certainly a great deal better than if they pursued a random course of search.

The reader may try the problem himself with the adjoining map. Two people parachute unexpectedly into the area shown, each with a map and knowing the

---

*Thomas C. Schelling, "Tacit Coordination," *The Strategy of Conflict*, Harvard University Press, 1960: 54-60; 72-74; 90-92. For permission to photocopy this selection, please contact Harvard University Press.

other has one, but neither knowing where the other has dropped nor able to communicate directly. They must get together quickly to be rescued. Can they study their maps and "coordinate" their behavior? Does the map suggest some particular meeting place so unambiguously that each will be confident tat the other reads the same suggestion with confidence?

The writer has tried this and other analogous problems on an unscientific sample of respondents; and the conclusion is that people often can coordinate. The following abstract puzzles are typical of those that can be "solved" by a substantial proportion of those who try. The solutions are, of course, arbitrary to this extent: any solution is "correct" if enough people think so. The reader may wish to confirm his ability to concert in the following problems with those whose scores are given in a footnote.[1]

1. Name "heads" or "tails." If you and your partner name the same, you both win a prize.
2. Circle one of the numbers listed in the line below. You win if you all succeed in circling the same number.

$$7 \quad 100 \quad 13 \quad 261 \quad 99 \quad 555$$

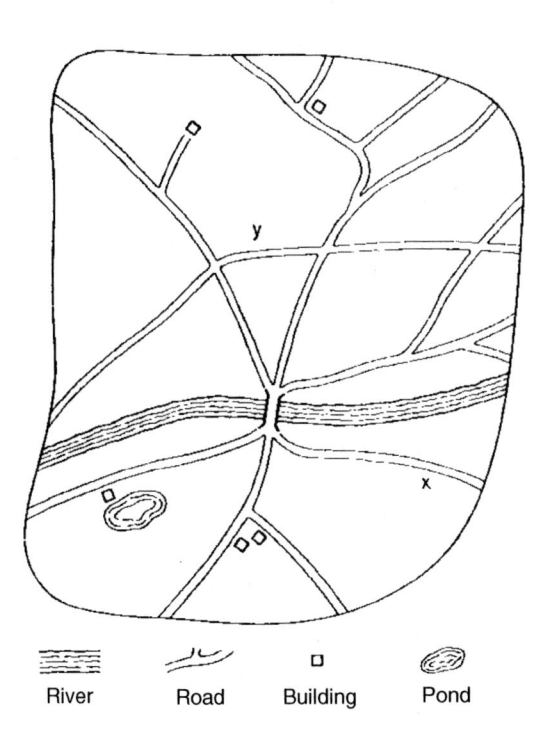

River Road Building Pond

3. Put a check mark in one of the sixteen squares. You win if you all succeed in checking the same square.

☐ ☐ ☐ ☐
☐ ☐ ☐ ☐
☐ ☐ ☐ ☐
☐ ☐ ☐ ☐

4. You are to meet somebody in New York City. You have not been instructed where to meet; you have no prior understanding with the other person on where to meet; and you cannot communicate with each other. You are simply told that you will have to guess where to meet and that he is being told the same thing and that you will have to try to make your guesses coincide.
5. You were told the date but not the hour of the meeting in No. 4; the two of you must guess the exact minute of the day for the meeting. At what time will you appear at the meeting place you elected in No. 4?
6. Write some positive number. If you all write the same number, you win.
7. Name an amount of money. If you all name the same amount, you can have as much as you named.
8. You are to divide $100 into two piles, labeled A and B. Your partner is to divide another $100 into two piles labeled A and B. If you allot the same amounts to A and B, respectively, that your partner does, each of you gets $100, if your amounts differ from his, neither of you gets anything.
9. On the first ballot, candidates polled as follows:

Smith 19   Robinson 29
Jones 28   White 9
Brown 15

The second ballot is about to be taken. You have no interest in the outcome, except that you will be rewarded if someone gets a majority on the second ballot and you vote for the one who does. Similarly, all voters are interested only in voting with the majority, and everybody knows that this is everybody's interest. For whom do you vote on the second ballot?

These problems are artificial, but they illustrate the point. People *can* often concert their intentions or expectations with others if each knows that the other is trying to do the same. Most situations—perhaps every situation for people who are practiced at this kind of game—provide some clue for coordinating behavior, some focal point for each person's expectation of what the other expects him to expect to be expected to do. Finding the key, or rather finding *a* key—any key that is mutually recognized as the key becomes *the* key — may depend on imagination more than logic; it may depend on analogy, precedent, accidental arrangement, symmetry, aesthetic or geometric configuration, casuistic reasoning, and who the parties are and what they know about each other. Whimsy may send the man and his wife to the "lost and found"; or logic may lead each to reflect and to expect the other to reflect on where they would have agreed to meet if they had had a prior agreement to cover the contingency. It is not being asserted that they will always find an obvious answer to the question; but the chances of their doing so are ever so much greater than the bare logic of abstract random probabilities would ever suggest.

A prime characteristic of most of these "solutions" to the problems, that is, of the clues or coordinators or focal points, is some kind of prominence or conspicuousness. But it is a prominence that depends on time and place and who the people are. Ordinary folk lost on a plane circular area may naturally go to the center to meet each other; but only one versed in mathematics would "naturally" expect to meet his partner at the center of gravity of an irregularly shaped area. Equally essential is some kind of uniqueness; the man and his wife cannot meet at the "lost and found" if the store has several. The writer's experiments with alternative maps indicate clearly that a map with many houses and a single crossroads sends people to the crossroads, while one with many crossroads and a single house sends most of them to the house. Partly this may reflect only that uniqueness conveys prominence; but it may be more important that uniqueness avoids ambiguousness. Houses may be intrinsically more prominent than anything else on the map; but if there are three of them, none more prominent than the others, there is but one chance in three of meeting at a house, and the recognition of this fact may lead to the rejection of houses as the "clue."

But in the final analysis we are dealing with imagination as much as with logic; and the logic itself is of a fairly casuistic kind. Poets may do better than logicians at this game, which is perhaps more like "puns and anagrams" than like chess. Logic helps—the large plurality accorded to the number 1 in problem 6 seems to rest on logic—but usually not until imagination has selected some clue to work on from among the concrete details of the situation.

Tacit Bargaining (Divergent Interests)

A conflict of interest enters our problem if the parachutists dislike walking. With communication, which is not allowed in our problem, they would have argued or bargained over where to meet, each favoring a spot close to himself or a resting place particularly to his liking. In the absence of communication, their overriding interest is to concert ideas; and if a particular spot commands attention as the "obvious" place to meet, the winner of the bargain is simply the one who happens to be closer to it. Even if the one who is farthest from the focal point knows that he is, he cannot withhold his acquiescence and argue for a fairer division of the walking; the "proposal" for the bargain that is provided by the map itself—if, in fact, it provides one—is the only extant offer; and without communication, there is no counterproposal that can be made. The conflict gets reconciled—or perhaps we should say ignored—as a by-product of the dominant need for coordination.

"Win" and "lose" may not be quite accurate, since both may lose by comparison with that they could have agreed on through communication. If the two are actually close together and far from the lone house on the map, they might have eliminated the long walk to the house if they could have identified their locations and concerted explicitly on a place to meet between them. Or it may be that one "wins" while the other loses more than the first wins: if both are on the same side of the house and walk to it, they walk together a greater distance than they needed to, but the closer one may still have come off better than if he had had to argue it out with the other.

This last case illustrates that it may be to the advantage of one to be unable to communicate. There is room here for a motive to destroy communication or to refuse to collaborate in advance on a method of meeting if one is aware of his advantage and confident of the "solution" he forsees. In one variant of the writer's test, A knew where B was, but B had no idea where A was (and each knew how much the other knew). Most of the recipients of the B-type questionnaire smugly sat tight, enjoying their ignorance, while virtually all the A-questionnaire respondents grimly acknowledged the inevitable and walked all the way to B. Better still may be to have the power to send but not to receive messages: if one can announce his position and state that his transmitter works but not his receiver, saying that he will wait where he is until the other arrives, the latter has no choice. He can make no effective counteroffer, since no counteroffer could be heard.

* * *

The writer has tried a sample of conflicting-interest games on a number of people, including games that are biased in favor of one party or the other; and on the whole, the outcome suggests the same conclusion that was reached in the purely cooperative games. All these games require coordination; they also, however, provide several alternative choices over which the two parties' interests differ. Yet, among all the available options, some particular one usually seems to be the focal point for coordinated choice, and the party to whom it is a relatively unfavorable choice quite often takes it simply because he knows that the other will expect him to. The choices that cannot coordinate expectations are not really "available" without communication. The odd characteristic of all these games is that neither rival can gain by outsmarting the other. Each loses unless he does exactly what the other expects him to do. Each party is the prisoner or the beneficiary of their mutual expectations; no one can disavow his own expectation of what the other will expect him to expect to be expected to do. The need for agreement overrules the potential disagreement, and each must concert with the other or lose altogether.

Two opposing forces are at the points marked X and Y in a map similar to the [previous map]. The commander of each force wishes to occupy as much of the area as he can and knows the other does too. But each commander wishes to avoid an armed clash and knows the other does too. Each must send forth his troops with orders to take up a designated line and to fight if opposed. Once the troops are dispatched, the outcome depends only on the lines that the two commanders have ordered their troops to occupy. If the lines overlap, the troops will be assumed to meet and fight, to the disadvantage of both sides. If the troops take up positions that leave any appreciable space unoccupied between them, the situation will be assumed "unstable" and a clash inevitable. Only if the troops are ordered to occupy identical lines or lines that leave virtually no unoccupied space between them will clash be avoided. In that case, each side obtains successfully the area it occupies, the advantage going to the side that has the most valuable area in terms of land and facilities. You command the forces located at the point marked X (Y). Draw on the map the lines that you send your troops to occupy.

The ability of the two commanders to recognize the stabilizing power of the river—or, rather, their inability not to recognize it —is substantiated by the evidence that if their survival depended on some agreement about where to stabilize their lines *and communication were not allowed*, they probably could perceive and appreciate the qualities of the river as a focus for their tacit agreement. So the tacit analogy at least demonstrates that the idea of "coordinating expectations" is meaningful rather than mystical.

Perhaps we could push the argument further still. Even in those cases in which the only distinguishing characteristic of a bargaining result is its evident "fairness" by standards that the participants are known to appreciate, we might argue that the moral force of fairness is greatly reinforced by the power of a "fair" result to focus attention, if it fills the vacuum of indeterminacy that would otherwise exist. Similarly, when the pressure of public opinion seems to force the participants to the obviously "fair" or "reasonable" solution, we may exaggerate the "pressure" or at least misunderstand the way it works on the participants unless we give credit to its power to coordinate the participants' expectations. It may, to put it differently, be the power of *suggestion*, working through the mechanism described in this paper, that makes public opinion or precedent or ethical standards so effective. Again, as evidence for this view, we need only to suppose that the participants had to reach ultimate agreement without communicating and visualize public opinion or some prominent ethical standard as providing a strong suggestion analogous to the suggestions contained in our earlier examples. The mediator in problem 7 is a close analogy. Finally, even if it is truly the force of moral responsibility or sensitivity to public opinion that constrains the participants, and not the "signal" they get, we must still look to the source of the public's own opinion; and there, the writer suggests, the need for a simple, qualitative rationale often reflects the mechanism discussed in this paper.

But, if the general line of reasoning is valid, any analysis of explicit bargaining must pay attention to what we might call the "communication" that is inherent in the bargaining situations, the signals that the participants read in the inanimate details of the case. And it means that tacit and explicit bargaining are not thoroughly separate concepts but that the various gradations from tacit bargaining up through types of incompleteness or faulty or limited communication to full communication all show some dependence on the need to coordinate expectations. Hence all show some degree of dependence of the participants themselves on their common inability to keep their eyes off certain outcomes.

This is not necessarily an argument for expecting explicit outcomes as a rule to lean toward exactly those that would have emerged if communication had been impossible; the focal points may certainly be different when speech is allowed, except in some of the artificial cases we have used in our illustrations. But what may be the *main* principle in tacit bargaining apparently may be at least *one* of the important principles in the analysis of explicit bargaining. And, since even much so-called "explicit" bargaining includes maneuver, indirect communication, jockeying for position, or speaking to be overheard, or is confused by a multitude of participants and divergent interests, the need for convergent expectations and the role of signals that have the power to coordinate expectations may be powerful.

Perhaps many kinds of social stability and the formation of interest groups reflect the same dependence on such coordinators as the terrain and the circumstances can provide: the band wagon at political conventions that often converts the slightest sign of plurality into an overwhelming majority; the power of constitutional legitimacy to command popular support in times of anarchy or political vacuum; the legendary power of an old gang leader to bring order into the underworld, simply because obedience depends on the expectation that others will be obedient in punishing disobedience. The often expressed idea of a "rallying point" in social action seems to reflect the same concept. In economics the phenomena of price leadership, various kinds of nonprice competition, and perhaps even price stability itself appear amenable to an analysis that stresses the importance of tacit communication and its dependence on qualitatively identifiable and fairly unambiguous signals that can be read in the situation itself.

"Spontaneous" revolt may reflect similar principles: when leaders can easily be destroyed, people require some signal for their coordination, a signal so unmistakably comprehensible and so potent in its suggestion for action that everyone can be sure that everyone else reads the same signal with enough confidence to act on it, thus providing one another with the immunity that goes with action in large numbers. (There is even the possibility that such a signal might be provided from outside, even by an agent whose only claim to leadership was its capacity to signal the instructions required for concerted action.)

* * *

It is usually the essence of mob formation that the potential members have to know not only where and when to meet but just when to act so that they act in concert. Overt leadership solves the problem; but leadership can often be identified and eliminated by the authority trying to prevent mob action. In this case the mob's problem is to act in unison without overt leadership, to find some common signal that makes everyone confident that, if he acts on it, he will not be acting alone. The role of "incidents" can thus be seen as a coordinating role; it is a substitute for overt leadership and communication. Without something like an incident, it may be difficult to get action at all, since immunity requires that all know when to act together. Similarly, the city that provides no "obvious" central point or dramatic site may be the one in which mobs find it difficult to congregate spontaneously; there is no place so "obvious" that it is evident to everyone that it is obvious to everyone else. Bandwagon behavior, in the selection of leadership or in voting behavior, may also depend on "mutually perceived" signals, when a part of each person's preference is a desire to be in a majority or, at least, to see some majority coalesce.

Excessively polarized behavior may be the unhappy result of dependence on tacit coordination and maneuver. When whites and Negroes [*sic*] see that an area will "inevitably" become occupied exclusively by Negroes [*sic*], the "inevitability" is a feature of convergent expectation. What is most directly perceived as inevitable is not the final result but the *expectation* of it, which, in turn, makes the result inevitable. Everyone expects everyone else to expect everyone else to expect the result; and everyone is powerless to deny it. There is no stable focal point except at the extremes. Nobody can expect the tacit process to stop at 10, 30 or 60 percent; no *particular* percentage commands agreement or provides a rallying point. If tradition suggest 100 percent, tradition could be contradicted only by explicit agreement; if coordination has to be tacit, compromise may be impossible. People are at the mercy of a faulty communication system that makes it easy to "agree" (tacitly) to move but impossible to agree to stay. Quota systems in housing developments, schools, and so forth, can be viewed as efforts to substitute an explicit game with communication and enforcement for a tacit game that has an undesirably extreme "solution."

The coordination game probably lies behind the stability of institutions and traditions and perhaps the phenomenon of leadership itself. Among the possible sets of rules that might govern a conflict, tradition points to the particular set that everyone can expect everyone else to be conscious of as a conspicuous candidate for adoption; it wins by default over those that cannot readily be identified by tacit consent. The force of many rules of etiquette and social restraint, including some (like the rule against ending a sentence with a preposition) that have been divested of their relevance or authority, seems to depend on their having become "solutions" to a coordination game: everyone expects everyone to expect everyone to expect observance, so that nonobservance carries the pain of conspicuousness. Clothing styles and motorcar fads may also reflect a game in which people do not wish to be left out of any majority that forms and are not organized to keep majorities from forming. The concept of *role* in sociology, which explicitly involves the expectations that others have about one's behavior, as well as one's expectations about how others will behave toward him, can in part be interpreted in terms of the stability of "convergent expectations," of the same type that are involved in the coordination game. One is trapped in a particular role, or by another's role, because it is the only role that in the circumstances can be identified by a process of tacit consent.

Endnotes

[1] In the writer's sample, 36 persons concerted on "heads" in problem 1, and only 6 chose "tails." In problem 2, the first three numbers were given 37 votes out of a total of 41; the number 7 led 100 by a slight margin, with 13 in third place. The upper left corner in problem 43 received 24 votes out of a total of 41, and all but 3 of the remainder were distributed in the same diagonal line. Problem 4, which may reflect the location of the sample in New Haven, Connecticut, showed an absolute majority managing to get together at Grand Central Station (information booth), and virtually all of them succeeded in meeting a 12 noon. Problem 6 showed a variety of answers, but two-fifths of all persons succeeded in concerting on the number 1; and in problem 7, out of 41 people, 12 got together on $1,000,000 , and only 3 entries consisted of numbers that were not a power of 10; of those 3, 2 were $64 and, in the more up-to-date version, $64,000! Problem 8 caused no difficulty to 36 out of 41, who split the total fifty-fifty. Problem 9 secured a majority of 20 out of 22 for Robinson. An alternative formulation of it, in which Jones and Robinson were tied in the first ballot at 28 votes each, was intended by the author to demonstrate the difficulty of concerting in case of tie; but the respondents surmounted the difficulty and gave Jones 16 out of 18 votes (apparently on the basis of Jones's earlier position on the list), proving the main point but overwhelming the subsidiary point in the process. In the map most nearly like the one reproduced here, 7 out of 8 repsondents managed to meet at the bridge.

13

Laughter in the Clinic: Humor as Social Organization

William C. Yoels and Jeffrey Michael Clair

Humans, Rose Laub Coser has noted, are the only animals that laugh. This study of the uses of humour in social settings builds on Coser's earlier study of the functions of humour. Humour is explored here, not in terms of how individuals use it as a strategy for their own social purposes, but in terms of the intended and unintended consequences for the maintenance of the entire social organization of which these individuals are a part. Based on this study of a hospital clinic, what are the sociological functions of humour? Does humour perform similar social functions in other organizational settings?

Introduction

While Shakespeare's "To be or not to be" surely ranks among the most memorable lines in English literature, a more sociological phrasing might pose the issue in terms of "To belong or not to belong." The question of how much one's self should be "surrendered" to the collectivity is an abiding one in social psychology (see, especially Fromm 1941; Simmel 1909). As Goffman (1961, p. 320) so perceptively noted:

> Without something to belong to, we have no stable self, and yet total commitment and attachment to any social unit implies a kind of selflessness. Our sense of being a person can come from being drawn into a wider social unit; our sense of selfhood can arise through the little ways in which we resist the pull. Our status is backed by the solid buildings of the world, while our sense of personal identity often resides in the cracks.

William C. Yoels and Jeffrey Michael Clair, "Laughter in the Clinic: Humor as Social Organization," *Symbolic Interaction*, 18(1) 1995: 39-47; 49-50; 54-57.

On a more structural level, the problem of attachment or separation takes the form of an inquiry into the nature of the social bond (see Nisbet 1966; Bellah et al. 1985), that is to say, a concern with how society is knit together through the interweaving of its various "parts." Integration and differentiation, then, at both the micro and macro levels are central issues of longstanding sociological concern (Durkheim [1893] 1933; Parsons 1937).

Humor provides an important perspective on the integration/differentiation issue. It reflects tensions in the social structure created by status inequality and the efforts of lower-ranking participants to come to grips with their place in the social order (Douglas 1975; Radcliffe-Brown 1940, 1949). In addition, through members' joking about common concerns and work tasks, humor may cut across status lines and knit the collectivity together. Humor, then, can serve as a prism through which we observe the conflicts and commonalities of life in organizations.

This article focuses on the usages of humor in an university-based outpatient clinic. We report how humor operates as both an integrating and differentiating feature of social organization. We analyze interactions between key clinic participants: attending physicians and residents; the residents themselves; residents and nurses; and residents/attending physicians and patients....

There is some work about the place of humor in medical settings but that literature is largely anecdotal, didactic, or focused on the therapeutic effects of laughter and joking (see Bennett 1991; Carroll and Shmidt 1992; Klass 1987; Lieber 1986). In one of the few observational studies touching on humor in medicine, Smith and Kleinman (1989) observed medical students using humor to relieve tensions, bond with faculty, and sympathetically communicate with one another about shared problems....

With the exception of the two previous studies, Coser's analysis of a private psychiatric hospital (1959; 1960) remains the only first-hand, observational study of humor in a medical setting. In her first article, Coser (1959) focused on joking between patients on a private psychiatric hospital ward. She found that "jocular griping" collectively represented personal complaints while emphasizing patients' equal status within a hierarchically organized social structure (1959, p. 179); as such, it facilitated a sense of group membership among persons who were not likely to establish longstanding relationships with one another.

In a second article, Coser (1960) examined relationships between the hospital's status hierarchy and the flow of humor between staff members. Based on recorded observations of staff meetings over a three-month period, she found humor flowed along the top-down hierarchical lines of the social structure:

> Those who were of higher status position more frequently took the initiative to use humor; more significant still, the target of witticism, if he was present, was never in a higher authority position than the initiator. (1960, p. 95).

...This article extends Coser's work by examining the meanings of humor in the context of an university-based residency outpatient clinic. More importantly, we examine the place of humor in the interactions between key participants in clinic life.

Setting and Method

The qualitative data presented below are part of a larger study of doctor-new patient encounters. They were generated over a two-year period through field observations of clinic activities and doctor-patient medical encounters taking place in an ambulatory medical resident clinic housed in a Division of General Internal Medicine at a major university medical center....

Patients at this clinic were primarily nonwhite (80%) and female (55%)....The clinic patient population was one representative of the general population in terms of socioeconomic status (SES), being disproportionately of lower income and education. Fifty-three percent of this population was uninsured or on Medicaid.

Throughout the study period, we worked with 150 housestaff, that is, about 50 PGY1s, 50 PGY2s, and 50 PGY3s (postgraduate year), as well as 24 different Attendings (supervising physicians). Essentially, every medical resident at some point throughout the year served as a housestaff physician in this clinic....

Resident housestaff in this clinic were primarily male (76%) and white (89%)....

The use of a field method is crucial for understanding behaviors which are taking place in both the front and backstage regions of the setting (Goffman 1959). We participated in this clinical setting as researchers playing the role of "observer as participant." When playing this role, we were defined by all parties as outsiders, members of neither the patient nor health care provider groupings. We participated in group activities through our presence in the setting but made no claims about sharing the skills background, or fate of group members.

We acknowledge that there are crucial questions about the validity of observations made under the conditions of observer as participant. It is possible, for example, that we witnessed only what the residents wanted us to see. Such a problem diminished, however, as we became a familiar part of the surroundings. Since the residents also were involved in demanding jobs requiring intense concentration, such as providing patient care, the risk of altered behavior was lessened. Thus, while it is likely that physicians acted in ways they believed we would approve of, we are confident that being with them for long periods of time over a two-year period minimized any threat to validity. In fact, as our fieldnote data reveal, physicians were very open with their opinions and even joked with us about shared clinic experiences.

We wanted to be just another part of the setting and wore white lab coats with our names and titles indicated to help blend in. As our relationship became well established, our obvious strategy was to be purely observers and as unobtrusive as possible. The possibility of remaining detached, however, was made problematic by physicians, patients, caregivers, and at times one's self. As far as the health care and service providers were concerned, it was implicit that we were sympathetic to their concerns, otherwise we would not be in the clinic for such an extended period of time. This is further evidenced by the fact that we spent many hours around the nursing stations, joining doctors during medical encounters, delivering a message to a doctor, helping a nurse locate someone, answering an occasional telephone, sitting around in the conference room, sharing food, coffee, opinions, goals, and a reciprocal obligation to pass time in general. Patients learned of us as something other than a health care or service provider. As far a they were concerned, we were there to support them and to help make things better during their visit.

Social scientists in clinical contexts must take a stance that is intrinsically divided. Such a dilemma required us to be collegial by expressing concern with the practical resolution of clinical problems; yet, at the same time, we remained autonomous by focusing our attention on the generation of sociologically relevant data about clinic work....

Humor as Bond and Divisor

Humor as a central dimension of social organization may bond members through laughter about common concerns and problems, while also marking them off from others with differing concerns. As a persuasive and universal feature of social life, humor is a powerful vehicle for exploring how persons do things together which, in the final analysis, as Becker (1986) reminds us, is what sociology is fundamentally about.

Through humor, we can observe how persons negotiate (Strauss 1978) their place in the organization. As such, it beautifully illustrates the ongoing dialectic between structural contexts and face-to-face relations. In the following sections, we examine how humor operates in the interactions between clinic participants, We illustrate humor's multidimensional qualities as a medium which adapts itself to a wide variety of problematic situations.

Humor between Attending Physicians and Residents

Humor between Attendings (i.e., supervising physicians) and residents seems to flow along the downward hierarchical lines first reported by Coser (1959, 1960) in her study of a private psychiatric hospital; that is, the higher ranks (Attendings) poke fun as the lower-ranking residents, although the humor we observed here was generally not of a highly critical nature. So an Attending, for example, can chide a PGY-2 who missed a softball game because his mother was in town, saying "So you need to ask your mother's permission to play." Or, in talking with two residents about a patient of one of them who has got something no one can figure out, the Attending jokingly says to the resident, "It's a humbling profession and you're a humble guy." Even though more playful in nature than critical, we did not observe similar instances of residents poking fun at Attendings.

Another important theme in the humor between Attendings and residents concerns the issue of workloads, the effort to manage the workflow through controlling schedules, and more specifically, the time spent with patients. Mizrahi (1986) documented such concerns in her study of residents in a teaching hospital. She used the acronym "GROP," that is, getting rid of patients, to refer to this issue.

Interns, that is, PGY-1s, are particularly sensitive to the lack of control over schedules and work conditions, especially since their work with patients must be overseen by the Attending physicians, whereas PGY-2s and 3s have much more autonomy in this regard. Additionally, since residents work anywhere from 70–80 hours per week during this three-year residency, workload schedules are of great concern....Schedule changes occasion much conversation and material for humor.

> In one instance, a PGY-3, 2 interns, and an Attending get in a conversation about the changing of the teams of residents at the VA clinic from 8 to 6 teams. Both the interns are worried that they will now be on call much more frequently as a result. The attending laughs and asks somewhat lightheartedly if they ever imagined that things might actually get better as a result, say, for example, that they might be on call even less than now, perhaps only every 6th night? Why do *you always imagine the worst*, he asks, while jokingly suggesting at the same time that he somewhat agrees with their projection. One of the interns responds by joking that they do that because their projections are supported by *huge reams of data*! Everyone laughs.

This is a very revealing incident. Reflected here are residents' concerns about time and pressure—being overworked (see Yoels and Clair 1994); and also issues of uncertainty and powerlessness—the schedule changes suddenly without their having any control or input into working conditions. Solidarity of residents versus others such as Attendings, for example, is indicated as well, with the Attending addressing them collectively as "why do *you*." The Attending's point about *always* also suggests that this is a very *common* and perhaps almost *predictable* response for residents in general. Finally, the residents respond to the Attending's question about their projections by falling back on scientific, *medical* metaphor—their subjective impressions are supported by "hard" *data*. In so doing, they are making a claim as well for their membership as full participants in the medical "universe of discourse" (Mead 1934). We see here how the residents' humor voices a very serious complaint about the structural context of their work—their lack of control over the work process—while stopping far short of a full-scale critique of the organization.

Humor as a bonding process can be seen in Attendings taking the role of socializing agents through mentorship activities. In a discussion between an Attending and a PGY-1 about public versus private hospitals, the Attending makes a joke that "public hospitals are the places where residents can get practice and *make mistakes*," meaning that they can learn their craft there. But since residents also can learn their craft in private hospitals, something else is left unsaid. Implicit here is the fact that the lower SES clientele, often uninsured, of the public hospitals are the more "appropriate material" for such activities. It would seem, then, that those who can afford to pay should not be practiced upon. In addition, Attendings also can teach residents how to control workloads by humorously conveying the "GROP" message through joking that the way to deal is "to tell them to just shut up and take the damn medicine." We might note, however, that such sympathetic responses by Attendings to residents' problems also reinforce the idea of the patient as the "other" — as someone who responses need to be controlled....

Humor between Residents

Humor between the residents themselves falls into three general categories: (1) issues related to workloads and "GROP," (2) mentoring, and (3) jokes reflecting moral judgments about particular social characteristics of patients.

In reference to workload-related matters, lower-level residents learn from higher-ranking ones the most effective procedures for controlling the workflow:

> Two interns are talking about an Attending who has a reputation for keeping the wards full, which is why one of them is so tired and busy. A PGY-2 joins the conversation and they talk about being MOD-Medical Officer of the Day, The PGY-2 says that he writes the whole time while the patient is talking and then when the patient is done, he looks up and says, "Sorry, I didn't hear what you were saying. I was writing. Here's your prescription." Everyone laughs. Another PGY-2, mentioned as someone who is an artist at *GROP* tactics, stops by and adds that, "If you let the patients talk, you'll be there the whole day."

This interchange reveals some persuasive and continual features of resident life that we noticed on countless occasions during our two years in this clinic. First, the control of one's time is a top priority. Second, in the effort to control one's own time, patients come to be seen as almost an obstacle to be gotten over.

One key way to achieve that control of time is to limit how much patients can speak. By controlling the verbal "airways," so to speak, residents establish the temporal rhythms (Snow and Brissett 1986) for social arrivals and departures....

The combination of humor and viewing patients as the "other," along with the time pressures of heavy workloads, contribute toward the residents' tendency to embrace ready-made societal labels when referring to patients. Many of the minority, low-income female patients in this clinic are overweight, for example, and one PGY-2 refers to his patients as belonging to his "Two Hundred Club," since they all weigh more than 200 pounds. Residents also joke about problems with patients who have histories of psychiatric treatment—"schizos," as they are often termed....

When dealing with patients face-to-face, residents generally treated them humanely and with respect. As outside observers and sociologists, however, we were continually struck by the ease with which labels—especially psychiatric ones—carrying implicit moral judgments, were constructed from materials in patients' medical records and then used as shorthand descriptors of the patient. The danger here, of course, is that the time constraints of residency work contribute toward possibly stereotypical treatments of patients (see Yoels et al. 1993; Ritchey et al., forthcoming). In fact, experimental studies reviewed by Jamieson and Zann (1989, p. 387) make the connection between time pressures and stereotyping a plausible one. Their analysis suggests that "stereotype-based categories organized perceptions and *biased judgments* when subjects were situationally motivated to come to rapid decisions" (italics added).

Such humor also reflects, we believe, a feeling of frustration, or perhaps thwarted idealism, among residents regarding health problems associated with obesity, drinking, and psychological functioning, which depend so heavily upon patients' own discipline and motivation for their resolution as opposed to the doctor's skill and knowledge. Residents genuinely want to help patients by having an impact on their health. They want to fell like they have made a contribution, a difference in someone's life; thus, health problems of these kinds pose real obstacles to their achieving that kind of work satisfaction.

Humor between Residents/Attendings and Nurses

While residents joke with nurses in general, most of what we observed in this regard involved joking between residents and/or Attendings and the clinic's Nurse Coordinator (hereafter referred to as NC). Such incidents nicely support Mary Douglas' (1975, p. 98) argument that humor takes as its subject "the joke in the social structure," which is present when one group challenges the official hegemony of another. In this clinic setting, that "joke" concerned the place of the NC in the clinic social structure. She was in an awkward situation of "status inconsistency" since she occupied a position of much lower societal prestige than the residents, but in the clinic she had the final say over scheduling....

Humor between residents and the NC generally fell in two categories: (1) she critiquing them in general as well as in terms of their ability and/or commitments to medical care; and (2) the residents joking with her about her power in the clinic.

One way perhaps for the NC to siphon off her own frustration about how much work she had to do and the responsibilities it entailed, was to derive satisfaction from critiquing those of higher status who, in this clinic at least, were subject to her decisions. There also may be some thwarted idealism here as well since she was a dedicated nurse who enjoyed helping people and remarked on occasion that the nurses did so much bureaucratic paperwork that "They can't do any nursing around here." She may envy, then, the residents who, despite their long hours and scheduling constraints, can do some real "doctoring."...

Humor between Residents/Attendings and Patients

Of all the interactions in the clinic, the joking between residents/Attendings and patients most clearly reflects the dual effects of humor as both integrating and differentiating. When used by residents and Attendings, humor may blur status lines by establishing both their and patients' membership in a *common* "universe of discourse." During one examination, for example, the Attending physician has joined the intern in the examination:

> Just after we enter the room, she jokingly tells the patient, after he responds rather slowly to one of her questions, "That's OK. I'm having the same kind of day you are"—meaning tiring and exhausting. Everyone laughs....

Residents/Attendings also use humor to ask questions of a possible intrusive kind about the patient's psychological world. Humor here allows them to "intrude" without causing a commotion, that is, without damaging the patient's self-esteem; more importantly, it also prevents the directing of too much attention to the residents' *power* to ask the question in the first place. In an examination with an intern, a patient mentioned that she was getting lots of headaches and they started four months ago. She had gotten married one month after the headaches started, and the intern jokingly asked if there was any connection there. She replied jokingly that there was and that her husband and his sister were the cause of her headaches.

The use of humor is significant here in that the intern asks an important, invasive kind of question about her marriage while simultaneously neutralizing it through joking about it. The expectation, of course, is that in a new marriage everything should be rosy, so how could the marriage be related to her headaches. The patient's joking response disguises some of her nervous discomfort and possible embarrassment about having to acknowledge that her marriage of only a few short months is causing some serious headache problems.

As we also can see in the above incident...for patients, humor can function as a way of warding off possibly negative reactions when responding to questions about one's private life or one's "character," which may evoke moral judgments from others, especially high-status, powerful others such as doctors. As such, it distances and protects them from the negative self that the residents may be constructing from their answers....

[Discussion]

Rarely has the study of humor been viewed as germane to the long-established debate about social structure and yet, because of its bonding and differentiating consequences, humor can be seen as a central dimension of social organization. Humor also ideally illustrates the ongoing, mesostructural dialectic between the daily experiences of face-to-face relations and the world behind our backs, the domain of history and social structure. While one laughs in the present, what is laughed about, who initiated the laughter, and who is targeted are all issues circumscribed by the historically based structural factors of status and power (Kemper 1978). As an important ingredient of the mesostructural domain, humor is a place where process and structure meet as social practice....

We suggest that humor functions as an organizational, emotional thermostat of sorts. Persons are continually responding to situations in terms of their ease or "dis-ease" with power and status, two critical dimensions of the organization's emotional climate. When discomforted by feelings of powerlessness or low status persons can try to recalibrate the situation; through the "liberated imagination" (Stark 1987, p. 161), they can "play" with the social structure by joking and laughter. So, residents can toy with the idea of Nurse Coordinator as their boss, as can she in her joking admonitions to them. Similarly, those of higher status and power can ease both their own as well as others' dis-ease about power differences through establishing a bond via humor with those lower down in the social order. As an example, we have shown how residents joke with patients about common elements in their lives. In such instances, people are trying to manage their own as well as others' emotions in order to keep interaction moving along nonproblematic, comfortable lines (Francis 1994).

Humor, then, can cool down situations when overheated, or warm up and enliven the atmosphere when frigid or icy. It is an ideal vehicle for relaxing tensions or resolving threatening status conflicts (Stark 1987). Our analysis of humor clearly evidences how social expectations regulate emotional expression, how society is both *inside* and outside our skins.

In terms of that particular form of *social practice* known as medicine, Foucault (1973, p. xv) has noted how modern medicine originates in a clinical experience that increasingly takes on the character of a nonreciprocal situation, "a confrontation of a gaze and a face, or a glance and a silent body." Medical practitioners face the central dilemma of dealing with patients who present themselves simultaneously as both physical and social "objects," as silent bodies and as discourse-producing selves with identities and social relationships. Medicine employs a biomedical model to diagnose and remedy the body's physical problems. In doing so, however, it often implicitly takes into account the social characteristics of the body (Wrigley et al. 1994; Zola 1983).

As we have seen in our discussions of communications between the residents themselves and between residents and patients, humor plays a central role in allowing both doctors and patients to navigate the ambiguous boundaries of *body* and *self* intrinsic to medical encounters. So, residents joke among themselves about negative social characteristics of patients while maintaining a professional image as helpful experts.... When examining patients, doctors may subtly invoke their power to cross at will from the physical into the social by joking with patients while raising possible intrusive questions about personal life-style matters. Through their own nervously humorous responses to such medically legitimated intrusions by residents into the personal/social realms, patients, in turn, distance and protect the self occupying their body.

An important aspect of medical socialization, noted above, concerns the negative casting of patients as "others." Smith's and Kleinman's (1989, p. 64) study of medical students also illustrates how such humor promotes bonding between students and faculty:

> Joking about patients and procedures means sharing something special with the faculty, becoming a colleague. The idea implicit in the humor, that feelings are real despite the rule against discussing them, is combined with an important sense of "we-ness" that the students value.

Our work and Smith's and Kleinman's (1989) indicate that the process of creating a sense of "we-ness" usually occurs, backstage, in areas off-limits to patients. We should note here, however, the flip side of this process, namely, a sense of "them-ness" vis-à-vis patients. We have indicated how residents sometimes portray patients negatively, for example, when they joke about patients' excessive talk and their poor health habits. Humor, then, often embodies aspects of interactional conflict in which "higher-ups" affirm what they see as their rightful claims to control the work process when dealing with "lower-downs," while commiserating with one another about arduous, burdensome aspects of their work that are little appreciated by outsiders.

As medicine encounters increased demands for a more empathetic focus on the person "in" the body, the boundaries between disease and psyche will become even more porous. We expect that humor will play a role in how doctors and patients negotiate this historical transformation in medical practice....

References

...Alexander, J. G. Giessen, R. Munch, and N. Smelser. 1987. *The Micro-Macro Link*. Berkeley: University of California Press.
Becker, Howard. 1986. *Doing Things Together*. Evanston, IL: Northwestern University Press....
Bellah, Robert, R. Madsen, W. Sullivan, Ann Swidler, and Steven Tipton. 1985. *Habits of the Heart*. Berkeley: University of California Press.
Bennett, Howard J. (ed.) 1991. *The Best of Medical Humor*. Philadelphia: Hanley and Belfus.
Caplow, Theodore. 1968. *Two Against One: Coalitions in Triads*. Englewood Cliffs, NJ: Prentice-Hall.
Carroll, James, and Jerry Shmidt. 1992. "Correlations between Humorous Coping Style and Health." *Psychological Reports*, 70 (2): 402....
Coser, Rose Laub. 1960. "Laughter among Colleagues." *Psychiatry* 23: 81-95.
Coser, Rose Laub. 1959. "Some Social Functions of Laughter." *Human Relations*. 12: 171-182.
Douglas, Mary. 1975. *Implicit Meanings*. New York: Routledge, Kegan and Paul....
Durkheim, E. 1933 [1893]. *The Division of Labor in Society*. New York: Macmillan Co....
Foucault, Michel, 1973. *The Birth of the Clinic: An Archeology of Medical Perception*. New York: Vintage....
Francis, Linda. 1994. "Laughter, the Best Medication: Humor as Emotional Management in Interaction." *Symbolic Interaction* 17:147-163.
Fromm, Erich. 1941. *Escape from Freedom*. New York: Rinehart.
Goffmann, Erving. 1959. *The Presentation of Self in Everyday Life*. New York: Doubleday.
Goffmann, Erving. 1961. *Asylums*. New York: Doubleday....
Jamieson, D.W., and M.P. Zann. 1989. "Need for Structure in Attitude Formation and Expression." Pp. 383–406 in *Attitude Structure and Function*, edited by A. Pratkanis, S. Beckler, and A. Greenwald. Hillsdale, NJ: Lawrence Erlbaum.
Kemper, Theodore. 1978. *A Social Interactionist Theory of Emotion*. New York: Wiley.
Klass, Perri. 1987. "Sick Jokes." *Discovery* 8: 30-35.
Kleinman, Arthur. 1988. *The Illness Narratives*. New York: Basic Books.
Lieber, Deborah. 1986. "Laughter and Humor in Critical Care." *Dimensions of Critical Care Nursing* 5: 162-170....
Mead, George Herbert. 1934. *Mind, Self and Society*. Chicago: University of Chicago Press.
Mizrahi, Terri. 1986. *Getting Rid of Patients*. New Brunswick, NJ: Rutgers University Press.
Nisbet, Robert. 1966. *The Sociological Tradition*. New York: Basic Books.
Parsons, Talcott. 1937. *The Structure of Social Action*. New York: McGraw-Hill.
Pogrebin, Mark, and Eric Poole. 1988. "Humor in the Briefing Room." *Journal of Contemporary Ethnography*, 17: 183-210.
Radcliffe-Brown, A.R. 1940. "On Joking Relationships." *Africa* 13: 195-210.
Radcliffe-Brown, A.R. 1949. "A Further Note on Joking Relationships." *Africa* 19: 133-140.

Ritchey, Ferris, William Yoels, Jeffrey Clair, and Richard Allman. Forthcoming. "Competing Medical and Social Ideologies and Communication Accuracy in Medical Encounters." *Research in the Sociology of Health Care*....

Simmel, Georg. 1909. "The Problem of Society." Translated by A. Small. *American Journal of Sociology* 15: 289-320....

Smith, Allen C. and Sherryl Kleinman. 1989. "Managing Emotions in Medical School: Students' Contacts with the Living and the Dead." *Social Psychology Quarterly* 55:56-69.

Snow, Robert, and Dennis Brissett. 1986. "Pauses: Explorations in Social Rhythm." *Symbolic Interaction* 9: 1-18.

Stark, Werner, 1987. *The Social Bond*. Volume V. New York: Fordham University Press.

Strauss, Anselm. 1978. *Negotiations*. San Francisco: Jossey-Bass....

Taylor, Steven, and Robert Bogdan. 1984. *Introduction to Qualitative Research Methods*. New York: John Wiley and Sons.

Wrigley, J. Michael, William Yoels, Carole Webb, and Phillip R. Fine. 1994. "Social and Physical Factors in the Referral of People with Traumatic Brain Injury to Rehabilitation." *Archives of Physical Medicine and Rehabilitation* 75: 149-155.

Yoels, William, and Jeffrey Michael Clair. 1994. "Never Enough Time: How Medical Residents Manage a Scarce Resource." *Journal of Contemporary Ethnography* 23: 185-213.

Yoels, William, Jeffrey Clair, Ferris Ritchey, and Richard Allman. 1993. "Role-Taking Accuracy in Medical Encounters: A Test of Two Theories." *Sociological Focus* 26: 183-201.

Zola, Irving K. 1983. *Socio-medical Inquiries*. Philadelphia: Temple University Press.

14

The Black Male in Public

Elijah Anderson

This excerpt from a larger study focuses on interactions involving young black males on the streets of adjoining black and white neighbourhoods in an American city. Anderson finds that black males are typically identified and reacted to by others as potentially dangerous and untrustworthy. However, he also finds that young black men often confirm this expectation inadvertently or purposefully as part of assuming a "cool," aggressive pose. Anderson argues that the practice results in a vicious circle of mistrust between blacks and whites, which perpetuates racial divisions in America. Are the typifications and practices equally visible and consequential in Canadian cities?

From summer 1975 through summer 1989, I did fieldwork in the general area I call the Village-Northton, which encompasses two communities—one black and low-income to very poor (with an extremely high infant-mortality rate), the other racially mixed but becoming increasingly middle- to upper-income and white. When my wife Nancy and I moved to the Village in 1975, I had not planned to study the area; but this changed, as I encountered the local community and discovered what seemed an ideal urban laboratory.

Particularly during the 1980s, the problems of United States cities grew more and more insistent, if not intractable, to many. With rising unemployment, brought on in part by increasing "deindustrialization" and the exodus of major corporations, the local black community suffered. The employment lives of its members are further complicated by continuing racial prejudice and discrimination, which often frustrate efforts to make effective adjustments to these changes and the emerging reality. Many who have difficulty finding work in the regular economy become even poorer and may join the criminal

---

Elijah Anderson, "The Black Male in Public," from *Streetwise*, University of Chicago Press, 1990: 164-168; 173-182. Copyright © 1990 the University of Chicago Press. Reprinted with permission of the University of Chicago Press.

underground, which promises them huge financial rewards, a certain degree of "coolness," and happiness—that seems never to fully materialize. Yet, in hot pursuit, many alienated young people commit themselves to this way of life, adopting its morality and norms and serving as role models for other youths. In this way, the drug economy has become elaborated, and drug use has grown widespread among the local poor. As the black community of Northton has undergone social deterioration, the adjacent Village has experienced "spill-over" crime and public incivility.

These developments have profound consequences for the more general area I was studying, requiring further refinement of my research plans from a limited ethnographic representation of the gentrifying neighborhood of the Village to a more inclusive study of the relationship between it and the adjacent black ghetto of Northton. I found that I could not truly understand the Village independent of Northton, and vice versa, particularly where the two communities met; and that realization posed insistent sociological...questions. How do these diverse peoples get it on? How are their everyday public lives shaped and affected by the workings of local social institutions? What is the culture of the local public spaces? What is the public social order? Is there one? How are the social changes in the two communities affecting the residents of both?

I mean my descriptions and analysis to convey...how individuals come to interpret and negotiate the public spaces in the community I have been studying. Much of what I have learned came through informal interviews and direct ethnographic observation over an extended period, and it draws on my experiences in the Village-Northton and in nearby communities that share some of the area's more prominent features....

Anonymous black males occupy a peculiar position in the social fabric of the Village. The fear and circumspection surrounding people's reactions to their presence constitute one of the hinges that public race relations turn on. Although the black male is a provocative figure to most others he encounters, his role is far from simple. It involves a complex set of relationships to be negotiated and renegotiated with all those sharing the streets. Where the Village meets Northton, black males exercise a peculiar hegemony over the public spaces, particularly at night or when two or more are together. This influence often is checked by the presence of the local police, which in turn has consequences for other public relationships in the Village.

The residents of the areas, including the black men themselves, are likely to defer to unknown black males who move convincingly through the areas as though they "run it," exuding a sense of ownership. They are easily perceived as symbolically inserting themselves into any available social space, pressing against those who might challenge them. The young black males, the "big winners" of these little competitions, seem to feel very comfortable as they swagger confidently along. Their looks, their easy smiles, and their spontaneous laughter, singing, cursing, and talk about the intimate details of their lives, which can be followed from across the street, all convey the impression of little concern for other pedestrians. The other pedestrians, however, are very concerned about them.

When young black men appear, women (especially white women) sometimes clutch their pocketbooks. They may edge up against their companions or begin to walk stiffly and deliberately. On spotting black males from a distance, other pedestrians often cross the street or give them wide berth as they pass. When black males deign to pay attention to passersby, they tend to do so directly, giving them a deliberate once-over; their eyes may linger longer than the others consider appropriate to the etiquette of "strangers in the streets." Thus, the black males take in all the others and dismiss them as a lion might dismiss a mouse. Fellow pedestrians, in turn, avert their eyes from the black males, deferring to figures who are seen as unpredictable, menacing, and not to be provoked—predators.

People, black or white, who are more familiar with the black street culture are less troubled by sharing the streets with young black males. Older black men, for instance, frequently adopt a refined set of criteria. In negotiating the streets, they watch out particularly for a certain kind of young black male; "jitterbugs," or those who might belong to "wolf packs," small bands of black teenage boys believed to travel about the urban areas, accosting and robbing people.

Many members of the Village community, however, both black and white, lack these more sophisticated insights. Incapable of making distinctions between law-abiding black males and others, they rely for protection on broad stereotypes based on color and gender, if not outright racism. They are likely to misread many of the signs displayed by law-abiding black men, thus becoming apprehensive of almost any black male they spot in public....

Two general sociological factors underlie the situation in which the black man in the Village finds himself. The first, the "master status-determining characteristic" of race (Hughes 1945), is at work in the most casual street encounter.... In the minds of many Village residents, black and white, the master status of the young black male is determined by his youth, his blackness, his maleness, and what these attributes have come to stand for in the shadow of the ghetto. In the context of racism, he is easily labeled "deviant."... In public, fellow pedestrians are thus uncertain about his purpose and have a strong desire to make sense of him quickly, so that they can get on with their own business. Many simply conclude that he is dangerous and act accordingly. Thus, in social encounters in the public spaces of the Village, before he can be taken for anything as an individual...he is perceived first and foremost as a young black man from the ghetto.... Here, the second element comes into play. An assessment like this is really a *social definition*, normally something to be negotiated between labeler and labeled....

In a city, one has many encounters with anonymous figures who are initially viewed as strangers, about whom little is known or understood. As Goffman (1959) suggests, there are ways strangers can rapidly become known or seen as less strange. In negotiating public spaces, people receive and display a wide range of behavioral cues and signs that make up the vocabulary of public interaction. Skin color, gender, age, companions, clothing, jewelry, and the objects people carry help identify them, so that assumptions are formed and communication can occur. Movements (quick or slow, false or sincere, comprehensible or incomprehensible) further refine this public communication. Factors like time of day or an activity that "explains" a person's presence can also affect in what way and how quickly the image of "stranger" is neutralized....

If a stranger cannot pass inspection and be assessed as "safe" (either by identity or by purpose), the image of predator may arise, and fellow pedestrians may try to maintain a distance consistent with that image. In the more worrisome situations—for example, encountering a number of strangers on a dark street—the image may persist and trigger some form of defensive action.

In the street environment, it seems, children readily pass inspection; white women and white men do so more slowly; black women, black men, and black male teenagers most slowly of all. The master status assigned to black males undermines their ability to be taken for granted as law-abiding and civil participants in public places: young black males, particularly those who don the urban uniform (sneakers, athletic suits, gold chains, "gangster caps," sunglasses, and large portable radios or "boom boxes"), may be taken as the embodiment of the predator. In this uniform, which suggests to many the "dangerous underclass," these young men are presumed to be troublemakers or criminals. Thus, in the local milieu, the identity of predator is usually "given" to the young black male and made to stick, until he demonstrates otherwise, something not easy to do in circumstances that work to cut off communication....

In the Village, a third, concrete factor comes into play. The immediate source of much of the distrust the black male faces is the nearness of Northton. White newcomers in particular continue to view the ghetto as a mysterious and unfathomable place that breeds drugs, crime, prostitution, unwed mothers, ignorance, and mental illness. It symbolizes persistent poverty and imminent danger, personified in the young black men who walk the Village streets (see Katz 1988, pp. 195-273). The following narrative of a young black indicates one response of Villagers to the stereotype they fear so much:

> A white lady walkin' down the street with a pocketbook. She start walkin' fast. She get so paranoid she break into a little stride. Me and my friends comin' from a party about 12:00. She stops and goes up on the porch of the house, but you could tell she didn't live there. I stop and say, "Miss, you didn't have to do that. I thought you might think we're some wolf

pack. I'm twenty-eight, he's twenty-six, he's twenty-nine. You ain't gotta run from us." She said, "Well, I'm sorry." I said, "You can come down. I know you don't live there. We just comin' from a party." We just walked down the street and she came back down, walked across the street where she really wanted to go. So she tried to act as though she lived there. And she didn't. After we said, "You ain't gotta run from us," she said, "No, I was really in a hurry." My boy said, "No you wasn't. You thought we was gon' snatch yo' pocketbook." We pulled money out. "See this, we work." I said, "We grown men, now. You gotta worry about them fifteen-, sixteen-, seventeen-year-old boys. That's what you worry about. But we're grown men." I told her all this. "They the ones ain't got no jobs; they're too young to really work. They're the ones you worry about, not us." She understood that. You could tell she was relieved and she gave a sigh. She came back down the steps, even went across the street.

We stopped in the middle of the street. "You all right, now?" And she smiled. We just laughed and went on to a neighborhood bar.

Experiences like this may help modify the way individual white residents view black males in public, by establishing conditions under which blacks pass inspection by disavowing the image of the predator; but they do little to change the prevailing public relationship between blacks and whites in the community. Common racist stereotypes persist, and black men who successfully make such disavowals are often seen not as the norm but as the exception—as "different from the rest"—thereby confirming the status of the "rest."

In the interest of security and defense, residents adopt the facile but practical perspective that informs and supports the prevailing view of public community relations: whites are law-abiding and trustworthy; anonymous young black males are crime-prone and dangerous. Ironically, this perceived dangerousness has become important to the public self-identity of many local black men....

[B]oth blacks and whites are cautious with strangers and take special care in dealing with anonymous young blacks. This caution is encouraged by a certain style of self-presentation that is common on the street. Many black youths, law-abiding or otherwise, exude an offensive/defensive aura, because they themselves regard the streets as a jungle. A young black man said:

A friend of mine got rolled. He was visiting this girl up near Mercer Street. He come out of this house, and somebody smacked him in the head with a baseball bat. He had all these gold chains on. Had a brand new $200 thick leather jacket,

$100 pair of Michael Jordan sneakers, and they were brand new, first time he had them on his feet. He had leather pants on, too. And I'm surprised they didn't take his leather pants. I mean, he had a gold chain this thick [shows quarter-inch with his fingers]. I mean pure gold—$800 worth of gold. He came out this girl's house, after visiting his baby. Cats hit him in the head with a baseball bat, and they took everything. Took his sneaks, his coat, everything. When the paramedics got there, he had no coat, no sneaks on. They took his belt, took his Gucci belt, the junkies did. I went to visit him in the hospital, and I'm sorry I went in there. I seen him. The boy had stitches...they shaved his head, stitches from here to all the way back of his head. Beat him in the head with a baseball bat. They say it was two guys. They was young boys, typical stupid young boys. Now, my boy's life is messed up. He home now, but poor guy has seizures and everything. It's a jungle out here, man. But he sold drugs; the cops found cocaine in his underwear. They [the muggers] got what they wanted.

The young black males' pose is generally intended for people they perceive as potentially aggressive toward them. But at the same time, it may engender circumspection and anxiety in law-abiding residents, both black and white, whose primary concern is safe passage on the streets.

In this public environment, pedestrians readily defer to young black males, who accept their public position. They walk confidently, heads up and gazes straight. Spontaneous and boisterous, they play their radios as loud as they please, telling everyone within earshot that this is their turf, like it or not. It may be that this is the one of the arenas where they can assert themselves and be taken seriously, and perhaps this is why they are so insistent.

Other pedestrians withdraw, perhaps with a defensive scowl, but nothing more. For the Village is not defended in the way many working-class neighborhoods are. As the black youths walk through late at night with their radios turned up, they meet little or no resistance. This lack of challenge shows how "tame," weak, or undefended the neighborhood is, except in certain areas where white college students predominate and fraternity boys succeed in harassing apparently defenseless blacks, such as women with children, lone women, and an occasional single black man. Black youths tend to avoid such areas of the Village, unless they are in groups.

The same black youths might hesitate before playing a radio loud in the well-defended territories of Northton, however. There they would likely be met by two or three "interceptors," who would promptly question their business, possibly taking the radio and punching one of the boys, or worse, in the process. No such defending force exists within the Village....

Another aspect of claiming turf rights is public talk—its idiom, duration, intensity, and volume. At times, the language of young black males, even those who are completely law-abiding, is harsh and profane. This language is used in many public spaces, but especially at trolley stops and on trolleys and buses. Like the rap music played loudly on boom boxes, it puts others on the defensive. The "others" tend not to say much to the offenders; rather, they complain to one another (though some residents have, in fact, come to appreciate the young males and enjoy the music).

On public transportation, young blacks, including some girls, may display raucous behavior, including cursing and loud talk and play. Because most people encounter the youths as strangers, they understand them through the available stereotypes. Law-abiding black youths often don the special urban uniform and emulate this self-presentation, a practice known as "going for bad" and used to intimidate others. As one young black man said:

> You see the guys sometimes on the bus, having this air about them. They know that the grown people on the bus hope that these guys are not problems. The boys play on that. I'm talking about with women old enough to be their mothers. Now, they wouldn't be doing this at home. But they'll do it on that bus. They'll carry on to such an extent.... Now, I know, especially the young boys. I know they [older people] be scared. They really wondering, 'cause all they know is the headlines, "Juvenile Crime...," "Problems of Youth Kids," or "Chain Snatchers." This is what they know. And these people are much more uncertain than I am, 'cause I know.

In some cases, black males capitalize on the fear they know they can evoke. They may "put on a swagger" and intimidate those who must momentarily share a small space on the sidewalk. When passing such a "loud" dark-skinned person, whites usually anticipate danger, though they hope for a peaceful pass. Whites and middle-income blacks are often more than ready to cross the street to avoid passing a "strange" black person at close range. Young blacks understand this behavior and sometimes exploit the fear, as illustrated in the following narrative by a young white woman:

> I went out for something at the store at about 9:00, after it was already dark. When I came back, there was no place to park in front of my house anymore. So I had to park around the corner, which I generally don't do, because there's a greater chance of getting your car broken into or stolen over there, since a lot of foot traffic goes by at night. So I parked the car, turned out

the lights, and got out. I began walking across the street, but I got into a situation I don't like to get into—of having there be some ominous-looking stranger between me and my house. So I have to go around or something. And he was a black fellow between twenty and thirty, on the youngish side. He certainly wasn't anybody I knew. So I decided not really to run, just sort of double-time, so I wouldn't meet him at close distance at the corner. I kind of ran diagonally, keeping the maximum distance between him and me. And it must have been obvious to him that I was running out of fear, being alone at night out in the street. He started chuckling, not trying to hide it. He just laughed at what I was doing. He could tell what he meant to me, the two of us being the only people out there.

At times, even civil and law-abiding youths enjoy this confusion. They have an interest in going for bad, for it is a way to keep other youths at bay. The right look, moves, and general behavior ensure safe passage. However, this image is also a source of subtle but enduring racial and class distinctions, if not overt hostility, within the community.

Some black youths confront others with behavior they refer to as "gritting," "looking mean," "looking hard," and "bumping." Youths have a saying, "His jaws got tight." Such actions could easily be compared to threatening animal behavior, particularly dogs warning other dogs away from their territory or food. Gritting is a way of warning peers against "messing with me." To grit is to be ready to defend one's interests, in this case one's physical self. It conveys alertness to the prospect of harmful intent, communicating and defining personal boundaries. As one black man said, concerning strategies for negotiating the Northton streets near the Village:

When I walk the streets, I put this expression on my face that tells the next person I'm not to be messed with. That "You messing with the wrong fellow. You just try it." And I know when cats are behind me. I be just lookin' in the air, letting them know I'm checkin' them out. Then I'll put my hand in my pocket, even if I ain't got no gun. Nobody wants to get shot, that shit burns, man. That shit hurt. Some guys go to singing. They try to let people know they crazy. 'Cause if you crazy [capable of anything], they'll leave you alone. And I have looked in they face [muggers] and said, "Yo, I'm not the one." Give 'em that crazy look, then walk away. 'Cause I know what they into. They catch your drift quick....

The youth is caught up here in a cultural catch-22: to appear harmless to others might make him seem weak or square to those he feels a need to impress. If he does not dress the part of a young black man on the streets, it is difficult for him to "act right." If he is unable to "act right," then he may be victimized by strangers in his general peer group. The uniform—radio, sneakers, gold chain, athletic suit—and the selective use of the "grit," the quasi-military swagger to the beat of "rap" songs in public places, are all part of the young man's pose. Law-abiding and crime-prone youths alike adopt such poses, in effect camouflaging themselves and making it difficult for more conventional people to know how to behave around them, since those for whom they may not be performing directly may see them as threatening. By connecting culturally with the ghetto, a young black may avoid compromising his public presentation of self, but at the cost of further alienating law-abiding whites and blacks.

In general, the black male is assumed to be streetwise. He also comes to think of himself as such, and this helps him negotiate public spaces. In this sense, others collectively assist him in being who he is. With a simple move one way or the other, he can be taken as a "dangerous dude." He is then left alone, whereas whites may have more trouble.

Civility and law-abidingness are stereotypically ascribed to the white male, particularly in the public context of so many "dangerous" and "predatory" young blacks. (In fact, white men must campaign to achieve the status of being seen as dangerous in public places.) The white male is not taken seriously on the streets, particularly by black men, who resist seeing him as a significant threat. They think that most white men view conflict in terms of "limited warfare," amounting to little more than scowls and harsh words. It is generally understood that blacks from Northton do not assume this but are open to unlimited warfare, including the use of sticks, stones, knives, and guns, perhaps even a fight to the death.

Most conventional people learn to fear black youths from reading about crimes in the local papers and seeing reports of violence on television, but also by living so near and having the chance to observe them. Every time there is a violent crime, this image of young blacks gains credibility. Such public relations attribute to blacks' control over the means and use of violence in public encounters, thus contributing to dominant stereotypes and fear....

Whereas street interactions between black strangers tend to be highly refined, greetings of whites toward blacks are usually ambiguous or have limited effectiveness. This general communication gap between blacks and whites is exacerbated by the influx of white newcomers. In contrast to the long-time residents, the newcomers are unaccustomed to and frequently intolerant of neighboring blacks and have not learned a visible street etiquette. The run-ins such new people have with blacks contribute to a general black view of "the whites" of the Village as prejudiced, thus undermining the positive race relations promoted over many years by egalitarian-minded residents.

The result is that the white and black communities become collapsed into social monoliths. For instance, although blacks tend to relate cautiously to unknown black youths, they are inclined to look at them longer, inspecting them and noting their business to see whether they deserve to be trusted. Whites, on the other hand, look at blacks, see their skin color, and dismiss them quickly as potential acquaintances; then they furtively avert their gaze, hoping not to send the wrong message, for they desire distance and very limited involvement. Any follow-up by black youths is considered highly suspect, unless there are strong mitigating factors, such as an emergency where help is needed.

A common testimonial from young blacks reflects the way whites encounter them. They speak about the defensiveness of whites in general. White women are said to plant broad grins on their faces in hopes of not being accosted. The smile may appear to be a sign of trust, but it is more likely to show a deference, especially when the woman looks back as soon as she is at a safe distance. When the black stranger and the perceived danger have passed, the putative social ties suggested by the smile are no longer binding, and the woman may attempt to keep the "dangerous" person in view, for a sudden move could signal an "attempted robbery" or "rape."...

Out of a sense of frustration, many young blacks mock or otherwise insult the whites they see in public places, trying to "get even" with them for being part of the "monolithic" group of whites. When they encounter whites who display fear, they may laugh at them or harass them. They think, "What do I have to lose?" and may purposely create discomfort in those they see as "ignorant" enough to be afraid of them. Of course, the whites of the Village are anything but a monolithic group. But it is convenient for certain blacks to see things this way, placing all whites, whom they see as the source of their troubles, into an easily manageable bag. In this way, blacks as well as whites become victims of simplistic thinking.

Black men's resentment, coupled with peer-group pressure to act tough, may cause them to shift unpredictably from being courteous to whites to "fulfilling the prophecy" of those who are afraid and uncomfortable around blacks. When confronting a white woman on the streets, some youths may make lewd or suggestive comments, reminding her that she is vulnerable and under surveillance. The following account describes such an encounter:

> On a Wednesday afternoon in June at about 2:00, Sandra Norris pushed her nine-month-old daughter down Cherry Street. The gray stone facades of the Victorian buildings sparkled in the sun. The streets seemed deserted, as the Village usually is at this time. Suddenly, three black youths appeared. They looked in their late teens. As they approached her, one of the young men yelled to the others, "Let's get her! Get her!" Making

sexual gestures, two of the youths reached for her menacingly. She cringed and pulled the stroller toward her. At that, the boys laughed loudly. They were playing with her, but the feigned attack was no fun for Mrs. Norris. It left her shaking.

As indicated above, an aggressive presentation—though certainly not usually so extreme—is often accepted as necessary for black youths to maintain regard with their peers. They must "act right" by the toughest ghetto standards or risk being ridiculed or even victimized by their own peers. Feeling a certain power in numbers, some groups will readily engage in such games, noisily swooping down on their supposed "prey" or fanning out in a menacing formation. Children, white and black, sometimes are intimidated and form fearful and negative feelings about teenage "black boys."

Such demeanor may be a way of identifying with the ghetto streets, but it is also a way of exhibiting "toughness" toward figures who represent the "overclass," which many view as deeply implicated in the misfortunes of their communities. Such conduct is easily confused with and incorporated into ordinary male adolescent behavior, but the result is complicated by race and gender and the generalized powerlessness of the black community. Understandably, middle-class residents, black and white, become even more likely to place social distance between themselves and such youths, conceptually lumping anonymous black males together for self-defense.

Of course, not everyone is victimized by crime, but many people take incivility as an indication of what could happen, if they did not keep up their guard. When representatives of Northton walking through the Village intimidate residents either verbally or physically, many middle-class people—whites in particular—become afraid of black males in general. They may have second thoughts about "open" and, to some degree, friendly displays they may previously have made toward blacks in public. Blacks and whites thus become increasingly estranged. In fact, there is a vicious circle of suspicion and distrust between the two groups and an overwhelming tendency for public relations between them to remain superficial and guarded.

References

Goffman, Erving. 1959. *The Presentation of Self in Everyday Life*. Garden City, NY: Doubleday.

Hughes, Everett. 1945. "Dilemmas and Contradictions of Status." *American Journal of Sociology, 50*:353-359.

Katz, Jack. 1988. *Seductions of Crime: Moral and Sensual Attraction in Doing Evil*. New York: Basic Books.

Section Four

Socialization

If persons have a universal human nature, they themselves are not to be looked to for an explanation of it. One must look rather to the fact that societies everywhere, if they are to be societies, must mobilize their members as self-regulating participants in social encounters. One way of mobilizing the individual for this purpose is through ritual; he is taught to be perceptive, to have feelings attached to self and a self expressed through face, to have pride, honor and dignity, to have considerateness, to have tact and a certain amount of poise. These are some of the elements of behavior which must be built into the person if practical use is to be made of him as an interactant, and it is through these elements that are referred to in part when one speaks of universal human nature.

Erving Goffman, *Interaction Ritual: Essays on Face-to-Face Behavior*, Anchor/Doubleday, 1967: 44-5.

15

Historical Emergence of Children and Child's Play

Gregory P. Stone

In this article Stone examines from a social historical standpoint how play prepares children for meaningful participation in society. What do children learn through play? What can we learn from examining children playing? The reader here is counselled to use the historical perspective as a backdrop for deriving any conclusions regarding contemporary social relations.

Physical educators too often have a restricted view of play, exercise, and sport, asking only how such activities contribute to the motor efficiency and longevity of the organism. Yet, the symbolic significance of recreation is enormous, providing a fundamental bond that ties the individual to his society. Indeed, many of society's forms—its myths and legends—endure only in play. Play is recreation, then, because it continually re-creates the society in which it is carried on. Social psychology, concerned as it is with the meaningful aspects of human life, is well suited to the analysis of play as a symbolic process.

Social psychologists have long recognized the significance of play for preparing young children to participate later on in adult society. But social psychology, when viewed against the backdrop of history, is very young. Furthermore, there is a disquieting tendency for many social science disciplines to lose their sense of history and develop what they conceive to be universal propositions based on observations made in quite spatially and temporally delimited milieux. This article is primarily designed to place the play of children in historical perspective and, then, to set forth some functions of contemporary child's play, reserving judgment about the universality of such functions. It is hoped that the very tentativeness with which such assertions are set forth will inspire the curiosity of others and encourage them to extend the spatial and

---

Gregory P. Stone, "The Play of Little Children," *Quest*, (1965), IV: 23-27. [as reprinted in Chris Jenks, *The Sociology of Childhood: Essential Readings*, Bastford Academic and Educational Ltd., 1982: 195-199.]

temporal focus of their studies of childhood. Play, like other collective enterprises, is a collective representation: it *re*presents the arrangements of the society and historical era in which it is carried on.

Historical Emergence of Children and Child's Play

In an extraordinary work (Ariès, 1962), Philippe Ariès asks the seemingly naïve question: where do children come from? He is not, of course, concerned with the biological origins of infants, but with the historical origins of the social *identity*, 'child.' Although the classical Greek civilization (and those it influenced directly) had distinguished children socially from babes and adults if only as objects of aesthetic appreciation, children did not emerge as social entities in the subsequent history of Western civilization until the early seventeenth century.

France as an Early Source of Children

Prior to the seventeenth century there were babes and adults in Western civilization, but no in-betweens. Babes were swaddled; adults attired; children were, in fact, *homunculi*. There was no distinctive dress to differentiate them, and expectations directed toward them were not age-specific. The elaborate record of the life of Louis XIII kept by his doctor, Heroard, amazes us today. The Dauphin was betrothed by his first birthday. At seventeen months, he was singing and playing the violin. By the age of two years, he was dancing various kinds of dances. At three and a half, he was reading, and he was writing at four. It must be emphasized here that the child, Louis, was not thought of as particularly brilliant. Such activities were merely expected of the little people we call children today. Nor was this seemingly precocious activity necessarily confined to children of royalty and aristocracy, although such intricate play forms were undoubtedly concentrated in that estate. Paintings of the period, as well as earlier paintings, show the children of commoners and peasants freely participating in what we think of today as adult settings, e.g., taverns and wine shops.

It is not as though there were no play at that time. Louis had his hobby horse, tops, and balls. Rather, play permeated all segments of the society. Ariès chides the contemporary historian Van Marle for his amazement upon discovering that the games played by grown-ups were no less childish than those played by children, retorting, 'Of course not: they were the same'. Festivals were another matrix of community-wide play in medieval Europe. Despite the fact, however, that play was general in the society, its unanticipated consequences were probably different for children and adults as they are today. Certainly some child's play provided young people with a vehicle for anticipatory socialization, permitting them to rehearse roles they would enact or encounter in later life, as in military play. Then as now, the play of children pulled them into the larger society. Adult play, on the other hand, undoubtedly released the players at times from everyday social demands and obligations. That adults and children played the same games makes such differences difficult to verify.

If play was general in the society of medieval Europe, attitudes toward play were not. In fifteenth and sixteenth century France, the Catholic clergy took a dim view of play, unless it followed the performance of work, and this view was subsequently adopted by police and other authorities. Yet, play could not be suppressed by such moralizers in a society where play was general in the population and work did not have the significance it was to acquire with industrialization. The only enforceable suppression of play was accomplished in universities where clergy were recruited and trained, and there is evidence to suggest that this was not very effective. Possibly for this very reason, the Jesuits assimilated the play of the larger society in the seventeenth century. Play was redefined as educational and incorporated in college curricula. At the end of the eighteenth century, emerging nationalism provided a further legitimation of play. Play was conceived as a way of preparing young people for military service. The inclusion of play forms in military training programs is a frequent mode of legitimation. Thus, boxing or 'prize-fighting' became legal in the United States in 1917 when it became an integral part of the U.S. Army's physical training program.

As play acquired the approval of the moral custodians of seventeenth and eighteenth century French society, childhood also became established as a separate social identity in the human biography, and play became rather more of a childish thing. Ariès interprets this emergence of the child in the social morphology as one consequence of the rise of an entrepreneurial stratum in European society. As work moved to the center of social arrangements, play became increasingly relegated to childhood, and *pari passu*, children were established as identifiable social beings. This may have been the case with France, but play and children were to have a more painful birth in the Protestant nations.

Play in the History of England and America

Protestantism provided a religious justification for the tremendous expansion of work in the emerging industrial societies. Work was the key to the gates of the Protestant heaven: by your works are ye known. In contrast to the relegation of play to childhood in seventeenth and eighteenth century France, play had been generally suppressed in England by the end of the eighteenth century. In particular, the legislated inclosures of open areas deprived much of the population of play space. Play was further suppressed by legislation in English towns which, for example, forbade children from playing with tops in the streets or running races on the roads. When Wesley drew up the rules for his school at Kingswood, no time was set aside for play, because, in his view, 'he who plays as a boy will play as a man'.

In America, the status of play in the seventeenth and eighteenth century is less clear. We do know, of course, that child labor persisted in the United States into the twentieth century. Tocqueville thought that the Americans of his time were so wrapped up in work that they could not enjoy play: 'Instead of these frivolous delights, they prefer those more serious and silent amusements which are like business and which do not drive business wholly out of their minds.' On the other hand, Green has observed that play was smuggled into many areas of earlier American life in the guise of work, as in quilting parties and barn-raisings, and, by the end of the nineteenth century, Bryce was impressed by the 'brighter' life afforded the factory workers in New England through their 'amusements than that of the clerks and shopkeepers of England'. The picture is, at best, a confused one. Moreover, what seemed 'serious and silent' to a Frenchman may well have seemed 'bright' to an Englishman....

Ariès may well be correct in his assertion that the emergence of an entrepreneurial stratum in France established the identity of child and cloaked that identity with distinctive play forms, but in England and America it is a very different matter. It required a social movement *against the excesses of capitalism*, in the Protestant countries, to release children from the bonds of work and confer the privileges of play. The movement had its inception in the reformist and revolutionary thought of the mid-nineteenth century and persisted until the twentieth. Indeed, Ritchie and Kollar maintain that, for the United States, the 'institutionalization of children's play and games is largely a twentieth century phenomenon'. It is even possible that this institutionalization was not formally secured until the formulation of the Children's Charter of the 1930 White House Conference on Child Health and Protection which proclaimed: 'With the young child, his work is his play and his play is his work'.

Implications for the Social Psychology of Play

Children and child's play, then, emerged much later on the social scene in the Protestant than in the Catholic countries. As I have pointed out elsewhere, this difference persists today in contrasting Protestant and Catholic attitudes toward gaming or gambling. Nevertheless, the fact remains that children and child's play have not always been with us, particularly as we know them today. Thus, when we speculate upon the social significance of child's play, we may well be developing hypotheses that have relevance only for a particular and relatively recent era of Western civilization. I have often wondered whether or not this is the best any social scientist can do—to dramatize effectively his own socio-historical era....

References

Philippe Ariès. *Centuries of Childhood: A Social History of Family Life*. New York: Vintage, 1982.

16

Behavioural Study of Obedience

Stanley Milgram

In this social psychological study Milgram set out to discover why, and under what circumstances, people obey authority. Are some people naturally inclined to obey or is it a matter of socialization? Under what conditions will an individual act in ways that he or she finds morally reprehensible?

Obedience is as basic an element in the structure of social life as one can point to. Some system of authority is a requirement of all communal living, and it is only the man dwelling in isolation who is not forced to respond, through defiance or submission, to the commands of others. Obedience, as a determinant of behaviour, is of particular relevance to our time. It has been reliably established that from 1933-45 millions of innocent persons were systematically slaughtered on command. Gas chambers were built, death camps were guarded, daily quotas of corpses were produced with the same efficiency as the manufacture of appliances. These inhumane policies may have originated in the mind of a single person, but they could only be carried out on a massive scale if a very large number of persons obeyed orders.

Obedience is the psychological mechanism that links individual action to political purpose. It is the dispositional cement that binds men to systems of authority. Facts of recent history and observation in daily life suggest that for many persons obedience may be a deeply ingrained behaviour tendency, indeed, a prepotent impulse overriding training in ethics, sympathy, and moral conduct. C.P. Snow (1961) points to its importance when he writes:

> When you think of the long and gloom history of man, you will find more hideous crimes have been committed in the

---

Stanley Milgram, "Behavioural Study of Obedience," *Journal of Abnormal and Social Psychology*, 1963, 67: 371-378. [as reprinted in Amy Halberstadt and Steve Ellyson, *Social Psychology Readings*, McGraw Hill, 1990: 362-372.]

name of obedience than have ever been committed in the name of rebellion. If you doubt that, read William Shirer's *Rise and Fall of the Third Reich*. The German Officer Corps were brought up in the most rigorous code of obedience...in the name of obedience they were party to, and assisted in, the most wicked large scale actions in the history of the world (p.24).

While the particular form of obedience dealt with in the present study has its antecedents in these episodes, it must not be thought all obedience entails acts of aggression against others. Obedience serves numerous productive functions. Indeed, the very life of society is predicated on its existence. Obedience may be ennobling and educative and refer to acts of charity and kindness, as well as to destruction.

General Procedure

A procedure was devised which seems useful as a tool for studying obedience (Milgram, 1961). It consists of ordering a naive subject to administer electric shock to a victim. A simulated shock generator is used, with 30 clearly marked voltage levels that range from 15 to 450 volts. The instrument bears verbal designations that range from Slight Shock to Danger: Severe Shock. The responses of the victim, who is a trained confederate of the experimenter, are standardized. The orders to administer shocks are given to the naive subject in the context of a "learning experiment" ostensibly set up to study the effects of punishment on memory. As the experiment proceeds the naive subject is commanded to administer increasingly more intense shocks to the victim, even to the point of reaching the level marked Danger: Severe Shock. Internal resistances become stronger, and at a certain point the subject refuses to go on with the experiment. Behaviour prior to this rupture is considered "obedience," in that the subject complies with the commands of the experimenter. The point of rupture is the act of disobedience. A quantitative value is assigned to the subject's performance based on the maximum intensity shock he is willing to administer before he refuses to participate further. Thus for any particular subject and for any particular experimental condition the degree of obedience may be specified with a numerical value. The crux of the study is to systematically vary the factors believed to alter the degree of obedience to the experimental commands.

The technique allows important variables to be manipulated at several points in the experiment. One may vary aspects of the source of command, content and form of command, instrumentalities for its execution, target object, general social setting, etc. The problem, therefore, is not one of designing increasingly more numerous experimental conditions, but of selecting those that best illuminate the process of obedience from the socio-psychological standpoint.

Related Studies

The inquiry bears an important relation to philosophic analysis of obedience and authority (Arendt, 1958; Friedrich, 1958; Weber, 1947), an early experimental study of obedience by Frank (1944), studies in "authoritarianism" (Adorno, Frenkel-Brunswik, Levinson and Sanford, 1950; Rokeach, 1961), and a recent series of analytic and empirical studies in social power (Cartwright, 1959). It owes much to the long concern with suggestion in social psychology, both in its normal forms (e.g., Binet, 1900) and in its clinical manifestations (Carcot, 1881). But it derives, in the first instance, from direct observation of a social fact; the individual who is commanded by a legitimate authority ordinarily obeys. Obedience comes easily and often. It is a ubiquitous and indispensable feature of social life.

Method

Subjects

The subjects were 40 males between the ages of 20 and 50, drawn from New Haven and the surrounding communities. Subjects were obtained by a newspaper advertisement and direct mail solicitation. Those who responded to the appeal believed they were to participate in a study of memory and learning at Yale University. A wide range of occupations is represented in the sample. Typical subjects were postal clerks, high school teachers, salesmen, engineers, and labourers. Subjects ranged in educational level from one who had not finished elementary school, to those who had doctorate and other professional degrees. They were paid $4.50 for their participation in the experiment. However, subjects were told that payment was simply for coming to the laboratory, and that the money was theirs no matter what happened after they arrived. Table 1 shows the proportion of age and occupation types assigned to the experimental condition.

Personnel and Locale

The experiment was conducted on the grounds of Yale University in the elegant interaction laboratory. (This detail is relevant to the perceived legitimacy of the experiment. In further variations, the experiment was dissociated from the university, with consequences for performance.) The role of experimenter was played by a 31-year-old high school teacher of biology. His manner was impassive, and his appearance somewhat stern throughout the experiment. He was dressed in a grey technician's coat. The victim was played by a 47-year-old accountant, trained for the role; he was of Irish-American stock, whom most observers found mild-mannered and likable.

Table 1 Distribution of Age and Occupational Types in the Experiment

Occupations	20-29 years n	30-39 years n	40-45 years n	Percentage of total occupations
Workers, skilled and unskilled	4	5	6	37.5
Sales, business, and white-collar	3	6	7	40.0
Professional	1	5	3	22.5
Percentage of total (Age)	20	40	40	

Note: Total N = 40.

Procedure

One naive subject and one victim (an accomplice) performed in each experiment. A pretext had to be devised that would justify the administration of electric shock by the naive subject. This was effectively accomplished by the cover story. After a general introduction on the presumed relation between punishment and learning, subjects were told:

> But actually, we know very little about the effect of punishment on learning, because almost no truly scientific studies have been made of it in human beings.
>
> For instance, we don't know how much punishment is best for learning—and we don't know how much difference it makes as to who is giving the punishment, whether an adult learns best from a younger or an older person than himself—or many things of the sort.
>
> So, in this study we are bringing together a number of adults of different occupations and ages. And we're asking some of them to be teachers and some of them to be learners.
>
> We want to find out just what effect different people have on each other as teachers and learners, and also what effect punishment will have on learning in this situation.
>
> Therefore, I'm going to ask one of you to be the teacher here tonight and the other one to be the learner.
>
> Does either of you have a preference?

Subjects then drew slips of paper from a hat to determine who would be the teacher and who would be the learner in the experiment. The drawing was rigged so that the naive subject was always the teacher and the accomplice always the learner. (Both slips contained the word "Teacher." Immediately after the drawing, the teacher and learner were taken to an adjacent room and the learner was strapped into an "electric chair" apparatus.

The experimenter explained that the straps were to prevent excessive movement while the learner was being shocked. The effect was to make it impossible for him to escape from the situation. An electrode was attached to the learner's wrist, and electrode paste was applied "to avoid blisters and burns." Subjects were told that the electrode was attached to the shock generator in the adjoining room.

In order to improve credibility the experimenter declared, in response to a question by the learner: "Although the shocks can be extremely painful, they cause no permanent tissue damage."

Learning Task

The lesson administered by the subject was a paired-associate learning task. The subject read a series of word pairs to the learner, and then read the first word of the pair along with four terms. The learner was to indicate which of the four terms had originally been paired with the first word. He communicated his answer by pressing one of four switches in front of him, which in turn lit up one of four numbered quadrants in an answer-box located atop the shock generator.

Shock Generator

The instrument panel consists of 30 lever switches set in a horizontal line. Each switch is clearly labelled with a voltage designation that ranges from 15 to 450 volts. There is a 15-volt increment from one switch to the next going from left to right. In addition, the following verbal designations are clearly indicated for groups of four switches going from left to right: Slight Shock, Moderate Shock, Extreme Intensity Shock, Danger: Severe Shock. (Two switches after this last designation are simply marked xxx.)

Upon depressing a switch: a pilot light corresponding to each switch is illuminated in bright red; an electric buzzing is heard; an electric blue light, labelled "voltage energizer," flashes; the dial on the voltage meter swings to the right; various relay clicks are sounded.

The upper left-hand corner of the generator is labelled Shock Generator, Type ZLB, Dyson Instrument Company, Waltham, Mass. Output 15 Volts - 450 Volts.

Details of the instrument were carefully handled to ensure an appearance of authenticity. The panel was engraved by precision industrial engravers, and all components were of high quality. No subject in the experiment suspected that the instrument was merely a simulated shock generator.[1]

Sample Shock

Each naive subject is given a sample shock on the shock generator, prior to beginning his run as teacher. This shock is always 45 volts, and is applied by pressing the third switch of the generator. This shock is applied to the wrist of the naive subject, and has its source in a 45-volt battery wired into the generator. This further convinces the subject of the authenticity of the generator.

Shock Instruction

The subject is told to administer a shock to the learner each time he gives a wrong response. Moreover—and this is the key command—the subject is instructed to "move one level higher on the shock generator each time the learner flashes a wrong answer." He is also instructed to announce the voltage level before administering a shock. This serves to continually remind subjects of the increasing intensity of shock administered to the learner.

Preliminary and Regular Run

Pretests revealed that the procedure of reading words and administering shocks requires some practice before it can be handled smoothly. Therefore, immediately preceding the regular run, the teacher is given a preliminary series of 10 words to read to the learner. There are 3 neutral words in the practice series (i.e., words that the learner answers correctly), so that shocks are administered for 7 of the words, with the maximum shock at 105 volts (moderate shock). Almost all subjects master the procedure by the time the preliminary run is over.

Subjects are then presented with a second list, and are told that the procedure is the same as for the first list; the experimenter adds, however:

> When you get to the bottom of the list, repeat it over again, and continue giving shocks, until the learner has learned all the pairs correctly.

The instructor instructs the subject to start from 15 volts and increase the shock level one step each time the learner gives a wrong answer.

Feedback from the Victim

In all conditions the learner gives a predetermined set of responses to the word pair test, based on a schedule of approximately three wrong answers to one correct answer. In the present experimental condition no vocal response or other sign of protest is heard from the learner until Shock Level 300 is reached. When the 300-volt shock is administered, the learner pounds on the wall of the room in which he is bound to the electric chair. The pounding can be heard by the subject. From this point on, the learner's answers no longer appear on the four-way panel.

At this juncture, subjects ordinarily turn to the experimenter for guidance. The experimenter instructs the subject to treat the absence of a response as a wrong answer, and to shock the subject according to the usual schedule. He advises the subjects to allow 5-10 seconds before considering no response as a wrong answer, and to increase the shock level one step each time the learner fails to respond correctly. The learner's pounding is repeated after the 325-volt shock is administered; afterwards he is not heard from, nor do his answers reappear on the four-way signal box.

Experimenter Feedback

At various points in the experiment the subject may turn to the experimenter for advice on whether he should continue to administer shocks. Or he may indicate that he does not wish to go on. It was important to standardize the experimenter's response to these inquiries and reactions.

If the subject indicated his unwillingness to go on, the experimenter responded with a sequence of "prods," using as many as necessary to bring the subject into line.

Prod 1: Please continue *or* Please go on.

Prod 2: The experiment requires that you continue.

Prod 3: It is absolutely essential that you continue.

Prod 4: You have no other choice, you *must* go on.

The prods were always made in a sequence: Only if Prod 1 had been unsuccessful, could Prod 2 be used. If the subject refused to obey the experimenter after Prod 4, the experiment was terminated. The experimenter's tone of voice was at all times firm, but not impolite. The sequence was begun anew on each occasion that the subject balked or showed reluctance to follow orders.

Special Prods

If the subject asked if the learner was liable to suffer permanent physical injury, the experimenter said:

> Although the shocks may be painful, there is no permanent tissue damage, so please go on. [Followed by Prods 2, 3, and 4 if necessary.]

If the subject said that the learner did not want to go on, the experimenter replied:

> Whether the learner likes it or not, you must go on until he has learned all the word pairs correctly. So please go on. [Followed by Prods 2, 3, and 4 if necessary.]

Dependent Measures

The primary dependent measure for any subject is the maximum shock he administers before he refuses to go any further. In principle this may vary from 0 (for subject who refuses to administer even the first shock) to 30 (for a subject who administers the highest shock on the generator). A subject who breaks off the experiment at any point prior to administering the thirtieth shock level is termed a *defiant* subject. One who complies with experimental commands fully, and proceeds to administer all shock levels commanded, is termed an *obedient* subject....

Interview and Dehoax

Following the experiment, subjects were interviewed; open-ended questions, projective measures, and attitude scales were employed. After the interview, procedures were undertaken to assure that the subject would leave the laboratory in a state of well being. A friendly reconciliation was arranged between the subject and the victim, and an effort was made to reduce any tensions that arose as a result of the experiment.

Results

Preliminary Notions

Before giving an account of the experimental results, it is instructive to consider how persons predict others will perform when commanded to administer powerful shocks to another person. Fourteen Yale seniors, all psychology majors, were provided with a detailed description of the experimental situation. They were asked to reflect carefully on it, and to predict the behaviour of 100 hypothetical subjects. More specifically, they were instructed to plot the distribution of obedience of "100 Americans of diverse occupations, and ranging in age from 20 to 50 years," who were placed in the experimental situation.

There was considerable agreement among the respondents on the expected behaviour of hypothetical subjects. All respondents predicted that only an insignificant minority would go through to the end of the shock series. (The estimates ranged from 0 to 3%; i.e., the most "pessimistic" member of the class predicted that of 100 persons, 3 would continue through to the most potent shock available on the shock generator—450 volts.) The class mean was 1.2%. The question was also posed informally to colleagues of the author, and the most general feeling was that few if any subjects would go beyond the designation Very Strong Shock.

Result of Experiment 1

Subjects Accept Situation

With few exceptions subjects were convinced of the reality of the experimental situation, that they were administering shocks to another person, and the most potent shocks were extremely painful. In the post-experimental interview subjects were asked: "How painful to the learner were the last few shocks that you administered to him?" Subjects were instructed to indicate their answers on a printed 14-point scale ranging form "Not at all painful" to "Extremely painful." The modal response was 14 (Extremely painful) with the mean at 13.42.

Signs of Extreme Tension

Many subjects showed signs of nervousness in the experimental situation, and especially upon administering the more powerful shocks. In a large number of cases the degree of tension reached extremes that are rarely seen in socio-psychological laboratory studies. Subjects were observed to sweat, tremble, stutter, bite their lips, groan, and dig their fingernails into their flesh. These were characteristic rather than exceptional responses to the experiment.

One sign of tension was the regular occurrence of nervous laughing fits. Fourteen of the 40 subjects showed definite signs of nervous laughter and smiling. The laughter seemed entirely out of place, even bizarre. Full-blown, uncontrollable seizures were observed for 3 subjects. On one occasion we observed seizure so violently convulsive that it was necessary to call a halt to the experiment. The subject, a 46-year-old encyclopedia salesman, was seriously embarrassed by his untoward and uncontrollable behaviour. In the post-experimental interviews, subjects took pains to point out that they were not sadistic types, and that the laughter did not mean they enjoyed shocking the victim.

Distribution of Scores

It had been conjectured that persons would not, in general, agree to administer shocks beyond the level designated as Very Strong Shock. The distribution of maximum shocks for this experiment is shown in Table 2. The obtained distribution of scores deviates radically from the prediction.

Upon command of the experimenter, each of the 40 subjects went beyond the expected break-off point. No subject stopped prior to administering Shock Level 20. (At this level—300 volts—the victim kicks on the wall and no longer provides answers to the teacher's multiple-choice questions.)

Of the 40 subjects, 5 refused to obey the experimental commands beyond the 300-volt level. Four more subjects administered one further shock, and then refused to go on. Two broke off at the 330-volt level, and 1 each at 345, 360, and 375 volts. Thus a total of 14 subjects defied the experimenter. It is instructive to reprint their remarks at the point of defiance, as transcribed from the tape recordings:

> [0124] I think he's trying to communicate, he's knocking.... Well it's not fair to shock the guy...these are terrific volts. I don't think this is very humane.... Oh, I can't go on with this; no, this isn't right. It's a hell of an experiment. The guy is suffering in there. No, I don't want to go on. This is crazy. [Subject refused to administer more shocks.]
>
> [0123] He's banging in there. I'm gonna chicken out. I'd like to continue, but I can't do that to a man...I'm sorry I can't do that to a man. I'll hurt his heart. You take your check.... No really, I couldn't do it.

These subjects were frequently in a highly agitated and even angered state. Sometimes, verbal protest was at a minimum, and the subject simply got up from his chair in front of the shock generator, and indicated that he wished to leave the laboratory.

Of the 40 subjects, 26 obeyed the orders of the experimenter to the end, proceeding to punish the victim until they reached the most potent shock available on the shock generator. At that point, their experimenter called a halt to the session. (The maximum shock is labelled 450 volts, and is two steps beyond the designation: Danger: Severe Shock.) Although obedient subjects continued to administer shocks, they often did so under extreme stress. Some expressed reluctance to administer shocks beyond the 300-volt level, and displayed fears similar to those who defied the experimenter; yet they obeyed.

After the maximum shocks had been delivered, and the experimenter called a halt to the proceedings, many obedient subjects heaved sighs of relief, mopped their brows, rubbed their fingers over their eyes, or nervously fumbled cigarettes. Some shook their heads, apparently in regret. Some subjects had remained calm throughout the experiment, and displayed only minimal signs of tension from beginning to end.

Discussion

The experiment yielded two findings that were surprising. The first finding concerns the sheer strength of obedient tendencies manifested in this situation. Subjects have learned from childhood that it is a fundamental breach of moral conduct to hurt another person against his will. Yet, 26 subjects abandoned this tenet in following the instructions of an authority who has no special powers to enforce his commands. To disobey would bring no material loss to the subject; no punishment would ensue. It is clear from the remarks and outward behaviour of many participants that in punishing the victim they are often acting against their own values. Subjects often expressed deep disapproval of shocking a man in the face of his objections, and others denounced it as stupid and senseless. Yet the majority complied with the experimental commands. This outcome was surprising from two perspectives: first, from the standpoint of predictions made in the questionnaire described earlier. (Here, however, it is possible that the remoteness of the respondents from the actual situation, and the difficulty of conveying to them the concrete details of the experiment, could account for the serious underestimation of obedience.) But the results were also unexpected to persons who observed the experiment in progress, through one-way mirrors. Observers often uttered expressions of disbelief upon seeing a subject administer more powerful shocks to the victim. These persons had a full acquaintance with the details of the situation, and yet systematically underestimated the amount of obedience that subjects would display.

The second unanticipated effect was the extraordinary tension generated by the procedures. One might suppose that a subject would simply break off or continue as his conscience dictated. Yet, this is very far from what happened. There were striking reactions of tension and emotional strain. One observer related:

> I observed a mature and initially poised businessman enter the laboratory smiling and confident. Within 20 minutes he was reduced to a twitching, stuttering wreck, who was rapidly approaching a point of nervous collapse. He constantly pulled on his earlobe, and twisted his hands. At one point he pushed his fist into his forehead and muttered: "Oh God, let's stop it."

Table 2 Distribution of Breakoff Points

Verbal designation and voltage indication		Number of subjects for whom this was maximum shock
Slight Shock	15	0
	30	0
	45	0
	60	0
Moderate Shock	75	0
	90	0
	105	0
	120	0
Strong Shock	135	0
	150	0
	165	0
	180	0
Very Strong Shock	195	0
	210	0
	225	0
	240	0
Intense Shock	255	0
	270	0
	285	0
	300	5
Extreme Intensity Shock	315	4
	330	2
	345	1
	360	1
Danger: Severe Shock	375	1
	390	0
	405	0
	420	0
XXX	435	0
	450	26

And yet he continued to respond to every word of the experimenter, and obeyed to the end.

Any understanding of the phenomenon of obedience must rest on an analysis of the particular conditions in which it occurs. The following features of the experiment go some distance in explaining the high amount of obedience observed in the situation.

1. The experiment is sponsored by and takes place on the grounds of an institution of unimpeachable reputation, Yale University. It may be reasonably presumed that the personnel are competent and reputable. The importance of this background authority is now being studied by conducting a series of experiments outside of New Haven, and without any visible ties to the university.

2. The experiment is, on the face of it, designed to attain a worthy purpose—advancement of knowledge about learning and memory. Obedience occurs not as an end in itself, but as an instrumental element in a situation that the subject construes as significant and meaningful. He may not be able to see its full significance, but he may properly assume that the experimenter does.

3. The subject perceives that the victim has voluntarily submitted to the authority system of the experimenter. He is not (at first) an unwilling captive impressed for involuntary service. He has taken the trouble to come to the laboratory presumable to aid the experimental research. That he later becomes an involuntary subject does not alter the fact that, initially, he consented to participate without qualification. Thus he has in some degree incurred an obligation toward the experimenter.

4. The subject, too, has entered the experiment voluntarily, and perceives himself under obligation to aid the experimenter. He has made a commitment, and to disrupt the experiment is a repudiation of this initial promise of aid.

5. Certain features of the procedure strengthen the subject's sense of obligation to the experimenter. For one, he has been paid for coming to the laboratory. In part this is cancelled out by the experimenter's statement that:

    Of course, as in all experiments, the money is yours simply for coming to the laboratory. From this point on, no matter what happens, the money is yours.[2]

6. From the subject's standpoint, the fact that he is the teacher and the

other man the learner is purely a chance consequence (it is determined by drawing lots) and he, the subject, ran the same risk as the other man in being assigned the role of learner. Since the assignment of positions in the experiment was achieved by fair means, the learner is deprived of any basis of complaint on this count. (A similar situation obtains in Army units, in which—in the absence of volunteers—a particularly dangerous mission may be assigned by drawing lots, and the unlucky soldier is expected to bear his misfortune with sportsmanship.)

7. There is, at best, ambiguity with regard to the prerogatives of a psychologist and the corresponding rights of his subject. There is a vagueness of expectation concerning what a psychologist may require of his subject, and when he is overstepping acceptable limits. Moreover, the experiment occurs in a closed setting, and thus provides no opportunity for the subject to remove these ambiguities by discussion with others. There are few standards that seem directly applicable to the situation, which is a novel one for most subjects.

8. The subjects are assured that the shocks administered to the subject are "painful but not dangerous." Thus they assume that the discomfort caused the victim is momentary, while the scientific gains resulting from the experiment are enduring.

9. Through Shock Level 20 the victim continues to provide answers on the signal box. The subject may construe this as a sign that the victim is still willing to "play the game." It is only after Shock Level 20 that the victim repudiates the rules completely, refusing to answer further.

These features help to explain the high amount of obedience obtained in this experiment. Many of the arguments raised need not remain matters of speculation, but can be reduced to testable proportions to be confirmed or disproved by further experiments.[3]

The following features of the experiment concern the nature of the conflict which the subject faces.

10. The subject is placed in a position in which he must respond to the competing demands of two persons: the experimenter and the victim. The conflict must be resolved by meeting the demands of one or the other; satisfaction of the victim and the experimenter are mutually exclusive. Moreover, the resolution must take the form of a highly visible action, that of continuing to shock the victim or breaking off the experiment. Thus the subject is forced into a public conflict that does not permit any completely satisfactory solution.

11. While the demands of the experimenter carry the weight of scientific authority, the demands of the victim spring from his personal experience of pain and suffering. The two claims need not be regarded as equally pressing and legitimate. The experimenter seeks an abstract scientific datum; the victim cries out for relief from physical suffering caused by the subject's actions.

12. The experiment gives the subject little time for reflection. The conflict comes on rapidly. It is only minutes after the subject has been seated before the shock generator that the victim begins his protests. Moreover, the subject perceives that he has gone through but two-thirds of the shock levels at the time the subject's first protests are heard. Thus he understands that the conflict will have a persistent aspect to it, and may well become more intense as increasingly more powerful shocks are required. The rapidity with which the conflict descends on the subject, and his realization that it is predictably recurrent may well be sources of tension to him.

13. At a more general level, the conflict stems from the opposition of two deeply ingrained behaviour dispositions: first, the disposition not to harm other people, and second, the tendency to obey those whom we perceive to be legitimate authorities.

Endnotes

[1] A related technique, making use of a shock generator, was reported by Buss (1961) for the study of aggression in the laboratory. Despite the considerable similarity of technical detail in the experimental procedures, both investigators proceeded in ignorance of the other's work. Milgram provided plans and photographs of his shock generator, experimental procedure, and first results in a report to the National Science Foundation in January 1961. This report received only limited circulation. Buss reported his procedure 6 months later, but to a wider audience. Subsequently, technical information and reports were exchanged.

[2] Forty-three subjects, undergraduates at Yale university, were run in the experiment without payment. The results are very similar to those obtained with paid subjects.

[3] A series of recently completed experiments employing the obedience paradigm is reported in Milgram (1964).

References

Adorno, T.W., Frenkel-Brunswik, E., Levinson, D., and Sanford, R.N. (1950). *The authoritarian personality*. New York: Harper. [35], [RI-35].

Arendt, H. (1958). "What was authority?" In C.J. Friedrich (ed.), *Authority* (pp. 81-112). Cambridge, MA: Harvard University Press.

Binet, A. (1900). *La suggestibilité*. Paris: Schleicher.
Cartwright, S. (ed.), (1959). *Studies in social power.* Ann Arbor: University of Michigan Institute for Social Research.
Milgram, S. (1961, Jan. 25). *Dynamics of obedience*. Washington: National Science Foundation.
Milgram, S. (1964). Some conditions of obedience and disobedience to authority. *Human Relations*, 18, 57-76.
Rokeach, M. (1961). "Authority, authoritarianism, and conformity." In I.A. Berg and D.M. Dass (eds.), *Conformity and deviation* (pp. 230-237). New York: Harper.
Snow, C.P. (1961, Feb.) *Either or progressive.* 24.
Weber, M. (1947). *The theory of social and economic organization*. Oxford: Oxford University Press.

17

Equality to Benefit from Schooling: The Issue of Educational Opportunity

Stephen Richer

As a primary site and instrument of socialization our education system purportedly provides an equal opportunity for all members of society to fulfil their potential. But is this actually the case? In this excerpt Richer argues that the pedagogy and the curriculum content, particularly at an elementary level, effectively reproduce inequalities persistent in the social order. The uniformity of structure and content across schools, classrooms and teachers masks a "hidden curriculum" that, says Richer, contributes to the reproduction of the inequality between men and women and the lower and middle classes.

...Do we therefore dismiss the notion of the school as reproducer of the social order? The answer is no, but in order to analyse the role of the school in this regard we must be sensitive to the dynamics of *classroom interaction*, particularly at the early elementary level. My contention is that it is precisely the *lack* of interschool and intraschool variation in pedagogical structure and curriculum content, particularly at the elementary level, which is partially responsible for the data alluded to above on inequality of returns to education. I shall argue that *it is the uniformity of schooling juxtaposed against the variability in children which is salient.* I shall take the position that there is an inequality to benefit from the schooling experience due to the exposure of different children to the *same* educational experience.[1] The reason for focusing on early elementary schooling arises out of the increasing conviction of many researchers in education that it is in these initial years that basic processes are set in motion which to a large extent determine educational and perhaps even occupational mobility. It is at this level that children are the most malleable and hence most vulnerable to the school as an agent of socialization.

Stephen Richer, "Equality to Benefit from Schooling: The Issue of Educational Opportunity," from Dennis Forcese and Stephen Richer (ed) *Social Issues: Sociological Views of Canada* (2nd ed), Scarborough: Prentice-Hall, 1988: 271; 272-277; 279; 283-286.

Cultural Capital and the Hidden Curriculum

Given this desired focus, how can we begin to investigate equality to benefit from education in elementary schools? Two useful concepts are those of cultural capital and the notion of the hidden curriculum. The former, most fully developed by Bourdieu (1964, 1966, 1970) connotes the idea of a differential distribution in society of cultural trappings which are essential for success. Kennett (1973), in summarizing the thrust of Bourdieu's work, explicates five postulates underlying it:

1. Society is essentially a repressive system.
2. There is diffused within society a cultural capital "transmitted by inheritance and invested in order to be cultivated."
3. The education system functions to "discriminate in favour of those who are the inheritors of this cultural capital."
4. The notion of school failure as due to lack of talents, or of groups lacking certain characteristics which makes them unfit for success, is "a mystification, an ideology of the dominant group."
5. Culture has a political function.

There are thus two sides of the cultural capital coin:
1. People vary with respect to their possession of cultural capital.
2. Schools operate within the assumptions underlying this cultural capital.

The latter point leads us to the so-called hidden curriculum, the name given to the bundle of values and norms implicitly transmitted in the schools. To quote Giroux and Penna (1977), the concept refers to "...those unstated norms, values and beliefs that are transmitted to students through the underlying structure of classrooms, as opposed to formally recognized and sanctioned dimensions of classroom experience."

I am convinced that in order for students to be successful in school they would be better to master the hidden rather than the formal curriculum. The point is, of course, that certain students (those already imbued with the cultural capital underlying the hidden curriculum) have a greater capacity to learn its subtleties than other children. In the rest of this paper I shall do two things:
1. Outline the content of the hidden curriculum.
2. Develop links between school success and certain types of children based on compatibility with the demands of the hidden curriculum.

I rely heavily for our discussion on my longitudinal study of Ontario kindergarten children.

Content of the Hidden Curriculum

The study just alluded to was carried out in Ottawa and involved four years of observation in six kindergarten classrooms. With the aid of video tapes and a team of observers, it was possible to collect detailed data on the organization and daily workings of such classrooms. A thematic analysis of the tapes and researchers' diaries led to the following description of what has been termed the "hidden curriculum." Basically, we identified two major aspects of the hidden curriculum: the cognitive (i.e., the way in which school knowledge is organized), and the social, which we discuss at two levels—the societal level and the level of schooling as an institution.

Cognitive Dimensions of the Hidden Curriculum

To understand the way knowledge is organized in our society, it is helpful to begin with a typical kindergarten activity schedule.

Table 1 presents such a schedule for one particular class (although it is very similar to that of other classes observed).[2] The important implicit aspect of this curriculum structure is the relatively clear demarcation which exists among subjects, even at this very early level of schooling. As Table 1 indicates, the day is divided into clearly defined time-space-activity blocks which have virtually no linkages or connections among them. That is, "knowledge" is presented to the child as a set of relatively discrete, self-contained subjects. In Bernstein's words, this exemplified a strong "classification" type of knowledge organization. Classification refers to "the nature of the differentiation" among curriculum contents—"where classification is strong, contents are well insulated from each other by strong boundaries. Where classification is weak, there is reduced insulation between contents for the boundaries between contents are weak and blurred" (Bernstein, 1971: 49). Such a knowledge code clearly reflects wider trends in industrial societies towards increased specialization in the division of labour (see also Esland, 1971; Young 1971).

The point is that children have to learn in a way that forces them to think in terms of relatively fragmented units of information, as opposed to thinking styles which preserve the gestalt or interconnectedness of the social and/or physical world. We shall return to this issue at a later point.

Social Dimensions of the Hidden Curriculum

This aspect of the hidden curriculum consists, I suggest, of two major levels of information—information about the society the children will eventually be entering, and information about public schooling as an institution.

Table 1 A Typical Kindergarten Schedule (Ottawa School, 1978)

Activity	Space	Time
Good Morning Time (Series of songs, e.g., Good Morning, If You're Happy & You Know It)	Piano area	9:00–9:10 a.m.
Demonstration by teacher of how to cut and paste a fire engine	Piano area	9:10–9:20 a.m.
Coordination exercises	Piano area	9:20–9:25 a.m.
Game (Simon Says)	Area in front of doll's house	9:25–9:35 a.m.
Walking across hall to French	Hall	9:35–9:38 a.m.
French	French Teacher's room across the hall	9:38–9:50 a.m.
1/2 class—construction of fire engine	Work-table area	9:50–10:15 a.m.
Others—Free Play	Doll's house area, Jungle Gym, Block area	
Rotation of above		10:15–10:40 a.m.
Snack	Piano area	10:40–10:55 a.m.
Show and Tell (children speak a little about materials brought from home)	Piano area	10:55–11:00 a.m.
Story (read by teacher)	Piano area	11:00–11:15 a.m.
Prepare for going home	Counter area	11:15 a.m.

The Societal Level

Talcott Parsons, writing about the school class as a social system, delineated the function played by formal schooling in preparing children for life in an industrial society. Utilizing his set of pattern variables as basic value and role configurations, he argues convincingly, albeit rather abstractly, that the school weans the child away from the particularism and affectivity characteristic of family life, gradually replacing these with the values of universalism and affective neutrality. The school experience is thus the child's first encounter with the kind of roles he or she will have to engage in when out in the work world (Parsons, 1959). My own study of several kindergarten classes found Parsons' arguments still relevant. Underlying the various classroom activities, even at this initial stage of schooling, can be discerned a set of general values characteristic of the wider society. The major themes involve:

1. the ethic of interindividual competition;
2. an emphasis on materialism;
3. the primacy of work over play; and
4. the submission of self.

First, the child from the first day of formal schooling finds himself competing with other children. Differentiation of the children in terms of success or failure is evident in the games played, early printing exercises, proper school comportment and achieving attention from the teacher. Some children do better than others in motor coordination events and are rewarded accordingly. Games such as Simon Says and Cross the River produced a winner—the first, the best in attentiveness and reflex, and the second, the best jumper in the class. By the middle of the second month in the classes observed, stars were allotted for especially neat printing, usually accompanied by verbal praise. Show and Tell, a period where children talked briefly about items brought from home, became a period where they sought to impress the teacher with their favourite doll, toy soldier or truck, this inevitably at the expense of their peers. At a more covert level, the children were placed in the position of competing throughout the day for both teacher approval and attention. Regarding the former, children adhering to the teacher's conception of proper school behaviour were clearly treated differently from those behaving otherwise. While there were children in the class who rejected this competition for a while and refused to participate, by the end of the first two months of school all the children were actively seeking the teacher's approval. This was accomplished by the teacher through various types of rewards and punishments. Regarding competition for teacher attention, Jackson has given a good description of the competition that constantly exists for this commodity. Given the situation of 30 or so children in a teacher-centred communication structure, "delay, denial and interruption" are no doubt inevitable and frequent occurrences (Jackson, 1968).

The institution of Show and Tell, we argue, became a competition along the axis of material possessions. This period, which occurred every day in the classes studied (and in virtually all elementary classes I have observed), was ostensibly established in schools to provide children the opportunity to speak before their peers about an object or objects familiar to them. Confidence in front of others and verbal skills are assumedly enhanced in the process. While these certainly may occur, an unanticipated consequence of Show and Tell would appear to reinforce interindividual competition and simultaneously to inculcate the values of materialism and private property. In a typical session, a child stands before the group exhibiting a toy or watch, or perhaps a new article of clothing. The teacher usually comments positively on its "niceness" and asks various questions about the object; for example, "Where did you get this?" "Who gave it to you?" "What is it supposed to do?" and "Does anyone else here have something like this?" For the child who has many toys and games at home, this activity becomes an exciting one. He or she proudly produces possessions day after day. Rewarded for bringing them by teacher as well as peer attention, he or she cannot help but see the value of material possessions.

The activities for which tangible rewards are allotted provide a clue as to which types of activities are valued in a group. In kindergarten, rewards such as paper stars, animal picture stamps or coloured check marks were distributed only for "3 R" type activities; that is, letter and number printing and various puzzle worksheets. Play activities, including games and songs, produced occasional praise if well done but no further recognition. In short, those we would term school work activities were associated with tangible rewards, while play activities were not. This, along with the physical centrality of the teacher's desk, the blackboard, and the children's work area, served, I would argue, to convey to the child the primacy of work over play, a primacy to be reinforced from that point on in his/her life.

Perhaps the least "hidden" aspect of the hidden curriculum is the transmission of what we would call submission of self. The theme of "man" as essentially wild, self-interested and aggressive in the pursuit of his interests appears in the writings of many philosophers and social scientists. Parsons, for example, in *The Structure of Social Action* wrestles with the contradiction between these attributes of man and the existence of order, eventually coming to his solution of the internalization of norms regulating social action (Parsons, 1939). The kindergarten classroom, although at first glance an unlikely arena for the acting out of the Parsonian solution, nevertheless evoked for me time and again the struggle between individual voluntarism and societal constraint. What the child learns here, sometimes painfully, is that the collectivity has precedence over his or her own desires and wishes.

In Parsons' terms, there is a move from a self to a collectivistic orientation (Parsons, 1951). The child learns that he/she must put aside his or her own wishes in favour of the wishes of a recognized authority figure in adult society, in this case the teacher. He/she is to accept as natural and right that people above him/her in a status hierarchy can dictate his or her own behaviour, an acceptance that is to be generalized to other organizations he or she will encounter.

From the first day of school, the teachers observed made this their primary task. Convinced, as are the large majority of teachers I have observed, that "You cannot teach them a thing if you can't control them," a great deal of effort was expended on achieving classroom order. Through an elaborate set of rewards and punishments, orderly behaviour was reinforced and its opposite punished. The concern of the teachers with their initial inability to effect control was also evident in the teacher interviews conducted regularly after each observation session. Two standard questions were asked during these interviews: "What were your impressions today?" and "Which children stood out today?" The questions were purposely phrased very generally so that teachers could raise anything they wished. Nevertheless, in the first several weeks, both questions were answered with regard to the presence or absence of control on that particular day:

> The class is too big to handle. They don't know enough to sit in groups. We have to have some conformity. While some are sitting at the piano others are wandering around. (September 5)

> It was better today, there was a little more control over the children. They didn't abuse the free playtime. The end of the day is a very disappointing time. I just can't control them any more. You cannot teach them a thing if you can't control them. In all, they are responding to me better as a person of authority and resource. (September 6)

> Monday mornings always seem to be good. It's a good teaching day. I'm refreshed from the weekend and the children are too. It gets worse up to the end of the week and by Friday they're right up there. (September 10)

The question "Which children stood out today?" might theoretically have resulted in discussions of particularly "bright" children, of conspicuous articles of clothing, or of children with various physical attributes. Instead, the children who "stood out" for the teacher were those she perceived as behaviour problems: "There are three problem boys, John, Mark, Phillip." (September 5) or "Billy—I can't get through to him." (September 6) or "Robert I can't figure him out. I can't reason with him." (September 7) or "Billy needs constant discipline. I believe things would be better with a smaller class" (September 12).[3]

The relationships between the teacher and six or seven of the children observed in the first month or so thus consisted largely of a contest of wills. The following exchanges, one from September 5 and another from September 8, provide vivid illustrations:

(September 5)
Teacher: "Billy, join the group please."
Billy: "I don't feel like coming."
Teacher: "Yes, you do."
Billy: "No, I don't. You might think I do, but I don't."

(September 8)
Teacher: "You're not doing what everyone else is doing."
Robert: "I know, I don't want to."
Teacher: "But I want you to. Come on."

It is clear, then, that for the child there is no alternative but to eventually submit. In terms of resources, the contest is inherently unequal, the teacher possessing greater age and physical size, not to mention legitimate authority. The latter is manifested both in the support of fellow professionals as well as in the tacit backing of the larger community who, in effect, grant a mandate to teachers to socialize their sons and daughters.

The outcome, then, undoubtedly functional from a societal perspective, is that the children learn to accept external authority and concomitantly to repress their own egocentric interest, a requisite for later participation in large-scale bureaucratic organizations.

The Institution of Public Schooling

From the first day of kindergarten, the child is presented with a set of values about appropriate school behaviour which he/she will encounter time and again throughout his/her formal education. These are in large part school-specific counterparts of the societal level values alluded to above. School is presented as a place where children compete with one another along the work axis for various rewards which are meted out by an adult to whom they are expected continually to defer. This last aspect, the submission of self, is expressed in schools in terms of a set of normative expectations clustered into the role of student. These expectations are transmitted by the teacher and involve attentiveness, ways of receiving attention and ways of overall comportment.

First, children are expected to listen when the teacher speaks. One of the teachers, for example, experimented with two major techniques of obtaining attention. In the first week, she told the children that when she called "All hands up," they were to stop whatever they were doing, raise their hands and "close their mouths." This signified her desire to address the class. This was abandoned, however, as it proved unsuccessful after the third or fourth attempt. The second technique, eventually adopted, was to require certain types of behaviour in particular parts of the classroom. We refer here to the association between spatial area and appropriate activity, exemplified in Table 1. The most relevant area was the piano area. When the children were gathered here, the teacher expected the exhibition of "piano manners." These entailed being quiet, sitting up straight, and listening when others were talking. An excerpt from October 29, is a typical illustration of the way in which the teacher sought to bring about the acceptance of the manners idea:

Teacher:	"Can we have piano manners? (pause) What are piano manners?"
Two or three children:	"Sitting up straight and listening."
Teacher:	"That is right. If I have people who don't give me piano manners, they'll put their hands on top of their heads."

By the end of the first week in November, piano manners were virtually automatically displayed by the children in this area of the room, and the teacher was able to drop explanatory repetitions of the kind quoted above.

Children were thus expected to give attention on demand to the teacher. They were also expected to conform to a set of rules concerning the *seeking* of attention. As early as September 5, in all the classes the children were told to raise their hands if they wished to speak and not to interrupt when someone else was speaking. It should be pointed out that most of the children were quite familiar with the hand-raising phenomenon before the teacher held forth on it, which implies some anticipatory socialization in the home *vis-à-vis* student behaviour.

As for general comportment, the children were to learn that school was a place where one behaves differently than one does away from school. This difference is expressed in one teacher's distinction between "inside" and "outside" voices—school is a place for the former; that is, quiet talk, hushed voices. A set of expected behaviours called "hall manners" by the same teacher are also a good illustration. When the children left the classroom to go to French or Gym, or to a school assembly, they were expected to line up in single file, place their two hands on their head, and walk directly to the appropriate area. In short, as a student is attentive to the teacher, one seeks recognition through appropriate channels, and one generally behaves docilely.

Student Cultural Capital and the Hidden Curriculum

The argument to be made here is that certain children, because of the cultural capital which they carry, are more compatible than others with the above aspects of schooling. Specifically, it is my contention that middle-class children and females are better "matched" to the demands of schooling than their lower-class and male counterparts. This accounts to a large extent, I suggest, for their differential success in the schools.

There has been much work done in the U.S. on cultural differences among the social classes (classic works are Hyman, 1954; Kohn, 1963, 1969; Kluckhohn and Strodbeck, 1961; Reissman, 1962). Despite some inconsistencies among studies, there is general agreement in this literature that one can differentiate the American lower and middle classes along four lines; attitudes towards achievement; future versus present orientation; extent to which competition versus cooperation characterizes life style; and extent to which materialism is a salient value. With some caution, one can produce a fair amount of evidence consistent with the following: members of the lower as opposed to the middle class are less motivated to achieve, more likely to stress the present as opposed to the future as the major source of rewards, more inclined to value cooperation as opposed to competition, more inclined to respond to material as opposed to symbolic rewards and, related to this latter point, more inclined to settle disputes through physical rather than verbal means.

The relevant research in Canada, although less abundant than that in the U.S., is nevertheless consistent with these typifications. (For general summaries see Elkin and Handel, 1972; Elkin, 1964; Pike and Zureik, 1975; Jones and Selby, 1972.)

By way of summarizing the above social class discussion, I am suggesting that certain middle-class characteristics, notably the tendency to defer gratification, the greater concern with interindividual competition, the tendency towards an analytical-goal orientation, the greater reliance on verbal rather than physical skills, and the greater likelihood of responding to non-material rewards, ensure a rather distinct advantage from the first days of formal schooling.

Endnotes

[1] Clearly, at the secondary level one finds greater differentiation of schools by curriculum content and perhaps teaching style. As I shall be arguing, however, it is the focus on elementary schooling (particularly the early grades) which is most salient.

[2] Much of the data reported in this paper came from one classroom, the central one in our study. The findings, however, hold without exception for all the classes observed.

[3] Observations made in other classes as well as the literature on classroom research (Jackson, 1968) indicate that the concern with order is by no means unique to this study. Indeed, it seems to pervade the atmosphere in most, if not all, traditional schools.

References

Bernstein, B. 1971. "On the Classification and Framing of Educational Knowledge." In M.F.D. Young, ed., *Knowledge and Control*. London: Collier-Macmillan.

Bourdieu, P. 1966. "L'Ecole conservatrice: Les inegalities devant l'ecole et devant la culture," *Review Francaise de Sociologie*, 7:325-347.

Bourdieu, P. 1970. *La Reproduction*. Paris: Editions de Minuit.
Bourdieu, P. and J.C. Passeron. 1964. *Les Heritiers*. Paris: Editions de Minuit.
Elkin, F. 1964. *The Family in Canada*. Ottawa: Canadian Conference on the Family.
Elkin, F. and G. Handel. 1972. *The Child and Society: The Process of Socialization*. New York: Random House.
Esland, G.M. 1971. "Teaching and Learning as the Organization of Knowledge." In Michael Young, ed., *Knowledge and Control*. London: Collier-Macmillan.
Giroux, H. and A. Penna. 1977 "Social Relations in the Classroom: The Dialectic of the Hidden Curriculum," *Edcentric* 40-41: 39-46.
Hyman, H.H. 1954. "The Value-System of Different Classes." In R. Bendix and S. Lipset, eds., *Class Status and Power*. London: Routledge and Kegan Paul.
Jackson, P.W. 1968. *Life in the Classroom* New York: Holt, Rinehart and Winston.
Jones, F. and J. Selby. 1973. "School Performance and Social Class." In T.J. Ryan, *Poverty and the Child*. Toronto: McGraw-Hill Ryerson.
Kennett, J. 1973. "The Sociology of Pierre Bourdieu," *Educational Review*, 25.
Kluckholn, F.R. and F. L. Strodtbeck. 1961. *Variations in Value Orientations*. Chicago: Row Peterson.
Kohn, M. 1963. "Social Class and Parent-Child Relationships: An Interpretation," *American Journal of Sociology*, 68: 471-480.
Kohn, M. 1969. *Class and Conformity*. Homewood: Dorsey Press.
Parsons, T. 1939. *The Structure of Social Action*. Glencoe: The Free Press.
Parsons, T. 1951. *The Social System*. Glencoe. The Free Press.
Parsons, T. 1959. "The School Class as a Social System," *Harvard Educational Review*, 29: 297-318.
Pike, R.M. and E. Zureik, eds. 1975. *Socialization and Values in Canadian Society*, Vol. 2. Toronto: McClelland and Stewart.
Riessman, F. 1962. *The Culturally Deprived Child*. New York: Harper and Row.
Young, M. 1971. "Curricula, Teaching and Learning as the Organization of Knowledge." In M. Young, ed., *Knowledge and Control*. London: Collier-Macmillan.

18

The Professionalization of Medical Students: Developing Competence and a Cloak of Competence

Jack Haas and William Shaffir

Socialization does not cease after childhood or adolescence, but is also part of the world of work. In this paper the socialization of adults is examined within the context of a formal organization, namely medical school. The specific focus is on the process through which medical students become "competent." This competence is found to reside less in a technical mastery of scientific methods or knowledge of "objective" facts, than in an ability to appear competent by demonstrating an understanding of what is expected.

Introduction

This paper[1] describes the adoption of a cloak of competence as a critical part of the professionalizing process. We observed medical students in an innovative three-year program attempting to come to grips with the problem of meeting exaggerated expectations.[2] The profound anxiety they feel about learning medicine and becoming competent is complicated by the pressing practical demands of the situation, particularly faculty, staff and institutional expectations.

As students move through the program they are converted to the new culture and gradually adopt those symbols which represent the profession and its generally accepted truths. These symbols (language, tools, clothing, and demeanour) establish, identify and separate the bearer from outsiders, particularly client and paraprofessional audiences. Professionalization, as we observed it, involves the adoption and manipulation of symbols and symbolic behaviour to create an imagery of competence and the separation and elevation of the profession from those they serve....

Jack Haas and William Shaffir, "The Professionalization of Medical Students: Developing Competence and a Cloak of Competence," *Symbolic Interaction* Volume 1, Number 1 (1978) [as reprinted in Lorne Tepperman and James Curtis (ed), *Readings in Sociology: An Introduction*, Toronto: McGraw-Hill Ryerson, 1988: 139-147.]

The Expectations of Competence

Medicine is a distinctively powerful and unique profession. Freidson outlines the characteristics of this occupation that set it apart from others. These are:
1. A general public belief in the consulting occupation's competence, in the value of its professed knowledge and skill.
2. The occupational group...must be the prime source of the criteria that qualify a man to work in an acceptable fashion.
3. The occupation has gained command of the exclusive competence to determine the proper content and effective method of performing some tasks (1970a: 10-11).

Medicine's position, Freidson notes, is equivalent to that of a state religion: "it has an officially approved monopoly of the right to define health and illness and to treat illness" (1970a: 5)....

Becoming Professional

From the outset, students are impressed by the tremendous responsibility of the physician. During their examination of various "psychosocial" problems, in Phase I,[3] students recognize that the physician's role is very broad. They learn that the medical profession not only deals with medical problems *per se*, but also with many apparently non-medical problems. The small group tutorial sessions, which form the major vehicle for learning at this stage of medical school, help shape students' enlarging conception of medicine and its practice. While early sessions are intended essentially to introduce students to the school's philosophy—the educational rationale underlying the distinctive structure and organization of the medical curriculum—they also serve to teach students the duties and responsibilities of the medical profession. An excerpt from the Phase I manual for incoming students illustrates this point:

> You are also becoming health professionals—members of an historic community concerned with the alleviation of human illness, the maintenance of health and the understanding of disease. You will begin to realize the special nature of the 'doctor-patient relationship.' Some of you will have initial difficulty with some of the physical things—blood, operations, injury, autopsies. Other experiences are more difficult to incorporate into your growth as a health professional—deformity, chronic illness, death, pain. You will see that physicians and other health professionals are ordinary human beings—with tempers, insensitivities and varied motivations (Phase I Manual, 1974: 25).

The physicians' influence on the way students learn about and define medical situations is critical to the professionalizing process. From the earliest stages of their medical training, and as they advance through the program, students continually watch doctors' working habits, listen to their philosophies of medical practice, take note of their competencies and incompetencies, and reflect upon the nature of their own present and future relationships with patients....

A dramatic shift in the professionalization process occurs when the students are given greater responsibility for patient health care and management. This occurs during the clerkship phase. Students become more integral members of a health care team, are delegated some tasks requiring personal responsibility, and become accountable in ways almost entirely new to them. As they assume increased responsibilities and make medical judgments for which they must account to a variety of professionals, they develop an increasingly sympathetic outlook towards their future profession....

As students observe and experience the problems of medical care and practice, they develop an understanding and identification with the profession and the ways its members confront their problems. Students are less quick to voice criticisms of what they see, as they come to take the role, directly or indirectly, of those they will soon follow....

The Symbols of Professionalism

The professionalization of medical students is facilitated by symbols the neophytes take on which serve to announce to insiders and outsiders how they are to be identified. During the first weeks of their studies students begin wearing white lab jackets with plastic name tags identifying them as medical students. In addition, since clinical skill sessions are included in the curriculum from the beginning, students participate in a variety of settings with the tools of the doctoring trade carried on their person. This attire clearly identifies students to participants and visitors of the hospital/school setting. Along with their newly acquired identity kit, students begin to learn and express themselves in the medical vernacular....

The significance of these symbols to the professionalization process is critical. The symbols serve, on the one hand, to identify and unite the bearers as members of a community of shared interests, purposes and identification (Roth, 1957). Simultaneously, the symbols distinguish and separate their possessors from lay people, making their role seem more mysterious, shrouded, and priest-like (Bramson, 1973). The early possession of these symbols serves to hasten their identification and commitment to the profession, while, at the same time, facilitating their separation from the lay world.

At this point, their very selection of medicine as a career has produced a set of reactions by friends, family and others which reinforce in the students' minds the idea that they are becoming very special people. Immediately upon acceptance into medical school, students perceive themselves being related to, in typified fashion, as medical students and future physicians. This reaction of others intensifies as students enter training and immerse themselves in it. At the same time, students see that they must devote more and more time and energy to their studies, and less time to past relationships and interests....

One of the first difficult tasks that faces students is to begin to learn and communicate in the symbolic system that defines medical work and workers. Immediately in tutorials, readings, demonstrations and rounds, students are inundated with a language they know they are expected to become facile in. Their task is even more difficult because this exotic language is used to describe very complex processes and understandings. Students are taken aback at the difficulty of learning to communicate in their new language. They begin carrying medical dictionaries to help them translate and define terms and phrases....

The separation between "we" and "they" becomes clearer to students as they are absorbed into the medical culture. As they move through the culture, they learn how the symbols are used to communicate and enforce certain definitions of the situation. Students learn how practising physicians use these symbols of the profession to shape and control the definition of the situation....

Turning Off Your Feelings

Previous research on medical students has shown that a major effect of medical education is to make the medical student more cynical and less idealistic. Our data also suggest that as students move through school and develop a professional self-image, and thus begin to take on the identity of a doctor, their views on medicine become transformed from what they describe as an idealistic phase to what they believe is a more realistic one. Accounting for this transition, one student claims:

...first of all, the exposure to what really goes on. You sort of keep your eyes open and you really get an idea of the real world of medicine.... The other part of it is when you're allowed responsibility...and you really become involved with patients.

Students become less vocal in their questioning and criticisms of the medical profession. They attribute many of their earlier concerns to naivete, and argue for a more sympathetic view of doctors and the profession as a whole.

> I think I went through a phase, as I went from knowing very little about medicine to a little bit.... You go through a sort of stage of disillusion in which you sort of expect doctors to be perfect, and the medical profession and treatment and everything else to be perfect. And you find out that it's not. So you sort of react to that. I think now, after about two years, I'm starting to get to the phase now where I'm quite pleased

with it really. Part of it is getting into arguments about other professions and this brings out things that you've thought about but not really verbalized.... A particular friend of mine is in law and he was talking about malpractice suits and it really makes you think that knowing doctors the way you do, and I've seen them operate, if other professions were as self-critical as doctors were and had a good sense of responsibility to duty, then I think a lot of the professions would be a lot better off....

Though not entirely pleased by the outcome of this transformation, students know that their views of medicine are being altered. They describe these changes as part of their personal and professional growth. They argue that they are becoming more mature personally and developing a clearer and sharper understanding of the world of medicine. Most importantly, they admit a willingness to accept the situation as a small price for becoming more competent. With only minor exceptions they accept the present sacrifice of their ideals as a necessary condition of medical training, and hope to recapture their idealism at a later time....

The hope and belief that they will be in a more opportune position to express and act upon their initial idealism after graduation is coupled, for many, with a more sombre realization that matters are unlikely to change. On the basis of their observations and deliberations many students become resigned to their behaviour as physicians always coming under close scrutiny and control from their colleagues. Most students do not have high hopes of being able to change medicine.

Although they are often initially dismayed by how physicians and other hospital staff treat patients, they come to accept that the objectification of patients is a routine feature of doctor-patient relationships. It is the "professional" way to deal with medical situations.[4] In time they accept the view that patients must be objectified and depersonalized or the doctor will be unable to maintain clinical objectivity (Coombs and Powers 1975; Emerson, 1970). While initially bothered, even offended, by this detachment, they come to see it as part of the professional situation over which they have little control....

Striving for competence is the primary student rationale to explain avoiding or shutting off emotional reactions. As they progress through the program students come to express the belief that their relationship with the patient should be governed strictly by the patient's medical problem; emotional feelings are a hindrance. They believe that they do not have time for both learning and caring, and learn to stifle their feelings because of the higher value they and others place on competence.

Students also believe that they are being trained for busy lives. Accepting the hectic pace as inevitable, they recognize that it is not temporary, but will continue throughout their medical career. Their work in the hospitals impresses on them the long hours that physicians devote to their work:

> If you look around at people who are teaching you, they often have a pretty rough life as far as time commitment and work. The work doesn't end when you get out of medical school and you can see somebody who is forty-five or fifty and married and has a couple of kids, in on Saturday afternoons working away, and being on call in the evenings.

Students recognize that many physicians work long and irregular hours. As they embark upon the clerkship phase of the program, they discover that the hospital routine they must fit demands that their everyday lives be organized around medicine....

The dominant concern with learning medicine leads students to maintain their learning efficiency and productivity. Students come to believe that they have no time for the frills of emotional involvement and quickly learn to close off feelings that interfere with their work (Lief and Fox, 1963). The following statement by a student emphasizes the idea of productivity:

> You can't function if you think about things like that [death and dying]. Everything you see sort of gets in there and turns about in your mind and you aren't productive. The reason you have to shut it off is because you won't be productive.... I think that my prime objective is to learn the pathology and just to know it and then, understanding that, I can go back to these other things and worry about the personal part of it.

During the first ten weeks of the curriculum the students are introduced to, among other things, the psychosocial component of health care. As many students are interested in working with and helping people, and are aware that medical problems have many different causes, the emphasis on the psychosocial issues gives them an opportunity to express their views concerning social, economic, political and moral aspects of medicine. However, even before Phase I is completed, they are eager to start what they consider to be their "real" medical studies. Reflecting the views of others in the class, a student says:

> [In Phase I] you really concentrate on a lot of psychosocial issues. But it becomes really obvious before the ten weeks are up that you are getting tired of talking about that kind of stuff, and you want to get on with it.

The students' concern for the psychosocial aspects of medicine are not entirely ignored when they enter Phase II of their program. As they are gradually introduced to the content and "core" of medicine, they begin to realize that there is too much to know and little time in which to learn it all. Like the religious or political convert who becomes fanatically observant and committed, students devote themselves to the task of learning medicine. Time becomes a commodity that must be spent wisely. They become very concerned about not misusing or wasting their time studying certain topics deemed unproductive. In this context, the psychosocial component becomes less important.

> One thing you have to do at medical school is pick up all the pathophysiology and to pick up all of the anatomy and pick up the clinical histories, the presentations, the clinical skills and so on. So psychosocial time is really a luxury, it can't really be afforded sometimes....

Although they put them aside, students continue to recognize that psychosocial matters are important. They believe this area must be neglected, however, in the interest of acquiring as much medical knowledge and competence as possible. They believe that if they feel for their patients and become involved with them they will not become professionally competent....

Most students move to the view that personal concerns for the patient should not intrude on the physician's professional responsibility....

Student concerns about learning medicine, making the most efficient use of time, and establishing some bases of certainty and security in their work are all reflected in the selected interest they take in patients with unusual pathology (Becker et al., 1961). Discussing the kind of patients that he looked forward to seeing, a student claims:

> A patient who has physical findings. Gees, I don't care what the findings are. It's a fantastic experience to see that physical finding. They may only have two or even one.... In order to do a physical exam you've got to have something there to feel. Someone can tell you this is the way to feel for a lump in the stomach, but if there is no lump there you are not going to learn how to feel it.... I think that's what I get the most out of, getting exposure to the pathology, feeling things that I may not feel.

The high point for students is making a correct diagnosis by sleuthing out relevant material, and knowing with some assurance the diagnosis is valid and the treatment competent....

Students alter their understanding of how medicine should be practiced.

Unable to feel as deeply concerned about the patient's total condition as they believe they should, they discover an approach that justifies concentrating only on the person's medical problem. As a student remarks:

> Somebody will say "Listen to Mrs. Jones' heart. It's just a little thing flubbing on the table." And you forget about the rest of her. Part of that is the objectivity and it helps in learning in the sense that you can go in to a patient, put your stethoscope on the heart, listen to it and walk out.... The advantage is that you can go in a short time and see a patient, get the important things out of the patient and leave.

As students learn to objectify patients they lose their sensitivity for them. When they can concentrate on the interesting pathology of the patient's condition, students' feelings for the patient's total situation are eroded.... The students do not lose their idealism and assume a professional mask without a struggle. But even when they see and feel the worst, students recognize that they do not have the time to crusade. That would interfere with the learning of medicine and impede their efforts to become competent....

Acting the Professional Role

Students believe they are expected to act as if they are in the know, not in ways which might put their developing competence into question. The pressure to be seen as competent by faculty, fellow students, hospital personnel and patients narrows the range of alternative roles students can assume. Students recognize their low status in the hospital hierarchy and on hospital rotations. They realize that the extent of their medical knowledge can easily be called into question by fellow students, tutors, interns, residents and faculty. To reduce the possibility of embarrassment and humiliation which, at this stage in their medical career, is easily their fate, students attempt to reduce the unpredictability of their situation by manipulating an impression of themselves as enthusiastic, interested, and eager to learn. At the same time, students seize opportunities which allow them to impress others, particularly faculty and fellow students, with their growing competence and confidence....

Although a basic objective of the school's philosophy is to encourage learning through problem-solving and a questioning attitude throughout the medical career, the philosophy does not help students' overriding problem of appearing competent. A perspective shared by students to manage an appearance of competence is to limit their initiatives to those situations which will be convincing demonstrations of their competence. Some students decide, for example, to ask questions in areas with which they are already familiar, to cultivate an impression of competence.

> The best way of impressing others with your competence is asking questions you know the answers to. Because if they ever put it back on you: "Well what do you think?" then you tell them what you think and you'd give a very intelligent answer because you know it. You didn't ask it to find out information. You ask it to impress people.

The general strategy that the students adopt is to mask their uncertainty and anxiety with an image of self-confidence. Image making becomes recognized as being as important as technical competence. As one student remarks: "We have to be good actors, put across the image of self-confidence, that you know it all...." The pressure to conform is perhaps even more extreme at this school than at other medical schools because its evaluation system is much more pervasive and a large part of it is generated by students. Students observe each other, seeking to establish a base of comparison....

The students are acutely aware of the relationship between impression management and successful evaluation. While the evaluation ought to consist of an objective assessment of the students' abilities to conduct a diagnosis and prescribe a course of treatment, the outcome is, in fact, shaped by the students' abilities to behave as if they are able to accomplish these tasks....

Conclusion

Our findings should be analogous to other professions and their socialization processes. The process of making some expert and more competent separates professionals from those they are presumed to help and serves to create a situation where the exaggerated expectations of competence are managed by symbolically defining and controlling the situation to display the imagery of competence. Impression management is basic and fundamental in those occupations and professions which profess competence in matters seriously affecting others.

Edgerton (1967) believes that the central and shared commonality of the mentally retarded released from institutions was for them to develop themselves in a cloak of competence to deny the discomforting reality of their stigma. The development of a cloak of competence is, perhaps, most apparent for those who must meet exaggerated expectations. The problem of meeting other's enlarged expectations is magnified for those uncertain about their ability to manage a convincing performance. Moreover, the performer faces the personal problem of reconciling his private self-awareness and uncertainty with his publicly displayed image. For those required to perform beyond their capacities, in order to be successful, there is the constant threat of breakdown or exposure. For both retardates and professionals the problem and, ironically, the solution, are similar. Expectations of competence are dealt with by strategies of impression management, specifically, manipulation and concealment. Interactional competencies depend on convincing presentations and much of professionalism requires the masking of insecurity and incompetence with a symbolic-interactional cloak of competence.

Endnotes

1   This paper is based on data that were collected largely during the first two years of a three-year study we are conducting on the socialization of medical students at a medical school in Ontario, Canada. The data were collected by means of participant observation and interviews. We have observed students during the full range of their educational and informal activities and to date have interviewed fifty-five of the eighty students in the class. We are presently completing the fieldwork phase of the study as students approach their licensing examination and graduation. We will be writing a monograph, based on the research, in the coming year.
2   Unlike most medical schools, the school we are studying has a three-year program where long summer vacations are eliminated. Admission is not restricted to individuals with strong pre-medical or science backgrounds. The school de-emphasizes lectures and has no formal tests or grades. Students are introduced to clinical settings from the very beginning of their studies. Learning revolves around a "problem-solving" approach as students meet in six-person tutorial groups. An analysis of the consequences of such innovations will be described in subsequent writings.
3   The program is divided into fives Phases: Phase I lasts ten weeks; Phase II twelve weeks; Phase III forty weeks; Phase IV, essentially the last half of the three-year program, is the clinical clerkship. Student elective, vacations and a review phhase—PhaseV—make up the remainder of the M.D. program.
4   The core of the professional attitiude toward the patient is to be found in what Parsons (1951) has termed "effective neutrality." As Bloom and Wilson have written: "This orientation is the vital distancing mechanism which prevents the practitioner from becoming the patient's colleague in illness....Affective neutrality constitutes the physician's prime safeguard against the antitherapeutic dangers of countertransference" 1972: 321). The management of closeness and detachment in professional-client relations is discussed in Joan Emerson (1970), and in Charles Kadushin (1962). For a discussion of the socialization of medical students toward a detached attitude, see Morris J. Daniels (1960). For an insightful analysis of how student-physicians come to manage the clinical role pertaining to death and dying, and learn to retain composure, no matter how dramatic the death scene, see Coombs and Powers (1975).

References

...Becker, Howard S., Blanche Geer, Everett C. Hughes and Anselm Strauss. *Boys in White: Student Culture in Medical School.* Chicago: University of Chicago Press, 1961.

Bloom, Samuel W. and Robert N. Wilson. "Patient-Practitioner Relationships," pp. 315-39 in H.E. Freeman, S. Levine and L.G. Reeder (eds.), *Handbook of Medical Sociology*. Englewood Cliffs, N.J.: Prentice-Hall, 1972.

Bramson, Roy. "The Secularization of American Medicine," *Hastings Center Studies*, (1973), pp. 17-28.

Coombs, Robert H. and Pauline S. Powers. "Socialization for Death: The Physician's Role," *Urban Life*, Vol. 4 (1975), pp. 250-71.

Daniels, Morris J. "Affect and its Control in the Medical Intern," *American Journal of Sociology*, Vol. 66 (1960), pp. 259-67....

Edgerton, Robert B. *The Cloak of Competence: Stigma in the Lives of the Mentally Retarded*. Berkeley: University of California Press, 1967.

Emerson, Joan P. "Behaviour in Private Places: Sustaining Definitions of Reality in Gynecological Examinations," pp. 73-97 in Hans Peter Dreitzel (ed.), *Recent Sociology*. New York: The Macmillan Company, 1970....

Freidson, Eliot. *Profession of Medicine*. New York: Dodds Mead and Co., 1970a.

_____. *Professional Dominance*, New York: Atherton, 1970b....

Kadushin, Charles. "Social Distance between Client and Professional," *American Journal of Sociology*, Vol. 67 (1962), pp. 517-31.

Lief, Harold I. and Renée Fox. "Training for 'Detached Concern' in Medical Students," pp. 12-35 in Lief, H.I., V. Lief and N.R. Lief (eds.), *The Psychological Basis of Medical Practice*. New York: Harper and Row, 1963....

Parsons, Talcott. *The Social System*. London: Routledge and Kegan Paul, 1951.

_____. "Research with Human Subjects and the Professional Complex," *Daedalus*, Vol. 98 (1969), pp. 325-60.

Phase 1 Manual, 1974....

Roth Julius A. "Ritual and Magic in the Control of Contagion," *American Sociological Review*, Vol. 22 (1957), pp. 310-14....

Section Five

Work and Organizations

Experience tends universally to show that the purely bureaucratic type of administrative organization...is, from a purely technical point of view, capable of attaining the highest degree of efficiency and is in this sense formally the most rational known means of carrying out imperative control over human beings. It is superior to any other form in precision, in stability, in the stringency of its discipline and in its reliability. It thus makes possible a particularly high degree of calculability of results for the heads of the organization and for those acting in relation to it.... The development of the modern form of the organization of corporate groups in all fields is nothing less than identical with the development and continual spread of bureaucratic administration. This is true of church and state, or armies, political parties, economic enterprises, organizations to promote all kinds of causes, private associations, clubs and many others. Its development is...the most crucial phenomenon of the modern Western state.

Max Weber, *The Theory of Social and Economic Organization*, New York: The Free Press, 1947: 337.

19

The Educational Implications of Our "Technological Society"

James Turk

Microelectronics and the shift from a manufacturing to a service-based economy are two of the major developments that are altering the nature and organization of work today. What are the implications of these changes for our secondary and post-secondary schools? In a conference presentation on liberal education, Turk challenges conventional views about the direction of these changes and their educational implications.

In this talk, I want to do three things. One is to address a prevalent myth about new technologies and their implications for education. The second is to attempt to clarify some terms that are essential for any meaningful discussion of the issues before us. The third is to focus on the educational implications of new technologies for workers—both production workers and salaried workers.

As you may have already surmised, one difference of a labour perspective is that we do not assume a session on "Career Implications in Technology" need focus primarily or solely on management. Workers have "careers" too—jobs which they hope to pursue and do well. And post-secondary institutions like Ryerson have had, and should increasingly have, a role to play in the education of these workers for their "careers." More about that later.

Myth about the New "Technology Society"

The context for this conference is the oft-repeated and commonly held notion that the dramatic outpouring of new and sophisticated microelectronic technologies means that our educational system needs to be reshaped. Workers will need more sophisticated job skills, and schools, from the primary to the post-secondary levels, must prepare workers for the new high-tech age by giving greater emphasis to science, by making "computer literacy" a priority, and so forth.

James Turk, "The Educational Implications of our Technological Society," *Catalyst: Newsletter of Local 556, George Brown College*, February, 1991.

The underlying view is that the employment future lies with those able to perform professional and technically sophisticated work.

I want to call into question much of this conventional wisdom. Let me begin with a myth which does not serve us well in our discussions of education and technology, namely, that the new microelectronic technologies will require a more highly skilled, better trained workforce.

Generally, the opposite is the case. The history of the development of the microelectronic technologies, and of their subsequent use, is a history of designing and using machines which deskill work and diminish the role of workers. Insofar as possible, decision making, which formerly was undertaken on the shop or office floor, is removed to the confines of management.

The deskilling is not inherent in new technologies. There is nothing natural or inevitable about deskilling. The new technologies have been consciously designed to deskill work—to allow employers to draw from a larger (and therefore less highly paid) labour pool. Technologies could be designed which enhance and make use of workers' skills, but designers and purchasers of new technologies have little interest in such approaches.[1]

The result is that the design and use of the new technologies is creating a pear-shaped distribution of skills. On the one hand, jobs are being created for a relatively small number of highly skilled people to design, program, and maintain the equipment. On the other hand, the present skills of the great majority of workers are being diminished, and many of their jobs eliminated.

This pattern applies across the board. Let me give you three examples.

In manufacturing operations, machinists have been one of the more highly skilled trades. Roger Tulin, a skilled machinist who has spent his evenings getting a Ph.D. in social sciences, has written on the changing machinist's work with computer-controlled machine tools:

> For many jobs, the new machines are better and more reliable than conventional methods of machining...computer-numerical-controls could allow skilled machinists who can program, set up, and operate these machines to reach new levels of craftsmanship. The most highly skilled metal workers like to make perfect parts. That's the source of their satisfaction. The new technology could allow them to conceive and execute work that was previously beyond anyone's reach.
>
> However, this hasn't been what shop managers have wanted...their interest is to get the work out with the least amount of labour time possible. So the programming and setting up is usually done by a small group of specialists. "Operators," at lower wages and skill levels, run the production cycles. They are given only the bits of information necessary

to keep the cycle running. It's the unused capability, the frustration of the human potential for creative work, that makes the reality of work life so dismal for large numbers of NC and CNC operators.

As machine tools have been made more and more fully automatic, the areas of production which require a full set of conventional skills have been cut back further and further. The "monkey" in the machine shop, who pushes buttons on a task that's broken down to fit so-called monkey intelligence, [this comment is based on a popular ad for CNC equipment which shows a monkey producing "skilled" work] is but a symbol of how management sees the future.[2]

David Noble, in his exceptional work on the history of technology,[3] shows in painstaking detail the history of the development of computer-controlled machine tools and how, at each step in their development and use, the priority was to take skill away from the operator and subject the operator to more direct management control.

One can see the same deskilling in the development and use of office technologies. Evelyn Glenn and Roslyn Feldberg of Boston University have undertaken extensive examinations of the changing character of clerical work. Their conclusions are clear-cut:

...narrow, largely manual skills displace complex skills and mental activity...close external control narrows the range of worker discretion...impersonal relationships replace social give and take.[4]

Their study of a number of different organizations adds that "the larger organizations are leading the changes by developing technologies and organizational techniques [for achieving these ends]."[5]

The same pattern of deskilling has also been identified within technical professions. Phillip Kraft, of the State University of New York at Binghamton, has carefully examined the changing nature of programming or software production. His conclusions are remarkably similar to Tulin's, Noble's and Glenn and Feldberg's:

What is most remarkable about the work programmers do is how quickly it has been transformed. Barely a generation after its inception, programming is no longer the complex work of creative and perhaps even eccentric people. Instead, divided

> and routinized, it has become mass-production work parcelled out to interchangeable detail workers. Some software specialists still engage in intellectually demanding and rewarding tasks...but they make up a relatively small and diminishing proportion of the total programming workforce. The great and growing mass of people called programmers...do work which is less and less distinguishable from that of clerks or, for that matter, assembly line workers.[6]

The point of these comments is to argue that contrary to the widely held (and widely perpetrated) view that the new technologies are increasing the demand for a more highly skilled workforce, the opposite is the case.

Evidence for this claim comes not only from scholars studying the workplace, but also from organizations like the U.S. Bureau of Labor Statistics which projects job growth over the next decade or so.

Its projections, the most sophisticated in North America, are quite startling for proponents of the high-tech future. Not one technologically sophisticated job appears among their top 15 occupations which are expected to experience the largest job growth.

The category which will contribute the most new jobs through 1995 is janitors—alone accounting for 775,000 new jobs or 3% of all new jobs created in the United States. Following janitors, in order, are cashiers, secretaries, office clerks, sales clerks, nurses, waiters and waitresses, primary school teachers, truck drivers, nursing aides and orderlies.

If you want to go down the list further, the eleventh occupation with the most substantial growth is salespeople, followed by accountants, auto mechanics, supervisors of blue-collar workers, kitchen helpers, guards and doorkeepers, fast food restaurant workers.[7]

In a separate examination of high technology sectors, the Bureau concludes,

> It should be reiterated that even when high tech is very broadly defined...it has provided and is expected to provide a relatively small proportion of employment. Thus, for the foreseeable future the bulk of employment expansion will take place in non-high tech fields.[8]

In short, the persistent deskilling of the majority of existing jobs, and the best forecasts for the nature of future jobs, lead to the same conclusion: a pear, rather than an inverted pyramid, describes the emerging skills distribution in our "technological society."

The Meaning of "Skills"

Before, talking about educational implications, I mentioned that I wanted to say a word about definitions. The key term in much of this discussion is "skills."

Many who would dissent from my argument would point to the fact that workers are (and presumably therefore need to be) better educated now than twenty years or forty years ago. Certainly workers today—from the shop floor to the manager's office—on average, have far more schooling than in the past. But that is no evidence that they are, or need be, more skilled. The lengthening of the average period of schooling has relatively little to do with changing occupational requirements for most workers. Rather the lengthening of years in school has resulted from attempts to decrease unemployment levels (beginning in the 1930s), to use the educational system to absorb some of the returning service personnel after World War II, to changing social expectations about the right to more education, and so forth.

In response to the higher level of average grade attained, employers have introduced higher minimum levels of education as requirements for hiring—whether it be a retail clerk at Eaton's, a machine operator at Canadian General Electric or an entry-level management trainee at General Motors.

But there has been no study which has demonstrated that the higher levels were a result of the changing nature of the jobs rather than an increased supply of people who had spent longer in school.[9]

Moreover, one must recognize that traditional designations of "skill" have only an inexact relation to what we would commonly mean by "skill." To put it differently, the definition of "skill" must be understood politically as well as descriptively. For example, things that are required in jobs done primarily by women tend to be defined less as skill than things required in jobs done traditionally by men.[10]

Similarly, there are often necessary "skills" required in the most "unskilled" work—a point employers often discover when they open a new plant in a low-wage area and find that they cannot get the production they expected initially because the inexperienced workforce does not have the "skills" required by the "unskilled" work.

I mention this only to highlight for you the fact that the definition of "skill" is more problematic than we conventionally take it to be. When I have argued that work is being deskilled, I am not referring to job classifications of skill, nor to educational requirements imposed by employers, but to the mastery of craft, that is the knowledge of processes and materials; the ability to conceptualize the product of one's labour and the technical ability to produce it.

As Braverman notes, most discussions of skill use the term as "a specific dexterity, a limited and repetitious operation, 'speed as skill', etc."[11] He goes on to say that the concept of skill has been degraded to the point that:

> ...today the worker is considered to possess a 'skill' if his or her job requires a few days' or weeks' training, several months of training is regarded as unusually demanding, and the job that calls for a learning period of six months or a year—such as computer programming—inspires a paroxysm of awe. (We may compare this with the traditional craft apprenticeship, which rarely lasted less than four years and which was not uncommonly seven years long.)[12]

To this point I have attempted to argue that new technologies in workplaces from a manufacturing plant floor to software production houses to offices are designed and used to deskill the work of the vast majority of workers, and, concomitantly, the definition of skill is also being degraded, giving the impression that the real degradation of skill is not as stark as it is.

What has come to be defined as skills training is a distorted and narrow kind of job training of the sort described many years ago by the Gilbreths in the *Primer* on scientific management:

> Training a worker means merely enabling him to carry out the directions of his work schedule. Once he can do this, his training is over, whatever his age.[13]

Even today, with all the mystifying hype about job enrichment and new forms of work organization, Frank Gilbreth's characterization of training is a perfect description of most so-called "skills training."

Educational Implications

The implications of all this are what concern us today.

The most obvious and important implication is that there is little foundation to the view that rising skill levels for the labour force as a whole demand the reshaping of school, college and university curricula to provide more emphasis on mathematics, computer science, and technical training.

While some jobs will require a significant amount of this type of education, the great majority (and a growing percentage) will require little of this knowledge in order to fulfil the requirements of the work. If anything, on average, there will be a diminution of the need for this kind of technical education as essential job prerequisite.

The dangers of a misplaced emphasis on more technical knowledge at all levels of the educational system are several.

First, false expectations are being created. Students will be primed with the myth about the skills their future jobs will require, and then, when they get jobs (if they get jobs), they will discover the cruel joke of their skilled training for what they find to be deskilled jobs.

Second, the rush to emphasize computer literacy and a more technical curriculum can force a de-emphasis of more important educational priorities that today's and tomorrow's students will require, not only for their jobs but for greater fulfilment in their lives.

The deskilling of work means that people will have increasingly to find meaning outside their work. The rapidity of technological change means that people will likely shift jobs (regardless of whether they shift employers) more frequently in their working lives. The greater availability of information and the burgeoning quantity of that information will put greater pressures on people who want to be informed and active participants in their society.

All of these factors mean that the priorities for education from kindergarten through university, including technical and vocational programs, must be to provide people with the capabilities to think critically, and to develop their cognitive, expressive and analytical skills to the fullest. It must, as well, provide people with extensive knowledge of their social, cultural, political and economic institutions, and prepare and encourage them to participate actively in the shaping of decisions that affect their lives.

Far from de-emphasizing a solid general education in the humanities, social and natural sciences, the implications of the emerging "technological society" are that we should be stressing this type of education more than ever.

Certainly there is a necessary place for people specializing in technical matters, but that may be no greater a need in the future than it has been in the past. More likely, there will be a lesser need for such specialized education. Given the power of what can be done with the new technologies, even our scientists will need a sound, general education more than ever. It will be essential for them to have a humanistic perspective from which they pursue their scientific achievements. The quality of our everyday lives, even the future of humankind, is dependent on scientists realizing the broader implications of what they are doing.

Our production and office workers will need narrow job training, which should be provided by the employer. Our skilled craftspeople that survive the deskilling mania of technology designers will continue to need proper apprenticeships (which have increasingly disappeared over the past forty years).

But all will need, as well, a tough, critical, informative general education—beginning at the primary level through to the highest levels—if we are to achieve our fullest potential as individuals and as a society.

Endnotes

[1] See Noble, David. 1984. *Forces of Production: A Social History of Industrial Automation.* New York: Knopf; and Zimbalist, Andrew (ed.). 1979. *Case Studies on the Labor Process.* New York: Monthly Review Press.

2. Tulin, Roger. 1984. *A Machinist's Semi-Automated Life*. San Pedro, California: Singlejack Books, p. 14.
3. Noble, *op. cit.*
4. Glenn, Evelyn and Roslyn Feldberg. 1977. "Degraded and Deskilled: The Proletarianization of Clerical Work." *Social Problems* 24: 42.
5. *Ibid.*, p. 52.
6. Kraft, Phillip. 1977. *Programmers and Managers: The Routinization of Computer Programming in the United States*. New York: Springer-Verlag, p. 97. See also Greenbaum, Joan. 1979. *In the Name of Efficiency: Management Theory and Shopfloor Practices in Data Processing Work*. Philadelphia: Temple University Press.
7. U.S. Bureau of Labor Statistics. "Occupational Employment Projections Through 1995." *Monthly Labor Review* (Nov. 1983): 37-49.
8. U.S. Bureau of Labor Statistics. "High Technology Today and Tomorrow: A Small Slice of the Employment Pie." *Monthly Labor Review* (Nov. 1983): 58.
9. See Berg, Ivar. 1971. *The Great Training Robbery*. Boston. See also Braverman, Harry. 1974. *Labor and Monopoly Capital*. New York: Monthly Review Press, pp. 424-449.
10. Gaskell, Jane. 1983. "Conceptions of Skill and the Work of Women: Some Historical and Political Issues." *Atlantis* 8(2): 11 - 25.
11. Braverman, p. 443-444.
12. Braverman, p. 444.
13. Quoted in Braverman, p. 447.

20

Life in a Fast-Food Factory

Ester Reiter

In this article Reiter describes her experiences working in a fast-food restaurant in terms of the institutionalized structure of opportunities and constraints which exists for workers within this setting.

The growth of large multinational corporations in the service industries in the post-World War II years has transformed our lives. The needs and tastes of the public are shaped by the huge advertisement budgets of a few large corporations. The development of new industries has transformed work, as well as social life. This paper focuses on the technology and the labour process in the fast-food sector of the restaurant industry....

Since the late 1960s, fast-food restaurants have been growing at a much higher rate than independent restaurants, virtually colonizing the suburbs.[1] Local differences in taste and style are obliterated as each town offers the familiar array of trademarked foods: neat, clean, and orderly, the chains serve up the same goods from Nova Scotia to Vancouver Island. The casualties of the phenomenal growth are the small "mom and pop" establishments, rather than the higher-priced, full-service restaurants. Fast-food outlets all conform to a general pattern. Each has a limited menu, usually featuring hamburger, chicken, or fried fish. Most are part of a chain, and most require customers to pick up their own food at a counter.[2] The common elements are minimum delay in getting the food to the customer (hence "fast food") and prices that are relatively low compared to those at full-service restaurants....

[Burger King] store operations are designed from head office in Miami. In 1980, this office commissioned a study to find ways of lowering labour costs,

---

Ester Reiter, "Life in a Fast-food Factory," from Craig Heron and Robert Storey (eds.), *On the Job: Confronting the Labour Process in Canada.* Copyright © 1986 McGill-Queen's University Press, pp. 309-310; 315-318; 320-322; 324.

increasing worker's productivity, and maintaining the most efficient inventories. The various components of a restaurant's operations were defined: customer-arrival patterns, manning or positioning strategies, customer/cashier interactions, order characteristics, production-time standards, stocking rules and inventory. Time-motion reports for making the various menu items, as well as corporate standards for service were also included in the calculation, and the data were all entered into a computer. By late 1981, it was possible to provide store managers not only with a staffing chart for hourly sales—indicating how many people should be on the floor given the predicted volume of business for that hour—but also where they should be positioned, based on the type of kitchen design. Thus, although staffing had been regulated since the late 1970s, what discretion managers formerly had in assigning and utilizing workers had been eliminated. The use of labour is now calculated precisely, as is any other objectively defined component of the system, such as store design, packaging, and inventory.[3]

Having determined precisely what workers are supposed to be doing and how quickly they should be doing it, the only remaining issue is that of getting them to perform to specification. "Burger King University," located at headquarters in Miami was set up to achieve this goal. Housed in a remodelled art gallery, the multimillion-dollar facility is staffed by a group of "professionals" who have worked their way up in the Burger King system to the rank of district manager. Burger King trains its staff to do things "not well, but right," the Burger King way.[4] Tight control over Burger King restaurants throughout the world rests on standardizing operations—doing things the "right" way—so that outcomes are predictable. The manager of a Burger King outlet does not necessarily need any knowledge of restaurant operation because the company provides it. What Burger King calls "people skills" are required; thus a job description for a manager indicated that he/she
- Must have good verbal communication skills
- Must have patience, tact, fairness, and social sensitivity in dealing with customers and hourly employees
- Must be able to supervise and motivate team of youthful employees and conduct himself/herself in a professional manner
- Must present a neat, well-groomed image
- Must be willing to work nights, weekends and holidays[5]

In 1981, a new crew-training program, designed as an outcome of the computer-simulation study was developed. The training program is called "The Basics of Our Business" and is meant to "thoroughly train crew members in all areas of operations and to educate them on how Burger King and the restaurant where they work...fit into the American free-enterprise system." In addition, the training program involves supervised work at each station, and a new feature that requires every employee to pass a standardized test on appropriate procedures for each station in the store.

Burger King thus operates with a combination of control techniques: technology is used to simplify the work and facilitate centralization, while direct control or coercion is exercised on the floor to make sure the pace of the work remains swift. "If there's time to lean, there's time to clean," is a favourite saying among managers. In fact, workers are expected to be very busy *all* the time they are on shifts, whether or not there are customers in the store. Sitting down is never permissible; in fact, the only chair in the entire kitchen is in the manager's office in a glassed-in cubicle at the rear of the kitchen. From there, the manager can observe the workers at their jobs. The application of these techniques is supported by a legitimizing ideology that calls for "patience, fairness, and social sensitivity" in dealing with customers in order to increase sales and profits "for the betterment of Burger King corporation and its employees."[6]

Working at Burger King

I did field work in the fast-food industry by working at a Burger King outlet in suburban Toronto on 1980/1. The Burger King at which I worked was opened in 1979, and by 1981 was the highest volume store in Canada with annual sales of over one million dollars. Everything in the customer's part of the store was new, shiny, and spotlessly clean. Live plants lent a touch of class to the seating area. Muzak wafted through the air, but customers sat on chairs designed to be sufficiently uncomfortable to achieve the desired customer turnover rate of one every 20 minutes. Outside the store, customers could eat at concrete picnic tables and benches in a professionally landscaped setting, weather permitting. Lunches, particularly Thursdays, Fridays, and Saturdays, were the busiest times, and during those periods, customers were lined up at the registers waiting to be served. During the evenings, particularly on Friday nights, families with young children were very much in evidence. Young children, kept amused by the plastic giveaway toys provided by the restaurant and sporting Burger King crowns, sat contentedly munching their fries and sipping their carbonated drinks.

Workers use the back entrance at Burger King when reporting for work. Once inside, they go to a small room (about seven by twelve feet), which is almost completely occupied by an oblong table where crew members have their meals. Built-in benches stretch along both sides of the wall, with hooks above for coats. Homemade signs, put up by management, decorate the walls. One printed, framed, sign read;

> WHY CUSTOMERS QUIT
> 1% die
> 2% move away
> 5% develop other friendships
> 9% competitive reasons
> 14% product dissatisfactions

68% quite because of ATTITUDE OF INDIFFERENCE TOWARDS CUSTOMER BY RESTAURANT MANAGER OR SERVICE PERSONNEL

Another sign reminded employees that only 1/3 ounce of ketchup and 1/9 ounce of mustard is supposed to go on the hamburgers; a crew member using more is cheating the store, while one using less is not giving customers "value" for their dollar.

The crew room is usually a lively place. An AM/FM radio is tuned to a rock station while the teenage workers coming off or on shift talk about school and weekend activities or flirt with each other. Children and weddings are favourite topics of conversation for the older workers. In the evenings, the talk and horsing around among the younger workers gets quite spirited, and now and then a manager appears to quieten things down. Management initiatives are not all geared to control through discipline; social activities such as skating parties, baseball games, and dances are organized by "production leaders" with the encouragement of the managers—an indication that the potentially beneficial effects for management of channelling the informal social relationships at the workplace are understood. Each worker must punch a time card at the start of a shift.... A positioning chart, posted near the time clock, lists the crew members who are to work each meal, and indicates where in the kitchen they are to be stationed.

There are no pots and pans in the Burger King kitchen. As almost all foods enter the store ready for the final cooking process, pots and pans are not necessary.... The major kitchen equipment consists of the broiler/toaster, the fry vats, the milkshake and coke machines, and the microwave ovens.... Even when made from scratch, hamburgers do not require particularly elaborate preparation, and whatever minimal decision making might once have been necessary is now completely eliminated by machines. At Burger King, hamburgers are cooked as they pass through the broiler on a conveyor belt at a rate of 835 patties per hour. Furnished with a pair of tongs, the worker picks up the burgers as they drop off the conveyor belt, puts each on a toasted bun, and places the hamburgers and buns in a steamer. The jobs may be hot and boring, but they can be learned in a matter of minutes.

The more interesting part of the procedure lies in applying condiments and microwaving the hamburgers. The popularity of this tasks among Burger King employees rests on the fact that it is unmechanized and allows some discretion of the worker. As the instructions for preparing a "whopper" (the Burger King name for a large hamburger) indicates, however, management is aware of this area of worker freedom and makes strenuois efforts to eliminate it by outlining exactly how this job is to be performed.... Despite such directives, the "Burger and Whopper Board" positions continue to hold their attraction for the workers, for this station requires two people to work side by side, and thus allows the opportunity fo conversation. During busy times, as well, employees at this station also derive some work satisfaction from their ability to "keep up." At peak times, a supply of ready-made sandwiches is placed in chutes ready for the cashiers to pick up; the manager decides how many sandwiches should be in the chutes according to a formula involving sales predictions for that time period. At such times, the challenge is to keep pace with the demand and not leave the cashiers waiting for their orders. The managers will sometimes spur the "Whopper-makers" on with cries of "Come on guys, let get with it," or "Let's go, team."

...At Burger King, the goal is to reduce all skills to a common, easily learned level and to provide for cross-training. At the completion of the ten-hour training program, each worker is able to work at a few stations. Skills for any of the stations can be learned in a matter of hours; the simplest jobs, such as filling cups with drinks, or placing the hamburgers and buns of the conveyor belt, can be learned in minutes. As a result, although labour turnover cuts into the pace of making hamburgers, adequate functioning of the restaurant is never threatened by people leaving. However, if workers are to be as replaceable as possible, they must be taught not only to perform their jobs in the same way, but also to resemble each other in attitudes, disposition, and appearance. Thus, workers are taught not only to perform according to company rules, but also are drilled on personal hygiene, dress (shoes should be brown leather or vinyl, not suede), coiffure (hair tied up for girls and not too long for boys), and personality. Rule 17 of the handout to employees underlines the importance of smiling: "Smile at all times, your smile is the key to our success."

While management seeks to make workers into interchangeable tools, workers themselves are expected to make a strong commitment to the store.... Workers, especially teenagers, are, then, expected to adjust their activities to the requirements of Burger King. For example, workers must apply to their manager two weeks in advance to get time off to study for exams or attend family functions. Parents are seen by management as creating problems for the store, as they do not always appreciate Burger King's demand for priority in their children's schedules. Thus, the manager warns new trainees to "remember, your parents don't work here and don't understand the situation. If you're old enough to ask for a job, you're old enough to be responsible for coming."[7]

...Making us about 75 percent of the Burger King work force, the youngsters who worked after school, on weekends, and on holidays were called "part-timers." The teenager workers (about half of them boys, half girls) seemed to vary considerably in background....

The daytime workers—the remaining 25 percent of the workforce—were primarily married women on mixed economic backgrounds.... Although they were all working primarily because their families needed the money, a few women expressed their relief at getting out of the house, even to come to Burger King. One woman said: "At least when I come here, I'm appreciated. If I do a good job, a manager will say something to me. Here, I feel like a person. I'm sociable and I like being amongst people. At home, I'm always cleaning up after everybody and nobody ever notices...."[8]

Common to both the teenagers and the housewives was the view that working at Burger King was peripheral to their major commitments and responsibilities; the part-time nature of the work contributed to this attitude. Workers saw the alternative available to them as putting up with the demands of Burger King or leaving; in fact, leaving seemed to be the dominant form of protest. During my period in the store, on average, eleven people out of ninety-four hourly employees quit at each two-week pay period. While a few workers had stayed at Burger King for periods as long as a few years, many did not last through the first two weeks. The need for workers is constant; occassionally even the paper placemats on the customer's trays invited people to work in the "Burger King family." "If you're enthusiastic and like to learn, this is the opportunity for you. Just complete the application and return it to the counter." At other times, bounties where offered for live workers. A sign that hung in the crew room for a few weeks read:

> Wanna make $10?
> It's easy! All you have to do is refer a friend to me for employment. Your friend must be able to work over lunch (Monday-Friday). If your friend works here for at least one month, you get $20. (And I'm not talking Burger Bucks either.)

Burger King's ability to cope with high staff turnover means that virtually no concessions in pay or working conditions are offered to workers to entice them to remain at Burger King. In fact, more attention is paid to the maintenance of the machinery than to "maintaining" the workers; time is regularly scheduled for cleaning and servicing the equipment, but workers may not leave the kitchen to take a drink or use the bathroom during the lunch and dinner rushes.

The dominant form—in the circumstances, the only easily accessible form—of opposition to the Burger King labour process is, then, the act of quitting. Management attempts to head off any other form of protest by insisting on an appropriate "attitude" on the part of the workers. Crew members must constantly demonstrate their satisfaction with working at Burger King by smiling at all times. However, as one worker remarked, "Why should I smile? There's nothing funny around here. I do my job and that should be good enough for them." It was not, however, and this worker soon quit....

My findings in the fast-food industry are not very encouraging. In contrast to Michael Burawoy,[9] for example, who found that male workers in a unionized machine shop were able to set quotas and thereby establish some control over the labour process, I found that women and teenagers at Burger King are under the sway of a labour process that eliminates almost completely the possibility of forming a workplace culture independent of, and in opposition to, management.

...Unfortunately, there are indications that the teenagers and women who work in this type of job represent not an anomalous but an increasingly typical kind of worker, in the one area of the economy that continues to grow—the service sector. The fast-food industry represents a model for other industries in which the introduction of technology will permit the employment of low-skilled, cheap, and plentiful workers. In this sense, it is easy to be pessimistic and find agreement with Andre Gorz's depressing formulation of the idea of work:

> The terms "work" and "job" have become interchangeable: work is no longer something that one *does* but something that one *has*.
>
> Workers no longer "produce" society through the mediation of the relations of production; instead the machinery of social production as a whole produces "work" and imposes it in a random way upon random, interchangeable individuals.[10]

The Burger King system represents a major triumph for capital: it has established a production unit with constant and variable components that are almost immediately replaceable. However, the reduction of the worker to a single component of capital requires more than the introduction of a technology; workers' autonomous culture must be eliminated as well, including the relationships among workers, their skills, and their loyalties to one another. The smiling, willing, homogenous worker must be produced and placed on the Burger King assembly line....

Notes

[1] Foodservice and Hospitality Magazine, *Fact File—Canada's Hospitality Business*, 4th ed. (Toronto n.d.).
[2] This definition comes from the National Restaurant Association and is reprinted in Marc Leepson, "Fast Food, U.S. Growth Industry," *Editorial Research Reports* 7 (1978): 907.
[3] "Kitchen design—the drive for efficiency," insert in *Nation's Restaurant News*, 31 August 1981.
[4] Personal communication, Burger King "professor," 4 January 1982.
[5] Job description handout for Burger King managers, 1981.
[6] Handouts to Burger King crew members, 1981.
[7] Burger King training session in local outlet, July 1981.
[8] Personal communication, Burger King worker, 8 August 1981.
[9] Michael Burawoy, *Manufacturing Consent* (Chicago 1979).
[10] Andre Gorz, *Farewell to the Working Class* (Boston 1982), 71.

21

Is There a Future for the Canadian Labour Movement?

Mary Lou Coates

More than a third of Canada's non-agricultural workers belong to unions, compared to less than a fifth of non-agricultural workers in the United States. While the proportion of unionized workers in Canada remains relatively high, and while unions have been withstanding the political economic climate of the 1990s, Coates asks us to take a hard look at the present state and future of Canada's unions amid the changes and restructuring currently taking place. How should Canada's labour movement respond to the trends that are affecting the workplace as well as the broader society?

Introduction

At first glance, all seems well with the Canadian labour movement and the prognosis looks good. Four million Canadians belong to labour unions, a record high. Except for a short plateau in the early sixties and a decline in 1982-83, union membership in Canada has increased steadily each year and since the 1981-82 recession, union ranks have increased by one-half million members. During the past decade, membership growth has averaged almost two percent per year. Currently, over one-third (36.3 percent) of the total non-agricultural paid workforce in the country is unionized. Those who have studies the Canadian union movement have commented that:

> ...the Canadian labour movement remains strong, exhibiting a remarkable resiliency in the face of a difficult and

---

Mary Lou Coates, "Is There a Future for the Canadian Labour Movement?" abridged from *Current Issues Series*, Kingston: Industrial Relations Centre, Queen's University Press, 1992: 1-13. [as reprinted in J.S. Lowe and H. Krahn, *Work in Canada: Readings in the Sociology of Work and Industry*, Nelson Canada, 1993: 257-265.]

unfavourable economic, social and political environment. (Kumar 1991, 1)

...the strength and vitality of the Canadian labour movement has been reflected in greater organizing activity and success, widespread rejection of concession bargaining, and prowess in achieving legislative goals. (Chaison and Rose 1990, 596)

Canadian union leaders, as expected, also appear confident about the health of their labour movement:[1]

...we continue to grow, and have credibility. I think we have an exciting labour movement. *Shirley Carr, President, Canadian Labour Congress*

...I think we're holding our own. In some places we're moving ahead, in other places we're being forced onto the defensive, but we'll be around for a long time to come. *Jeff Rose, Past President, Canadian Union of Public Employees*

I think the percentage of organized non-agricultural people in Canada will continue to grow in the next 10 years. I think that the Canadian Labour Movement, in total, is healthy. *Cliff Evans, International Vice-President, United Food and Commercial Workers Union*

...I think that generally the labour movement is alive and well and fighting back. I think the future of the labour movement is not at all down, I think it can be up... the future for the labour movement is one in which the labour movement is going to continue to fight back and we'll continue to grow. *Bob White, National President, Canadian Auto Workers*

Declining Union Growth?

By international standards, unions in Canada have not suffered the steep membership losses that the United Kingdom, France and the United States have experienced during the 1980s (Visser 1991). Compared with the United States, the degree of unionization in Canada is twice as high.

However, there are indications that all is not well. Despite steady increases in union membership, union growth in Canada has certainly not been as robust in recent years as it was in the 1960s and 1970s. Furthermore, membership growth has failed to keep pace with the rise in the non-agricultural paid workforce and, as a result, union density, which hovered around 38 percent in the early 1980s, has declined to 36 percent in recent years. While some would argue that this pattern indicates 'stability' in union penetration, others brand it 'stagnation' or 'decline.'

There is even more cause to ponder the future of union activity in Canada when one moves beyond the aggregate measures to look at what has been happening in the private and public sectors and across industries. Two major concerns include the decline in private sector unionization and the union presence, or lack thereof, in the faster growing segments of the Canadian workforce.

In the traditionally strong sectors of unionization such as mining and manufacturing, union membership growth has fallen over the past ten years. In forestry, union growth has been marginal in the 1980s although healthier than it was in the 1970s while in construction it has slowed compared to the previous decade. In transportation, communications and utilities, union growth has been steady but not robust.

As a proportion of paid employment, union membership in forestry, mining and manufacturing has declined substantially over the past two decades. Over one-half of the paid workforce in construction and in transportation, communication and utilities remain unionized, roughly the same proportions as twenty years ago.

On the other hand, over four-fifths of the overall increase in union membership during the past decade has been in the service industries and public administration, evidence that unions have been expanding into new and growing areas of the economy. Nevertheless, the majority of workers in the service industries, trade and finance, insurance and real estate remain non-unionized. With three-quarters of employees organized in public administration, there is concern that unionization is at or near its saturation level in this sector. By occupation, density is less than average in professional occupations outside of teaching and medicine and health, in clerical and related occupations, sales occupations, service occupations such as food and accommodation and personal services, and wood, rubber, plastic and other product fabricating, assembling and repairing occupations.

Why the Decline?

Numerous reasons have been given to explain the decline or stagnation in unionization in the private sector and the relatively low levels of union representation in growing sectors: structural shifts in the economy, labour legislation and public policy that restricts organizing and collective bargaining, employer hostility to unions, and unfavourable public opinion. The 1981-82 recession appears to have marked a turning point for organized labour during the 1980s. The severe economic downturn had a deleterious impact on employment in the goods-producing industries and blue-collar occupations, traditional strongholds of union strength.

For the first time in recorded history, there was an actual reduction in the number of union members and many unions, faced with losses in their dues-paying memberships, were also forced to rationalize union administrative structures and cut back on staffing and servicing the membership. Union bargaining power was also weakened as many unions came face to face with concession bargaining (including wage cuts and freezes, wage settlements below the rate of inflation, lump-sum payments in lieu of wage increases, reductions in employee benefits and modified work rules) as well as public sector wage restraint legislation and restrictions on the right to strike.

Moreover, on the heels of the recession came massive corporate restructuring, rationalization and consolidation in response to international pressures which meant continued losses in jobs, many permanent, and related employment upheaval, particularly in the unionized sectors of manufacturing and the resource-based industries. Against the background of plant closures and relocation, privatization, deregulation, fallout from the Canada-US Free Trade Agreement, technological change, and contracting-out, the union's ability to bargain improved wages, benefits and working conditions and provide employment and income security has been severely hampered. Several of the larger private sector unions, such as the United Steelworkers, Carpenters, International Brotherhood of Electrical Workers, Machinists, Woodworkers and several construction unions have therefore been unable to regain the membership lost during the recession.

With unionization rates declining or stagnating in those areas where membership had traditionally been concentrated, unions are also facing the labour market realities of new workforce—a workforce with diverse interests from traditional rank and file members, one that unions have historically found more difficult to organize and where existing union structures, policies and practices have often been inadequate in reflecting some of the concerns of these new groups of workers. For example, women comprise 45 percent of the labour force but only 30 percent of employed women are union members and the proportion of Canadian women members elected to union executive boards remains relatively low. The rate of unionization tends to be relatively low among part-time workers (26.2 percent) who have accounted for over one-quarter of net employment creation in Canada in the 1980s (Economic Council of Canada 1991, 72). About two-thirds of the net employment growth in the 1980s was in managerial and professional occupations and the demand for highly skilled workers, particularly in managerial and administrative occupations, is expected to rise dramatically (Employment and Immigration Canada 1989). Many managerial and professional workers are not legally eligible to unionize at the present time and some of these groups consider themselves to be outside the mainstream of the trade union movement. Almost 90 percent of the net employment creation since the 1950s has taken place in the service sector (Economic Council of Canada 1991, 1), which tends to be characterized by high turnover, either very large employers (eg, banks, department stores) or small-sized firms, and a high proportion of women, part-time workers, professionals and youth—factors which have made union organizing more difficult.

Unions have also contended that labour legislation and labour board policy, while successful in extending collective bargaining to workers in the resource and manufacturing sectors, has not been conducive to organizing either part-time workers or workers in the growing finance and service industries (Partnership 1991, 3). Unions have also had problems making inroads in the private service sector because there tends to be more contact between the worker and the consumer which creates an incentive for employers to adopt human resource strategies that reinforce this identification (Betcherman 1989).

New Forms of Work Organization

This points up another area of concern for the future of the labour movement—increased employer demands for new forms of work organization, that is, alternative approaches to how work is organized and managed. In attempting to become more responsive to changing business conditions and to cope with a fiercely competitive environment, management is placing greater emphasis on flexibility in production methods as well as compensation and working arrangements. Employers have been flattening management structures by eliminating layers of management, pushing for fewer or broader job classifications and multiskilling, looking to more variable compensation schemes (eg, lump-sum or cash bonus payments, two-tier wage systems, pay for knowledge and pay for performance, productivity gain-sharing, incentive pay, employee stock ownership plans and profit-sharing) and making greater use of part-time and temporary employees and contracting-out.

With an erosion in the effectiveness of traditional competitive tools such as technology, product innovation, financial resources and access to raw materials, organizations are beginning to discover that their human resources represent a 'fundamental source of competitive advantage' and a 'significant force in achieving organizational effectiveness' (Benimadhu 1989). Many organizations feel a growing need to become more directly involved with employees, foster greater worker commitment and cooperation and make their human resources more involved in managing change and improving competitiveness. Quality circles, team concepts, quality of worklife, and other initiatives aimed at increasing worker participation and employee involvement are receiving increased attention. A recent survey of over 400 public and private sector organizations found that 'companies appear to be more active in responding to changing worker values and in building a new management style than in any other area' (Towers Perrin 1991, 19). For example, more than 50 percent of the survey group have introduced, or plan to introduce, a quality management or improvement program *involving employees* while almost 50 percent have adopted other types of programs that focus on greater productivity or morale enhancement. In terms of organizational strategy, over 40 percent of the companies had undertaken strategic changes ranging from the design of communication processes to help build employee commitment to business objectives, the reorganization of work tasks or activities to create greater labour efficiencies, programs to encourage innovation and productivity at the operating level, and the development of a more supportive 'culture' to reduce turnover and enhance productivity.

Unionism and the New HRM

The implementation of alternate forms of work organization has important implications for labour unions not only in unionized settings but also in terms of nonunionized workplaces where the desire for and ability to unionize may be thwarted by such schemes. Some of these issues were explored in a recent paper which examined the compatibility of strong unionism with alternate forms of human resource management (Wells 1991). Although some argue that the effectiveness of such human resource management strategies depends on the presence of strong unions, Wells' study of some of the alleged 'successful' experiments (eg, Shell, Eldorado Resources, Xerox, Dominion Stores and Willet Foods) points out that the 'new human resource management' leads to weak unions or the absence of unions.

The Canada/US Debate

Evidence that private sector unionization has been declining in Canada in recent years has led to a controversial debate on whether the path of Canadian unions is paralleling that of unions in the United States. In the United States, membership levels have steadily declined since 1975 and union density has fallen from a peak of 32.5 percent in 1953 to 16.1 percent in 1990, more than one-half of the current Canadian rate. Two contrasting views have emerged in this debate raising some startling and critical issues for the future direction of the Canadian labour movement.

Unionization in Canada—Is It Following the American Route?

The conventional view is that although unionization in the United States has been 'dying on the vine', Canadian unionism has been 'thriving' and that, given the close economic and institutional relationship between Canada and the United States, the United States has been unique with respect to this deunionization. More recently, however, this mainstream view has been challenged by the counterclaim that not only has declining unionization in the United States *not* been unique but the experience of private sector industrial relations in the US indicates that the size and strength of Canadian private unionism will be reduced (Troy 1991b).

Leo Troy, Distinguished Professor of Economics at Rutgers University in New Jersey, has taken strong exception to the comparisons made between the 'robust' and 'vibrant' Canadian labour movement and the 'flabby' American one and any suggestions that American labour relations policy emulate the Canadian model. Troy has long held the opinion that the conventional view of divergent trends in Canadian and US unionization, which relied on aggregate measures of union membership levels and density, misdiagnosed the invulnerability of Canada's private sector union movement because it failed to distinguish private from public sector markets, union movements, and industrial relations systems. Therefore, instead of diverging, trends in private sector density have been similar in Canada and the United States except that the US 'led the way'....

Troy believes that the robustness of Canadian unionism applies to the public not the private sector. Moreover, he argues that public sector unionism owes its strength to favourable government intervention which, unlike unions in the private sector, sheltered public sector unions from market forces and blunted the impact of competitive pressures. However, he feels that the economic costs of unionism in the public sector will encourage more privatization and public management will be under increased pressure to reduce negotiated wage increases in the public sector. Given the role that public policy and legislation has played in giving 'instant unionism' to the public sector, Troy questions whether public sector unions have the 'allegiance' of their members. The growth of public sector unionism 'ran out of steam' during the 1980s and was unable to offset the decline in private and therefore, overall union density. Over time, the Free Trade Agreement, privatization, technological change, public resistance and the growing weakness of private sector unions will mean that public sector unions will no longer be able to remain immune to the erosion taking place in private sector unions and Troy expects stagnation in Canadian public unionism (Troy 1990a and 1991a). In the private sector, Troy believes that as 'the Canadian labor market get[s] swept into the vortex of the more competitive North American free trade economy, Canadian private sector unionism, already in a state of decline, will become more vulnerable to the "American disease"' (Troy 1991b)....

Pradeep Kumar, Associate Director of the School of Industrial Relations at Queen's University in Kingston, Ontario also acknowledges that public sector unions in Canada have outperformed those in the United States and that private sector unionism has declined in both countries but debates whether the size of the decline is similar (Kumar 1991). In his paper, he carries the debate further to examine the more qualitative measures of the extent and influence of unionism. The difference in union strategies and approaches, he states, is what accounts for the growing divergence between the labour movements in Canada and the United States. In his analysis, Kumar transcends some of the 'gloom and doom' scenarios and offers a more optimistic outlook for the Canadian labour movement by focusing on the strategic role that unions have assumed in organizing, collective bargaining and in their political and social approaches.

According to Kumar, it is the broader 'social' concept of unionism in Canada which accounts for the strength of the labour movement in this country. In particular, he distinguishes between the Canadian unions' emphasis on social and political strategies compared to the American reliance on collective bargaining as a key factor in the divergence. This divergence is manifested in the more active and aggressive organizing efforts by Canadian unions, their opposition to concession bargaining and resistance to contingent compensation and employee involvement/participation programs, the negotiation of social issues (eg, pay and employment equity, child care, human rights, etc), legislative lobbying, coalition-building with various groups outside the labour movement, and the bilateral consultation and consensus-building initiatives with employers at the national and sectoral level (eg, the Canadian Labour Market and Productivity Centre, Canadian Steel Trade and Employment Congress).

Conclusion

Despite the various strategies and approaches taken by the labour movement, unions are still faced with the grim reality that unionization in the private sector has declined, remains relatively low among the faster growing segments of the Canadian workforce, and is near saturation in the public sector. Furthermore, there is no indication of any 'wave' of new organizing on the horizon. These developments raise serious questions about how the labour movement is preparing for the future and whether a transformation is taking place in Canadian industrial relations.

Endnote

[1] Based on interviews by Pradeep Kumar and Dennis Ryan with prominent business leaders (Kumar and Ryan 1988).

References

Benimadhu, Prem. 1989. *Human Resource Management: Charting a New Course.* Report 41-89. Ottawa: Conference Board of Canada.

Betcherman, Gordon. 1989. 'Union Membership in a Service Economy,' in Michel Grant, ed., *Industrial Relations Issues for the 1990s. Proceedings of the 26th Conference of the Canadian Industrial Relations Association,* 120-31.

Chaison, Gary N. and Joseph B. Rose. 1990. 'New Directions and Divergent Paths: The North American Labor Movements in Troubled Times.' *Proceedings of the Spring Meeting of the Industrial Relations Research Association.* 591-96. Madison, WI:IRRA.

Economic Council of Canada. 1991. *Employment in the Service Economy*. Ottawa: Supply and Services Canada.

Employment and Immigration Canada. 1989. *Success in the Works: A Profile of Canada's Emerging Workforce*. Ottawa: Employment and Immigration Canada.

Kumar, Pradeep and Dennis Ryan. 1988. *Canadian Union Movement in the 1980s: Perspectives from Union Leaders*. Research and Current Issues Series no. 53. Kingston: Industrial Relations Centre, Queen's University.

Partnership and Participation in the 1990s: Labour Law Reform in Ontario. 1991. Report of the Labour Representatives to the Labour Reform Committee of the Ministry of Labour. April 14.

Towers Perrin and the Hudson Institute of Canada. 1991. *Workforce 2000: Competing in a Seller's Market: Is Canadian Management Prepared?* Toronto: TPFC.

Troy, Leo. 1990a. 'Why Canadian Public Sector Unionism is Strong,' *Government Unions Review* 11, No. 3: 1-32.

Troy, Leo. 1990b. 'Is the US Unique in the Decline of Private Sector Unionism?' *Journal of Labor Research* 11: 111-43.

Troy, Leo. 1991a. *Convergence in International Unionism Et Cetera: The Case of Canada and the US*. Queen's Paper in Industrial Relations 1991-3. Kingston: Industrial Relations Centre.

Troy, Leo. 1991b. 'Can Canada's Labor Policies Be a Model for the US?' Paper prepared for the 28th Conference of the Canadian Industrial Relations Research Association, June.

Viser, Jelle. 1991. *Employment Outlook* (July). Paris: Organization for Economic Development and Cooperation.

Wells, Don. 1991. *What Kind of Unionism is Consistent with the New Model of Human Resource Management?* Queen's Papers in Industrial Relations 1991-9. Kingston: Industrial Relations Centre, Queen's University.

Section Six

Social Inequality

But what is social inequality, exactly?.... (M)ost would agree it involves such concerns as the gap between the rich and the poor, or the advantaged and the disadvantaged, in society. More generally, however, social inequality can refer to any of the differences between people (or the socially defined positions they occupy) that are consequential for the lives they lead, most particularly for the rights or opportunities they exercise and the rewards or privileges they enjoy. Of greatest importance here are those consequential differences that become structured, in the social sense of the term, that are built into the ways that people interact with one another on a recurring basis.

Edward Grabb, *Social Inequality: Classical and Contemporary Theories*, Holt, Rinehart and Winston of Canada, 1984: 3-4.

22

Poverty in Canada

National Council of Welfare

What is poverty in an affluent nation such as Canada, and why is it so difficult to determine? What proportion of Canadians are poor? Characteristically, who tends to comprise the poor? How severe are the financial conditions of the poor, and how much additional income would be required such that all Canadians could have a decent standard of living? The answers to questions such as these provide an important context for the more troublesome problem—why does poverty persist in modern society?

Introduction

The United Nations has designated 1996 as the International Year for the Eradication of Poverty, and the latest available statistics show that Canada still has a long way to go to meet this goal. Nearly 4.8 million children, women and men—one of every six Canadians—were living in poverty in 1994, and the overall national poverty rate was 16.6 percent. In a country as rich as Canada, these figures bear witness to the failure of successive federal, provincial and territorial governments to provide for the well-being of a significant portion of the people they were elected to represent....

As in previous years, families headed by single-parent mothers and "unattached" people or people living outside families were among the groups of Canadians most likely to be poor.

Single-parent mothers had poverty rates many times higher than husband-wife families. The poverty rate for all single-parent mothers under 65 with children under 18 was 57.3 percent in 1994. Single-parent mothers under age 25 had a poverty rate of 89.6 percent. Single-parent mothers who did not graduate

---

National Council of Welfare, "Poverty in Canada," from Poverty Profile 1994, Ottawa: Supply and Services, Spring, 1996: 1-2; 4-12; 14-17; 51-54; 59-61.

from high school had a rate of 82.3 percent. And single-parent mothers with children under seven had rates as high as 82.8 percent....

When we look at the actual dollars and cents that poor people had to live on, the picture is just as dismal. A total of 226,000 families and 367,000 unattached people had incomes in 1994 that amounted to less than half the poverty line.

Despite these grim realities, winning the war on poverty is not an unrealistic goal. Statistics Canada estimates that the cost of bringing all poor people out of poverty in 1994 would have been $15.2 billion. That's a huge, but not outrageous amount of money in a country where the federal, provincial and territorial governments spent in the order of $350 billion in 1994 and where the value of all the goods and services produced was $750 billion.

Better job opportunities, better income support programs and better pension programs all would help close the poverty gap....

Methodology and Definitions

Every year, Statistics Canada conducts a household survey known as the Survey of Consumer Finances to obtain information on the distribution of income and the nature and extent of poverty in Canada. The survey on which this report is based, conducted in April of 1995, sampled 37,594 private households from all part of the country except for Yukon, the Northwest Territories, Indian reserves, and institutions such as prisons, mental hospitals, and homes for the elderly. The survey looked at incomes for the 1994 calendar year....

Information about poverty is obtained by comparing the survey data with the low income cut-offs of Statistics Canada. The cut-offs represent levels of gross income where people spend disproportionate amounts of money for food, shelter and clothing. The Bureau has decided over the years—somewhat arbitrarily—that 20 percentage points is a reasonable measure of the additional burden. The average Canadian family spent 36.2 percent of gross income on food, shelter and clothing according to 1986 data on spending patterns, so it was assumed that low-income Canadians spent 56.2 percent or more on the necessities of life.

The low income cut-offs vary by the size of the family unit and the population of the area of residence. There are seven categories of family size from one person to seven or more persons, and five community sizes ranging from rural areas to cities with 500,000 or more residents. The result is a set of 35 cut-offs. The cut-offs are updated annually by Statistics Canada using the Consumer Price Index.

The cut-offs used in this report for the year 1994 are technically known as the 1986 base cut-offs, because of the year in which spending on food, shelter and clothing was surveyed. The entire set of 35 cut-offs for 1994 appears below as Table 1....

Table 1 Statistics Canada's Low Income Cut-offs (1986 Base) for 1994

Family Size	Cities of 500,000 +	100,000-499,999	30,000-99,999	Less than 30,000	Rural Areas
1	$15,479	$13,596	$13,282	$12,108	$10,538
2	20,981	18,430	18,004	16,411	14,286
3	26,670	23,426	22,884	20,860	18,157
4	30,708	26,969	26,348	24,019	20,905
5	33,550	29,467	28,787	26,242	22,841
6	36,419	31,983	31,246	28,483	24,792
7+	39,169	34,403	33,609	30,638	26,666

The National Council of Welfare, like many other social policy groups, regards the low income cut-offs as poverty lines and uses the term poor and low-income interchangeably. Statistics Canada takes pains to avoid references to poverty. It says the cut-offs have no official status, and it does not promote their use as poverty lines.

Regardless of the terminology, the cut-offs are a useful tool for defining and analyzing the significantly large portion of the Canadian population with low incomes. They are not the only measures of poverty used in Canada, but they are the most widely accepted and are roughly comparable to most alternative measures.

Graph A shows the 1986 base and 1992 low income cut-offs or LICOs of Statistics Canada along with seven other poverty lines sometimes seen in published reports....

Toronto SPC, the description of the first bar of Graph A, refers to the budget guides of the Metropolitan Toronto Social Planning Council updated to the year 1994. CCSD refers to the Canadian Council on Social Development's income guidelines, which are based on one-half of average family income and do not vary from one area of the country to another. The calculation for the bar labelled Croll uses the methodology first proposed in 1971 by a special Senate committee on poverty headed by Senator David Croll. The Gallup bar is an update of responses to a public opinion poll that asked: "What is the minimum weekly

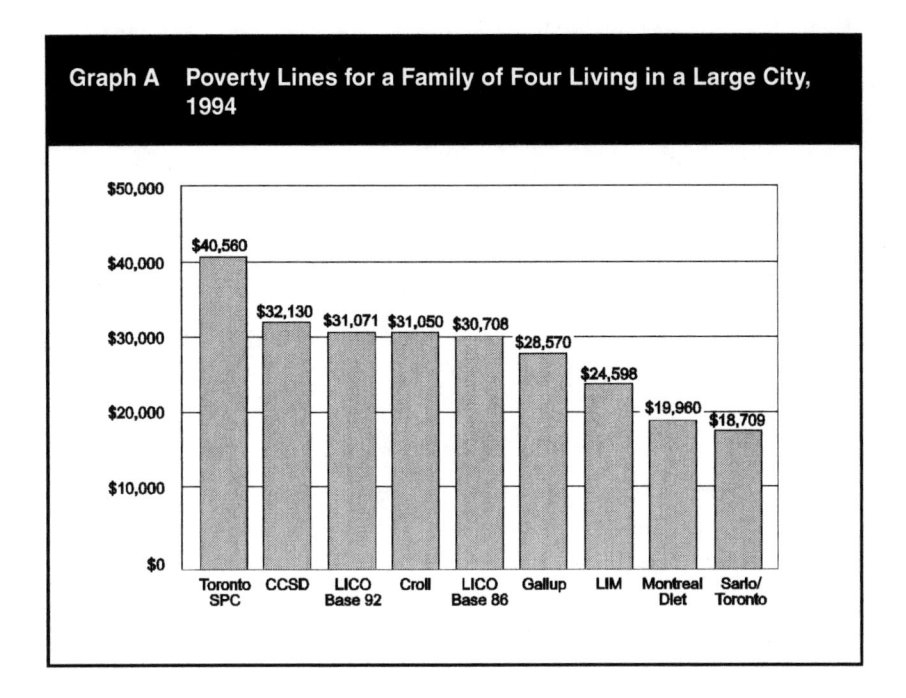

Graph A Poverty Lines for a Family of Four Living in a Large City, 1994

Toronto SPC	$40,560
CCSD	$32,130
LICO Base 92	$31,071
Croll	$31,050
LICO Base 86	$30,708
Gallup	$28,570
LIM	$24,598
Montreal Diet	$19,960
Sarlo/Toronto	$18,709

amount of income required for a family of four, consisting of two adults and two children?" LIM means the low income measures of Statistics Canada, an alternative measure based on one-half of median family income with no geographic variations. Montreal Diet refers to the income needed for a minimum adequate standard of living as calculated by the Montreal Diet Dispensary. The group also has basic needs guidelines strictly intended for short-term assistance that are somewhat lower. Sarlo/Toronto is the poverty line for Toronto calculated for 1992 by Christopher A. Sarlo and updated to 1994 by the National Council of Welfare. Professor Sarlo also has "social comfort lines" that are twice as high as his poverty lines.

Poverty statistics are often broken down according to families and unattached individuals. The survey which gathered the data defined a family as a group of individuals sharing a common dwelling unit and related by blood, marriage or adoption. The definition includes couples living in common-law relationships. Most of the data in this report is expressed in terms of families rather than the number of people in family units. Unattached individuals are defined as people living alone or in households where they are not related to other household members....

Income refers to money income reported by all family members 15 years or older and includes gross wages and salaries, net income from self-employment, investment income, government transfer payments (for example, the federal Child

Tax Benefit, Old Age Security, and provincial tax credits), pensions, and miscellaneous income (scholarships and child support payments, for example). The definition of income excludes gambling wins or losses, income tax refunds, loans received or repaid, lump sum settlements of insurance policies, and income in kind....

Recent Poverty Trends

...This [section] shows major national trends in poverty from 1980 through 1994 using two types of measures. One looks at Canadians as individual people, the other as members of families or as unattached people living outside families.

Poverty Trends for Individual Canadians

One type of poverty statistics published by Statistics Canada gives the number of poor people and the poverty rates for people as individuals.... In 1980, the number of people living in poverty was just over 3.6 million and the poverty rate was 15.3 percent. Both the number of poor people and the poverty rate rose following the recession of 1981-1982, declined slowly through 1989, and started rising again in 1990 through 1993. In 1994, the number of poor people in Canada was nearly 4.8 million and the poverty rate was 16.6 percent.

Many of the other poverty statistics followed the same general pattern as the figures for all persons. Child poverty, for example, increased in the early 1980s.... In 1984, well over 1.2 million children under the age of 18 were living in poverty and the poverty rate was 19.6 percent. The number of poor children and the poverty rate declined through 1989, then started to rebound through 1993. In 1994, the number of poor children was more than 1.3 million and the poverty rate was 19.1 percent....

Children are poor because their parents are poor, and one of the main reasons for poverty among parents is a lack of good jobs. It should come as no surprise that the poverty rates for adults under age 65 tend to move up and down in line with changes in the unemployment rate.

Graph B plots the average annual unemployment rate for people 15 and older against the poverty rate for people ages 18 to 65, the group most likely to be in the labour force. As the percentage of unemployed people in the work force rose and fell, so did the percentage of adults under 65 living in poverty. In 1980, the unemployment rate was 7.5 percent and the poverty rate for people 18 to 65 was 12.9 percent. In 1994, the unemployment rate was 10.4 percent and the poverty rate was 15.5 percent.

One group that is largely immune from high unemployment rates is seniors, because most of them are not in the labour force. The poverty rates for people 65 and older are more a reflection of the health of public and private pension programs than the health of the economy.

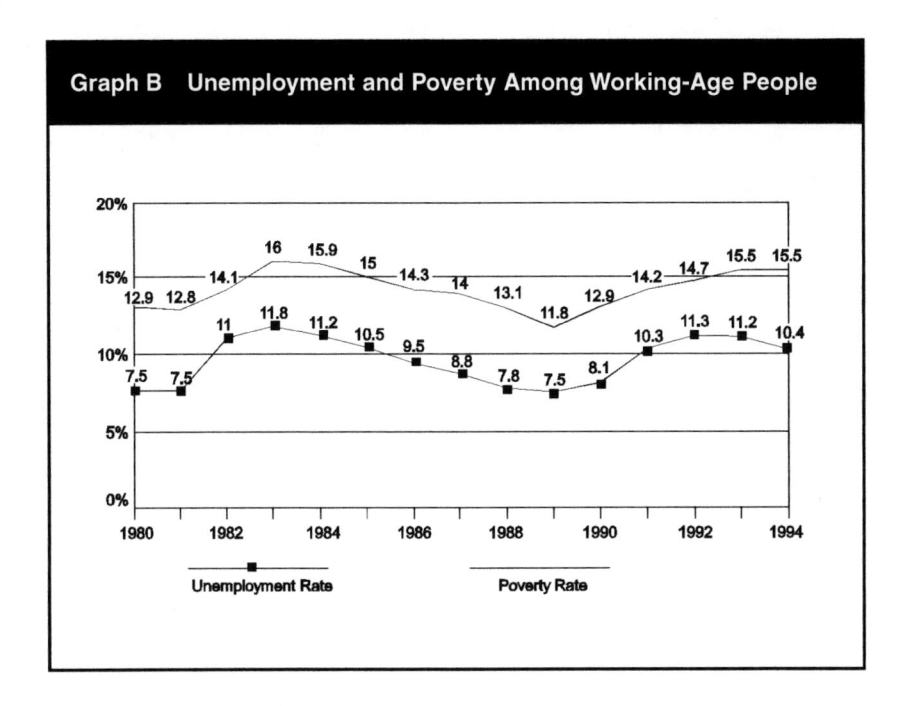

Graph B Unemployment and Poverty Among Working-Age People

Unemployment Rate: 7.5, 7.5, 11, 11.8, 11.2, 10.5, 9.5, 8.8, 7.8, 7.5, 8.1, 10.3, 11.3, 11.2, 10.4

Poverty Rate: 12.9, 12.8, 14.1, 16, 15.9, 15, 14.3, 14, 13.1, 11.8, 12.9, 14.2, 14.7, 15.5, 15.5

Pensions have improved tremendously during the last generation, and this is reflected in poverty rates and numbers for the elderly that have fallen more or less steadily since the first poverty statistics were published in Canada in 1969.

Poverty Trends for Families and Unattached Individuals

While the poverty statistics for persons give a good overview of poverty, it is often more revealing to look at poor people in terms of families or unattached individuals. Throughout most of the period 1980 to 1994, the poverty rates for unattached people were roughly three times higher than the rates for families. In 1994, for example, the poverty rate for families was 13.7 percent, and the rate for unattached individuals was 37 percent.

One reason that families have poverty rates that are consistently much lower than unattached individuals is they often have a second family member in the labour force. The percentage of younger married couples with both spouses in the work force has grown dramatically during the last generation, and two-earner couples now far outnumber one-earner couples. Many older families are couples where both spouses had careers outside the home and where both get pension benefits aside from the federal government's Old Age Security pension.

An even better view of poverty comes by breaking down families and unattached individuals into their major subcategories—which we call family

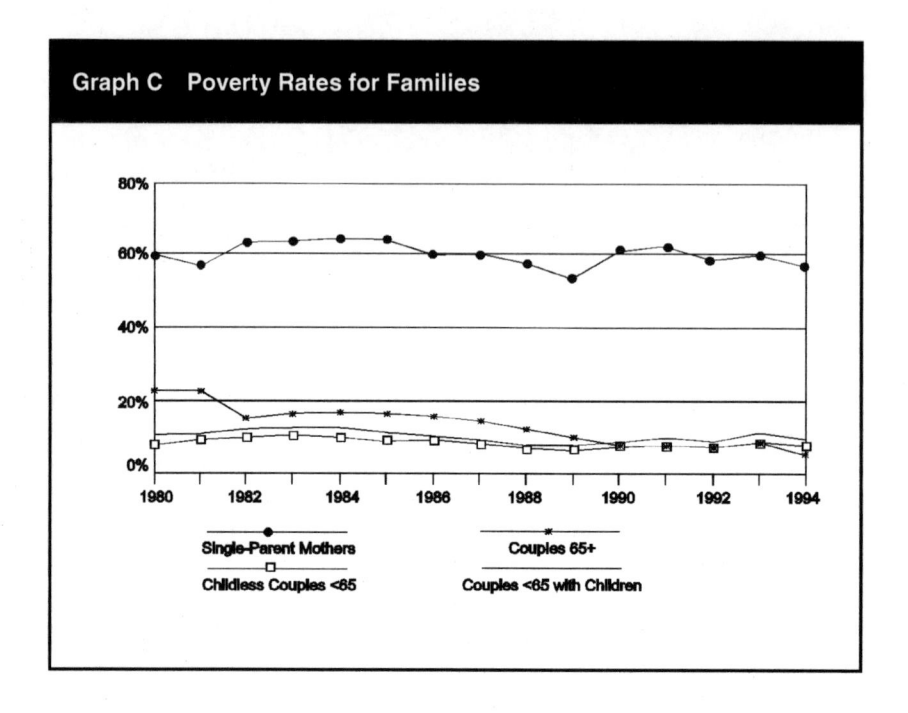

Graph C Poverty Rates for Families

- Single-Parent Mothers
- Childless Couples <65
- Couples 65+
- Couples <65 with Children

types for want of a better term. The four subcategories of families are: married couples where the head of the family is 65 or older; married couples under 65 with children under 18; married couples under 65 without children under 18; and single-parent mothers under 65 with children under 18. Altogether, these four subcategories accounted for 82 percent of all poor families in 1994. The other 18 percent was made up of less common family types, such as married couples living with children who were all 18 or older, single-parent fathers and their children, and brothers and sisters who lived together.

The four subcategories of unattached individuals are: unattached men under 65, unattached men 65 and older, unattached women under 65, and unattached women 65 and older. These four subcategories account for 100 percent of unattached individuals.

The importance of a second wage-earner or second source of pension income becomes obvious from the poverty statistics for the four subcategories of families in Graph C.... The poverty rates for married couples were all low, regardless of the age of the spouses or the presence of children at home. The poverty rates for families led by single-parent mothers were incredibly high....

Graph D Depth of Poverty by Family Type, 1994

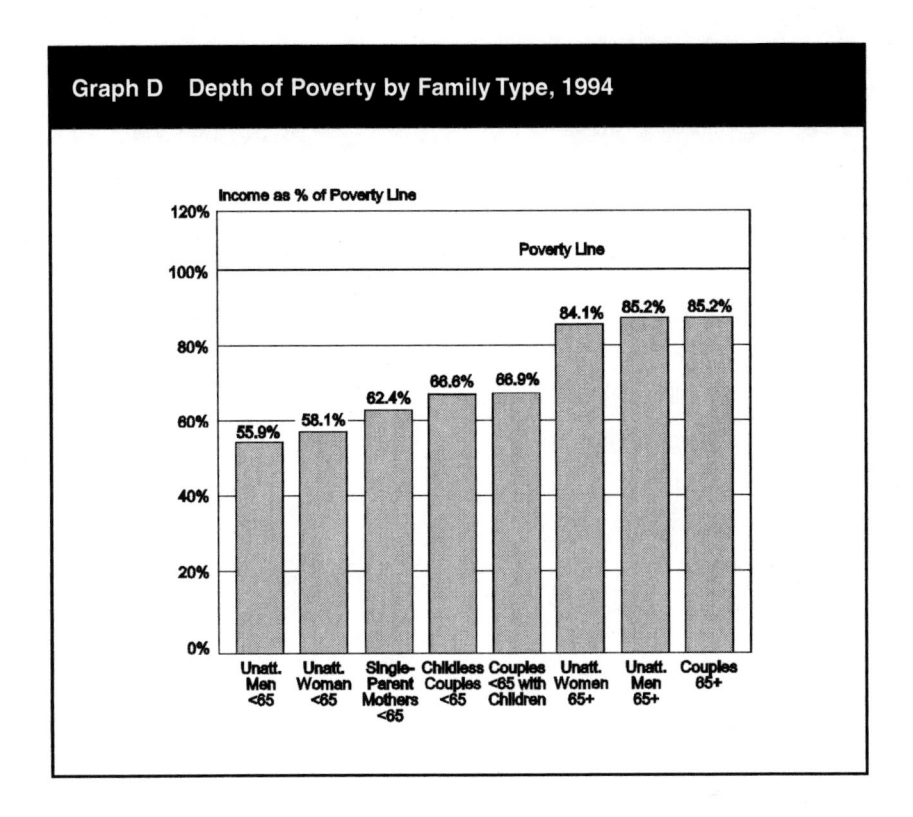

Income as % of Poverty Line

- Unatt. Men <65: 55.9%
- Unatt. Woman <65: 58.1%
- Single-Parent Mothers <65: 62.4%
- Childless Couples <65: 66.6%
- Couples <65 with Children: 66.9%
- Unatt. Women 65+: 84.1%
- Unatt. Men 65+: 85.2%
- Couples 65+: 85.2%

Depth of Poverty and the Poverty Gap

It is one thing to measure the risk of poverty and another to measure its severity. Poverty rates show the percentage of the population which is poor each year, but they do not show whether poor people are living in abject poverty or a few dollars below the poverty line. For that, we need measures of the "depth of poverty." Depth of poverty statistics also allow us to calculate the "poverty gap" to show how much additional income would be needed to bring all Canadians out of poverty.

Graph D shows the average incomes of poor Canadians as a percentage of the poverty line for the eight family types which were highlighted [earlier]. The groups are arranged with the poorest at the left of the graph and the least poor at the right. Unattached men under 65 were the poorest of the eight family types in 1994, with total incomes that were only 55.9 percent of the poverty line on average. Poor unattached men 65 and older and poor married couples 65 and older were at the other end, with average incomes of 85.2 percent of the poverty line.

Table 2   Average Depth of Poverty by Family Type in Constant 1994 Dollars, 1980 and 1994

Family Type	Dollars Below Poverty Line in 1980	Dollars Below Poverty Line in 1994
Single-Parent Mothers under 65 with Children under 18	$9,912	$8,535
Couples under 65 with Children under 18	$8,167	$8,203
Unattached Women under 65	$7,200	$5,943
Unattached Men under 65	$6,903	$5,902
Childless Couples under 65	$6,605	$5,999
Unattached Men 65 and Older	$4,051	$2,089
Unattached Women 65 and Older	$3,900	$2,322
Couples 65 and Older	$3,318	$2,870

Depth of poverty can also be expressed in dollars as the difference between the poverty line and the average income of poor families or unattached individuals. Table 2 shows the depth of poverty by family type for 1980 and 1994, with all the figures given in 1994 dollars to factor out the effects of inflation over the years.

Poor single-parent mothers under 65 with children under 18 were the worst off, living $9,912 below the poverty line on average in 1980 and $8,535 below the line in 1994. Poor couples under 65 with children under 18 were not much better off, with average incomes $8,167 below the poverty line in 1980 and $8,203 below the line in 1994....

Using the average depth of poverty in dollars for different family types and the number of families or unattached individuals in each group, it is possible to calculate Canada's total "poverty gap," or the amount of additional income that would be required to bring all Canadians above the poverty line in any given year.

The poverty gap in 1994 was $15.2 billion.... Four family types accounted for more than three-quarters of the gap: unattached men under 65, unattached women under 65, couples under 65 with children under 18, and single-parent mothers under 65 with children under 18. The ranking of these four groups

Table 3   Incomes of the Poor Compared to Average Incomes, 1994

Family Type	Average Income of Poor	Average Income of All	Income of Poor as Percentage of All
Unattached Men under 65	$8,201	$28,050	29%
Unattached Women under 65	$8,525	$22,521	38%
Unattached Women 65 and Older	$12,311	$17,106	72%
Unattached Men 65 and Older	$12,406	$23,782	52%
Childless Couples under 65	$12,699	$54,214	23%
Single-Parent Mothers under 65 with Children under 18	$14,397	$24,221	59%
Couples 65 and Older	$17,272	$37,387	46%
Couples under 65 with Children under 18	$19,022	$61,168	31%

changes from year to year, but no other family types come close to the size of their poverty gaps.

Canada's poverty gap rose and fell in recent years in much the same way that poverty rates rose and fell.... [D]ollar figures are expressed in constant 1994 dollars to show the trends with the effects of inflation removed. The gap was $12 billion in 1980, it rose to $14.4 billion in 1983 in the wake of the recession, and it fell for most of the rest of the decade. With the start of another recession in 1990, the gap rose once again.

Poor Canadians and their Sources of Income

One measure of the financial plight of poor people is how far they live below the poverty line. Another is how their incomes compare to average incomes. Table 3 gives the average income of poor Canadians by family type in 1994, the average income of *all* Canadians by family type, and the relationship between the two. For example, unattached men under 65 who were poor had a total income of $8,201 on average in 1994. The income of all unattached men under 65, both poor and non-poor, was $28,050 on average. The average income of the poor amounted to 29 percent of the average income of all unattached men under 65.

Table 4 Transfer Payments to the Poor by Family Type, 1994

Family Type	Average Transfer Payment	Average Income From All Sources	Transfers as Percentage of Total Income
Unattached Men under 65	$4,181	$8,201	51%
Unattached Women under 65	$4,238	$8,525	50%
Childless Couples under 65	$6,361	$12,699	50%
Couples under 65 with Children under 18	$9,067	$19,02	48%
Single-Parent Mothers under 65 with Children under 18	$10,551	$14,397	73%
Unattached Women 65 and Older	$11,183	$12,311	91%
Unattached Men 65 and Older	$11,558	$12,406	93%
Couples 65 and Older	$15,829	$17,272	92%

The differences between the average incomes of the poor and all Canadians are sometimes striking. Poor couples under 65 with children under 18 had an average family income of $19,022 in 1994, for example, while the average income of all couples with children under 18 was $61,168 or roughly three times as large.

The differences were much less in the case of unattached seniors and single-parent mothers, because average incomes were much less. The average income for poor single-parent mothers under 65 with children under 18 was $14,397 in 1994, but the average income of all single-parent mothers was only $24,221—much less than average incomes for all husband-wife families.

Obviously, many poor Canadians rely on government programs of one kind or another to help make ends meet. In some cases, the amounts provided by governments are surprisingly modest, and the amounts provided by earnings and non-government sources of income are substantial. In other cases, especially in the case of poor seniors, governments provide a very large portion of total income.

Table 4 shows the average amount of transfer payments received by poor families and unattached individuals in 1994. Transfer payments include Canada and Quebec Pension Plan benefits, unemployment insurance, welfare, the federal Child Tax Benefit and the federal GST credit. The Canada and Quebec Pension

Plans and unemployment insurance are government-run programs, but the money comes from contributions by workers and employers, not from government.

The family types in the table are ranked according to the average size of the transfer payments, with the smallest amounts first. The second column gives the average incomes of poor families and unattached individuals from all sources—the same figures as in Table 3. The third column gives the percentage of total income from transfers.

23

Who Owns Canada?

Edward G. Grabb

In capitalist societies like Canada ownership of property is probably the most significant dimension of material inequality and of economic classes. Within sociology, ownership doesn't just refer to the possession of material goods and resources for personal use or consumption. It refers primarily to the right and capacity to command the activities and systems involved in producing, accumulating, investing or expending society's material resources. So who does own Canada? Has economic power become more concentrated? Has foreign influence increased? How does the state compare with private business in terms of owning and controlling the Canadian economy? What is the role of organizations other than government or private business?

Introduction

One significant body of research in Canadian social science considers the overall structure of economic power. Some earlier works pertaining to the topic can be identified (e.g., Myers 1914; Creighton 1937), but only in the past twenty-five years have scholars compiled extensive information on economic control.

John Porter provided the initial impetus for this research. He found a heavy concentration of economic power within a relatively small number of corporations (Porter 1956, 1957, 1965). Wallace Clement's work in the 1970s suggested that the concentration of economic power among dominant corporations had become even more pronounced (Clement 1975, 1977a, 1977b).

Since these analyses, more has been learned about private-sector corporations in the Canadian economy, (e.g., Newman 1979, 1981; Marchak 1979; Niosi 1978, 1981, 1985; Ornstein 1976; Carroll, Fox, and Ornstein 1982;

Revised from Edward G. Grabb, "Who Owns Canada? Concentration of Ownership and the Distribution of Economic Assets, 1975-1985," *The Journal of Canadian Studies*, Vol. 25, No. 2 (Summer 1990), pp. 72-91.

Carroll 1982, 1984, 1986; Richardson 1982; Brym 1985; Francis 1986). A common thread in some of this subsequent research is that, if anything, Porter and Clement probably understated the degree to which economic power is concentrated in Canada.

The present paper addresses the question of economic concentration, but broadens and extends the discussion in several respects. First, it adds to the evidence on corporate economic concentration, particularly with regard to the assets held by large business enterprises. Second, it investigates the share of economic control retained by other organizations operating outside the private business sector. Overlaying these concerns is foreign ownership, which has long been of pivotal importance for shaping the structure of economic power in Canada. The analysis is concerned with determining more completely how Canada's economic "pie" is divided up.

Beyond private-sector businesses, other institutions are also influential in modern capitalist economies. Of these institutions, the government or state is perhaps the best known and most prominent. Contemporary social scientists have shown a growing interest in the nature of state involvement in economic activity (e.g., Miliband 1973; Poulantzas 1978; Wright 1978; Friedman and Friedman 1980; Offe 1984). Observers in Canada have explored the state's alleged role as the principal spender of the country's wealth, and the advisability of greater state control over economic affairs (e.g., Newman 1981: 458-62; Malcolm 1985: 253-54; Pantich 1977; Calvert 1984; Banting 1982, 1986a, 1986b; Albert and Moscovitch 1987). What has yet to be fully documented is the relative level of economic control held by government organizations. A related question is whether government economic involvement has grown appreciably over time.

In addition, several other institutional constituents remain that are usually overlooked in this context. The examples considered here include what are commonly referred to as non-profit organizations: religious organizations, educational institutions, charitable organizations, health and welfare organizations, and labour unions, in particular....

Analysis

Trends in the Concentration of Corporate Assets

Our first concern is the current level of economic concentration among corporate enterprises, and changes in this concentration level during the recent past. Various writers have considered this issue and have concluded that the pattern of high corporate concentration reported in the earlier work of Porter has become more pronounced over time. Often, however, the evidence used to support this conclusion has been unavoidably incomplete.

For example, using an approach generally similar to Porter's, Clement found that the 183 dominant corporations identified by Porter in the 1950s had been distilled down to just 113 in the early 1970s (Clement 1975: 125-26). This reduction in number suggests a process of concentration and centralization. Yet there are methodological disparities between the two studies, which make an exact comparison difficult (cf. Hunter 1986: 213). Newman has shown that the number of what he terms "major and significant" corporate mergers and takeovers rose steadily in each year of a six-year span, from 8 in 1975 to more than 80 in 1981 (Newman 1981: 467-531). Francis also reports that the takeovers occurring between 1974 and 1984 were more numerous and also involved larger businesses than those of the previous decade (Francis 1986: 3). In both cases these results are suggestive of increasing concentration but are not totally conclusive.

Such findings still give a distinct impression of continued consolidation over this period. They also seem to be consistent with evidence taken from earlier historical periods (cf. Niosi 1981: 18-21; Hunter 1986: 205-08). Other information from government sources can be used to assess the problem more completely. Table 2-1 presents figures derived from government statistics provided under the Corporations and Labour Unions Returns Act (CALURA). The CALURA data are not comprehensive, since they include only non-financial corporations. However, in 1985 such corporations accounted for about three-quarters of all the companies operating in Canada, as well as over 85 percent of the total business income; hence, the results in Table 2-1 do take in a large segment of the country's economic activity (Statistics Canada 1987a: 157).

The key unit of analysis in Table 2-1 is the "enterprise," which in this context refers to any "group of corporations under a single controlled interest" (Statistics Canada 1984a: 37). An example from the private sector is George Weston, one of Canada's top 10 business enterprises in 1985 and majority owner, through various intercorporate connections, of major firms such as Loblaws, which was also in the top 10 (Canadian Business 1986: 76-78). The enterprises have been divided into categories, to distinguish between private-sector businesses (both foreign and domestically-owned) and those controlled by various levels of government. Before any differences are discussed, some points about the entire set of leading enterprises should be noted.

First, as a group, the leading enterprises play a formidable role in our economy. Together, the top 100 enterprises controlled over 1400 corporations in both 1975 and 1985, with an overall average of between 14 and 15 corporations per enterprise in the two years. This clustering of businesses under a small number of enterprises is even more pronounced as we move up the scale. Thus, the leading 25 enterprises each subsumed an average of almost 23 companies in both 1975 and 1985.

These figures suggest a high degree of intercorporate ownership and centralization, especially at the very top. Such government statistics provide only a conservative estimate of the interconnections, since the data are based solely on cases of majority ownership and do not include situations of minority

Table 2-1 Leading Non-Financial Enterprises in Canada (Ranked by Sales), Showing Ownership, Number of Corporations Controlled, and Proportionate Share of Assets and Profits Held, 1975 and 1985

	1975				1985				Change 1975-1985			
	Priv. Sec.				Priv. Sec.				Priv. Sec.			
	For.	Can.	Gov't	Total	For.	Can.	Gov't	Total	For.	Can.	Gov't	Total
Leading 25 Enterprises												
% of Total Assets	9	12	4	25	10	11	4	25	+1	-1	0	-
% of Total Profits	5.4	10.0	13.8	29.2	6.1	11.3	16.0	33.5	+0.7	+1.3	+2.2	+4.3
No. of Corporations	10.2	8.5	3.5	22.2	17.3	7.3	6.9	31.5	+7.1	-1.2	+3.4	+9.3
Average Corporations	193	302	71	566	182	242	149	573	-11	-60	+78	+7
per Enterprise	21.4	25.2	17.8	22.6	18.2	22.0	37.3	22.9	-3.2	-3.2	+14.7	+0.3
Leading 100 Enterprises												
% of Total Assets	56	37	7	100	42	49	9	100	-14	+12	+2	-
% of Total Profits	14.5	16.7	15.4	46.5	11.5	21.8	18.7	52.0	-3.0	+5.1	+3.3	+5.5
No. of Corporations	23.8	15.0	4.3	43.1	25.5	15.8	8.6	49.9	+1.7	+0.8	+4.3	+6.8
Average Corporations	672	735	88	1495	515	739	189	1443	-157	+4	+101	-52
per Enterprise	12.0	19.9	12.6	15.0	12.3	15.1	21.0	14.4	+0.3	-4.8	+7.4	-0.6
All Non-Financial Corporations												
% of Total Assets	32.3	45.8	17.6	100.0	23.4	57.6	19.1	100.0	-8.9	+11.8	+1.5	-
% of Total Profits	45.3	45.1	5.6	100.0	40.7	50.0	9.3	100.0	-4.6	+4.9	+3.7	-
No. of Corporations	6,216	60,968	423	215,600**	5,027	408,198	219	413,444				

**Includes 147,993 "unclassified" corporations in 1975.

Source: CALURA Annual Reports for 1975 and 1985.

control of other businesses by the enterprises in question. Because it is possible for an enterprise to control another firm despite owning less than 50 percent of its shares, the data undoubtedly understate the actual number of companies under the effective ownership of these leading enterprises. This point is particularly relevant for "conglomerates" such as Argus and Power Corporation, which often employ the strategy of minority ownership.

The other data on Table 2-1 provide a good indication of economic concentration between 1975 and 1985. In 1985, the top 25 enterprises alone accounted for over one-third of all assets held by non-financial firms, as well as about one-third of all profits. The top 100 enterprises held over half of all assets and earned about half of all profits among non-financial corporations. Moreover, if we compare these figures for 1985 with the data for 1975, it is clear that the leading enterprises increased their share of the economic pie during this decade. The proportion of assets held by the top 100 enterprises rose significantly in the 10 years, from 46.5 to 52.0 percent of the total; the top 25 enterprises alone moved from 29.2 to 31.5 percent of total assets in the same period. The figures on profits are even more dramatic, with the leading 25 firms increasing their share from 22.2 to 31.5 percent and the leading 100 enterprises jumping from 43.1 to 49.9 percent of all the profits earned by non-financial companies.[1]

We should be reminded that financial enterprises are not included in these data; nevertheless, evidence indicates that concentration among financial firms is even more pronounced than for non-financial enterprises (e.g., Francis 1986: 242). There is also no reason to believe that this high level of concentration has declined in the financial sphere, since fewer than twenty banks, trust companies, and insurance firms controlled the vast majority of assets throughout this period (cf. Stewart 1982; Canadian Business 1986: 126-29).

The next task is to determine whether the tendency toward increased concentration varies for different segments of the corporate structure.

Changes in Foreign Economic Influence

Canada has a long history of foreign involvement in its economic affairs, although the more recent influx by American-based multinational corporations has been the main topic of concern among contemporary observers (e.g., Levitt 1970; Lumsden 1970; Clement 1975, 1977a). Research suggests that this American incursion occurred at different stages, but was particularly marked during a period of about twenty-five years after World War II. Since 1970, however, evidence indicates some decline in foreign ownership (e.g., Niosi 1981: 31-33).

The findings in Table 2-1 provide a more recent assessment of foreign ownership, and distinguish some changes during the decade from 1975 to 1985. First, if we use assets to measure ownership, we find that foreign ownership has declined for the entire set of non-financial corporations, from almost one-third of all assets in 1975 to less than a quarter of the total in 1985. In the top 100 enterprises, the proportion of assets held by foreign enterprises also dropped, from 14.5 percent of the total in 1975 to 11.5 percent in 1985. Similar declines occurred in the number of foreign corporations operating in Canada during this period, and in the number of foreign enterprises among the top 100.

Nevertheless, foreign involvement in Canada's non-financial sector was significant in both 1975 and 1985 and, in some comparisons, actually increased. This is most evident in profits earned. Despite their lower numbers in the top 100 enterprises, foreign businesses earned over 25 percent of total profits in 1985, up from 23.8 percent in 1975. For the leading 25 firms, just 10 foreign enterprises gained over 17 percent of all the profits generated by non-financial companies in 1985, compared to 10.2 percent a decade earlier. Many of these enterprises included the large American automobile and petroleum companies (cf. Canadian Business 1986).

One final point to note is that CALURA figures do not treat a corporation as foreign unless more than 50 percent of its ownership is foreign-based. Therefore, the results may understate the full extent of foreign influence, since companies under minority control by foreign interests are not defined as foreign in these data.

The State and Economic Control

The Canadian state, throughout our history, has shown a notable willingness to help guide or influence business activity in diverse, if sometimes contradictory, ways. These actions have included, for example, financing ventures and insuring loans for Canadian capitalists, imposing tariff barriers and trade restrictions on foreign interests so as to protect Canadian industries, offering tax relief and other incentives to encourage foreign investment, establishing government-run enterprises in some fields while privatizing state businesses in others, and so on (cf. Grant 1965; Levitt 1970; Clement 1975, 1977b; Whitaker 1977; Marchak 1979; Traves 1979; Malcolm 1985).

At times, government actions have made the state appear to be a close partner with private industry, but more recently the government has come to be viewed by many business people as an intruding competitor for Canadian capitalists (cf. Ornstein 1985). This view stems largely from the belief by some that the state has taken on an excessive share of ownership in the Canadian economy.

In fact, the government's economic participation has been expanding in some respects. One illustration is government spending. For example, in 1982 the various levels of government accounted for more than 47 percent of Canada's gross national expenditures, up from just 22 percent in 1950. Such an increase does signal a greater willingness (or necessity) to engage in certain types of economic action, although government spending in Canada during this period was still below average for major developed countries (Calvert 1984: 104, 17).

Table 2-1 provides evidence on economic ownership by the state in recent years, specifically within the non-financial sector. First of all, the number of state-owned corporations was relatively small and actually declined during the decade in question, from 423 in 1975 to just 219 in 1985. The proportion of government firms among the leading enterprises was more sizable but still small and virtually constant between 1975 and 1985: just 4 of the top 25 enterprises were state-owned in both years, while between 7 and 9 of the top 100 were government-run during this decade.

However, some indication of expanding government participation or control can be found in certain features of Table 2-1. For example, the average number of corporations subsumed by leading state enterprises rose significantly between 1975 and 1985, from 17.8 percent to 22.9 in the top 25 category. By comparison, the average number of corporations owned by the leading private-sector enterprises either declined or remained unchanged.

Other evidence of government involvement can be found in the data on assets and profits. Despite the state's comparatively small overall share, the very largest government non-financial enterprises did account for a significant and increasing proportion of total assets and total profits. The four largest government enterprises by themselves held 13.8 percent of all assets in 1975 and 16 percent in 1985; the comparable figures for profits were 3.5 percent in 1975 and 6.9 percent in 1985. Furthermore, almost all of the assets and profits controlled by government non-financial enterprises in 1985 were under the control of only nine state firms, 18.7 percent out of 19.1 for assets and 8.6 percent out of 9.3 for profits. In summary, the state has an increasing role in the economy, but it is still a minor player relative to private enterprise and its part is taken up mainly by a very few large government firms....

Overview: Who Owns Canada?

Keeping in mind the limits on some of the information we have reviewed, it is possible to arrive at an approximate depiction of how our assets are distributed, if this earlier information is combined with additional government data on Canada's "national balance sheet" (Statistics Canada 1986b).

By 1985, the estimated total assets held within Canada stood at just over 4,000 billion, or 4 trillion, dollars.[3] As shown in Figure 2-1, the largest single portion of these assets, about 44 percent of the total, belongs to private-sector businesses. Financial firms, virtually all of which are Canadian-controlled, hold almost half of this portion, or about 21 percent. Canadian non-financials own approximately 18 percent and foreign non-financials the remaining 5 percent.[4]

Another sizable share of assets is in the hands of various branches of the state. This share amounts to approximately 20 percent of the total, which entails 3 percent for government financial institutions, 5 percent for non-financial government enterprises, and 11 percent for other government agencies and organizations.[5]

The remaining assets in Figure 2-1, over 36 percent of the total, are held by persons and unincorporated businesses in the national balance sheet. Most of these assets involve the personal possessions, savings, real estate, private pension funds, and other material resources of individual citizens, including independent

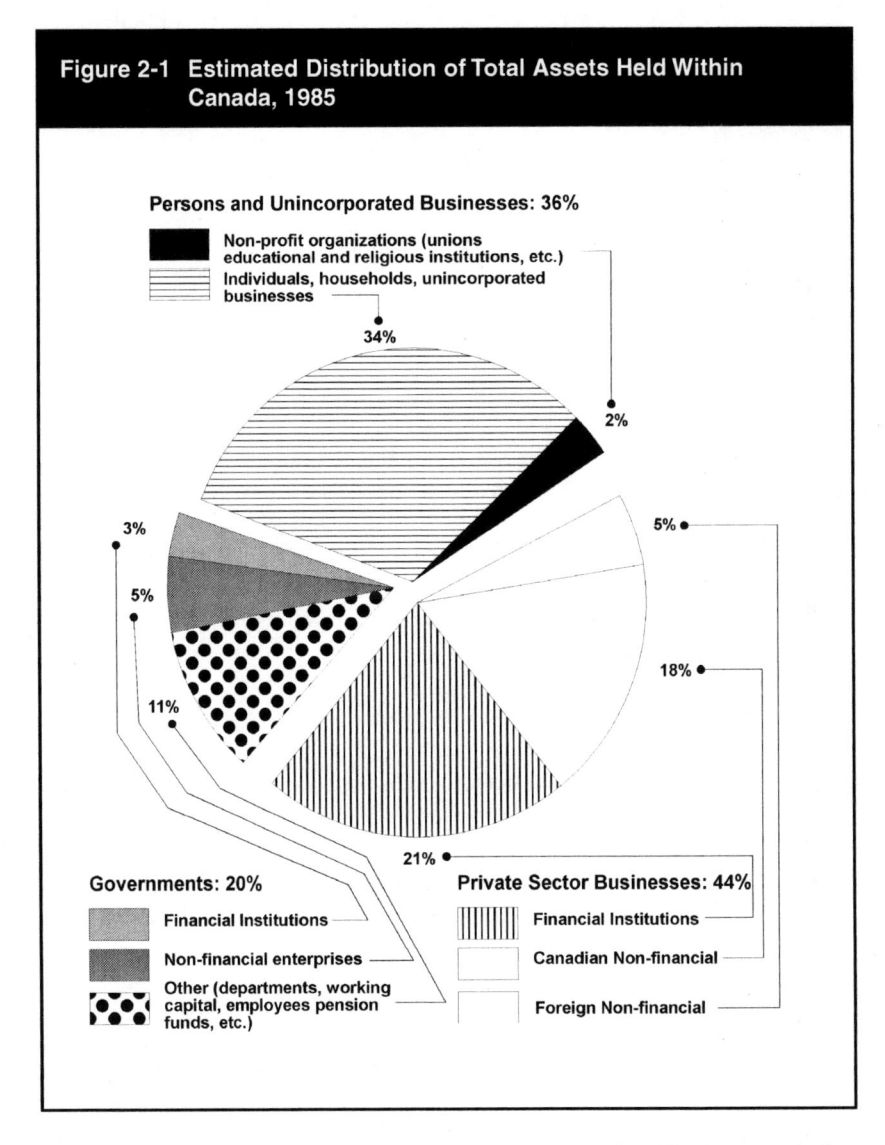

Figure 2-1 Estimated Distribution of Total Assets Held Within Canada, 1985

Persons and Unincorporated Businesses: 36%
- Non-profit organizations (unions educational and religious institutions, etc.) — 2%
- Individuals, households, unincorporated businesses — 34%

Governments: 20%
- Financial Institutions — 3%
- Non-financial enterprises — 5%
- Other (departments, working capital, employees pension funds, etc.) — 11%

Private Sector Businesses: 44%
- Financial Institutions — 21%
- Canadian Non-financial — 18%
- Foreign Non-financial — 5%

*Note: All percentages are approximate and may not add to 100 due to rounding
Source: National Balance Sheet Accounts 1961-1985 Catalogue 13-214

agricultural producers (Statistics Canada 1986b: 1-1vi).[6] However, this portion also subsumes the non-profit institutions examined earlier in the analysis: colleges, universities, labour unions, religious organizations, and so on (Statistics Canada 1985: xx). Based on our previous discussion, a conservative estimate would put the combined holdings of these non-profit organizations at about one or two percent of the total assets in Canada at this time.[7] This leaves approximately one-third of all assets in the hands of individual Canadian residents, including farmers and the proprietors of various unincorporated businesses.

Summary and Conclusions

This analysis has outlined the major contours of Canada's system of economic ownership, with special regard for understanding which organizations and institutions have the greatest command over the productive property, material resources, and various financial or non-financial assets of our society. The key conclusion is that private businesses continue to be the major force, and that their relative share of assets and economic influence grew between 1975 and 1985. The other major finding within the private sector is that foreign control has declined somewhat over the past decade, although profit shares, at least among the largest foreign enterprises, have increased during the same period.

The evidence suggests that some growth in state involvement has occurred, but that it is moderate and confined primarily to less than ten giant government enterprises at the top of the ownership structure. Moreover, even with the increase in government ownership activity, the overall share of the economy controlled by the state is relatively small. Thus, claims of an imminent takeover of our economy by an expansionist Canadian state clearly misrepresent the current situation in our society.

The final goal of the investigation has been to arrive at some approximation of the part played by organizations other than private business and government. While the nature of the evidence makes conclusions tentative, the best estimate is that these other organizations, both collectively and separately, fall well behind state institutions and private business enterprises in their share of economic control within Canada. Of the remaining organizations examined, health, welfare, and charitable institutions appear to rank after those in religious and education, with many of these organizations also overlapping at times with the state, with religious organizations, and with each other. Finally, labour unions do not retain sufficient assets to match those of any other organizations we have considered.

In determining how Canada's material assets are divided among the major institutional spheres, we are still left with a variety of other important questions. For example, a comprehensive assessment of the distribution of total income or revenues to major organizations would be a valuable supplement to the analysis of assets undertaken in this paper. In addition, a more systematic attempt to compare not only the magnitude of the assets but also the capacity of various institutions to put their assets to use would provide a better gauge of the relative economic power of different organizations. For, in somewhat the same way that some shares in a company (usually those owned by the major stockholders) are more crucial for deciding who retains effective ownership of the company, so too are certain assets more important when determining which groups or organizations actually wield the most economic power in society.

It seems likely that private businesses and their owners have more economic control than their share of material assets suggests: besides controlling the largest single portion of the country's assets, the heads of private corporations command the most usable and marketable assets, since the resources overseen by individual citizens, or even by leaders in the state or other spheres, tend to be less discretionary, more dispersed, and more constrained in how they can be used. These considerations suggest that the portrayal of the distribution of assets provided here is best seen as approximate.

Similar considerations should be kept in mind when interpreting the level of foreign control. It is likely that the modest proportion of foreign ownership suggested by our analysis understates the actual level of foreign influence in the Canadian economy. This underestimate is probable, both because the available evidence does not allow us to include cases of minority ownership by foreign interests and because foreign assets continue to be concentrated in that part of our economy where they are undoubtedly the most telling—within a small number of giant private enterprises at the top of the structure. Recent changes in government policy, including the free trade agreement and the easing of restrictions on foreign banks in Canada, could reverse whatever decline in foreign influence has occurred in recent years.

Endnotes

* I thank the following people and organizations for their suggestions and assistance: William Carroll, E.L. Davies, Jasna Krmpotic, Kevin McQuillan, Paul Whitehead, the Anglican Church of Canada, and the United Church of Canada

[1] Comparable trends are evident using two other indicators of economic influence: total equity and total sales. To preserve space, these are not presented in Table 2-1.

[2] Another institutional overlap here involves religious organizations, some of which operate their own colleges and schools. Estimates for such institutions are included in the total for religious organizations and are not part of the estimates provided in the educational sphere.

[3] This amount excludes over 357 billion dollars in Canadian assets held in the "rest of the world" and not part of the national account itself. It also excludes assets that could not be adequately valued on the basis of available information: undeveloped public lands, untapped mineral resources and fuel deposits, water, "human capital," and so on (cf. Statistics Canada 1986b: liv).

4   It should be noted, once again, that this figure may understate actual foreign control, since cases of minority control by foreign firms are not included.
5   Government financial institutions include federal and provincial housing corporations, economic development agencies, monetary authorities, and social security funds such as the Canada Pension and Quebec Pension Plans. Government non-financial organizations are mainly state-run corporations involved in transportation, communications, resources, and utilities. The "Other" category involves the assets of various government departments, working capital funds, public employee pension plans, government hospitals, and so on.
6   Assets held in credit unions and *caisses populaires*, which tend to be sizable, are included in the persons and unincorporated business sector, rather than under financial institutions (Statistics Canada 1986b: lix).
7   One percent of estimated total national assets in 1985 is about 40 billion dollars, which is close to our estimate for the combined holdings of religious and educational organizations. Based on our conclusion that the assets of health and welfare organizations, charities, and unions are smaller than for either religious or educational institutions, and allowing for some additional assets among other organizations not considered here (e.g., professional associations, voluntary organizations, political parties), the figure of between one and two percent overall appears to be the best estimate for the entire set of non-profit organizations.

References

Albert, James, and Allan Moscovitch. 1987. *The Growth of the Welfare State.* Toronto: Garamond....

Banting, Keith. 1982. *The Welfare State and Canadian Federalism.* Kingston and Montreal: McGill-Queen's University Press.

Banting, Keith. 1986a. *State and Society: Canada in Comparative Perspective.* Toronto: University of Toronto Press.

Banting, Keith. 1986b. *The State and Economic Interests.* Toronto: University of Toronto Press....

Barkans, John, and Norene Pupo. 1978. "Canadian universities and the economic order." In R.W. Nelson and D.A. Nock, eds., *Reading, Writing, and Riches: Education and the Socio-Economic Order in North America.* Kitchener: Between the Lines Press.

Brym, Robert J. 1985. "The Canadian capitalist class, 1965-1985." Pp. 1-20 in R.J. Brym, ed., *The Structure of the Canadian Capitalist Class.* Toronto: Garamond Press.

Calvert, John. 1984. *Government, Limited.* Ottawa: Canadian Centre for Policy Alternatives.

Canadian Business. 1985. "Canada's Top 500 Companies." Volume 58 (June).

Canadian Business. 1986. "Canada's Top 500 Companies." Volume 59 (June).

Carroll, William. 1982. "The Canadian corporate elite: Financiers or finance capitalists?" *Studies in Political Economy* 8: 89-114.

Carroll, William. 1984. "The individual, class, and corporate power in Canada." *Canadian Journal of Sociology* 9, 3: 245-68.

Carroll, William. 1986. *Corporate Power and Canadian Capitalism.* Vancouver: University of British Columbia Press.

Carroll, William, John Fox, and Michael Ornstein. 1982. "The network of directorship links among the largest Canadian firms." *Canadian Review of Sociology and Anthropology* 19, 1: 44-69....
Clement, Wallace. 1975. *The Canadian Corporate Elite. An Analysis of Economic Power.* Toronto: McClelland and Stewart.
Clement, Wallace. 1977a. *Continental Corporate Power.* Toronto: McClelland and Stewart.
Clement, Wallace. 1977b. "The corporate elite, the capitalist class, and the Canadian state." Pp. 225-48 in L. Panitch, ed., *The Canadian State.* Toronto: University of Toronto Press.
Council of Ontario Universities. 1984. Combined financial statements for the University of Western Ontario (photocopy)....
Creighton, Donald. 1937 (1956). *The Commercial Empire of the St. Lawrence.* Toronto: Macmillian of Canada.
Francis, Diane. 1986. *Controlling Interest.* Toronto: Macmillan of Canada.
Friedman, Milton, and Rose Friedman. 1980. *Free to Choose.* New York: Harcourt Brace Jovanovich....
Grant, George. 1965. *Lament for a Nation.* Toronto and Montreal: McClelland and Stewart.
Hunter, Alfred A. 1986. *Class Tells: On Social Inequality in Canada* (2nd. ed.). Toronto: Butterworths....
Levitt, Kari. 1970. *Silent Surrender.* Toronto: Macmillan of Canada.
Lumsden, Ian, ed. 1970. *Close the 49th Parallel Etc.* Toronto: University of Toronto Press.
Malcolm, Andrew H. 1985. *The Canadians.* Markham: Fitzhenry & Whiteside....
Marchak, M. Patricia. 1979. *In Whose Interests? An Essay on Multinational Corporations in a Canadian Context.* Toronto: McClelland and Stewart....
Miliband, Ralph. 1973. *The State in Capitalist Society.* London: Quartet Books....
Myers, Gustavas. 1914 (1972). *A History of Canadian Wealth.* Toronto: James Lewis and Samuel.
Newman, Peter C. 1979. *The Canadian Establishment* (rev. ed.). Toronto: McClelland and Stewart-Bantam..
Newman, Peter C. 1981. *The Acquisitors.* Toronto: McClelland and Stewart-Bantam.
Niosi, Jorge. 1978. *The Economy of Canada.* Montreal: Black Rose Books.
Niosi, Jorge. 1981. *Canadian Capitalism: A Study of Power in the Canadian Business Establishment.* Toronto: Lorimer..
Niosi, Jorge. 1985. *Canadian Multinationals.* Toronto: Garamond Press.
Offe, Claus. 1984. *Contradictions of the Welfare State.* Cambridge: MIT Press....
Ornstein, Michael. 1976. "The boards and executives of the largest Canadian corporations: Size, composition and interlocks." *Canadian Journal of Sociology* 1, 4: 411-37.
Ornstein, Michael. 1985. "Canadian capital and the Canadian state: Ideology in an era of crisis." Pp. 129-66 in R.J. Brym, ed., *The Structure of the Canadian Capitalist Class.* Toronto: Garamond Press.
Ornstein, Michael. 1986. "Extending the reach of capital: Corporate involvement in Canadian hospital and university boards, 1946-1977." Institute for Social Research, York University.
Ornstein, Michael. 1988. "Corporate involvement in Canadian hospital and university boards, 1946-1977." *Canadian Review of Sociology and Anthropology* 25, 3: 365-88.

Panitch, Leo, ed. 1977. *The Canadian State*. Toronto: University of Toronto Press.
Porter, John. 1956. "Concentration of economic power and the economic elite in Canada." *Canadian Journal of Economics and Political Science* 22 (May): 199-200.
Porter, John. 1957. "The economic elite and the social structure in Canada." *Canadian Journal of Economics and Political Science* 23 (August): 377-94.
Porter, John. 1965. *The Vertical Mosaic. An Analysis of Social Class and Power in Canada*. Toronto: University of Toronto Press.
Poulantzas, Nicos. 1978. *State, Power, Socialism*. London: New Left Books.
Richardson, R.J. 1982. "'Merchants against industry': An empirical study of the Canadian elite." *Canadian Journal of Sociology* 7, 3: 279-95.
Scott, Jack. 1978 *Canadian Workers, American Unions*. Vancouver: New Star Books.
Statistics Canada. 1979. *Corporations and Labour Unions Returns Act. Annual Report for 1976*. Part I: Corporations. Catalogue 61-210. Ottawa: Ministry of Supply and Services....
Statistics Canada. 1984a. *Corporations and Labour Unions Returns Act. Annual Report for 1981*. Part I: Corporations. Catalogue 61-210. Ottawa: Ministry of Supply and Services....
Statistics Canada. 1985. *The National Balance Sheet Accounts, 1961-1984*. Catalogue 13-214. Ottawa: Ministry of Supply and Services....
Statistics Canada. 1986b. *The National Balance Sheet Accounts, 1961-1985*. Catalogue 13-214. Ottawa: Ministry of Supply and Services.
Statistics Canada. 1987a. *Corporations and Labour Unions Returns Act. Annual Report for 1985*. Part I: Corporations. Catalogue 61-210. Ottawa: Ministry of Supply and Services....
Stewart, Walter. 1982. *Towers of Gold, Feet of Clay*. Toronto: Collins.
Traves, Tom. 1979. *The State and Enterprise: Canadian Manufacturers and the Federal Government, 1917-1931*. Toronto: University of Toronto Press....
Whitaker, Reg. 1977. "Images of the State in Canada." Pp. 28-68 in L. Panitch, ed., *The Canadian State*. Toronto: University of Toronto Press.
Wright, Eric Olin. 1978. *Class, Crisis, and the State*. London: New Left Books.

24

And So They Were Wed

Lillian Breslow Rubin

How do classes persist and perpetuate themselves as classes? Why are class differences and gender differences so difficult to eradicate? In this excerpt Rubin examines the culture of one segment of the working class to begin to develop answers to these questions. On the basis of interviews with relatively young, but long-married, men and women she uncovers differences in the ways men and women describe and understand love, courtship and the other sex. Rubin also discusses the socio-cultural and economic environment and pressures within which the meaning of marriage and children take root.

They were young when they met—sometimes just in high school, sometimes just out. They were young when they married for the first time—on the average, 18 for women, 20 for the men; the youngest, 15 and 16 respectively. And they were young when they divorced and remarried. One-fourth of the women and one-fifth of the men were married once before. And although the present marriages average almost nine years, the mean age of the women is only 28; of the men, 31:

How did you decide that this was the person you wanted to marry?

Most people hesitate, not quite sure how to respond to that question. When the answers do come, usually they are the expected ones—those that affirm the romantic ideals of American courtship and marriage. "We fell in love." "We were attracted to each other." "We were having fun." "He was the right one." As the conversation continues, however, the stories they tell about how they met

---

Lillian Breslow Rubin, "And So They Were Wed," from *Worlds of Pain: Life in the Working-Class Family*, Basic Books, 1976: Chapter 14 [as reprinted in William Feigelman (ed), *Sociology Full Circle: Contemporary Readings on Society* (4th ed), New York: Holt, Rinehart and Winston: 1985: 277-291.]

and why they married are inconsistent with those first socially acceptable responses.

Some describe meetings and matings that seemed to happen by chance:

> We met at the show where we all used to go on Friday nights. We started to go together right away. Four months later, I got pregnant so we got married. [Twenty-eight-year-old housewife, mother of four, married 11 years.]

...or marriages that took place almost by accident, without choice or volition:

> I don't know exactly why I married her instead of somebody else. I guess everybody always knows they're going to have to get married. I mean, everybody has to some time, don't they? What else is there to do but get married? [Thirty-four-year-old maintenance man, father of five, married 13 years.]

Some—the young divorcees—often married because they were exhausted from the struggle to support and care for their small children. One such woman, a 31-year-old mother of four, married eleven years to her second husband, was divorced at nineteen. With a husband who couldn't have supported her even if he wanted to, and a family who "would have helped, but [who] had their own problems," she recalls:

> I really wasn't sure I wanted to get married again. But financially, it was terrible. I got no support at all. I think even then I knew that I probably would have taken a lot more time about remarrying if I didn't have those really awful financial problems.
>
> I was so tired of working, and I felt like I was giving my kids so little. I began to be afraid that they wouldn't even know who their mother was. It was to the point where I was picking them up, taking them home, giving them a bath, putting them to bed, putting up my hair, and going to bed myself. I was too tired for anything else—not for them and not for me. On the weekends it was just about all I could do to get things straight in the house and get ready for the next week. Rest? Who knew about that then!
>
> It finally all caved in on me when I came to pick up my kids after work one night, and they didn't want to go home with me. [*Near tears.*] Can you believe it? They wanted to stay with the babysitter. I couldn't even blame them. I sure

wasn't any fun to be with; and it was getting so they knew her better than me.

So Johnny was around, and he really was different than my first husband. I figured he was a responsible guy, and he cared about me and my kids. So we got married. And, you know, now I still have to work. [*Then quickly, as if wanting to take the words back.*] But it's not as bad; in fact, you can't compare it. I work only part time, and we don't have such awful money problems. Besides, I don't have to do *everything* all by myself. Johnny helps out with the kids and stuff when I need him to.

How did you decide this was the person you wanted to marry?

Often wives and husbands disagree. For just as Jessie Bernard in her book *The Future of Marriage* found two marriages—his and hers—for many couples there are also two courtships—his and hers. A 29-year-old mother of three, married 11 years, recalls:

> We met at the coffee shop where some of us kids used to hang out. I guess we knew right away because we began to go steady right after. We just fell in love right away.
>
> I thought he was a big man. I was still in high school, and it was like—you know, he wasn't just another kid in school. He got out the year before, and he was working and making lots of money (it seemed like lots then anyway), and we could go out and do cool things. Then after a couple of months, he gave me his class ring. Boy, I was surprised. It was really big, so I put a tape around it so it wouldn't fall off. Then that wasn't comfortable, so after a while, I had the ring made smaller, and I figured if he didn't say anything—I mean, if he said it was okay to do it—this must be a sure thing. And it was! And we got married.

Her 30-year-old husband tells the story differently:

> We met at this place and I kind of liked her. She was cool and kind of fun to be with. Before I knew it, we were going steady. I don't exactly know how it happened. I had this class ring from high school and she kept wanting me to give it to her. So finally one night I took it off and did it. And the next thing I knew, she took it down and had it made smaller. She made a big thing out of it, and so did her family. Don't get me wrong;

> I like her good enough. But I just didn't think about getting married—not then anyhow. But then, after we were going together for almost a year, it just seemed like the thing to do. So we did.

Over and over such differences in recollections appear, each sex playing out its stereotypic role—the women more often focusing on the romantic view of the meeting and the marrying, the men on the "I-don't-know-how-she-caught-me" view. Typical of these differences is this couple, both 26, married eight years.

The wife:
> We just knew right away that we were in love. We met at a school dance, and that was it. I knew who he was before. He was real popular; everybody liked him. I was so excited when he asked me to dance, I just melted.

The husband:
> She was cute and I liked her, but I didn't have any intention of getting married. I went to this school dance and she was there. I sort of knew who she was, but I'd never talked to her before. Then that night she worked it so that her girlfriend who I knew introduced us. I felt kind of funny knowing she wanted me to dance with her, so I asked her. That started it.
>
> Then, I don't know, we just got to seeing each other; she always seemed to be there. And like I said, she was cute and fun. By the time we graduated, everybody was just expecting us to get married. I thought about breaking it off; I even tried, but she cried so much I couldn't stand it.

Although both wives and husbands frequently start a discussion about how they came to choose their mates with a certain defensiveness and a seeming lack of awareness, the women more often than the men move rather quickly to demonstrate a sophisticated self-awareness, as this couple, parents of three children, married 13 years, shows.

The wife:
> I guess the reason we got married was because he was out of a job, and he was being kicked out of his boardinghouse.
>
> *You weren't planning to marry, then?*
>
> Well, we had never really talked about marriage although maybe we both kind of knew it would happen. At the time it

all happened kind of sudden. I said, "What are you going to do about this situation?" He said, "I don't know; maybe we could get married." I said, "Okay, let's do it." And we did.

But what made you say "okay?" What attracted you most about him?

I think the fact that he liked me. I guess that was really important to me. I didn't date very much, and then this guy came along, and he liked me. Also, I guess I felt needed; that's important, especially when you're just a kid. Nothing makes you feel more important [*Pausing reflectively, then adding.*] Now that I look at him, I also see that he reminds me very much of my dad. I suppose that was part of it, too, even though back then I certainly didn't know it.

The husband:

What do you mean, how did we decide? *We* didn't really decide; *she* did mostly, if you know what I mean.

But what made you go along? What attracted you most about her?

I don't know. We were seeing each other every day, and what else was there to do but to get married. [*With a tight, angry laugh.*] She was hard to get, I guess. A lot of girls play that way, you know, because they know it gets to a guy. She sure knew how to get to me.

Undoubtedly, all these explanations speak to some part of the truth. Like women and men in all classes, however, these couples marry for a complex of reasons, many of them only dimly understood, if at all. First among those reasons may be the social-psychological milieu in which we all come to adulthood—the nuclear family which promises (even if it doesn't always deliver) intimacy, and leaves us yearning for more; a society in which almost everyone marries, and where those who don't are viewed as deviant and deficient. So we come together because we need to feel close to someone; because it's what most of us do at a certain stage of life; because it's the accepted and the expected, the thing to do if one is finally to be grown up. Still, there is a quality of urgency among the young people of the working class that is not so evident in a comparable group of middle-class, college-educated men and women—an urgency that is rooted in their class history and family backgrounds.

There are those—women and men—from hard-living families, aching with pain, needing a place in which to feel safe, a place to which they belong:

> My mother left us when I was nine. It was bad enough living in the house with just my father, but then when he got married, it was just awful.
>
> He married a real bad woman. They met in a bar. They both drink a lot—too much. And a little while after they met, she moved into our house with her two kids. I was so ashamed, I could have died—them living together in our house like that. After a year or so, they got married and things got even worse. She's got a foul mouth and she was really awful to us kids. She'd curse us and call us the most awful, terrible names. When she got drunk, she'd be even worse. She'd knock us down and kick us while she was cursing us out.
>
> It wasn't much of a family before she came, but it was a whole lot better. My father tried the best he could. Even though he was drunk a lot of the time, he wasn't mean. And we all felt we had *somebody*. After she came, there was just nobody, nobody.
>
> I used to dream all the time about a home of my own. I wanted so much to have a place where I'd be secure. So when I met Barney, I thought, "here's a guy who loves me and needs me." And that felt so good so we got married. [Twenty-four-year-old sales clerk, mother of two, married seven years.]

It was not only the children of hard-living families who married young, however. Whether hard-living or settled, most lived in relatively poor neighbourhoods where parents saw around them many young people whose lives were touched by the pain and delinquency that often accompanies a life of poverty. In such an environment, parents tend to be terribly fearful about their children's future—fearful that they will lose control, that the children will wind up "on the streets," or worse yet, in jail. Therefore, they try to draw the reins of control very tight—keeping a close watch, imposing strict rules about manners and behaviour, strict regulations about time and activities.

But these same parents and children live in a society where respect is accorded to the financially successful, where the mark of ability is represented by one's annual income. Such parents, believing that they haven't "made it," feel unsure of themselves, their worth, and their wisdom—a perception that often is shared by their children.

No words are necessary to convey these feelings. Children know. They know when their teachers are contemptuous of their family background, of the values they have been taught at home. They know that there are no factory workers, no truck drivers, no construction workers who are the heroes of the television shows they watch. They know that their parents are not among those who "count" in America. And perhaps most devastating of all, they know that their parents know these things as well. Why else would they urge their children on to do "better," to be "more" than they are? Why else would they carry within them so much generalized and free-floating anger—anger that lashes out irrationally at home, anger that is displaced from the world outside where its expression is potentially dangerous?

Such children, then, not only are exposed to the values of the larger society which denigrate their parents' accomplishments and way of life, but those values also are taught to them in implicit and explicit ways by their own parents. Under such circumstances, it is difficult, indeed, for working-class parents either to provide acceptable parental role models for their children or to enforce their authority.

The acceptance and transmission of definitions of self-worth that are tied to material accomplishments and acquisitions is one of the unacknowledged and most painful of the "hidden injuries" that this society has visited upon the working class. When the insecurities that derive from these injuries are denied, as they most often are (for who can face the humiliation of being debased in one's own and one's children's eyes), the response is to cling ever more tightly to old and familiar ways, and to shout ever more loudly about their value.

It is of such economic and sociocultural realities that child rearing patterns are born. And it is to those experiences that we must look to explain the origins of child rearing patterns in working-class families that, on the surface, appear rigid and repressive. In that context, the widely accepted theories that their authoritarian personalities are responsible for the observed relations between parents and children become highly questionable. Instead, those theories seem to reflect the inability of their middle-class creators to understand either the context in which the behaviour takes place or its subjective meaning to the actors involved.

These parenthetical comments aside, the fact remains that most working-class parents feel free to relax their vigilance only after children marry. For the young in those families, then, marriage becomes a major route to an independent adult status and the privileges that accompany it.

The fact that life is different for the college-educated, middle-class young needs little documentation; our television screens and newspaper headlines shouted the news to us through the decade of the sixties. The young people of that class find outside of marriage at least some of the independence and adult privileges that are available to the working-class young only within marriage. Thus, the children of the professional middle-class consistently marry later. Among those I met, the average age at marriage was 23 for women, 25 for men.

In other ways, too, the children of these classes have different experiences and are expected to assume different responsibilities within the family. In the working-class home, for example, the family economy generally rests on at least some help from grown or growing sons. Thus, boys are expected to work early and contribute a substantial part of their earnings to the family. And although they may have more freedom from certain kinds of parental surveillance and restraints than their sisters, they, too, generally live at home—in houses that are too small to permit even minimal privacy—until they marry:

> I had to work from the time I was 13 and turn over most of my pay to my mother to help pay the bills. By the time I was 19, I had been working for all those years and I didn't have anything—*not a thing*. I used to think a lot about how when I got married, I would finally get to keep my money for myself. I guess that sounds a little crazy when I think about it now because I have to support the wife and kids. I don't know *what* I was thinking about, but I never thought about that then. But even so, my wife doesn't get it all, you can bet on that. [Thirty-three-year-old automobile painter, father of three, married 13 years.]

For the girls, the culture dictates that "nice" girls remain under the parental roof until a husband comes to take them away. For them, there is no other road to womanhood and independence:

> I was only 17 when I got married the first time. I met him just after I graduated from high school, and we were married six weeks later. I guess that was kind of fast. I don't know, maybe it was rebound. I had been going with a boy in high school for a couple of years, and we had just broken up. Actually, I guess the biggest thing was that there was no other way if I wanted to get away from that house and to be a person in myself instead of just a kid in that family. All three of us girls married when we were very young, and I guess we all did it for the same reason. All three of us got divorced, too, only for my sisters it didn't work out as lucky as for me. They've both had a lot of trouble. [Thirty-year-old housewife, mother of three, married nine years.]

It is true that several couples did speak of living together before marriage, but in all but one instance, the women had been married before and had borne one or more children. One of these women said of that period of her life:

> We met and things just clicked, so we started living together right away. I know that sounds terrible, but that's the way it was. Before I'd ever gotten married, I'd never have thought of doing anything like that. But after all, I'd already been

married. And anyway, we only did it for a couple of months; then we got married.

Mostly, however, working-class teenagers chafe under living conditions that are oppressive and parental authority that feels repressive. Marriage often is seen as the only escape—a route they take very early in their lives.

But there are still other components to the urgency to marry. For while parents try desperately to circumscribe and control their children's behaviour, to make them into respectful and respectable adults, the children—especially the boys—often get into youthful trouble and are themselves frightened by those experiences. Thus, there are the men who recall those years as a time when they were facing the choice between a hard-living and a settled-living life, and who saw a "good woman" as the way to the settled-living path:

> I was 17 and hanging around with a loose crowd, and all of us got into a lot of trouble—you know, with the police and all that kind of stuff. I had this girlfriend who was also 17. She quit school when she was about 15, I guess, and she already had a kid (he was about two, I guess) when I knew her. So you can see, I was just asking for it, running around with people like that.
>
> I already had some run-ins with the police, just some juvenile, y'know, kid stuff. And then I got picked up for a heavy rap—robbery. That really scared me. While I was waiting for my trial and wondering what was going to happen to me (I used to have nightmares about going to jail), I met Ann. She was the sweetest, most honest, innocent girl I ever knew. I just knew I needed a girl like her to help me change my ways. She did, too. I beat that rap, and after that Ann would come and pick me up and take me to school every day; then she'd wait for me to take me home.
>
> We both finished high school, and I'm proud of that because nobody else in our families did. Then we got jobs and saved our money; and then we got married. I've never been sorry either, because she still keeps me straight. [Twenty-seven-year-old mechanic, father of two, married eight years.]

Not an exceptional story when one considers that well over one-third of the men and 10 percent of the women told of juvenile records—four boys and two girls being defined by the authorities as incorrigibles by age 12 or 13, the rest held on a variety of charges ranging from petty theft, to breaking and entering, to grand theft, to assault with a deadly weapon. These charges, which sound so serious, often grow out of such activities as breaking into a vacant house, stealing a two-by-four from a construction site, getting into a street fight, or joy-riding in a stolen car. As one young man, telling of his troubles with the police, said:

> You know, they always put those terrible names on it. They always make it sound so much worse than it is.

Not always; it depends on who is getting into trouble. Several men in a comparable group of professional middle-class adults recalled similar activities, yet not one had a juvenile record. Usually, they were not even picked up. On the rare occasion when they were, they were released immediately into the custody of their parents, leading one to assume that the police tend to view such behaviour differently depending upon the class composition of the neighbourhood in which it is found. In working-class neighbourhoods of any colour, these behaviours are called crimes; in middle-class neighbourhoods, they are just boyish pranks.

The rate of juvenile arrests among the working-class people I met suggests a very high level of police activity in white working-class communities—activity about which we hear almost nothing. We are accustomed to the cry of police harassment from black communities whose young people also have a very high rate of arrests. But such high juvenile arrest rates in white communities catch us by surprise since they receive so little publicity. Partly, that may be because whites experience black crime as more dangerous to the society than white crime and, therefore, attend less to the latter. Partly, and not unrelated to this kind of racist consciousness among whites, it may be a matter of what the media consider news. And partly, it may indicate a less troubled relationship between the police and white working-class communities—perhaps because policemen are often white and working class in origin. The last may also be the reason why—in contrast to black youth who tend to see the police as an alien and repressive enemy who harass and victimize them without cause—the whites tend to accept police definitions of themselves an to agree that they "got what was coming." One man, aged 24, recalling his juvenile troubles, says:

> Boy, I always felt like a big man every time I got into trouble. I got mad when I got caught sometimes, but I always knew the cops were right and I was wrong.

Another, aged 39, says flatly:

> I had plenty of run-ins with the police, but I can't say I didn't get what was coming to me. I got what I deserved, being the smart-alecky kid I was.

Finally, there are those—44 percent of the couples to whom I talked—who married because the woman became pregnant, another statistic that seems extraordinarily high but that is so prevalent among working-class youth that it is experienced as commonplace. Speaking of his first marriage, a 31-year-old machinist, now in a seven-year-old second marriage, remembers:

> I had gone with this girl for two years, and I suppose we expected to get married, but not yet. She was 18 and I was 19 when she got pregnant. Once that happened, there was nothing else to do but get married. My one consolation was that I outlasted everybody else. Everybody I knew then was getting married because the girl got pregnant; nobody got married without that. And most of them were getting caught a lot sooner than I did.

"Getting caught"—a phrase that was used over and over again:

> I got caught right away; it really happened quick. A lot of people I know got away with it much longer. [Twenty-two-year-old housewife mother of two children, married six years.]
>
> We had been fooling around for a few months, then all of a sudden, she got caught. [Thirty-year-old cook's helper, father of three, married nine years.]
>
> I felt so mad because I got caught when other people were doing the same thing and getting away with it. My sister-in-law and a couple of my girlfriends were doing it, too, and they didn't get caught so they got to have a big wedding, and to be all dressed up like a bride and all that stuff that I wanted so bad and couldn't have because I got caught. [Twenty-four-year-old clerk, mother of one, married six years.]

"Getting caught," with its clear implication of an accident. What does it really mean when 80 percent of these couples engaged in sexual relations before marriage—a figure that accords with the recent literature documenting the increase over earlier generations in the rate of premarital sex. Since class and education breaks differ in these studies, none shows data that are directly comparable to mine. But the best known, Morton Hunt's *Sexual Behaviour in the 1970s*, reports that among his married respondents aged 25-34, 92 percent of the men and 65 percent of the women *at all educational* levels experienced premarital coitus, not necessarily with their present spouse.

But the focus on the *rate* of behaviour or the *change* from earlier generations, while both impressive and sensational, ignores the way in which people *experience* their behaviour. And among the men and women in this study one thing is quite clear: while most people talked relatively openly about their premarital sexual experiences, most of the women, at least, were not free of guilt about them. Indeed, only one woman spontaneously commented positively about the experience of premarital sex with her husband:

> I think it's a hundred percent better to have it. I mean, I don't think you should sleep with just anybody, but I think it's better. If Joe and I had gotten married and had never had anything before, it could've been a disaster. I wouldn't like to marry a man and not know anything about what he needs or how he was; and I'd rather he knew something about me, too. Otherwise, I might be afraid of failing him, or maybe he might fail me. You know, I don't mean to sleep with just everybody and anybody, but if you fall in love.... [Twenty-five-year-old mother of two, married five years.]

A more typical response came from a woman who still speaks with pain of that period in her life:

> I was raised quite a strict Catholic, and I had many guilt feelings about having sex before we were married. Then when I got pregnant, I was so upset I almost died. It took me quite a while to get over those terrible feelings, and I still have problems. [Thirty-year-old mother of three, married 12 years.]

Another woman, aged 26, married seven years, says:

> My sexual adjustment after we were married was very hard. I think I felt guilty about what I had done before. I really felt terrible about it, and I just couldn't enjoy it because I felt so bad. In fact, I still have trouble with it and I worry about what my husband is *really* thinking about me because I let him have me before we were married.

"I let him have me before we were married"—words that suggest the very traditional ways in which so many of these working-class women think about and experience their sexual activities; words that suggest their bodies are something to be given away at the socially mandated moment; words that were not heard from the college-educated middle-class women. In fact, one of the interesting class differences is that the middle-class women—72 percent of whom also engaged in premarital coitus—generally spoke with less guilt about it. Partly, that may be due to class differences in the *expressed* attitudes about such behaviour. Among the working-class women—even though people around them engaged in premarital intercourse; even though they, too, were doing so—there seemed to be a wider gap than in the middle class between the ideal statements of the culture and the reality of the behaviour. Thus, among the working-class women, there was a greater sense that they were doing "wrong," an act to hide in shame from the world around them.

Such fears and the feelings that accompany them are mirrored in the women who resisted premarital intercourse, all of whom showed a decided sense of relief that they had not "given in," partly because it enabled them to feel superior to friends or sisters:

> I wanted so bad to have a white wedding and to not have to say he had to marry me. My sisters, they had to get married, and it was *so* important to me not to have to. I didn't want ever to lose my self-respect like so many girls I knew did. [Twenty-seven-year-old typist, married eight years.]

...and partly because experience has taught them that the women who did often were stigmatized and demeaned in the eyes of their husbands:

> I'm very glad we didn't because I've heard his friends throw it back in their wives' faces now. And when I've heard that, I think, "Boy, am I glad he doesn't have that as a weapon to use on me." [Twenty-eight-year-old housewife, married 10 years.]

These concerns suggest that the "good girl-bad girl" split remains alive for many of these women, and that their fears of being tagged with the "bad girl" label are rooted in social reality and reinforced in interactions with their men who "throw it back in their wives' faces." So deep is this fear, in fact, that it plays a vital part in most of the premarital pregnancies. In this era of The Pill, over three-quarters of the women who became pregnant before marriage pleaded innocent of knowledge about birth-control measures. Some may actually have known nothing. But for most, it turned out that it wasn't that they didn't know, but rather that they had believed that only "bad girls" engage in such advance planning. One woman in her early twenties, married five years, put it this way:

> You know, I was really an innocent. I thought only bad girls went out and got birth-control pills. I would never have done anything like that.

Another 26-year-old, married eight years, said:

> I was just a dumb kid. I didn't know hardly anything at all. And I certainly wasn't the kind of girl who'd go out and get pills or something like that.

The implication here is that unmarried sex is forgivable if she is carried away on the tide of some great, uncontrollable emotion—forgivable, that is, because she succumbed to a natural force stronger than she; she just couldn't help herself. In that context, birth-control planning, implying as it does preparation for the sex act, is incompatible with her definition of self as a "good girl." The formulation goes something like this: "good girls" do but don't plan; "bad girls" do and plan.

Viewed from this perspective, few, if any, of these pregnancies could be said to be accidental. Indeed, if we shift focus from the women to the men, we see that they, too, were participants in what appears to be an unconscious drama of getting pregnant and getting married. Both men and women shared the widespread fantasy that "It couldn't happen to me." Both repeated one version or another of "A lot of people I know got away with it, at least for a lot longer than I did;" or, "I just never thought about it happening to me." Not unexpectedly, however, when pushed about what they *did* think would happen, the women were more open than the men, more able to own their behaviour, too quick to take *sole* responsibility for the pregnancy. One woman who became pregnant at 17 explained how it happened:

> I guess I was really stupid. I wasn't taking precautions; we'd just do withdrawal. I guess we'd been sleeping together for about six months when one time I just said, "Leave it in; don't take it out." And I got caught.

The use of the first-person pronoun is striking. It seems not to have occurred to her that her partner in the act might share some responsibility for protecting against an unwanted pregnancy. Small wonder, however, since social attitudes generally assume that since it is the woman who gets pregnant, it behooves her to take care—an attitude shared by the man in this family who lamented:

> I felt like I got cornered, and I still get mad at her for that sometimes, even now. I never could figure out what she was thinking about, doing that. I sure wish she'd had enough sense to use some birth control.

What, one wonders, was this young man thinking about when he failed to have "enough sense" to do so? But it occurs to neither wife nor husband to ask him that question about his role in this "accidental" pregnancy.

While we can speculate about the underlying psychological causes of these pregnancies, once again, the sociocultural context in which these young people live gives us more grounded clues. Most come from poor families, live in homes with little or no privacy, feel hemmed in by parental restraints, and yearn for the freedom, independence, and adult status that marriage seems to offer. A young woman, married at 19, says:

> I thought finally there's be no one telling me what to do any more.

A young man, married at 20:

> I wanted to have something of my own finally. And I wanted to get my old man off my back, to be able to do what I wanted without having to answer to him all the time.

When asked directly to examine the reasons for their premarital pregnancies, however, the women speak more readily than the men, with more awareness of their needs and motivations. No surprise in a culture where women are trained from birth to attend to the emotional side of life, and men, the instrumental side. Exploring the "why's" of her behaviour, one woman who became pregnant at 18 mused:

> I think I was ready to move out of the house, and I knew the only way I could do that was to get married. [*Looking down at her hands hesitantly.*] Do you think that had something to do with my getting pregnant? I gotta admit, inside myself I was really thrilled. I wanted to be married, and I wanted a baby. I was scared to death to tell my parents, but I was really very happy. Wow! I hardly ever thought about those things before. I sure never thought I'd dare tell anybody that.

Another, pregnant at 17 and trying to understand that event in her life, said:

> I've wondered a lot about why that happened to me. I read somewhere that you psychologists think that everything that happens to us is our fault. I mean, that we sort of do things to ourselves. Maybe that's true sometimes, not all the time, but sometimes. I sure did want to get out of that house, but my father would never stand for us girls going any place without being married. And I just knew I *had* to get away.

But how could you be sure that getting pregnant meant that you'd get married?

She looked puzzled, as if the question made no sense, then replied:

> I don't understand. Of course, if you get pregnant, you get married; everybody does. Everybody just expected us to get married when I got pregnant—my parents, his parents, our friends.

Her husband confirmed that perception:

> I always figured if I messed around with anybody where it happened, I'd have to marry her. All of us guys did.

There were, of course, some pregnancies among those who did use birth control that may have been genuine accidents—cases in which the women, while never doubting that the men would marry them, vainly sought a way out. But they were defeated by a culture that offers no real options. One 28-year-old mother of three recalls that time:

> When I found out I was pregnant, I didn't tell anyone but my girlfriend—not my parents, not my boyfriend, nobody. I thought I would go to some unwed mothers' home and have the baby and then come back and say I was on vacation. I suppose that sounds silly now, but I wasn't able to make any other plans.

> *Did you ever consider abortion?*

> Never! I could never do that. God, I remember even now how terrified I was. I kept thinking it couldn't be true. I remember even thinking that I would take my mom's car and drive it off a cliff. I knew he'd marry me; I never doubted that. *But I didn't want to get married.* I wanted to *do* things, and to *have* things. I never had any clothes. In fact, it always seemed like I had less money, less everything, than anybody else. I don't mean it was my parents' fault; they gave us what they had. They just didn't have much.
>
> I still remember how much I didn't want to get married. I wanted to get a job and have some things. I was afraid if I got married it would be the end of my chance for a better life. I wasn't wrong about that either.
>
> But my girlfriend kept arguing with me, and finally she told my boyfriend. They both kept saying that I had to get married, and that I couldn't go away. Finally, they told my parents, and then it was all of them against me. So I got married. It never did work; we got divorced less than two years later. But by then I had two children. What a mess!

Some of the men also spoke of their panic on hearing the news:

> I just wasn't ready for that. I was too young; I was too irresponsible; I didn't want to settle down. I looked at myself

and I thought, "How did you get here?" I just didn't know what to do. And then at the same time, I knew there was nothing else I *could* do. No matter what I thought, I knew I'd have to marry her.

One recalled the wedding grimly:

> It's hard to think about it. I don't remember too much of that whole period. Something you don't want to remember, you just don't remember. I do remember that I was very nervous at the wedding. I felt like screaming and running out, but there was just no way out.

Retrospectively, several said that they felt they had been entrapped and might do otherwise if they had it to do over again:

> I'm not sure what I'd do if I had to face that again. A guy can't help but feel he got trapped into getting married when a girl gets pregnant like that. I don't know, maybe if I knew what I know now, I wouldn't marry her.

But most would agree with the man who said flatly:

> If a girl got pregnant, you married her. There wasn't no choice. So I married her.

Not one person, woman or man, even considered abortion—generally not because of religious scruples, but because the idea, they said, was "disgusting," "impossible," "not a choice," or because it "just never occurred" to them. Not one seriously considered *not* getting married. Despite the disclaimers of some of them, for most of the men as well as the women, marriage appears to have been the desired outcome. The culture, we know, inhibits men from giving voice to their needs for nurturance and to their fantasies about marriage and family, while encouraging women to do so. Women, therefore, find those dreams, needs and motivations more accessible to their consciousness. But the men's behaviour suggests that their unspoken, perhaps unconscious, dreams may not be so different. Thus, marriage comes young; courtships generally are short—counted in weeks or months, rarely years—even when not terminated by a pregnancy. For like young people in all classes, in all cultures, these young working-class men and women strive toward manhood and womanhood. And while what constitutes those estates differs in many ways, they are alike in one fundamental aspect. Both are tied closely to marriage and parenthood in the American culture—values that may be changing, but that still find their clearest and liveliest expression in the white working class.

25

Ideology and Social Organization

M. Patricia Marchak

The concept of ideology and its significance in the organization and understanding of collective life is the focus of Marchak's article. She provides us with a basic overview of competing ideologies that we draw upon to describe and justify how society is, or should be, organized.

Ideologies

Dominant and counter-ideologies grow out of the same social organization. They take the same economic arrangement, the same territorial boundaries, the same population as their units of analysis. But they posit different relationships between these units and different relationships between these units and different organizations within them. Although the two major ideologies of our time—which we will label liberalism and socialism—claim to explain society in historical and comparative perspective, they both originate in the period of the European Industrial Revolution, and both are unmistakably locked into industrial society as it emerged in Europe at that time.

Because they grow out of the same organization, they have much in common. They are the two sides of a single coin: one describing how the entire structure looks to one who accepts it and expects it to survive; the other, how it looks to one who rejects it and anticipates its demise....

Ideologies are explanations for the social organization, but they are, as well, evaluations of it. These evaluations tend to be circular: the social organization gives rise to certain beliefs about what is right, appropriate, and desirable, that

---

Patricia Marchak, "Ideology and Social Organization," from *Ideological Perspectives on Canada* (3rd ed). Toronto: McGraw-Hill Ryerson, 1988 [as reprinted in Lorne Tepperman and James Curtis (ed) *Readings in Sociology: An Introduction*, Toronto, McGraw-Hill Ryerson, 1988: 49-57.]

is, to certain values. These values are then assumed, and the society judges itself by those values. The liberal democracy gave rise to positive evaluations of equality, individualism, material prosperity and personal freedom. The society is then judged within that framework: does it allow for the realization of these values? The dominant ideology rests on an affirmative answer: yes, this society provides the necessary conditions for equality, material prosperity, and personal freedom. Where there are deficiencies, these are often not recognized. Where the deficiencies are recognized, they are explained not as symptoms of a system that fails but as aberrations or temporary problems in a system that succeeds.

Widespread acceptance of an ideology creates an incapacity for judgment of its truth. There is comfort in believing what so many others appear to believe, in accepting conventional wisdom. There is fear in doing otherwise. Sometimes there are, as well, serious social consequences. To many minds, the person who admits to a deviant perspective is out of bounds, somehow dirty and unacceptable.

Counter ideologies involve a good deal of imagination. They provide a critique of the present society and a creative vision of an alternative. Both socialism and the "new right" provide these critiques and creative visions; and whether we agree with them or despise them, we are indebted to their proponents for enabling us to imagine other ways of doing things.

Counter ideologies generally begin with a critical perspective which arises from recognition of inconsistencies between what the dominant ideology portrays as truth and what the senses suggest is reality. They begin, then, as reform movements and their members are social critics. Equality, material prosperity, and personal freedom may be assumed as "right" values, but the society it judges as deficient in providing for their realization. The negative judgment leads to an analysis of social organization which diverges from that propagated by those who hold the dominant ideology and believe it to meet its own objectives. Gradually the analysis turns into a fully developed counter ideology, and an entirely different way of viewing the society.

Some people think that ideology is something that happens to others, and generally to somewhat deranged others. That is not the sense in which the term is used here. We are all immersed in ideological understandings of our world.

We define ideology as shared ideas, perceptions, values, and beliefs through which members of a society interpret history and contemporary social events and which shape their expectations and wishes for the future.

A dominant ideology is defined as that particular set of ideas, perceptions, values, and beliefs which is most widely shared and has the greatest impact on social action at any particular time in any particular society.

A counter ideology is defined as a set of ideas, etc., which is held by a substantial minority and which has noticeable impact on social action. There may be many or few counter ideologies in any society at any historical period.

There is another definition of ideology: the ideas and values of the ruling class, disseminated through agencies controlled by that class in ways that obfuscate class realities for subservient classes. We are not using this definition here.

Ideology and theory are different entities, though they grow out of the same womb. Theory consists of explicit assumptions, a reasoning by which the assumptions are demonstrated to be linked to conclusions on the one hand, and such material evidence as can be gathered on the other. It is, by definition, open to challenge through the presentation of more complete or contesting evidence, or by a refutation of the logic that links assumptions to conclusions. It is not a faith. It is not unexamined.

In some ways, theories are rivals and enemies of ideologies because they tend to dissect them. Someone begins by saying, "Hmmm, I believe this and that, I think I'll write it all down in some systematic way so that others will think as I do." Then, in the writing of it, the author begins to see some inconsistencies, some flaws in logic, some mismatch between theory and evidence. And the reader, perusing the manuscript, says, "but this isn't good enough." Theories evolve over time, moving further and further away from their ideological base, becoming more sophisticated, more logical, more consistent—but often moving so far from their beginnings that they leave the majority of believers far behind.

Ideologies normally attract some people who want to make them public and systematic. In addition to theorists, there are scribes and prophets who define ideologies, trying to demonstrate how their particular beliefs are unique and true. For this reason, we can examine such ideologies through the writings of the scribes and the speeches of the prophets. And, as we begin to see which values they emphasize, which utopian visions they advance, we can label the ideologies and identify them relative to one another with reference to specific values. But for the same reason that we need to distinguish between theory and ideology, we need to recognize the possible differences between what the scribes and prophets say and what a majority of believers accept.

Ideologies may be phrased in terms we would recognize as political, that is, they are about the political world and how the public arena should be governed. Other ideologies may also have political implications but may be phrased as religious belief systems. Although the language of discourse may seem very different, there are usually close ties between what people believe about the meaning of human existence or the properties of nature and gods, and what they believe about political governance in the temporal world.

We are concerned here with the major ideologies of our society, the dominant and the counter ideologies which motivate large numbers of people. And we are concerned primarily, though not exclusively, with how these ideologies link up with economic and political events. There are, in addition to these central ideologies, other versions of the world espoused by smaller numbers of people. Some of these other versions take political forms, some take religious forms.

Political ideologies ultimately boil down to the relative emphasis placed on individualism versus collectivism, and on egalitarianism versus elitism. It is in these terms that we can identify the differences between one ideology and another. We have political labels for various positions in our own society, along two continuums: the first, from extreme individualists (society has absolutely no claims on the individual, and there should be no rules, government, or constraints on individual actions) to extreme collectivists (society always has precedence over individuals, and the right to demand conformance with rules for the public good): and the second, from extreme elitism (there should be rulers and the rulers should have complete power) to extreme egalitarianism (all people should be absolutely equal in condition, not just opportunities). The differences between these labelled positions can be noted by referring to the theories, scribes and prophets, but as observed above, we must be wary of assuming that all adherents to labelled positions are consistent in their beliefs.

Individualist and Market-Based Ideologies

Anarchism, libertarianism, and to a lesser degree, liberalism, treat society as a collection of individuals. Society does not exist in and of itself, it is not an organic whole. Individuals each strive to manufacture the necessary conditions for life, and the market mechanism has emerged as a means of coordinating their separate strivings without applying force. The preservation of individual liberty and of the "free market" becomes the major concerns of advocates of these positions.

Anarchism and Libertarianism

The individualist position is taken to the extreme in anarchist and libertarian ideologies; all other values become subordinate. Anarchists would do away with all government and social restrictions on personal liberty; libertarians (though with some differences between various groups) generally accept the necessity of government, but would restrict its functions to the defence of persons and property. Anything which prevents individuals from fully exercising their initiative, entrepreneurial skills, and talents is harshly judged: thus democracy and the welfare state are deemed to be impediments to individual growth. Inequality is viewed as inevitable because people are genetically unequal, and as necessary because the most talented provide the leadership which permits others to survive. Libertarians believe that "pure" capitalism is an ideal social and economic system because it includes a genuinely free market for absolutely all good and services.

Liberalism

Liberalism has a somewhat different meaning in Canada than in the United States. In Canada, it is an approach which emphasizes the individual but combines that emphasis with concern for the preservation of law, order, and public well-being in the society, and includes some concern for equality between citizens. In the United States, its connotation is more strongly connected to social and collective values, closer to what Canadians regard as "social democratic." It differs from the Canadian social democratic view in that while both take equality to be a positive value, the liberal view is that equality is largely achieved within the present social system. Social democrats argue in favour of greater equality of condition and perceive great inequalities of both opportunity and condition in the present social system.

Like libertarians, liberals believe in the virtues of a free enterprise market, in which all sellers and buyers compete on equal terms for the attention of consumers. Unlike libertarians, liberals temper this belief by acknowledgement of some services and goods which "ought" to be in the public realm. The free enterprise market is rarely called "capitalism" in liberal ideology; the phrase "free enterprise" becomes the euphemism for capitalism. Consonant with the belief that society is made up of individuals, liberals deny the existence of classes in capitalist society. A great deal of emphasis is placed on the education system because liberals believe that individuals have equal opportunity in that sphere, each achieving there what their innate talents and hard work permit and thus moving upward or downward in the social system according to ability.

The role of government is to regulate the market place and to ensure that the rules are fair and equitable; government is not itself an economic actor in a truly "free" enterprise system. Further, since there are no classes, government cannot be seen as the agent of any particular class; and since there is no ruling class, it cannot be seen as acting on behalf of that class.

Liberalism has been the dominant ideological perspective adopted by Canadians throughout the past 40 years. One political party is called "Liberal" but when we speak of liberalism, we do not refer exclusively to this party. In fact, throughout this period, the two major alternative parties, the Progressive Conservative and the New Democratic Parties, have shared much of the liberal version of Canadian society.

Collectivist Positions

Collectivist positions begin with the argument that the society is an organic whole. Society exists independent of the individuals who happen to live in it at any time. But there is enormous difference in the conclusions and policy positions taken by collectivists of the "left" and of the "right." The basic difference occurs between those who believe that society ought to be more egalitarian (social democratic, socialist, communist) and those who believe it should be more hierarchically ordered (conservative, corporatist, and fascist).

Social Democratic

Social democrats accept the basic values of liberalism but place more emphasis on equality. As well, they recognize the existence of classes, of class barriers, and of governments acting in the interests of a dominant or ruling class. They thus share some of the understandings of socialists. They are committed to the gradual and democratic evolution of a socialist society, which they understand to be a more egalitarian organization within which workers have decision making control over production, and private ownership rights over industrial units and natural resources are abolished. This is the position of various democratic socialist parties throughout the world, and of the CCF and NDP parties.

Socialist

Socialists perceive capitalism as a system where a ruling class extracts wealth from a subordinate class (or classes), sells products made by labour, and uses the profits to invest in more properties and new technologies which displace or further enslave labour. Classes exist, inequalities are essential to the system, and individual freedom is highly circumscribed by the fundamental requirements that labour must produce goods and services for capital. For the socialist these conditions are unacceptable.

Socialism involves a version of the future which differs markedly from that of liberalism. For liberals, the future is a continuum of the past and present. It is a highly optimistic ideology, assuming eternal progress and gradual elimination of imperfections in the social system. But socialism, identifying capitalism as an oppressive and exploitative system, involves the belief that only through the destruction of capitalism can a more egalitarian and humane system emerge. Capitalism is expected to self-destruct, because its internal contradictions must eventually cause a fatal blockage in the capacities of capitalists to continue accumulating new profits (this is called "a crisis of accumulation" in the socialist literature).

For the liberal, capitalism is a necessary reality and critiques of it are ideology. For the socialist, the liberal version of capitalism is ideology. It is understood by socialists as an essential feature of the capitalist system, because it induces workers to consent to their own exploitation. They are persuaded, rather than forced (although force may on occasion also be necessary), to believe that the system is fair even if it leads to extremely unequal distributions of material wealth and economic power. Part of the key to this persuasion is, in the opinion of socialists, the nature of democratic governments. These are either so constrained by the economic decisions of private capital (there are different theories on this) that they can do little more than facilitate private accumulation. They mediate class conflict by developing rules for employment, hours, welfare and the like, because the system could not continue with persistent or violent class conflict, but the appearance is of governments acting in the general public interest. As well, since governments are formally elected by the population at large, there is a widespread belief in their neutrality and representative character. The ideology of democracy, then, and the mechanics of democratic elections are important features of capitalism because they "legitimate" the economic system and provide the pretence of impartiality.

Conservatism

Conservatism—like liberalism not to be interpreted as necessarily coincident with a particular political party—shares with socialism a belief that there are classes, that capitalism necessarily involves inequality, and that the marketplace should not be the locus of most important social decisions. But unlike socialism, conservatism gives a high positive value to class inequalities: they are necessary because society requires leadership, and well established leaders look after less well established workers. Conservatism thus values a "natural" hierarchy, paternalistic relations between capital and labour. For the conservative, government properly has the right to establish norms for the conduct of social life, though it should have a restrained role in the economy.

The chief difference between conservatism and liberalism is in their respective views of society: conservatives viewing it as an organic whole within which individuals have assigned places; liberals as a collection of individuals each striving for personal goals. Thus true conservatives should be concerned with the collective moral fabric as well as the permanence of a dominant class. Logically, liberals would be less concerned with social and moral issues except where society infringes on individual rights.

Corporatism

Corporatism shares with conservatism the belief in a natural hierarchy of human beings, the importance of planning the economy, and the positive evaluation of social classes. It goes beyond conservatism in arguing that economic units—corporations—should make the decisions about the conduct of economic life. Democratic procedures typical of liberal societies are viewed as unacceptable, because they allow uninformed and unpropertied individuals and groups to choose leaders and policies and thus inhibit social progress.

This position is associated with Italy under Mussolini, and has not had much of a history in Canada though some Canadians flirted with it during the 1930s. At the present time, some Canadians are again flirting with it, and there are curious alliances between some of its advocates and libertarians.

Fascism

Fascism is an extreme form of corporatism, going beyond it in accepting the necessity for force in controlling dissidents. We usually associate it with Nazi Germany in the 1930s and 1940s, but there was a fascist party in Canada during the 1930s, and a very small group of followers have persisted throughout this century.

Dominant Ideology

If we identify the dominant ideology as the values and beliefs held in common by a majority, we would include the liberal, social democratic, and conservative positions as falling within its compass. Although they differ in the degree to which they emphasize individualism and egalitarianism, they share a number of assumptions. To begin with, proponents of these positions assume the legitimacy of private property rights, but at the same time recognize legitimate constraints on these. They accept (with varying degrees of approval) the economic drive for profits, but again, place limits on its capacity to drive the entire social system. They accept differential rewards for work associated with numerous social factors (education, skills, talent, etc.), but reject differences associated with gender, ethnicity, religion, or other "non-economic" attributes of individuals. Although both the conservative and social democratic positions include acknowledgement of the reality of class divisions in capitalist society, and liberalism does not, all three tend to explain social events in terms of individuals or non-class groups (e.g., men and women, ethnic groups, particular interest groups) more than in terms of classes. All positions involve notions of social progress toward a "better" society to be achieved through gradual evolution.

Political parties espousing these points of view make many more distinctions between the positions. It is in their interests to do so, of course, since they have to make their party appear to be the unique champion of individual rights or equal opportunity or whatever.

All societies arrive, whether through conscious political activity or tacit agreements and traditional activities, at some position between individualism and collectivism, egalitarianism and elitism. There is another set of values which cross-cuts these, providing a third dimension to social organization. It is attitudes toward nature.

Societies dependent on hunting and gathering, and some societies dependent on cultivation of foods, have developed understandings of people as components of nature on the same level with other animate beings. Most such societies also hold the view that there are unseen spirits guiding and judging their activities. Within these perceptions, animals and land are highly valued, and destruction of either is unacceptable behaviour. Thus the hunter must apologise to the beast he has killed, explaining his need for food and his sincere appreciation for the sacrifice made by the animal.

By contrast, the industrial society treats animals and humans as qualitatively different entities, with humans having the right to kill and conquer all other living things. Land is but a space where human activity takes place: it has no spiritual quality.

Within the past decade, new social movements have arisen within industrial societies opposed to the destruction of our environment. Some of these have taken on political aspects, organizing as political parties or as pressure groups. The anti-nuclear movement, the Green Party, and numerous groups devoted to the saving of particular territories are among these. To date, these groups have not developed consistent positions on individualism-collectivism, egalitarianism-elitism. They are, in a sense, outside the mainstream of public discourse, and adherents to environmentalist ideologies could, conceivably, place themselves anywhere within the other political spectrums.

Similarly, religious movements sometimes exist outside the main discourse of industrial society. While the major religions in Canada—Christian Catholicism and Protestantism and Judaism—have generally adopted and supported the dominant ideology, smaller and often sectarian groups have challenged these views. Some support highly individualistic positions (salvationist religions), others more collectivist positions (cultural renewal religions).

The industrial society is not a static social organization. The processes set in motion by the development of urban populations and competitive capitalism destroyed the feudal aristocracy and the peasantry. They created new forms of government. They destroyed societies and created new ones in far-off colonies. Change occurred at many levels simultaneously: at the level of the family unit, at the level of education. The liberal ideology explains these changes as cumulative growth. Society is always progressing, always adjusting to new conditions. Its growth is limitless, its perfection is a viable goal. The analogy is to a wheel turning over new territory and adding always to its conquest of distance.

Marx posited quite a different kind of change—cumulative, still, but fraught with internal contradictions. The growth in competitive capitalism would give rise to monopoly capitalism. The growth of wealth at the top would create the growth of poverty at the bottom. The more successful the capitalists were in developing technology and organizing the workforce for their own ends, the faster they brought about their own demise by an organized, efficient proletariat. The wheel in this analogy spins ever faster only to break down from over-use, and its riders are obliged to make a new wheel out of the parts. Marx envisioned the final stages in these words:

> One capitalist always kills many. Hand in hand with this centralization, or this expropriation of many capitalists by few, develop, on an ever-extending scale, the cooperative form of the labour process, the conscious technical application of science, the methodical cultivation of the soil, the

transformation of the instruments of labour into instruments of labour only usable in common, the economizing of all means of production by their use as the means of production of combined, socialized labour, the entanglement of all peoples in the net of the world market, and with this, the international character of the capitalistic regime. Along with the constantly diminishing number of the magnates of capital, who usurp and monopolise all advantages of this process of transformation, grows the mass of misery, oppression, slavery, degradation, exploitation; but with this too grows the revolt of the working-class, a class always increasing in numbers, and disciplined, united, organized by the very mechanism of the process of capitalist production itself.[1]

Whether one takes the progressional view of history or the dialectic view, one is struck by the observation that cumulative growth in any respect of social organization eventually becomes destructive of that organization. Whether we eventually arrive in a different town by riding the wheel from one place to another, or whether the journey itself transforms the travellers, the fact is that the industrial society of the 1980s is not the industrial society of the 1920s or the 1880s. It is qualitatively a different society. The technology has changed dramatically. The social organization has changed. The population balance has changed. The relations between nation states have changed. What has noticeably failed to change is the ideology.

The ideologies at the popular level are very much the same as they were in these other times. Speeches to the Chamber of Commerce reflect the same abiding faith in progress, material prosperity, and general affluence; the same evaluation of private property, individualism, and achievement; the same belief in the existence of equality and opportunity. The slogans of the Left are remarkably similar to those uttered in the trade union struggles of the turn of the century. There is the same belief in massive exploitation by a ruling class, the same faith in the nobility of labour, the same conviction that pervasive equality is both yet to come and highly desirable.

In Canada, for example, feudalistic values remained into the early twentieth century. While these were tinged by the values of liberalism as it was expressed in the United States and Britain, liberalism in its classic form did not emerge as a dominant ideology until very late in history by comparison with these other countries. Nearly a century after the American War of Independence had spawned the notion that individuals should pursue happiness and that this was a legitimate basis for social organization, as long again after the French Revolution had bannered the words "liberty, equality, fraternity," Canada continued to be ruled by a landed aristocracy which gained its wealth through the fur trade, export-import businesses, and banking. Its values were not those of industrial capitalists.

It was not engaged in competitive enterprise, and was not generating new wealth out of the production of goods for a market. At the other end of the social scale, the larger part of the population was engaged in farming rather than manufacturing, and Canada was largely a rural country before World War I; indeed, it remained predominantly rural until the 1930s. The slow development of industry and of an industrial urban labour force retarded the development of liberalism as an ideology.

Conservativism, then, has not been absent in Canada, but in the past half-century it has not been a dominant ideology either.

Liberalism and socialism can interpret one kind of society, one form of industrial organization. This is the society in transition within the political framework of nation states. Neither is suited to providing a popular interpretation or appropriate set of values for maintenance of a multi-national or non-national capitalism in which wage work is not available to many people, surplus is not created out of labour, communications technology becomes more central to political control, and corporations are the chief social as well as economic organizations. Those of us who continue to live in the "old world" like the peasant of the feudal period or the colonials of an imperial empire, are unable to envision or make sense of the developments around us which lead in such a direction. We attempt to interpret them through the ideological perspectives of a society already in decline. Subtly, scarcely intruding on our consciousness, a new set of perceptions and beliefs and their appropriate justifying values will develop around the new technologies and within the corporate empires. Some of this will be transmitted to the generations now living out what may well be the last state of national states and a social organization which divides the political, economic, and religious realms. These transmissions are phrased clumsily, to fit existing belief systems. Thus we have insights on what might be called "liberal corporatism" and we are puzzled by where the Soviet form of corporatism fits in to our theories of history. But if the past is an indication of the future, it will not be the case that liberalism as an ideology imperceptibly becomes corporatism; nor that socialism becomes totalitarianism, but rather that both are superseded by new ideologies emanating from a new society that has already grown within the old and destroyed its foundations.

Endnotes

[1] Karl Marx, *Capital* (1867), translated by Samuel Moore and Edward Aveling (New York International Publishers, 1967), Vol. 1, pp. 762-763.

Section Seven

Gender

According to usage and conventions which are at last being questioned but have by no means been overcome, the social presence of a woman is different in kind from that of a man. A man's presence is dependent upon the promise of power which he embodies [which] may be moral, physical, tempermental, economic, social, sexual—but its object is always exterior to the man.... To be born a woman has been to be born within an alloted and confined space, into the keeping of men. The social presence of women has developed as a result of their ingenuity in living under such tutelage within a limited space.... One might simplify this by saying: men act and women appear.
John Berger, *Ways of Seeing*, London: Penguin, 1972: 45-7.

26

Sex, Lies and Conversation:
Why is it so Hard for Men and Women to Talk to Each Other?

Deborah Tannen

Who talks more, men or women? Who says more? What is the role of talk in relationships? In this short article the author summarizes her findings about gender conversational patterns and compares them to our common-sense views of gender and talk.

I was addressing a small gathering in a suburban Virginia living room—a women's group that had invited men to join them. Throughout the evening, one man had been particularly talkative, frequently offering ideas and anecdotes, while his wife sat silently beside him on the couch. Toward the end of the evening, I commented that women frequently complain that their husbands don't talk to them. This man quickly concurred. He gestured toward his wife and said, "She's the talker in our family." The room burst into laughter; the man looked puzzled and hurt. "It's true," he explained. "When I come home from work I have nothing to say. If she didn't keep the conversation going, we'd spend the whole evening in silence."

This episode crystallizes the irony that although American men tend to talk more than women in public situations, they often talk less at home. And this pattern is wreaking havoc with marriage.

The pattern was observed by political scientist Andrew Hacker in the late '70s. Sociologist Catherine Kohler Riessman reports in her new book *Divorce Talk* that most of the women she interviewed—but only a few of the men—gave lack of communication as the reason for their divorces. Given the current divorce rate of nearly 50 percent, that amounts to millions of cases in the United States every year—a virtual epidemic of failed conversation.

In my own research, complaints from women about their husbands most often focused not on tangible inequities such as having given up the chance for

---

Deborah Tannen, "Sex, Lies and Conversation: Why is it so Hard for Men and Women to Talk to Each Other?" *Washington Post*, 1990, p. C3 [as reprinted in M. Schaum and C. Flanagan (ed), *Gender Images: Readings for Composition*. Houghton Mifflin Co., 1992: 113-117.]

a career to accompany a husband to his, or doing far more than their share of daily life-support work like cleaning, cooking, social arrangements and errands. Instead, they focused on communication: "He doesn't listen to me," "He doesn't talk to me." I found, as Hacker observed years before, that most wives want their husbands to be, first and foremost, conversational partners, but few husbands share this expectation of their wives.

In short, the image that best represents the current crisis is the stereotypical cartoon scene of a man sitting at the breakfast table with a newspaper help up in front of his face, while a women glares at the back of it, wanting to talk.

Linguistic Battle of the Sexes

How can women and men have such different impressions of communication in marriage? Why the widespread imbalance in their interests and expectations?

In the April issue of *American Psychologist,* Stanford University's Eleanor Maccoby reports the results of her own and others' research showing that children's development is most influenced by the social structure of peer interactions. Boys and girls tend to play with children of their own gender, and their sex-separate groups have different organizational structures and interactive norms.

I believe these systematic differences in childhood socialization make talk between women and men like cross-cultural communication, heir to all the attraction and pitfalls of that enticing but difficult enterprise. My research on men's and women's conversations uncovered patterns similar to those described for children's groups.

For women, as for girls, intimacy is the fabric of relationships, and talk is the thread from which it is woven. Little girls create and maintain friendships by exchanging secrets; similarly, women regard conversation as the cornerstone of friendship. So a woman expects her husband to be a new and improved version of a best friend. What is important is not the individual subjects that are discussed but the sense of closeness, of a life shared, that emerges when people tell their thoughts, feelings, and impressions.

Bonds between boys can be as intense as girls', but they are based less on talking, more on doing things together. Since they don't assume talk is the cement that binds a relationship, men don't know what kind of talk women want, and they don't miss it when it isn't there.

Boys' groups are larger, more inclusive, and more hierarchical, so boys must struggle to avoid the subordinate position in the group. This may play a role in women's complaints that men don't listen to them. Some men really don't like to listen, because being the listener makes them feel one-down, like a child listening to adults or an employee to a boss.

But often when women tell men, "You aren't listening," and the men protest, "I am," the men are right. The impression of not listening results from misalignments in the mechanics of conversation. The misalignment begins as soon as a man and a woman take physical positions. This became clear when I studied videotapes made by psychologist Bruce Dorval of children and adults talking to their same-sex best friends. I found that at every age, the girls and women faced each other directly, their eyes anchored on each other's faces. At every age, the boys and men sat at angles to each other and looked elsewhere in the room, periodically glancing at each other. They were obviously attuned to each other, often mirroring each other's movements. But the tendency of men to face away can give women the impression they aren't listening even when they are. A young woman in college was frustrated: Whenever she told her boyfriend she wanted to talk to him, he would lie down on the floor, close his eyes, and put his arm over his face. This signaled to her, "He's taking a nap." But he insisted he was listening extra hard. Normally, he looks around the room, so he is easily distracted. Lying down and covering his eyes helped him concentrate on what she was saying.

Analogous to the physical alignment that women and men take in conversation is their topical alignment. The girls in my study tended to talk at length about one topic, but the boys tended to jump from topic to topic. The second-grade girls exchanged stories about people they knew. The second-grade boys teased, told jokes, noticed things in the room and talked about finding games to play. The sixth-grade girls talked about problems with a mutual friend. The sixth-grade boys talked about 55 different topics, none of which extended over more than a few turns.

Listening to Body Language

Switching topics is another habit that gives women the impression men aren't listening, especially if they switch to a topic about themselves. But the evidence of the 10th-grade boys in my study indicates otherwise. The 10th-grade boys sprawled across their chairs with bodies parallel and eyes straight ahead, rarely looking at each other. They looked as if they were riding in a car, staring out the windshield. But they were talking about their feelings. One boy was upset because a girl had told him he had a drinking problem, and the other was feeling alienated from all his friends.

Now, when a girl told a friend about a problem, the friend responded by asking probing questions and expressing agreement and understanding. But the boys dismissed each other's problems. Todd assured Richard that his drinking was "no big problem" because "sometimes you're funny when you're off your butt." And when Todd said he felt left out, Richard responded, "Why should you? You know more people than me."

Women perceive such responses as belittling and unsupportive. But the boys seemed satisfied with them. Whereas women reassure each other by implying,

"You shouldn't feel bad because I've had similar experiences," men do so by implying, "You shouldn't feel bad because your problems aren't so bad."

There are even simpler reasons for women's impression that men don't listen. Linguist Lynette Hirschman found that women make more listener-noise, such as "mhm," "uhuh," and "yeah," to show "I'm with you." Men, she found, more often give silent attention. Women who expect a stream of listener-noise interpret silent attention as no attention at all.

Women's conversational habits are as frustrating to men as men's are to women. Men who expect silent attention interpret a stream of listener-noise as overreaction or impatience. Also, when women talk to each other in a close, comfortable setting, they often overlap, finish each other's sentences and anticipate what the other is about to say. This practice, which I call "participatory listenership," is often perceived by men as interruption, intrusion and lack of attention.

A parallel difference caused a man to complain about his wife, "She just wants to talk about her own point of view. If I show her another view, she gets mad at me." When most women talk to each other, they assume a conversationalist's job is to express agreement and support. But many men see their conversational duty as pointing out the other side of an argument. This is heard as disloyalty by women, and refusal to offer the requisite support. It is not that women don't want to see other points of view, but that they prefer them phrased as suggestions and inquiries rather than as direct challenges.

In his book *Fighting for Life*, Walter Ong points out that men use "agonistic" or warlike, oppositional formats to do almost anything; thus discussion becomes debate, and conversation a competitive sport. In contrast, women see conversation as a ritual means of establishing rapport. If Jane tells a problem and June says she has a similar one, they walk away feeling closer to each other. But this attempt at establishing rapport can backfire when used with men. Men take too literally women's ritual "troubles talk," just as women mistake men's ritual challenges for real attack.

The Sounds of Silence

These differences begin to clarify why women and men have such different expectations about communication in marriage. For women, talk creates intimacy. Marriage is an orgy of closeness: you can tell your feelings and thoughts, and still be loved. Their greatest fear is being pushed away. But men live in a hierarchical world, where talk maintains independence and status. They are on guard to protect themselves from being put down and pushed around.

This explains the paradox of the talkative man who said of his silent wife, "She's the talker." In the public setting of a guest lecture, he felt challenged to show his intelligence and display his understanding of the lecture. But at home, where he has nothing to prove and no one to defend against, he is free to remain silent. For his wife, being home means she is free from the worry that something she says might offend someone, or spark disagreement, or appear to be showing off; at home she is free to talk.

The communication problems that endanger marriage can't be fixed by mechanical engineering. They require a new conceptual framework about the role of talk in human relationships. Many of the psychological explanations that have become second nature may not be helpful, because they tend to blame either women (for not being assertive enough) or men (for not being in touch with their feelings). A sociolinguistic approach by which male-female conversation is seen as cross-cultural communication allows us to understand the problem and forge solutions without blaming either party.

Once the problem is understood, improvement comes naturally, as it did to the young woman and her boyfriend who seemed to go to sleep when she wanted to talk. Previously, she had accused him of not listening, and he had refused to change his behavior, since that would be admitting fault. But then she learned about and explained to him the differences in women's and men's habitual ways of aligning themselves in conversation. The next time she told him she wanted to talk, he began, as usual, by lying down and covering his eyes. When the familiar negative reaction bubbled up, she reassured herself that he really was listening. But then he sat up and looked at her. Thrilled, she asked why. He said, "You like me to look at you when we talk, so I'll try to do it." Once he saw their differences as cross-cultural rather than right and wrong, he independently altered his behavior.

Women who feel abandoned and deprived when their husbands won't listen to or report daily news may be happy to discover their husbands trying to adapt once they understand the place of small talk in women's relationships. But if their husbands don't adapt, the women may still be comforted that for men, this is not a failure of intimacy. Accepting the difference, the wives may look to their friends or family for that kind of talk. And husbands who can't provide it shouldn't feel their wives have made unreasonable demands. Some couples will still decide to divorce, but at least their decisions will be based on realistic expectations.

In these times of resurgent ethnic conflicts, the world desperately needs cross-cultural understanding. Like charity, successful cross-cultural communication should begin at home.

27

Woman's Place in Man's Life Cycle*

Carol Gilligan

In this excerpt from her book In a Different Voice *Gilligan challenges major developmental theorists from psychology with regard to their views on moral development and morality. Drawing on interviews with children and adults, Gilligan identifies differences in male and female worldviews and values, and in the kind of relationships they develop to support these. A guiding question for the reader: What are the differences between the masculine and feminine systems of valuing which emerge from her research?*

In the second act of *The Cherry Orchard*, Lopahin, a young merchant, describes his life of hard work and success. Failing to convince Madame Ranevskaya to cut down the cherry orchard to save her estate, he will go on in the next act to buy it himself. He is the self-made man who, in purchasing the estate where his father and grandfather were slaves, seeks to eradicate the "awkward, unhappy life" of the past, replacing the cherry orchard with summer cottages where coming generations "will see a new life." In elaborating this developmental vision, he reveals the image of man that underlies and supports his activity: "At times when I can't go to sleep, I think: Lord, thou gavest us immense forests, unbounded fields and the widest horizons, and living in the midst of them we should indeed be giants"—at which point, Madame Ranevskaya interrupts him, saying, "You feel the need for giants—They are good only in fairy tales, anywhere else they only frighten us."

Conceptions of the human life cycle represent attempts to order and make coherent the unfolding experiences and perceptions, the changing wishes and realities of everyday life. But the nature of such conceptions depends in part on the position of the observer. The brief excerpt from Chekhov's play suggests that when the observer is a woman, the perspective may be of a different sort.

---

* Carol Gilligan, "Woman's Place in Man's Life Cycle," from *In a Different Voice*, Harvard, 1982: 5-11; 14; 16-22. Copyright © 1982 Harvard University Press. For permission to photocopy this selection, please contact Harvard University Press.

Different judgments of the image of man as giant imply different ideas about human development, different ways of imaging the human condition, different notions of what is of value in life.

At a time when efforts are being made to eradicate discrimination between the sexes in the search for social equality and justice, the differences between the sexes are being rediscovered in the social sciences. This discovery occurs when theories formerly considered to be sexually neutral in their scientific objectivity are found instead to reflect a consistent observational and evaluative bias. Then the presumed neutrality of science, like that of language itself, gives way to the recognition that the categories of knowledge are human constructions. The fascination with point of view that has informed the fiction of the twentieth century and the corresponding recognition of the relativity of judgment infuse our scientific understanding as well when we begin to notice how accustomed we have become to seeing life through men's eyes.

The penchant of developmental theorists to project a masculine image, and one that appears frightening to women, goes back at least to Freud (1905), who built his theory of psychosexual development around the experiences of the male child that culminate in the Oedipus complex. In the 1920s, Freud struggled to resolve the contradictions posed for his theory by the differences in female anatomy and the different configuration of the young girl's early family relationships. After trying to fit women into his masculine conception, seeing them as envying that which they missed, he came instead to acknowledge, in the strength and persistence of women's pre-Oedipal attachments to their mothers, a developmental difference. He considered this difference in women's development to be responsible for what he saw as women's developmental failure.

Having tied the formation of the superego or conscience to castration anxiety, Freud considered women to be deprived by nature of the impetus for a clear-cut Oedipal resolution. Consequently, women's superego—the heir to the Oedipus complex—was compromised: it was never "so inexorable, so impersonal, so independent of its emotional origins as we require it to be in men." From this observation of difference, that "for women the level of what is ethically normal is different from what it is in men," Freud concluded that women "show less sense of justice than men, that they are less ready to submit to the great exigencies of life, that they are more often influenced in their judgments by feelings of affection or hostility" (1925, pp. 257-258).

Thus a problem in theory became cast as a problem in women's development, and the problem in women's development was located in their experience of relationships. Nancy Chodorow (1974), attempting to account for "the reproduction within each generation of certain general and nearly universal differences that characterize masculine and feminine personality and roles," attributes these difference between the sexes not to anatomy but rather to "the fact that women, universally, are largely responsible for early child care." Because this early social environment differs for and is experienced differently by male and female children, basic sex differences recur in personality development. As a result, "in any given society, feminine personality comes to define itself in relation and connection to other people more than masculine personality does" (pp. 43-44).

In her analysis, Chodorow relies primarily on Robert Stoller's studies which indicate that gender identity, the unchanging core of personality formation, is "with rare exception firmly and irreversibly established for both sexes by the time a child is around three." Given that for both sexes the primary caretaker in the first three years of life is typically female, the interpersonal dynamics of gender identity formation are different for boys and girls. Female identity formation takes place in a context of ongoing relationship since "mothers tend to experience their daughters as more like, and continuous with, themselves." Correspondingly, girls, in identifying themselves as female, experience themselves as like their mothers, thus fusing the experience of attachment with the process of identity formation. In contrast, "mothers experience their sons as a male opposite," and boys, in defining themselves as masculine, separate their mothers from themselves, thus curtailing "their primary love and sense of empathic tie." Consequently, male development entails a "more emphatic individuation and a more defensive firming of experienced ego boundaries." For boys, but not girls, "issues of differentiation have become intertwined with sexual issues" (1978, pp. 150, 166-167).

Writing against the masculine bias of psychoanalytic theory, Chodorow argues that the existence of sex differences in the early experiences of individuation and relationship "does not mean that women have 'weaker' ego boundaries than men or are more prone to psychosis." It means instead that "girls emerge from this period with a basis for 'empathy' built into their primary definition of self in a way that boys do not." Chodorow thus replaces Freud's negative and derivative description of female psychology with a positive and direct account of her own: "Girls emerge with a stronger basis for experiencing another's needs or feelings as one's own (or of thinking that one is so experiencing another's needs and feelings). Furthermore, girls do not define themselves in terms of the denial of preoedipal relational modes to the same extent as do boys. Therefore, regression to these modes tends not to feel as much a basic threat to their ego. From very early, then, because they are parented by a person of the same gender...girls come to experience themselves as less differentiated than boys, as more continuous with and related to the external object-world, and as differently oriented to their inner object-world as well" (p. 167).

Consequently, relationships, and particularly issues of dependency, are experienced differently by women and men. For boys and men, separation and individuation are critically tied to gender identity since separation from the mother is essential for the development of masculinity. For girls and women, issues of femininity or feminine identity do not depend on the achievement of separation from the mother or on the progress of individuation. Since masculinity is defined through separation while femininity is defined through attachment, male gender identity is threatened by intimacy while female gender identity is threatened by separation. Thus males tend to have difficulty with relationships, while females tend to have problems with individuation. The quality of embeddedness in social interaction and personal relationships that characterizes women's lives in contrast to men's, however, becomes not only a descriptive difference but also a developmental liability when the milestones of childhood and adolescent development in the psychological literature are markers of increasing separation. Women's failure to separate then becomes by definition a failure to develop.

The sex differences in personality formation that Chodorow describes in early childhood appear during the middle childhood years in studies of children's games. Children's games are considered by George Herbert Mead (1934) and Jean Piaget (1932) as the crucible of social development during the school years. In games, children learn to take the role of the other and come to see themselves through another's eyes. In games, they learn respect for rules and come to understand the ways rules can be made and changed.

Janet Lever (1976), considering the peer group to be the agent of socialization during the elementary school years and play to be a major activity of socialization at that time, set out to discover whether there are sex differences in the games that children play. Studying 181 fifth-grade, white, middle-class children, ages ten and eleven, she observed the organization and structure of their play-time activities. She watched the children as they played at school during recess and in physical education class, and in addition kept diaries of their accounts as to how they spent their out-of-school time. From this study, Lever reports sex differences: boys play out of doors more often than girls do; boys play more often in large and age-heterogeneous groups; they play competitive games more often, and their games last longer than girls' games. The last is in some ways the most interesting finding. Boys' games appeared to last longer not only because they required a higher level of skill and were thus less likely to become boring, but also because, when disputes arose in the course of a game, boys were able to resolve the disputes more effectively than girls: "During the course of this study, boys were seen quarrelling all the time, but not once was a game terminated because of a quarrel and no game was interrupted for more than seven minutes. In the gravest debates, the final word was always, to 'repeat the play,' generally followed by a chorus of 'cheater's proof'" (p. 482). In fact, it seemed that the boys enjoyed the legal debates as much as they did the game itself, and even marginal players of lesser size or skill participated equally in these recurrent squabbles. In contrast, the eruption of disputes among girls tended to end the game.

Thus Lever extends and corroborates the observations of Piaget in his study of the rules of the game, where he finds boys becoming through childhood increasingly fascinated with the legal elaboration of rules and the development of fair procedures for adjudicating conflicts, a fascination that, he notes, does not hold for girls. Girls, Piaget observes, have a more "pragmatic" attitude toward rules, "regarding a rule as good as long as the game repaid it" (p.83). Girls are more tolerant in their attitudes towards rules, more willing to make exceptions, and more easily reconciled to innovations. As a result, the legal sense, which Piaget considers essential to be moral development, "is far less developed in little girls than in boys" (p.77).

The bias that leads Piaget to equate male development with child development also colours Lever's work. The assumption that shapes her discussion of results is that the male model is the better one since it fits the requirements for modern corporate success. In contrast, the sensitivity and care for the feelings of others that girls develop through their play have little market value and can even impede professional success. Lever implies that, given the realities of adult life, if a girl does not want to be left dependent on men, she will have to learn to play like a boy.

To Piaget's argument that children learn the respect for rules necessary for moral development by playing rule-bound games, Lawrence Kohlberg (1969) adds that these lessons are most effectively learned through the opportunities for role-taking that arise in the course of resolving disputes. Consequently, the moral lessons inherent in girls' play appear to be fewer than in boys'. Traditional girls' games like jump rope and hopscotch are turn-taking games, where competition is indirect since one person's success does not necessarily signify another's failure. Consequently, disputes requiring adjudication are less likely to occur. In fact, most of the girls whom Lever interviewed claimed that when a quarrel broke out, they ended the game. Rather than elaborating a system of rules for resolving disputes, girls subordinated the continuation of the game to the continuation of relationships.

Lever concludes that from the games they play, boys learn both the independence and the organizational skills necessary for coordinating the activities of large and diverse groups of people. By participating in controlled and socially approved competitive situations, they learn to deal with competition in a relatively forthright manner—to play with their enemies and to compete with their friends—all in accordance with the rules of the game. In contrast, girls' play tends to occur in smaller, more intimate groups, often the best-friend dyad, and in private places. This play replicates the social pattern of primary human relationships in that its organization is more cooperative. Thus, it points less, in Mead's terms, toward learning to take the role of "the generalized other," less toward the abstraction of human relationships. But it fosters the development of the empathy and sensitivity necessary for taking the role of "the particular other" and points more toward knowing the other as different from the self.

These observations about sex difference support the conclusion reached by David McClelland (1975) that "sex role turns out to be one of the most important determinants of human behaviour; psychologists have found sex differences in their studies from the moment they started doing empirical research." But since it is difficult to say "different" without saying "better" or "worse," since there is a tendency to construct a single scale of measurement, and since that scale has generally been derived from and standardized on the basis of men's interpretations of research data drawn predominantly or exclusively from studies of males, psychologists "have tended to regard male behaviour as the 'norm' and female behaviour as some kind of deviation from that norm" (p. 81). Thus, when women do not conform to the standards of psychological expectation, the conclusion has generally been that something is wrong with the women.

"It is obvious," Virginia Woolf says, "that the values of women differ very often from the values which have been made by the other sex" (1929, p. 76). Yet, she adds, "it is the masculine values that prevail." As a result, women come to question the normality of their feelings and to alter their judgments in deference to the opinion of others. In the nineteenth-century novels written by women, Woolf sees at work "a mind which was slightly pulled from the straight and made to alter its clear vision in deference to external authority." The same deference to the values and opinions of others can be seen in the judgments of twentieth century women. The difficulty women experience in finding or speaking publicly in their own voices emerges repeatedly in the form of qualification and self-doubt, but also in intimations of a divided judgment, a public assessment and private assessment which are fundamentally at odds.

Yet the deference and confusion that Woolf criticizes in women derive from the values she sees as their strength. Women's deference is rooted not only in their social subordination but also in the substance of their moral concern. Sensitivity to the needs of others and the assumption of responsibility for taking care lead women to attend to voices other than their own and to include in their judgment other points of view. Women's moral weakness, manifest in an apparent diffusion and confusion of judgment, is thus inseparable from women's moral strength, an overriding concern with relationships and responsibilities. The reluctance to judge may itself be indicative of the care and concern for others that infuse the psychology of women's development and are responsible for what is generally seen as problematic in its nature.

Thus women not only define themselves in a context of human relationship but also judge themselves in terms of their ability to care. Women's place in man's life cycle has been that of nurturer, caretaker, and helpmate, the weaver of those networks of relationships on which she in turn relies. But while women have thus taken care of men, men have, in their theories of psychological development, as in their economic arrangements, tended to assume or devalue that care. When the focus on individuation and individual achievement extends into adulthood and maturity is equated with personal autonomy, concern with relationships appears as a weakness of women rather than as a human strength (Miller, 1976).

The discrepancy between womanhood and adulthood is nowhere more evident than in the studies on sex-role stereotypes reported by Broverman, Vogel,

Broverman, Clarkson, and Rosenkrantz (1972). The repeated finding of these studies is that the qualities deemed necessary for adulthood—the capacity for autonomous thinking, clear decision making, and responsible action—are those associated with masculinity and considered undesirable as attributes of the feminine self. The stereotypes suggest a splitting of love and work that relegates expressive capacities to women while placing instrumental abilities in the masculine domain. Yet looked at from a different perspective, these stereotypes reflect a conception of adulthood that is itself out of balance, favouring the separateness of the individual self over connection to others, and leaning more toward an autonomous life of work than toward the interdependence of love and care.

The discovery now being celebrated by men in mid-life of the importance of intimacy, relationships, and care is something that women have known from the beginning. However, because that knowledge in women has been considered "intuitive" or "instinctive," a function of anatomy coupled with destiny, psychologists have neglected to describe its development. In my research, I have found that women's moral development centres on the elaboration of that knowledge and thus delineates a critical line of psychological development in the lives of both of the sexes. The subject of moral development not only provides the final illustration of the reiterative pattern in the observation and assessment of sex differences in the literature on human development, but also indicates more particularly why the nature and significance of women's development has been for so long obscured and shrouded in mystery.

The criticism that Freud makes of women's sense of justice, seeing it as compromised in its refusal of blind impartiality, reappears not only in the work of Piaget but also in that of Kohlberg. While in Piaget's account (1932) of the moral judgment of the child, girls are an aside, a curiosity to whom he devotes four brief entries in an index that omits "boys" altogether because "the child" is assumed to be male, in the research from which Kohlberg derives his theory, females simply do not exist. Kohlberg's (1958, 1981) six stages that describe the development of moral judgment from childhood to adulthood are based empirically on a study of eighty-four boys whose development Kohlberg has followed for a period of over twenty years. Although Kohlberg claims universality for his stage sequence, those groups not included in his original sample rarely reach his higher stages (Edwards, 1975; Holstein, 1976; Simpson, 1974). Prominent among those who thus appear to be deficient in moral development when measured by Kohlberg's scale are women, whose judgments seem to exemplify the third stage of his six-stage sequence. At this stage morality is conceived in interpersonal terms and goodness is equated with helping and pleasing others. This conception of goodness is considered by Kohlberg and Kramer (1969) to be functional in the lives of mature women insofar as their lives take place in the home. Kohlberg and Kramer imply that only if women enter the traditional arena of male activity will they recognize the inadequacy of this moral perspective and progress like men toward higher stages where relationships are subordinated to rules (stage four) and rules to universal principles of justice (stages five and six).

Yet herein lies a paradox, for the very traits that traditionally have defined the "goodness" of women, their care for and sensitivity to the needs of others, are those that mark them as deficient in moral development. In this version of moral development, however, the conception of maturity is derived from the study of men's lives and reflects the importance of individuation in their development. Piaget (1970), challenging the common impression that a developmental theory is built like a pyramid from its base in infancy, points out that a conception of development instead hangs from its vertex of maturity, the point toward which progress is traced. Thus, a change in the definition of maturity does not simply alter the description of the highest stage but recasts the understanding of development, changing the entire account.

When one begins with the study of women and derives developmental constructs from their lives, the outline of a moral conception different from that described by Freud, Piaget, or Kohlberg begins to emerge and informs a different description of development. In this conception, the moral problem arises from conflicting responsibilities rather than from competing rights and requires for its resolution a mode of thinking that is contextual and narrative rather than formal and abstract. This conception of morality as concerned with the activity of care centres moral development around the understanding of responsibility and relationships, just as the conception of morality as fairness ties moral development to the understanding of rights and rules.

This different construction of the moral problem by women may be seen as the critical reason for their failure to develop within the constraints of Kohlberg's system. Regarding all constructions of responsibility as evidence of a conventional moral understanding, Kohlberg defines the highest stages of moral development as deriving from a reflective understanding of human rights. That the morality of rights differs from the morality of responsibility in its emphasis on separation rather than connection, in its consideration of the individual rather than the relationship as primary, is illustrated by two responses to interview questions about the nature of morality. The first comes from a twenty-five-year-old man, one of the participants in Kohlberg's study:

> [*What does the word morality mean to you?*] Nobody in the world knows the answer. I think it is recognizing the right of the individual, the rights of other individuals, not interfering with those rights. Act as fairly as you would have them treat you. I think it is basically to preserve the human being's right to existence. I think that is the most important. Secondly, the human being's right to do as he pleases, again without interfering with somebody else's rights.

> [*How have your views on morality changed since the last interview?*] I think I am more aware of an individual's rights now. I used to be looking at it strictly from my point of view, just for me. Now I think I am more aware of what the individual has a right to.

Kohlberg (1973) cites this man's response as illustrative of the principled conception of human rights that exemplifies his fifth and sixth stages. Commenting on the response, Kohlberg says: "Moving to a perspective outside of that of his society, he identifies morality with justice (fairness, rights, the Golden Rule), with recognition of the rights of others as these are defined naturally or intrinsically. The human's being right to do as he pleases without interfering with somebody else's rights is a formula defining rights prior to social legislation" (pp. 29-30).

The second response comes from a woman who participated in the rights and responsibilities study. She also was twenty-five and, at the time, a third-year law student:

> [*Is there really some correct solution to moral problems, or is everybody's opinion equally right?*] No, I don't think everybody's opinion is equally right. I think that in some situations there may be opinions that are equally valid, and one could conscientiously adopt one of several courses of action. But there are other situations in which I think there are right and wrong answers, that sort of inhere in the nature of existence, of all individuals here who need to live with each other to live. We need to depend on each other, and hopefully it is not only a physical need but a need of fulfilment in ourselves, that a person's life is enriched by cooperating with other people and striving to live in harmony with everybody else, and to that end, there are right and wrong, there are things which promote that end and that move away from it, and in that way it is possible to choose in certain cases among different courses of action that obviously promote or harm that goal.
>
> [*Is there a time in the past when you would have thought about these things differently?*] Oh, yeah, I think that I went through a time when I thought that things were pretty relative, that I can't tell you what to do and you can't tell me what to do, because you've got your conscience and I've got mine.
>
> [*When was that?*] When I was in high school. I guess that it just sort of dawned on me that my own ideas changed, and

because my own judgment changed, I felt I couldn't judge another person's judgment. But now I think even when it is only the person himself who is going to be affected, I say it is wrong to the extent it doesn't cohere with what I know about human nature and what I know about you, and just from what I think is true about the operation of the universe, I could say I think you are making a mistake.

[*What led you to change, do you think?*] Just seeing more of life, just recognizing that there are an awful lot of things that are common among people. There are certain things that you come to learn promote a better life and better relationships and more personal fulfilment than other things that in general tend to do the opposite, and the things that promote these things, you would call morally right.

This response also represents a personal reconstruction of morality following a period of questioning and doubt, but the reconstruction of moral understanding is based not on the primacy and universality of individual rights, but rather on what she describes as a "very strong sense of being responsible to the world." Within this construction, the moral dilemma changes from how to exercise one's rights without interfering with the rights of others to how "to lead a moral life which includes obligations to myself and my family and people in general." The problem then becomes one of limiting responsibilities without abandoning moral concern. When asked to describe herself, this woman says that she values "having other people that I am tied to, and also having people that I am responsible to. I have a very strong sense of being responsible to the world, that I can't just live for my enjoyment, but just the fact of being in the world gives me an obligation to do what I can to make the world a better place to live in, no matter how small a scale that may be on." Thus while Kohlberg's subject worries about people interfering with each other's rights, this woman worries about "the possibility of omission, of your not helping others when you could help them."

The issue that this woman raises is addressed by Jane Loevinger's fifth "autonomous" stage of ego development, where autonomy, placed in a context of relationships, is defined as modulating an excessive sense of responsibility through the recognition that other people have responsibility for their own destiny. The autonomous stage in Loevinger's account (1970) witnesses a relinquishing of moral dichotomies and their replacement with "a feeling for the complexity and multifaceted character of real people and real situations" (p. 6). Whereas the rights conception of morality that informs Kohlberg's principled level (stages five and six) is geared to arriving at an objectively fair or just resolution to moral dilemmas upon which all rational persons could agree, the responsibility conception focuses instead on the limitations of any particular resolution and describes the conflicts that remain.

Thus it becomes clear why a morality of rights and non-interference may appear frightening to women in its potential justification of indifference and unconcern. At the same time, it becomes clear why, from a male perspective, a morality of responsibility appears inconclusive and diffuse, given its insistent contextual relativism. Women's moral judgments thus elucidate the pattern observed in the description of the developmental differences between the sexes, but they also provide an alternative conception of maturity by which these differences can be assessed and their implications traced. The psychology of women that has consistently been described as distinctive in its greater orientation toward relationships and interdependence implies a more contextual mode of judgment and a different moral understanding given the differences in women's conceptions of self and morality, women bring to the life cycle a different point of view and order human experience in terms of different priorities.

The elusive mystery of women's development lies in its recognition of the continuing importance of attachment in the human life cycle. Woman's place in man's life cycle is to protect this recognition while the developmental litany intones the celebration of separation, autonomy, individuation, and natural rights.

References

Broverman, I., Vogel, S., Broverman, D., Clarkson, F., and Rosenkrantz, P. "Sex-role Stereotypes: A Current Appraisal." *Journal of Social Issues* 28 (1972): 59-78.

Chodorow, Nancy. "Family Structure and Feminine Personality." In M. Z. Rosaldo and L. Lamphere, eds., *Woman, Culture and Society*. Stanford: Stanford University Press, 1974.

Chodorow, Nancy. *The Reproduction of Mothering*. Berkeley: University of California Press, 1978.

Edwards, Carolyn P. "Society Complexity and Moral Development: A Kenyan Study." *Ethos* 3 (1975): 505-527.

Freud, Sigmund. *The Standard Edition of the Complete Psychological Works of Sigmund Freud*, trans. and ed. James Strachey. London: The Hogarth Press, 1961.

Freud, Sigmund. *Three Essays on the Theory of Sexuality* (1905). Vol. VII.

Freud, Sigmund. "Some Psychical Consequences of the Anatomical Distinction Between the Sexes" (1925). Vol. XIX.

Holstein, Constance. "Development of Moral Judgment: A longitudinal Study of Males and Females." *Child Development* 47 (1976): 51-61.

Kohlberg, Lawrence. "The Development of Modes of Thinking and Choices in Years 10 to 16." Ph.D. Diss., University of Chicago, 1958.

Kohlberg, Lawrence. "Stage and Sequence: The Cognitive-Development Approach to Socialization." In D. A. Goslin, ed., *Handbood of Socialization Theory and Research Chicago*: Rand McNally, 1969.

Kohlberg, Lawrence. "Continuities and Discontinuities in Childhood and Adult Moral Development Revisited." In *Collected Papers on Moral Development and Moral Education*. Moral Education Research Foundation, Harvard University, 1973.

Kohlberg, Lawrence. *The Philosophy of Moral Development*. San Francisco: Harper and Row, 1981.

Kohlberg, L., and Kramer, R. "Continuities and Discontinuities in Child and Adult Moral Development." *Human Development* 12 (1969): 93-120.

Lever, Janet. "Sex Differences in the Games Children Play." *Social Problems* 23 (1976): 478-487.

Loevinger, Jane, and Wessler, Ruth. *Measuring Ego Development*. San Francisco: Jossey-Bass, 1970.

McClelland, David C. *Power: The Inner Experience*. New York: Irvington, 1975.

Mead, George Herbert. *Mind, Self, and Society*. Chicago: University of Chicago Press, 1934.

Miller, Jean Baker. *Toward a New Psychology of Women*. Boston: Beacon Press, 1976.

Piaget, Jean. *The Moral Judgment of the Child* (1932). New York: The Free Press, 1965.

Piaget, Jean. *Structuralism*. New York: Basic Books, 1970.

Simpson, Elizabeth L. "Moral Development Research: A Case Study of Scientific Cultural Bias." *Human Development* 17 (1974): 81-106.

Stoller, Robert, J. "A Contribution to the Study of Gender Identity." *International Journal of Psycho-analysis* 45 (1964): 220-226.

Woolf, Virginia. *A Room of One's Own*. New York: Harcourt, Brace and World, 1929.

28

Men as Success Objects and Women as Sex Objects

Simon Davis

How far have we come in achieving gender equality? What are women and men looking for in a mate? How do we import stereotypes into our consideration of what constitutes a desirable partner? The author of this study does a content analysis of personal advertisements as a means of examining sex stereotyping. What can this method of analysis tell us? How might we, as researchers, continue to build on these findings?

Editor's Introduction

Some people believe that we've come a long way toward gender equality. But this excerpt casts doubt on the validity of their optimistic beliefs. In it, Simon Davis shows that women and men still play traditional roles when looking for a mate.

Generally, when people mate they look for qualities that complement their own and compensate for their weaknesses. What sociologists call "heterogamy" offers a large range of possibilities. It allows a person to trade off one quality or characteristic for another: for instance, youth and beauty for wealth and status. However, all such exchanges occur within a context of acquiring "erotic (or sexual) property".

Sociologist Randall Collins believes that sexual property is the key to family structure. According to him, when people mate they take possession of erotic property, that is, exclusive sexual rights to someone's body. Even in our society, marriage is a system of property relations, and men have far more property rights over women then women have over men.

Consider our society's ideas about infidelity. Adultery is treated as a serious infraction because (Collins claims) it violates the right to exclusive sexual access.

Simon Davis, "Men as Success Objects and Women as Sex Objects: A Study of Personal Advertisements," *Sex Roles*, 23(1/2), 1990: 100-106. [as reprinted in L. Tepperman and J. Curtis (ed), *Everyday Life: A Reader* (2nd ed) McGraw-Hill, Inc. Primus, 1995: 100-106.]

The same reasoning explains why most societies have placed a heavy emphasis on the virginity of the bride—but not the groom—at marriage. In almost every case, the property system underlying marriage is one in which men own women's bodies.

Today, of course, women enjoy an unparalleled degree of independence in our society. Yet an examination of the newspaper advertisements that people use to attract mates still reveals men looking for sex objects—erotic property—and women looking for steady, successful partners. Previous research has indicated that, to a large extent, selection of opposite-sex partners is dictated by traditional sex stereotypes (Urberg, 1979). More specifically, it has been found that men tend to emphasize sexuality and physical attractiveness in a mate to a greater extent than women (e.g. Harrison and Saeed, 1977; Deaux and Hanna, 1984; Nevid, 1984); this distinction has been found across cultures, as in the study by Stiles and colleagues (1987) of American and Icelandic adolescents.

The relatively greater preoccupation with casual sexual encounters demonstrated by men (Hite, 1987, p. 184) may be accounted for by the greater emotional investment that women place in sex; Basow (1986, p. 80) suggests that the "gender differences in this area (different meaning attached to sex) may turn out to be the strongest of all gender differences."

Women, conversely, may tend to emphasize psychological and personality characteristics (Curry and Hock, 1981; Deaux and Hanna, 1984), and to seek longevity and commitment in a relationship to a greater extent (Basow, 1986, p. 213).

Women may also seek financial security more so than men (Harrison and Saeed, 1977). Regarding this last point, Farrell (1986, p. 25) suggests that the tendency to treat men as success objects is reflected in the media, particularly in advertisements in women's magazines. On the other hand, men themselves may reinforce this stereotype in that a number of men still apparently prefer the traditional marriage with working husband and unemployed wife (Basow, 1986, p. 210).

Men have traditionally been more dominant in intellectual matters, and this may be reinforced in the courting process: Braito (1981) found in his study that female coeds feigned intellectual inferiority with their dates on a number of occasions. In the same vein, Hite, in her 1981 survey, found that men were less likely to seek intellectual prowess in their mate (p. 108).

The mate selection process has been characterized in at least two ways. Harrison and Saeed (1977) found evidence for a matching process, where individuals seeking particular characteristics in a partner were more likely to offer those characteristics in themselves. This is consistent with the observation that "like attracts like" and that husbands and wives tend to resemble one another in various ways (Thiessen and Gregg, 1980). Additionally, an exchange process may be in operation, wherein a trade-off is made with women offering "domestic work and sex for financial support" (Basow, 1986, p. 213).

With respect to sex stereotypes and mate selection, the trend has been for "both sexes to believe that the other sex expects them to live up to the gender stereotype" (Basow, 1986, p. 209).

Theoretical explanations of sex stereotypes in mate selection range from the socio-biological (Symons, 1987) to radical political views (Smith, 1973). Of interest in recent years [have] been demographic influences, that is, the lesser availability of men because of population shifts and marital patterns (Shaevitz, 1987, p. 40). Age may differentially affect women, particularly when children are desired; this, combined with women's generally lower economic status (particularly when unmarried [Halas, 1981, p. 124]), may mean that the need to "settle down" into a secure, committed relationship becomes relatively more crucial for women.

The present study looks at different mate selection by men and women as reflected in newspaper companion ads. Using such a forum for the exploration of sex stereotypes is not new; for instance, in the study by Harrison and Saeed (1977) cited earlier, the authors found that in such ads women were more likely to seek financial security and men to seek attractiveness; a later study by Deaux and Hanna (1984) had similar results, along with the finding that women were more likely to seek psychological characteristics, specific personality traits, and to emphasize the quality and longevity of the relationship. The present study may be seen as a follow-up of this earlier research, although on this occasion using a Canadian setting. Of particular interest was the following: Were traditional stereotypes still in operation, that is, women being viewed as sex objects and men as success objects (the latter defined as financial and intellectual accomplishments)?

Method

Personal advertisements were taken from the *Vancouver Sun*, which is the major daily newspaper serving Vancouver, British Columbia. The *Sun* is generally perceived as a conservative, respectable journal—hence it was assumed that people advertising in it represented the "mainstream." It should be noted that people placing the ads must do so in person. For the sake of this study, gay ads were not included. A typical ad would run about 50 words, and included a brief description of the person placing it and a list of the attributes desired in the other party. Only the parts pertaining to the attributes desired in the partner were included for analysis. Attributes that pertained to hobbies or recreations were not included for the purpose of this study.

The ads were sampled as follows: Only Saturday ads were used, since in the *Sun* the convention was for Saturday to be the main day for personal ads, with 40-60 ads per edition—compared to only 2-4 ads per edition on weekdays. Within any one edition *all* the ads were included for analysis. Six editions were randomly sampled, covering the period of September 30, 1988, to September 30, 1989.

The attempt to sample through the calendar year was made in an effort to avoid any unspecified seasonal effect. The size of the sample (six editions) was large enough to meet goodness-of-fit requirements for statistical tests.

The attributes listed in the ads were coded as follows:
1. *Attractive*: specified that a partner should be, for example, "pretty" or "handsome."
2. *Physique*: similar to 1; however, this focused not on the face but rather on whether the partner was "fit and trim," "muscular," or had "a good figure." If it was not clear if body or face was being emphasized, this fell into variable (1) by default.
3. *Sex*: specified that the partner should have, for instance, "high sex drive," or should be "sensuous" or "erotic," or if there was a clear message that this was an arrangement for sexual purposes ("lunchtime liaisons—discretion required").
4. *Picture*: specified that the partner should include a photo in his/her reply.
5. *Profession*: specified that the partner should be a professional.
6. *Employed*: specified that the partner should be employed, e.g., "must hold steady job" or "must have steady income."
7. *Financial*: specified that the partner should be, for instance, "financially secure" or "financially independent."
8. *Education*: specified that the partner should be, for instance, "well educated" or "well read," or should be a "college grad."
9. *Intelligence*: specified that the partner should be "intelligent," "intellectual," or "bright."
10. *Honest*: specified, for instance, that the partner should be "honest" or have "integrity."
11. *Humor*: specified "sense of humor" or "cheerfulness."
12. *Commitment*: specified that the relationship was to be "long term" or "lead to marriage," or some other indication of stability and longevity.
13. *Emotion*: specified that the partner should be "warm," "romantic," "emotionally supportive," "emotionally expressive," "sensitive," "loving," "responsive," or similar terms indicating and opposition to being cold and aloof.

In addition to the 13 attribute variables, two other pieces of information were collected: The length of the ad (in lines) and the age of the person placing the ad. Only if age was exactly specified was it included; if age was vague (e.g., "late 40s") this was not counted.

Variables were measured in the following way: Any ad requesting one of the 13 attributes was scored once for that attribute. If not explicitly mentioned, it was not scored. The scoring was thus "all or nothing," e.g., no matter how many times a person in a particular ad stressed that looks were important it was only counted as a single score in the "attractive" column; thus, each single score represented one person. Conceivably, an individual ad could mention all, some, or none of the variables. Comparisons were then made between the sexes on the basis of the variables, using percentages and chi-squares. Chi-square values were derived by cross-tabulating gender (male/female) with attribute (asked for/not asked for). Degrees of freedom in all cases equaled one. Finally, several of the individual variables were collapsed to get an overall sense of the relative importance of (a) physical factors, (b) employment factors, and (c) intellectual factors.

Results

A total of 329 personal ads were contained in the six newspaper editions studied. One ad was discarded in that it specified a gay relationship, leaving a total sample of 328. Of this number, 215 of the ads were placed by men (65.6%) and 113 by women (34.5%).

The mean age of people placing ads was 40.4. One hundred and twenty seven cases (38.7%) counted as missing data in that the age was not specified or was vague. The mean age for the two sexes was similar: 39.4 for women (with 50.4% of cases missing) and 40.7% [sic] for men (with 32.6% of cases missing).

Sex differences in desired companion attributes are summarized in Table 1. It will be seen that for 10 of the 13 variables a statistically significant difference was detected. The three largest differences were found for attractiveness, professional and financial status. To summarize the table: in the case of attractiveness, physique, sex, and picture (physical attributes) the men were more likely than the women to seek these. In the case of professional status, employment status, financial status, intelligence, commitment, and emotion (nonphysical attributes) the women were more likely to seek these. The women were also more likely to specify education, honesty and humor, however not at a statistically significant level.

The data were explored further by collapsing several of the categories: the first 4 variables were collapsed into a "physical" category, Variables 5-7 were collapsed into an "employment" category, and Variables 8 and 9 were collapsed into an "intellectual" category. The assumption was that the collapsed categories were sufficiently similar (within the three new categories) to make the new larger categories conceptually meaningful; conversely, it was felt the remaining variables (10-13) could not be meaningfully collapsed any further.

Sex differences for the three collapsed categories are summarized in Table 2. Note that the Table 2 figures were not derived simply by adding the numbers in the Table 1 categories: recall that for Variables 1-4 a subject could specify all, one, or none; hence simply adding the Table 1 figures would be biased by those individuals who were more effusive in specifying various physical traits. Instead, the Table 2 categories are (like Table 1) all or nothing: whether a subject specified

Table 1 Gender Comparison for Attributes Desired in Partner

Variable	Desired by men (n = 215)	Desired by women (n = 113)	Chi-square
1. Attractive	76 (35.3%)	20 (17.7%)	11.13[a]
2. Physique	81 (37.7%)	27 (23.9%)	6.37[a]
3. Sex	25 (11.6%)	4 (3.5%)	6.03[a]
4. Picture	74 (34.4%)	24 (21.2%)	6.18[a]
5. Profession	6 (2.8%)	19 (16.8%)	20.74[a]
6. Employed	8 (3.7%)	12 (10.6%)	6.12[a]
7. Financial	7 (3.2%)	22 (19.5%)	24.26[a]
8. Education	8 (3.7%)	8 (7.1%)	1.79 (ns)
9. Intelligence	22 (10.2%)	24 (21.2%)	7.46[a]
10. Honest	20 (9.3%)	17 (15.0%)	2.44 (ns)
11. Humor	36 (16.7%)	26 (23.0%)	1.89 (ns)
12. Commitment	38 (17.6%)	31 (27.4%)	4.25[a]
13. Emotion	44 (20.5%)	35 (31.0%)	4.36[a]

[a]Significant at the .05 level.

one or all four of the physical attributes it would only count once. Thus, each score represented one person.

In brief, Table 2 gives similar, although more exaggerated results to Table 1. (The exaggeration is the result of only one item of several being needed to score within a collapsed category.) The men were more likely than the women to specify some physical attribute. The women were considerably more likely to specify that the companion be employed, or have a profession, or be in good financial shape. And the women were more likely to emphasize the intellectual abilities of their mate.

One can, incidentally, also note from this table an overall indication of attribute importance by collapsing across sexes, i.e., it is apparent that physical characteristics are the most desired regardless of sex.

Table 2 Gender Comparison for Physical, Employment, and Intellectual Attributes Desired in Partner

Variable	Desired by men (n = 215)	Desired by women (n = 113)	Chi-square
Physical (collapsing Variables 1-4)	143 (66.5%)	50 (44.2%)	15.13[a]
Employment (collapsing variables 5-7)	17 (7.9%)	47 (41.6%)	51.36[a]
Intellectual (collapsing 8 and 9)	29 (13.5%)	31 (27.4%)	9.65[a]

[a]Significant at the .05 level.

Discussion

Sex Differences

This study found that the attitudes of the subjects, in terms of desired companion attributes, were consistent with traditional sex role stereotypes. The men were more likely to emphasize stereotypically desirable feminine traits (appearance) and deemphasize the nonfeminine traits (financial, employment, and intellectual status). One inconsistency was that emotional expressiveness is a feminine trait but was emphasized relatively less by the men. Women, on the other hand, were more likely to emphasize masculine traits such as financial, employment, and intellectual status, and values commitment in a relationship more highly. One inconsistency detected for the women concerned the fact that although emotional expressiveness is not a masculine trait, the women in this sample asked for it, relatively more than the men, anyway. Regarding that last point, it may be relevant to refer to Basow's (1986, p. 210) conclusion that "women prefer relatively androgynous men, but men, especially traditional ones, prefer relatively sex-typed women."

These findings are similar to results from earlier studies, e.g., Deaux and Hanna (1984), and indicate that at this point in time and in this setting sex role stereotyping is still in operation.

One secondary finding that was of some interest to the author was that considerably more men than women placed personal ads—almost a 2:1 ratio. One can only speculate as to why this was so; however, there are probably at least two (related) contributing factors. One is that social convention dictates that women should be less outgoing in the initiation of relationships: Green and Sandos (1983) found that women who initiated dates were viewed less positively than their male counterparts. Another factor is that whoever places the ad is in a "power position" in that they can check out the other person's letter and photo, and then make a choice, all in anonymity; one could speculate that this need to be in control might be more an issue for the men.

Methodological Issues

Content analysis of newspaper ads has its strengths and weaknesses. By virtue of being an unobtrusive study of variables with face validity, it was felt some reliable measure of gender-related attitudes was being achieved. That the mean age of the men and women placing the ads was similar was taken as support for the assumption that the two sexes in this sample were demographically similar. Further, sex differences in desired companion attributes could not be attributed to differential verbal ability in that it was found that length of ad was similar for both sexes.

On the other hand, there were some limitations. It could be argued that people placing personal ads are not representative of the public in general. For instance, with respect to this study, it was found that the subjects were a somewhat older group—mean age of 40—than might be found in other courting situations. This raises the possibility of age being a confounding variable. Older singles may emphasize certain aspects of a relationship, regardless of sex. On the other hand, there is the possibility that age differentially affects women in the mate selection process, particularly when children are desired. The strategy of controlling for age in the analysis was felt problematic in that the numbers for analysis were fairly small, especially given the missing data, and further, that one cannot assume the missing cases were not systematically different (i.e., older) from those present.

References

Basow, S. (1986). *Gender stereotypes: Traditions and alternatives*. Brooks/Cole Publishing Co.

Braito, R. (1981). The inferiority game: Perceptions and behavior. *Sex Roles*, 7, 65-72.

Curry, T., and Hock, R. (1981). Sex differences in sex role ideals in early adolescence. *Adolescence*, 16, 779-789.

Deaux, K., and Hanna, R. (1984). Courtship in the personals column: The influence of gender and sexual orientation. *Sex Roles*, 11, 363-375.

Farrell, W. (1986). *Why men are the way they are*. New York: Berkley Books.

Green, S., and Sandos, P. (1983). Perceptions of male and female initiators of relationship. *Sex Roles*, 9, 849-852.

Halas, C. (1981). *Why can't a woman be more like a man?* New York: Macmillan Publishing Co.

Harrison, A., and Saeed, L. (1977). Let's make a deal: An analysis of revelations and stipulations in lonely hearts advertisements. *Journal of Personality and Social Psychology*, 35, 257-264.

Hite, S. (1981). *The Hite report on male sexuality.* New York: Alfred A. Knopf.

Hite, S. (1987). *Women and love: A cultural revolution in progress.* New York: Alfred A. Knopf.

Nevid, J. (1984). Sex differences in factors of romantic attraction. *Sex roles*, 11, 401-411.

Shaevitz, M. (1987). *Sexual static.* Boston: Little, Brown and Co.

Smith, D. (1973). Women, the family and corporate capitalism. In M. Stephaneson (Ed.), *Women in Canada.* Toronto: New Press.

Stiles, D., Gibbon, J., Hardardottir, S., and Schnellmann, J. (1987). The ideal man or women [sic] as described by young adolescents in Iceland and the United States. *Sex Roles*, 17, 313-320.

Symons, D. (1987). An evolutionary approach. In J. Geer and W. O'Donohue (Eds.), *Theories of human sexuality.* New York: Plenum Press.

Thiessen, D., and Gregg, B. (1980). Human assortive mating and genetic equilibrium: An evolutionary perspective. *Ethology and Sociobiology*, 1, 111-140.

Urberg, K. (1979). Sex role conceptualization in adolescents and adults. *Developmental Psychology*, 15, 90-92.

Review Questions

1. Why have personal advertisements in newspapers become a popular way of finding mates? Why did people not use, or need to use, this method in the past?

2. In Davis's study, only the men who place personal ads seem intent on capturing erotic property. How does this finding fit with Randall Collins's notion that all mating (and marriage) have the same goal?

3. Sample 30 or more personal ads—half by men and half by women—from your local newspaper to find out whether Davis's results still hold up. If they don't, offer some possible reasons.

4. Write two personal ads of your own. In one, describe the kind of partner you are looking for; do so in a way that is likely to bring results! In the other, imagine that *you* are the mate you are looking for. Write an advertisement from another's viewpoint that would have the effect of getting you to reply.

The Language of Sex: The Heterosexual Questionnaire

M. Rochlin

What do we assume when we identify someone's sexual orientation? How are these assumptions reinforced by our cultural, political and economic institutions? What else do the following questions force us to confront?

1. What do you think caused your heterosexuality?
2. When and how did you decide you were a heterosexual?
3. Is it possible that your heterosexuality is just a phase you may grow out of?
4. Is it possible that your heterosexuality stems from a neurotic fear of others of the same sex?
5. If you have never slept with a person of the same sex, is it possible that all you need is a good gay lover?
6. Do your parents know that you are straight? Do your friends and/or roommate(s) know? How did they react?
7. Why do you insist on flaunting your heterosexuality? Can't you just be who you are and keep it quiet?
8. Why do heterosexuals place so much emphasis on sex?
9. Why do heterosexuals feel compelled to seduce others into their lifestyles?
10. A disproportionate majority of child molesters are heterosexual. Do you consider it safe to expose children to heterosexual teachers?
11. Just what do men and women *do* in bed together? How can they truly know how to please each other, being so anatomically different?
12. With all the societal support marriage receives, the divorce rate is spiraling. Why are there so few stable relationships among heterosexuals?
13. Statistics show that lesbians have the lowest incidence of sexually transmitted diseases. Is it really safe for a woman to maintain a heterosexual lifestyle and run the risk of disease and pregnancy?

M. Rochlin, "The Language of Sex: The Heterosexual Questionnaire," *Changing Men* (Spring, 1982). Waterloo, Ont.: University of Waterloo.

14. How can you become a whole person if you limit yourself to compulsive, exclusive heterosexuality?
15. Considering the menace of overpopulation, how could the human race survive if everyone was heterosexual?
16. Could you trust a heterosexual therapist to be objective? Don't you feel s/he might be inclined to influence you in the direction of her/his own leanings?
17. There seem to be very few happy heterosexuals. Techniques have been developed that might enable you to change if you really want to. Have you considered trying aversion therapy?
18. Would you want your child to be heterosexual, knowing the problems that s/he would face?

Section Eight

Family

The first family to really interest me was my own. I still know less about it than I know about many other families. This is typical.... The most common situation I encounter in families is when what I think is going on bears almost no relation to what anyone in the family experiences or thinks is happening...
R.D. Laing, *The Politics of Experience: The Massey Lectures 1968*, CBC, 1969: 1, 9.

Less love, more courtesy, please.
Kurt Vonnegut, *Slapstick*

30

Old Order Mennonites Provide Support While at the Same Time Preserving the Independence of Their Elderly

John B. Bond Jr.

The dramatic and continuing increase in Canadians' life expectancy has significantly altered family life, and prompted questions about its organization and responsibilities. Models of the family often overlook the elderly, who have become the fastest-growing group in our society. How should they best be cared for? In this brief article one community's response is documented. Are these solutions feasible in (our) wider society? What lessons might we draw from this arrangement?

Two of the most significant changes of the twentieth century have been an increase in average age of death and an increase in life expectancy from birth.

In 1921 the average age of death of Canadian men was 39 years, while for women it was 41. Sixty years later, these ages had increased to 69.7 years for men and 75.8 years for women. Similarly, life expectancies at birth increased from 60 years (1931) to 71.9 years (1981) for men, and from 62.1 years (1931) to 79 years (1981) for women. These dramatic shifts can be attributed to control of many diseases which cause death in childhood, as well as treatment of a variety of causes of death of the elderly (pneumonia, chronic heart conditions, better medical care for accident victims, etc.).

These changes, however, have caused significant alterations in family life. While families have fewer childhood deaths to confront, the care of elderly family members is now a concern. Earlier in the century, there were few frail older people in society; widowhood occurred at an earlier age, at a healthier time of life, and lasted for fewer years. Children generally did not have very old parents, let alone elderly grandparents. Now, there are significant numbers of older family members, who may live for decades following retirement from the work force and departure of children from the home.

John B. Bond Jr., "Old Order Mennonites Provide Support While at the Same Time Preserving the Independence of Their Elderly," *Mennonite Mirror*, November, 1988 [as reprinted in Mark Novak (ed), *Aging and Society: A Canadian Reader*, Nelson Canada, 1995: 50-54.]

Given these changes, those in the middle years of life have been called the "new pioneers": there has never before been a time when the middle-aged have had significant responsibilities to their elderly parents as well as their children. There are no models of how families can best provide care to their older members. Each life experience with an older parent seems to be unique.

With these factors in mind, for the last several years Carol Harvey and I have been examining patterns of family life and the elderly in rural communities, first in Manitoba, and now in Ontario on a more restricted basis. We believe that family ties may be more cohesive and stable in rural areas than in urban settings where social and medical services are usually more available.

Of additional interest has been an examination of the family lives of Mennonites for whom strong family linkages have been a concern throughout history. We think that by comparing Mennonite with non-Mennonite families, much can be learned about successful intergenerational relations, and how family interactions can be improved. We have been extremely fortunate that the Social Sciences and Humanities Research Council of Canada (SSHRC) and the Centre on Aging, University of Manitoba, have financially supported the projects. Most important, however, has been the willingness of hundreds of family members to share their views with us. During the past two years, we have collected interviews from almost 200 parents over the age of 65, and have received responses to our questionnaires from more than 650 middle-aged offspring.

Most of the data we have collected are still being analyzed, using fairly complex statistical procedures. I can, however, offer some of my observations on the family life of Old Order Mennonites as it relates to the elderly. The nine families who shared their insights live near Kitchener-Waterloo, Ontario. They were not randomly selected, but volunteer participants, so my observations may not represent all Old Order families. But I believe that these families honestly and openly presented their lives, and to that extent, we can all profit. All of the parents who were interviewed were males; they ranged in age from 67 to 89. Two parents were widowed, for almost 20 years, and all but one had at least one living sibling. The numbers of living children ranged from two to 11.

The communities in which the interviewees live are a few kilometers from a moderately sized city. All of the Old Order Mennonites we contacted live on family farms, each approximately 100 acres in size. The farms generally produce a number of crops, as well as maintaining some livestock. The homes and farm operations are usually non-electrified, with the exception of those who need refrigeration for milk from dairy cattle. In some instances tractors are used, while horse-drawn plows are also common. There are no telephones on home or farm premises. Local transportation is typically by horse and buggy.

Two significant characteristics of the lives of the parental generation are continuity and independence. These themes can be seen in the home, marital, financial, work and spiritual aspects of life.

On the first day that I was to meet a member of the community, to determine whether my research project would be welcomed, I drove to his home and faced a house with what appeared to be two main entrances. In fact, the house contained two separate homes, one for the son and one for the parents (the *doddy* house). After subsequent visits to a number of homes, I observed that in some situations there is an inner passage between the two homes, while in others no passageway exists. The houses are completely self-contained, with no common areas. The homes can be described as side-by-side, but the lives of the families are independent. One elderly mother said that, even though she and her son lived in adjacent homes, she only saw her son once or twice a week during winter. The ability to maintain a separate household, although having family nearby, is a consistent concern of many elderly in North America. Governments are now realizing that the maintenance of older persons in their own home environments is cost-effective and psychologically beneficial to the older person.

Reliance Network

A second network of continuity and independence is the reliance on the lifetime marital partner, rather than adult children, to meet the tasks of daily life. It was not uncommon for an older husband to continue to rely upon his wife for meals, although a daughter-in-law lived next door, who could easily set another couple of places at meal time. Keep in mind that the stoves might be wood burning and the pots and pans cast iron. Some modernization has taken place, and propane stoves are accepted by some. Similarly, the elderly wife relies upon her husband for the maintenance of the home, care of the horse and carriage, assistance with canning of food, and other household chores. At the same time, should strength and abilities fail, younger family members step in and provide whatever is needed, careful not to infringe upon the independence of the older parents.

The financial arrangements established between the generations to maintain economic independence of the elderly caught my attention. As a cautionary note, only three families discussed their financial arrangements, so the generalizability of their comments is suspect; the specifics are noteworthy, in any event. When an older father is ready to "retire" from the farm, and subsequently move to the *doddy* house, he sells the farm and the current family house to the youngest son. ("Why the youngest son?" I asked. At the time the eldest son is ready to establish his own farm, the father is typically in his 40s and not ready to leave farming for the next 40 years. So, the father assists all but the youngest son in relocating to another farm.) As the youngest son is not in a financial position to buy the farm outright, the father provides the mortgage, approximating current interest rates, with the son repaying over time; this provides a consistent source of income to the parental generation. The fair market price of the farm is established by an independent assessor. In one case, the father stated that, as part of the land transfer, he and his wife are entitled to unlimited farm crops for personal consumption, and he pays his son a fixed sum each year for meat. The fathers help other sons in the financing of their farms. They repay the fathers over time, thus contributing to later life income.

In addition to the consistent income from the sale of the farm, most of the older fathers still earn an income. One repairs harnesses and horse collars, another assists his wife in production and marketing of cheese, a third is a wood-worker, and a fourth serves as a broker for the community in purchasing horses for the carriages, receiving only a nominal fee for his help. It was clear to me that the income received is far less important than the desire to be a productive member of the community. One gentleman shared his financial "books" with me, which indicated that he earns less than $1 per hour for his work; but it is important to him that he still has a work role, rather than just being an inactive burden on the community.

Faith in God is fundamental to the activities of the older parents as well as their children. Daily prayer and Bible reading are the norm. The religious beliefs and practices are not newly found, as the end of life approaches, but have been consistently verified by a lifetime of experiences. The willingness to do God's work while on this earth is a theme that I heard time and again. Their faith provides a strength to withstand cultural pressures for change in their lifestyle, a tolerance of people different from themselves, and an acceptance of their own frailties.

Given the desires of the parents to remain independent for as long as possible, it would seem that there is little for the middle-aged offspring to provide their parents. This was reflected in the responses to the questionnaires which they returned. Generally, little help is given on a consistent basis for lengthy periods of time. It is not, however, because they are unwilling to give, but because the parents are not viewed by either generation as needing significant help. When the help is needed, however, it is easily forthcoming. Responses to the question "What do you feel is the most important service of support you provide for your parent?" included: "provide a home alongside our family; share and care; care when ill or sick"; "living side by side"; "companionship"; "just being there when they need us."

The motivation to provide care to older parents is simply ascribed to God's instruction to honour one's father and mother, the Golden Rule, or Jesus' love for us all. A more extensive response was provided by one son: "When I was a child, my parents took care of me, and saw to my needs, emotionally as well as others. Now when they are older, it is the turn of the child to help. Where there is mutual love, this is easy; but even where this is lacking, it is a Christian duty to take care of our older people."

As all of the older participants in this study were fairly healthy and independent, our results do not reflect what happens as the older person loses his or her health, and needs substantial care. I was told of a variety of family settings where extensive support was provided by the family. In one instance, the widowed mother was incontinent, and appeared to have reached a stage of Alzheimer's disease which included continual wandering and periods of violence. The family had organized such that, for each day of the week, a different family member was responsible to move into the *doddy* house and care for the older mother. The family size was sufficiently large and nearby that this placed no undue strain on any individual family member. In instances where the family can no longer provide the needed care, a home has been established by some Old Order women to receive the elderly. In cases where hospitalization is needed, the individual must pay for the services, as the Old Order Mennonites are not participants in the Ontario Health Insurance Plan (OHIP). The individual, family and church community collectively pay for the needed medical costs.

It can be seen that the family lives of Old Order Mennonites foster the independence and self-sufficiency of nuclear families. This can be seen in the domestic and economic roles of the families. As health and abilities become problematic, extended family members dutifully provide support to the extent that it is needed. Intergenerational interdependence, maintaining autonomy wherever possible, is the goal. It is only when the family and spiritual community are unable to provide support that assistance is sought from the larger society. Throughout these changes, faith and the desire to do God's work pervade.

31

Thinking About the Future

Meg Luxton

While few would disagree that the family in North America is in transition, there is considerable debate about the significance of these changes and the future of families. In this article Luxton points out that the debate over the family is bound up with the deeper question of how society generally should be organized. The debate has also been heavily influenced by an ideology of familialism. If we liberate the discussion from this prevailing ideology and look more carefully at the reality of families today, what does the future hold?

Introduction

There is no question but that families are now in a state of very rapid transformation. Since the early 1960s there have been dramatic increases in divorce rates, the number of single-parent families, teenage pregnancies, individuals co-habiting without getting married, openly lesbian and gay couples, the ages at which people are having their first child, the number of people having only one or two children, and married women's employment. All of these changing statistical patterns reflect profound changes in people's experience of daily life. As a result, much effort is devoted to the task of interpreting the significance of these changes. Why are they occurring? Will they continue to occur, and will they in turn provoke further, as yet unanticipated, changes? What will the consequences be? All of these changes raise important questions about the future of families.

These questions get raised in a range of different ways, from individuals contemplating their personal future to government legislators and policy analysts designing legislation that can shape the course of an entire nation for several generations. So these are not abstract academic issues but life-and-death concerns

---

Meg Luxton, "Thinking About the Future," from K.L. Anderson, et al., *Family Matters*, Nelson Canada, 1988: 237-260.

affecting everyone. Questions that are asked about what is happening to families today and what such changes will mean for the future reflect both deep confusion about what is possible and profound social disagreement about the way society *should* be organized. Contending visions are at stake, of how we want our future to be.

In this section I explore a number of questions about family life in the future. Because the shape of the future results from developments in the present, I argue that in thinking about families of the future, we must determine first what we include in the concept of "family." Then we can assess what currently exists, what the trends are, and where they might lead. We can uncover varying visions of the future, and anticipate what the world might look like if those visions came to pass.

The Ideology of "The Family"

One of the reasons why it is so difficult for people to discuss visions of future family life is that there is little consensus about what "the family" actually is. As Michele Barrett and Mary McIntosh (1982) have shown, to understand "the family" we have to differentiate between *ideology* and the actual ways in which people interact, co-reside, have sexual relations, have babies, marry, divorce, raise children and so on. In other words, "the family" exists in two quite distinct forms: as "familialism," a widespread and deeply embedded ideology about how people *ought* to live; and as economic and social groups which in fact organize domestic and personal life (Gittins, 1985). The ideology of "familialism" is a belief system which argues that the best way for adults to live is in nuclear families; that is, as a socially and legally recognized heterosexual couple (a woman and man) who normally expect to have children (Rapp, 1978). The ideal way for children to be raised is in such a family, according to this belief system (Bloom 1976; Blumenfeld 1976), the nuclear family being thought to provide the most stable, intimate, loving environment possible (Spock, 1968). The more people live in ways that deviate from this idealized model, the less likely they are, again according to this ideology, to get intimacy, love, and stability, and the more likely they are to be in some way socially unstable (Riley, 1983). This ideology also assumes that the prevailing organization of family life profoundly affects the total organization of society. Thus, it is argued, the more that people deviate from the nuclear family, the more the fundamental organization of contemporary society is undermined.

Basic to the ideology of familialism are patriarchal definitions and ideals of how men, women, and children should behave. While men are defined primarily by their occupation (the origin of many surnames, e.g., in English, Smith, Taylor, Steward), women and children have for centuries been defined by their relation to the kinship system through men (taking the surname of their fathers and husbands) (Gittins, 1985: 35). Because "the family," by definition, has referred to the authority of the male head over his wife and children, the ideology of the nuclear family implies male power over women and children and a wife's subordination to her husband (Weber, 1967).

This ideology about the way we *should* live shapes our lives profoundly. First, most individuals carry some form of that belief system around with them throughout their lives, and it affects the way they assess their own circumstances (Barrett and McIntosh, 1982). Too often, people marry and have children, not because they are certain that is what they want, but because they feel they should. Other people who have clearly chosen a different route are still affected by this ideology, and may have residual anxieties about whether their decision was actually the right one.

Second, the ideology of familialism permeates the assumptions made about and for other people. So young women will be asked by their well-intentioned relatives whether they have found "Mr. Right" yet, and young men will be asked when they are going to find a nice "girl" and settle down. A daughter's husband who she has married after a short acquaintance will be much more welcome at family gatherings than another daughter's female lover and companion of 20 years. Someone in hospital for a major illness is permitted to have "immediate family" visit, while friends are excluded, even though these friends may in fact provide the only real love and caring in the patient's life and the "proper" family may be estranged and uncaring. In schools it may be assumed that children who do not live in nuclear families will be less able to perform well and more likely to present behaviour problems. Children who actually do have problems may find them attributed to their "abnormal" domestic situation rather than to perceptual difficulties (Griffith, 1983).

Third, the ideology of familialism has shaped social policy and government legislation for much of the 20th century (Eichler, 1983). For example, in many workplaces employees are able to obtain benefits for spouses of the opposite sex but not for those of the same sex. Women can get maternity leave if they give birth or adopt but not if their woman partner gives birth and both are going to be closely involved in raising the child. Married individuals cannot obtain a mortgage without their spouse's involvement, even when the couple keep entirely separate finances. Income tax laws are similarly based on certain assumptions about family. Neighbourhood zoning laws and building codes, as well as the types of housing constructed, impose material constraints on domestic arrangements (Hayden, 1981). For example, in certain areas, *by law*, only people legally related to each other are allowed to share a house. Though a married woman and man and their children can share a dwelling in such areas, three friends cannot.

Controversies about "The Family"

The prevailing ideology of familialism, or the concept of "the family," has recently become a centre of major controversy. The most serious challenge to it comes from reality—the way people actually organize their domestic and personal lives. Yet, while we have quite exact figures on the number of people employed in the labour force and what their earning are, we have very little information about the actual relations between co-habiting individuals (Rubin, 1976), about how housework is done, or who pays for what in a household (Luxton, 1980; Luxton and Rosenberg, 1986). Precisely because such information on how people actually live is so difficult to obtain, the myths about family life are hard to challenge. However, increasing evidence reveals that, while it is most likely that the greatest number of people will live in a nuclear family for some part of their lives, they may well do so for only a few years; at any given time the majority of the population does not live that way.

Another challenge to the prevailing ideology has emerged with the revelation that the nuclear family is often not the centre of love and security its proponents claim. For example, one of the most prevalent myths about "the family" is that young children grow best when raised exclusively by their (biological) parents and that other ways of raising children, in group daycare, for instance, are only second best. And yet there is no evidence to support this myth at all (Gallager Ross, 1978). Indeed, the few studies that have been done suggest that daycare is excellent for children (Zigler and Gordon, 1983); and there is evidence to show that the nuclear family is too often the site of violence against children, of sexual assault and psychological deformation (Guberman and Wolfe, 1985). Similarly, the idea that women will find their greatest pleasure and satisfaction as wives and mothers has been undermined by women articulating needs for additional sources of self-worth (Friedan, 1963), and is overtly contradicted by the evidence of violence against women in the home (MacLeod, 1980) and by married women's persistent economic vulnerability (Wilson, 1986).

Another powerful challenge to the prevailing family ideology comes from increasing numbers of women who, in their personal lives, have challenged the authority of patriarchal ideology and domination and are insisting on their rights to equality both in the paid workplace within their families (FitzGerald et al., 1982; Briskin and Yanz, 1983). Collectively, the feminist movement has played a part in revealing the differences between the ideology of the ideal family and the lived reality of daily life (Luxton and Rosenberg, 1986: 10-11). Feminists demand that society as a whole provide quality social services (such as health care and childcare) for all people, rather than expecting individuals or families (usually, in practice, women) to bear these costs themselves. Many feminists demand that the term "family" be stretched to include any adult-child groupings such as single parents, lesbian or gay parents, and all intimate co-habitating or self-consciously committed support groups including childless couples, communes, or networks of friends. Such demands raise the issue of public legitimization for people whose existence in the past was always private, sometimes secret. All of them challenge the concept of family which dominates ideologically.

In reaction, conservatives have organized to defend the legitimacy of familial ideology and to attempt to enforce conformity to it. These anti-feminist "backlash" movements, the so-called "pro-family" movements (such as REAL Women), derive some popular appeal from fears evoked by the new definitions of the family, especially as most people's experience with these ideas come through the media's distorted images.[1] But today's anti-feminism (like its earlier versions) is also closely linked with hostility to the principle of government provision of social services; it disguises a call for cutbacks by claiming that "the family" (meaning unpaid women) is the best group for providing care. They oppose government intervention in business decisions (e.g., regarding affirmative action and equal pay, health and safety) and in education; they are even averse to the promotion of sexual and racial equality. Indeed, conservatives have used family politics to call for a re-privatization which is a wholly political project, and which demonstrates the links between support for private property and free enterprise on the one hand, and support for the nuclear family's structure of breadwinner husband/dependent wife on the other. It includes not only bolstering the authority of the husband/father as family head, but also increased autonomy for corporate heads—whose control over their private domains in each case has been in dispute for at least a decade (Gordon and Hunter, 1978).

It is worth noting that, though current, conservative politics of "the family" are not new. Concerns about the future of the family are often used to mask various political intentions. They have reappeared with regularity in the history of Western Europe, the United States and Canada, especially at times when "underclasses" (such as women, working-class people, socialists or communists, blacks, or people of the First Nations in Canada) are perceived as politically mobilized and therefore dangerous. The discontent of such groups is often attributed to failures in their family life, rather than to the material conditions that motivate their rebellion. In the past several centuries there has been constant flux in *all* social institutions, including families. Equally constantly, community leaders, both religious and secular, have worried about the implications of aspirations for change, and have predicted general doom as a result.[2]

At present, a dual concern, about the apparent "crisis of the family" and about the "future of the family," prevails in much of contemporary political discourse. The Canadian government formally recognized the importance of this controversy in the 1986 Speech From the Throne, which promised to place "the family" on the formal political agenda. "The family" is at the centre of a major social controversy, as various interest groups compete to ensure that their model of the family wins widespread acceptance and is legislated into social policy. The future of "the family" depends on the outcome of their struggles.

Sociology and the Future of the Family

Sociology is a science which studies human interaction, social organization, and social structure. It provides both an analytic framework and methods of study which can interpret the influence of the past in shaping the present, analyse the present, identify and assess current developments, and project their potential consequences. In this way sociology can help in the combined effort to both predict the future and formulate realistic visions of what might be.

However, "the family" is one of the most problematic and difficult areas to study (Morgan, 1975). First of all, families are relatively private, and it is very difficult for an investigator to study what actually goes on in family relationships. Whereas a researcher can get hired on in a factory and learn fairly accurately on the job what that work experience is like (Westwood, 1984), her colleague hoping to study families will have to rely on interviews in which people describe their family life (Rubin, 1976). The discrepancies between what people say about their families (and often even genuinely believe) and the actuality of family life may never be caught by the research (Luxton, 1980: 142).

Second, everyone has had an experience of family life, and therefore each of us brings a certain expertise to the topic. Because family experiences are so important and the emotions generated by them are so deeply felt, people often find it very difficult to separate their personal experiences and feelings from their analysis of "the family." While individuals may be very clear that their experiences with paid work are quite specific, and that it is not possible to generalize to all paid work situations from that one particular experience, they may find it much more difficult to remember when talking about families that generalizing from their own family life is not appropriate in that case, either. Individual sociologists are just as vulnerable as everyone else's to myths of "family," and that vulnerability can affect their analysis. As Karen Anderson and Margrit Eichler have demonstrated, instead of investigating the reality of "family" life, historians and sociologists have all too often developed contending theories of the family which correspond to the contending popular ideologies (Segal, 1983).

These problems become even more difficult when sociology tackles the future. The task requires cutting through the ideology of familialism, dispelling the myths surrounding "the family," and holding our personal dreams and fears in careful perspective as we investigate current trends and their implications for the future.

Defining "The Family"

Before we can begin to think about the future of families, we must determine how to think about the differences between myth and reality, between how we think people should live and how they actually do. Once we have some sense about what "the family" actually is and why it is that way, we can begin to assess the implications of the competing models of family currently advocated and begin to develop realistic visions of what it might be. Central to that task is the problem of clarifying what is meant by "the family." In everyday language, the term "family" is used variously to refer to a number of different groupings. A "single-family dwelling" is intended for a married woman and man and their children; when a university student living in residence says he is going home to his family at Thanksgiving, we usually assume he means his parents; when a mature adult talks about missing her family she is probably referring to her grown-up children. But when someone says that most of her family were killed in the holocaust, she is referring to a wide range of extended kin; and when a man invites a group of friends to celebrate his success and tells them they are his real family, he means those from whom he receives loving support and encouragement.

The flexibility with which the term "family" is used in regular conversation reflects the complexity of social relations and activities which are commonly included in the term. What is assumed in these usages are notions of "blood" or kinship and strong emotional bonds; family is associated with belonging—those people who have to take you in no matter what.

In academic discourse, "the family" is a term used widely and often uncritically. There are several problems with it. First, it assumes that there is, and has been, and in the future will be one single phenomenon that can be called "the family." So adult sexual and emotional relations get lumped with parent-child relations, or kinship is merged with emotional caring. And it is assumed, despite profound historical changes in all those relationships, that there is something common to all of them throughout time.

Second, it presents a variety of different family forms as though they were really the same thing. For example, an extended matrilineal kin network of immigrants from the Caribbean is equated with a white, middle-class, nuclear family from Ottawa, and both are seen as being the same as a Métis kin group in Saskatchewan; a wealthy factory owner and his heirs in Vancouver and considered in the same light as a single welfare mother in a fishing village in Nova Scotia. Third, the notion of "the family" tends to assume that all individuals within "the family" are in a similar situation sharing similar resources and life chances (despite extensive research which shows that men and women, boys and girls, do not have equal access to family resources, nor do they share equal life chances). Assuming one identical family form throughout denies important differences based on class, race, ethnicity, age, and gender (Thorne and Yalom, 1982). Finally, such usage tends to imply that the model of the nuclear family represented by familial ideology is normative, and actually exists in real life. As a result, other family forms and relationships appear to be deviant. Thus the term "the family" both obscures reality and contributes to the maintenance of familial ideology, instead of recognizing the multiplicity of relationships and activities that are actually subsumed by the terms (Collier, Rosaldo, and Yanagisako, 1982).

Analytically, sociologists include within the definition of family such relations and activities as kinship and marriage, economic inheritance, pooling and sharing, conceiving and bearing children, raising children, domestic labour, sexuality, love and caring, and forms both of power and domination and of intimacy. So, when people talk about the future of the family, they are actually discussing the ways in which that whole range of relations and activities might be organized. And when others advocate that certain legal and social practices be implemented in relation to any one of those items, they are shaping the future of families in Canada.

Kinship and Marriage

Throughout the history of capitalist societies, kinship and marriage have decreased in importance as primary forms of social organizing. Increasingly through the 20th century, adult men have been able to arrange their lives independently of kin and marriage relationships (Ehrenreich, 1983). More recently, increasing numbers of women have also been able to get jobs which pay enough to allow them to live independently as well. However, kinship and marriage still form the basis for one of the main ways in which groups or networks of people are organized. Kinship is a system which demarcates socially recognized and legitimated relations between people. Marriage is a legal relationship which links two different kinship groups and regulates gender relations between men and women. Together, kinship and marriage operate on a number of somewhat distinct levels.

For many people, their kinship and marriage connections form an extended family from which they receive an important sense of identity and belonging. The vast majority of children are raised by kin, and those relationships are among the most significant in their lives. For many adults, the commitment represented by marriage signifies a dedication to the partner greater than any an individual is willing or able to make to other people. For many people, kinship and marriage are the main, most stable, enduring, and committed of relationships. As a result, many people hold a very strong attachment to family and are very suspicious of any criticisms raised over it.

For subordinated social groups, extended family ties are often the means by which cultural, political, religious, and language traditions are maintained and preserved (Stack, 1974; Lamoureux, 1987). When such groups are subject to discrimination or persecution, extended family ties may provide a basis for defence and resistance (Caulfield, 1974).

Politically, kinship and marriage systems are one of the most important ways by which nation states—national governments—control and regulate individuals. First and foremost, kinship establishes an individual's right to citizenship and hence to access to national resources, (rights which vary enormously from country to country but in Canada include such things as the right to seek paid employment; access to social security benefits like unemployment insurance, mother's allowance, old age pensions and welfare; the right to certain legal protections; and the right to vote). The legal citizenship of the newborn child is derived from its kin, that is, from the citizenship of one or both of its parents. While immigration laws determining which adults can acquire Canadian citizenship are constantly changing, kinship or marriage ties are usually regarded as the significant grounds for admitting immigrants.[3]

The regulation of marriage is one way the state exerts social control over individuals. Legal marriage both enforces and privileges heterosexuality and regulates interpersonal relationships. The legal structure of marriage traditionally has reinforced male power and privilege over women and, although in recent years pressure from feminists has forced certain legal changes in family law which gesture in the direction of equality in marriage, its current structure is still fundamentally unequal. More significantly, marriage and kin relations are used by the state to hold certain individuals economically and socially responsible for others (i.e., their family) as a way of avoiding demands that the government provide adequate social services for everyone.

Kinship and marriage are also central to the ways in which individuals have access to and are required to provide certain kinds of economic resources. On a more structural level, kinship and marriage relations are fundamental to the organization of certain kinds of property relations and, consequently, as will be seen in what follows, are the chief way in which classes and class hierarchies are maintained and reproduced.

Family Economics: Inheritance, Pooling and Sharing

Because family is one way to organize access to economic resources, family patterns vary by class. One of the features of a capitalist economy is that wages or salaries are paid to individuals and legally belong to those individuals. Similarly, investment income is usually owned either by large corporate organizations or by individuals. However, there are well-established patterns of pooling and sharing by which wealth owned privately is redistributed among kin and household relations.

The economic resources of their family of birth largely shape the opportunities available to children, and therefore profoundly influence their class location as adults. Children from well-off families will have a much easier time establishing themselves as well-to-do adults than will the children of poor families (Porter, 1965). Class privilege and class disadvantage are seen most clearly with the passing of wealth from one generation to the next through inheritance....

For many people, the economics of daily subsistence are organized through families. A family is a pooling, sharing group through which individuals obtain much of their food, clothing, and shelter. Legal obligations, cultural values, and common social practices assume that the economic support for individuals unable to support themselves should come from "their family." So governments resist giving greater access to welfare or social services, on the grounds that families have the "real responsibility" for such care. One of the most common of such patterns is found in the particular family form advocated as ideal by familial ideology; that is, a family in which the male is the breadwinner who takes on financial responsibility for the other members of his nuclear family and the female is the housewife-homemaker who takes responsibility for domestic labour including the raising of the children. Under the law the man is required to share his (privately owned) income with his wife and their children.

The fact that women are supposed to be wives and mothers supported by their husbands has been used since the 19th century to justify excluding women from many paid jobs, particularly the most skilled and best paid (Armstrong and Armstrong, 1983; Connelly, 1978). Young women are discouraged from obtaining the education and training that would enable them to qualify for such work, on the grounds that their main occupation will be as wife and mother (Russell, 1987). Jobs held primarily by women (especially in clerical work, sales, and services) are systematically paid less than jobs which require the same or even less training but are held predominantly by men; this discrimination is explained by claiming that women are secondary wage earners (Abella, 1984).

This economic discrimination in the paid labour force provides a major economic compulsion on the part of women toward marriage. Because they are unlikely to earn enough to support themselves very well, and definitely cannot support children on a typical woman's wages, women need marriage to provide them with basic economic resources (Ehrenreich, 1983). As a consequence, married women, whether they are employed or not, are economically dependent on their husbands. If the marriage is a loving and co-operative one, this economic dependency may seem insignificant, but the minute the marriage breaks down, through death, separation, or divorce, the economic consequences reassert themselves. Many women living comfortable lives have suddenly found themselves plunged into poverty when their breadwinner is gone. It is this economic inequality which results in the harsh reality of contemporary Canadian life that poverty is female; the vast majority of poor people in this country are either women with young children to support or older women trying to get by on their old-age pensions (Canadian Advisory Council on the Status of Women, 1983; National Council of Welfare, 1979).

The major social change of the last 20 years has been the dramatic increase in married women's participation in the paid labour force. In 1970, 38.3 percent of women were in the labour force and constituted 33.6 percent of it. By 1980, 50.4 percent of women were in the labour force, and they constituted 40.1 percent of the total. By (December) 1986 this had increased to 55.1 percent of women, becoming 49.7 percent of the total (Labour Force Annual Averages, Statistics Canada Catalogue 71-001; Historical Labour Force Statistics, Statistics Canada Catalogue 71-201). Most significantly, the greatest increase of women in the labour force has been amongst women with pre-school children, 58.2 percent. While such shifts mean that women have some independent income, which begins to alleviate the negative consequences of their economic dependency on men, their lower incomes mean that the problem still remains.

This economic basis for family relations means that the future of family life depends more than anything else on what happens economically. Changing patterns of male and female employment will have profound economic consequences for households. As long as women are unable to earn enough to support themselves and their children, they will be subject to strong economic pressures to marry and thus to be dependent on and hence subject to men. Only when women have equal training, equal access to all jobs, equal pay, and equal pay for work of equal value will they be able to genuinely choose whether or not to marry. Hours of work, levels of pay, parental-leave benefits, security of employment, childcare arrangements, and access to housing all affect the way people organize their personal lives and their ability to care for children. So debates about the economy (on issues such as free trade, unemployment insurance, "acceptable" levels of unemployment, a guaranteed annual income, and a shorter work week) and about government spending (who should provide economic support for those unable to support themselves: children, the disabled, the elderly, the ill, and the unemployed) are also debates about family life. At the heart of those economic debates are contending visions of how social life "should" be organized; more than anything else, future economic developments will shape constraints and possibilities for future families.

Conceiving and Bearing Children

While conceiving and bearing children appear to be private individual actions, rooted in biological processes, they are in fact profoundly social. Individual women have children for a variety of reasons, but in so doing they are reproducing the human species and their own particular population. The proportion of women who have children, and the numbers of children they bear, are determined by numerous complex social forces (Gittins, 1982), and in turn shape the population profile of the next generation (Seccombe, 1983).

Familial ideology has prescribed and proscribed appropriate behaviour for conception and child bearing. Fundamental to familial ideology is the assumption that adults marry to have children and that children should only be born to married couples.

> Heterosexuality, marriage, and having children are thus all part of the western patriarchal parcel of rules for appropriate sexual relations and behaviour between men and women. Indulging in one without accepting the rest of the "parcel" has been, and still is, widely condemned (Gittins, 1985: 92).

Until recently, because women's economic survival depended on marriage, and because of male power over women's sexuality, having children was, in part, a price women paid for economic security. However, as increasing numbers of women have gained relative economic independence from men, it has become possible for them to exercise greater control over their biological reproduction. This control has been dramatically increased by developments in medical knowledge and reproductive technology.

Relatively effective (though not entirely safe nor cheap) birth control and abortions have made it possible for those fertile women who have access to them to choose when and if to have children. Increasing knowledge about human fertility has increased the chances of conceiving and carrying a pregnancy to term for people who might previously have been unable to do so. Childbirth itself, which was often extremely dangerous for both mother and child is now, for those who have access to modern medical knowledge and technology, much safer (McLaren and Tigar McLaren, 1986). Amniocentesis, genetic testing, fetal monitoring, and *in utero* surgery provide enormous possibilities for control over the types of children who are born.

The new knowledge and the reproductive technology which accompanies it has opened up tremendous possibilities for the future. What is at present completely unclear, however, is what that future might look like. On the one hand, these new developments have offered great hope for people previously unable to have children. On the other hand, a preference for male children has prompted the abortion of some female babies, a practice which could result in dramatic imbalances in future population (Mies, 1986). While genetic testing and manipulation have eliminated for some parents the grief of producing genetically abnormal children, the various drugs and surgical techniques connected with this research are often tested on poor, immigrant, black, native, or third-world women before they are deemed safe for white, middle-class, Western women (Melrose, 1982). For some lesbians, the new knowledge has permitted them to use donated sperm to impregnate themselves without either having intercourse or seeking the intervention of the medical profession. Some people have called for the creation of a "super" population, and have established sperm banks to preserve the genes of (usually white) middle-class professional men. On the other hand, some women have become concerned that, with surrogate mothering, women will be reduced to being merely egg farmers (Murphy, 1984).

At present we simply do not have enough experience to know what the future consequences of such developments might be, but a number of issues have already emerged. There is a complex politics which determines what kind of research gets done and what does not get done. Evidence indicates that the large pharmaceutical companies determine what research is done into birth control, because they fear the loss of their profits if cheaper, more effective methods were to be found. Some of the recent research into genetic engineering was prompted by military strategies for limited nuclear war. At present this knowledge, and control over access to it, is in the hands of the medical profession, a predominantly white, male, middle-class group....

Concerns about the future consequences of these developments have prompted some people to call for a moratorium on reproductive research. The Roman Catholic Church has declared all aspects of reproductive technology unacceptable for its members. In contrast, feminist groups have called for increased access for all, and have challenged the control of the medical profession, advocating clinics under the control of the community.

The larger question underlying all these debates is who should have the right and the power to make decisions about if, when, and how women give birth (Petchesky, 1985; Gavigan, 1987). Do individual (white male) doctors have the right to decide which women can benefit from medical reproductive techniques? Should governments have the right to legislate (as China does currently) the number of children women can have? Should religious organizations have the right to impose compulsory motherhood on their members? Should individual women have the right to abort a fetus because they don't like its sex? Does anyone have the right to force women to have babies if they do not want to—the logical extension of making abortion illegal or restricted....

Raising Children

The bottom line in debates about the future of family life is always the question, "But what about the children?" The promoters of the ideology of familialism respond to proposals for alternative family forms by arguing that only the nuclear family can provide the best environment for raising children, and that mothers are the best caregivers for infants and young children. In practice, lived experience and systematic research (Zigler and Gordon, 1983) demonstrate over and over that this is not necessarily the case.

In the same way, women are not innately more skilled at childcare than men, nor are biological parents automatically good parents. What all the research shows is that many different forms of childcare can be equally effective. What matters is that the child is both emotionally and physically nurtured and stimulated, and that the caregivers are not isolated and lacking in support. What we know is that making mothers primarily responsible for their children without providing supporting social services such as daycare renders those women vulnerable to poverty (because they cannot take paid work), extraordinary stress (when they take paid work and juggle two jobs while worrying about childcare), and burnout from bearing too much responsibility in isolation (Rosenberg, 1987).

A current political issue revolves around the question of who should bear the cost of raising children. On the one hand, feminist and daycare activists call for free, universal daycare funded by the government and controlled by the parents, the staff, and the community. They argue that childcare is a social responsibility to be shared by all. In contrast, conservatives insist that the costs of caring for young children should be born by the individual parents. The outcome of this struggle could result in a continuation of current practices of ad hoc, unregulated, and often unsatisfactory childcare arrangements whose cost may keep a couple from having more children; or, on the other hand, if a system of quality daycare centres were to become available across the country, parents could have a much wider range of options available to them.

The question of who cares for the children is a much larger one than that, however. It is really about whether children are the private property and responsibility of their individual parents or whether a larger community of involved and concerned adults will share the work, the responsibility, and the joy of them. Why, for example, should people only have intimate access to children if they are their actual parents? Can we imagine a future society where the choice about who cares for children (and by extension, all those needing special care such as the handicapped, the ill, and the elderly), is not restricted to either their "family" (read "woman") or an institution (the horrors of which have been well documented) but is shared collectively by their community?

Domestic Labour

Domestic labour is the work of looking after the home and the people living in it (which is one reason why it is so easily assumed that anyone primarily responsible for domestic labour will provide caregiving to all who need it). It includes housework (activities such as cooking, cleaning, and laundry), childcare, care of disabled, sick, or elderly people, and a whole series of vital but intangible loving and nurturing tasks which go into "making a home." Overwhelmingly, domestic labour is primarily a woman's responsibility (Oakley, 1974, 1976; Luxton, 1980). It is usually private, individual, and unpaid.

The ideology of familialism offers an explanation for why domestic work should be done on a private, volunteer basis by individual women in their own homes. Because it claims that the best family form is a combination of a male, breadwinner husband/father and a female housewife/mother, it implies that women are "naturally" the best qualified to do domestic labour, and argues that the home and the activities which go on inside it are a world apart from the spheres of economics and politics. To reinforce that argument, this ideology claims that women have always worked in the home and that homemaking is women's "traditional" occupation.

That myth obscures the reality that the work done in the home for "love" rather than pay is indeed influenced by economic pressures and political decisions. Sociologists have shown that the structure of private family households and all the work activities which have historically gone on inside them have been transformed by corporate decisions made to ensure profitability (Strasser, 1982). For one thing, production and marketing strategies develop in the home. Moreover, future changes in tax structures, social service provisions, housing policies, and in the relative wages of women and men will all combine to profoundly affect the supposedly private sphere of the family household.

Intimacy and Sexuality

In contemporary Canadian society "family" is at the heart of emotional life and is understood to be the centre of personal life. Family life establishes our expectations and promises to fulfil our deepest, most fundamental needs. As a result, family relations are among our dearest and most important. At the same time, precisely because of the way familial ideology results in privileging one type of social relationship—the nuclear family—over any others, it is very difficult for people to get intimacy elsewhere and, when they do, it is hard for them to get those alternative relationships validated or supported. As Barrett and McIntosh point out:

> It is the overvaluation of family life that devalues these other lives. The family sucks the juice out of everything around it, leaving other institutions stunted and distorted (1982: 78).

Because family relations are supposed to provide love and intimacy, and because it is so difficult to get these elsewhere, family relations give us strength and undermine us simultaneously. The contradictory nature of the demands placed upon family life mean that those dynamics are also often the most harmful and damaging (Wilson, 1983). When family relations cannot provide what the ideology claims they should, when families are the site of violence, murder, sexual assault, or psychological terrorism, the disappointment generated may be nearly as damaging as the violence itself.

Familial ideology restricts sexuality to the heterosexual adult relations of marriage, claiming that other types of sexual relations are immature, inappropriate, or degenerate. Such notions first of all deny the reality experienced by, on the one hand, thousands of people who enjoy alternative sexual practices. On the other hand they also deny the misery and pain experienced by those people who remain in a heterosexual marital relation because they believe they must. Such compulsory heterosexuality is essential in maintaining the nuclear family in which men control women's sexuality and children are identified as the "property" of particular individuals (something that is absolutely critical in societies where wealth is redistributed through kin-based inheritance).

So, when thinking about the future, we need to focus on how people can best be assured of getting the secure, long-term, committed relationships they need. What the sociological evidence shows is that by restricting sexuality and intimacy to a small family group, and

> ...in privileging the intimacy of close kin, it has made the outside world cold and friendless (Barrett and McIntosh, 1982: 80).

By undermining the potential for community-based love and caring, the pressures on the individual family are enormous and the potential for pain and disappointment great. This suggests that unless other kinds of relations are strengthened and given legal, economic, and social support, "the family" will continue to appear to be a "haven in a heartless world" (Lasch, 1977), an appearance which masks the actual extent to which "the family" is anti-social:

> Caring, sharing and loving would be more widespread if the family did not claim them for its own (Barrett and McIntosh, 1982: 80).

The way society is currently organized, many needs formerly provided by communities are now offered for sale: childcare, therapy, even giving birth and affection. At the same time, anything which is wanted but is outside of a cash nexus or cannot be afforded is now redeposited in "the family." So "the family" is simultaneously the place where one gets what is not available elsewhere and a structure which prevents people getting those things elsewhere except for payment.

Developing New Visions: Strategies for Change

The activities, needs, and satisfactions that are usually embodied in the term "family"—security, affection, sexuality, love, parenting, who we live with and how our households are managed—are centrally important aspects of life. But, as I have tried to suggest, the ways they are actually met at the present time are highly problematic. Some people respond to these problems by reinforcing familial ideology and attempting to compel uniform social compliance to that ideology (Harding, 1981). Arguing that the family is in crisis and that the future of the family is threatened, they urge total social compulsion, from individual behaviour through to government legislation. They are particularly threatened by efforts to legitimize alternative sexual, emotional, economic, and parenting practices.

But attempts to impose universal conformity to an idealized model of how "the family" should be will not solve the problem, precisely because the source of the problem lies in the ideology of familialism and the way its associated practices restrict and limit how needs for love and sustenance are met.

Instead, we must develop a vision of the future in which more people can more easily rely on having those needs met regularly. However, our capacity to envision such a future is shaped and limited by our present experience. Because "the family" is currently one of the few places where people can hope to find security, love, intimacy, and so on, people tend to cling to it tenaciously, fearing that to let go would be to usher in something far worse—a cold, unfeeling, individualized, and competitive world. An analysis of familial ideology and of current practices of family life suggest that:

> ...the iniquities of the family and its appeal are closely related—they are two sides of the same coin. The benefits of family life depend upon the suffering of those who are excluded. The idea of the family life brings in its train many a bitter marriage and disappointed parents. If the family were not the only source of a range of satisfactions, were it not so massively privileged, it would not be so attractive (Barrett and McIntosh, 1982: 133).

So what does an analysis of the present suggest for the future? First, it illustrates the problems inherent in familial ideology and the social practices that go with it. Compulsory conformity to a single model creates situations where people cannot ensure that their needs are met. Instead, we need multiple options which permit people to make real choices about how they will live their lives, and which allow people to live differently at different times of their lives. And those options need to be based on collectivities or communities, networks of people living and working together who can contribute, collectively, to the support needed by each of them.

Second, such an analysis suggests that we need to appreciate that social change occurs in many ways, and that families are changed by forces which may appear to be quite remote. And yet human agency, the actions of individuals organizing together, can play a major role in shaping how that change occurs. Social change involves the complex interaction of many forces, of which a good number are unintentional, but it can also be affected by deliberate intervention such as social policy legislation or political organizing by special interest groups. For example, economic forces lead to changing patterns in labour force participation for women and men; developments in science and technology such as birth control or abortion affect biological reproduction; new ideologies, social norms, and expectations can lead to new practices (for example, the growing involvement of men in the care of young babies); the underlying assumptions shaping various legislative policies can profoundly affect family life (for example, through income taxes, zoning laws, and building codes); and, finally, large social movements and organized political campaigns can either win new possibilities or constrict and limit them (for example, the inclusion of sexual orientation in the human rights code or the current battle over whether to remove abortion from the Criminal Code). The point is that social change occurs; our only hope for shaping a future we want to live in will come from committing ourselves to understanding the implications of contemporary issues and acting on that understanding.

Endnotes

[1] For a critique of media representations of the women's movement, see the 1981 video *Rising Up Strong* by Lorna Weir and Linda Briskin, DEC Films, Toronto.
[2] For a powerful fictionalized projection of that position into the future, see Margaret Atwood's novel, *The Handmaid's Tale*. Toronto: McClelland and Stewart, 1985.
[3] One terrible exception to this rule occurs when women (usually non-white women) are admitted as domestic workers and are expressly forbidden to bring their children, even after they have established themselves in Canada (Brand, 1984).

References

Abella, Rosalie. 1984. *Equality in Employment: A Royal Commission Report*. Ottawa: Minister of Supply and Services Canada.

Anderson, Karen. 1987. "A Gendered World: Women, Men and the Political Economy of the Seventeenth Century Huron." In *Feminism and Political Economy: Women's Work, Women's Struggles,* Heather Jon Maroney and Meg Luxton, eds. Toronto: Methuen Publications.

Armstrong, Pat and Hugh Armstrong. 1983. *A Working Majority: What Women Must Do for Pay*. Ottawa: Canadian Advisory Council on the Status of Women.

Barrett, Michele and Mary McIntosh. 1982. *The Anti-Social Family*. London: Verso.

Bloom, Lynn. 1976. "'It's All For Your Own Good': Parent-Child Relationships in Popular American Child Rearing Literature, 1820-1970." *Journal of Popular Culture* 10.

Blumenfeld, Emily. 1976. "Child Rearing Literature as an Object of Content Analysis." *The Journal of Applied Communications Research,* November.

Brand, Dionne. 1984. "A Working Paper on Black Women in Toronto: Gender, Race and Class." *Fireweed* No. 19 Summer/Fall: 26-43.

Briskin, Linda, and Lynda Yanz, eds. 1983. *Union Sisters: Women in the Labour Movement*. Toronto: The Women's Press.

Canadian Advisory Council on the Status of Women. 1983. *As Things Stand*. Ottawa: Canadian Advisory Council on the Status of Women.

Caulfield, Mina. 1974. "Imperialism, the Family and Cultures of Resistance." *Socialist Revolution 4,* No. 20, October.

Collier, Jane, Michelle Rosaldo and S. Yanagisako. 1982. "Is There a Family? New Anthropological Views." In Thorne and Yalom, *Rethinking the Family*. New York: Longmans.

Connelly, Pat. 1978. *Last Hired, First Fired: Women and the Canadian Work Force*. Toronto: The Women's Press.

Ehrenreich, Barbara. 1983. *The Hearts of Men: American Dreams and the Flight from Commitment*. London: Pluto.

FitzGerald, Maureen, Connie Guberman and Margie Wolfe. 1982. *Still Ain't Satisfied: Canadian Feminism Today*. Toronto: The Women's Press.

Friedan, Betty. 1963. *The Feminine Mystique*. New York: Dell.

Gallager Ross, Kathleen. 1978. *Good Day Care: Fighting for It, Getting It, and Keeping It*. Toronto: The Women's Press.

Gavigan, Shelley. 1987. "Women and Abortion in Canada: What's Law Got To Do With It?" In Heather Jon Maroney and Meg Luxton, eds., *Feminism and Political Economy: Women's Work, Women's Struggles.* Toronto: Methuen Publications.

Gittins, Diana. 1982. *Fair Sex, Family Size and Structure in Britain, 1900-39.* London: Hutchison.

Gittins, Diana. 1985. *The Family in Question: Changing Households and Familiar Ideologies.* London: Macmillan.

Gordon, Linda and Allen Hunter. 1978. *Sex, Family and the New Right: Anti-feminism as a Political Force.* Somerville, Mass.: 1978 (reprinted from Radical America, Nov. 1977-February 1978.)

Griffith, Alison. 1983. "Skilling for Life, Living for Skill: The Social Construction of Life Skill in Ontario Schools," unpublished Ph.D thesis, University of Toronto, Toronto, Ontario.

Guberman, Connie and Margie Wolfe, eds. 1985. *No Safe Place: Violence Against Women and Children.* Toronto: The Women's Press.

Harding, Susan. 1981. "Family Reform Movements: Recent Feminism and its Opposition." *Feminist Studies,* vol. 7, No. 5:57-75.

Hayden, Delores. 1981. *The Grand Domestic Revolution: A History of Feminist Designs for American Homes, Neighborhoods and Cities.* Cambridge: MIT Press.

Lamoureux, Diane. 1987. "Nationalism and Feminism in Quebec: An Impossible Attraction." In Heather Jon Maroney and Meg Luxton, eds. *Feminism and Political Economy: Women's Work, Women's Struggles.* Toronto, Methuen Publications.

Lasch, Christopher. 1977. *Haven in a Heatless World.* New York.

Luxton, Meg. 1980. *More Than Labour of Love: Three Generations of Women's Work in the Home.* Toronto: The Women's Press.

Luxton, Meg and Harriet Rosenberg. 1986. *Through the Kitchen Window: The Politics of Home and Family.* Toronto: Garamond.

Maroney, Heather Jon and Meg Luxton, eds. 1987. *Feminism and Political Economy: Women's Work, Women's Struggles.* Toronto: Methuen.

McLaren, Angus and Arlene Tigar McLaren. 1986. *The Bedroom and the State.* Toronto: McClelland and Stewart.

Meis, Maria. 1986. *Patriarchy and Accumulation on a World Scale: Women in the International Division of Labour.* Atlantic Highlands, New Jersey: Zed Books.

Melrose, Dianna. 1982. *Bitter Pills: Medicines and the Third World Poor.* Oxford: Oxfam.

Morgan, D.J.H. 1975. *Social Theory and the Family.* London: Routledge & Kegan Paul.

Murphy, Julie. 1984. "Egg Farming and Women's Future." In *Test-Tube Women,* Rita Arditti, Renate D. Klein, Shelley Minden, eds. New York: Methuen Publications.

National Council of Welfare. 1979. *Women and Poverty: A Report.* Ottawa: National Council of Welfare.

Oakley, Ann. 1974. *The Sociology of Housework.* Bath: Martin Robinson.

Oakley, Ann. 1976. *Women's Work: The Housewife Past and Present.* New York: Vintage Books.

Petchesky, Rosalina. 1988. *Abortion and Women's Choice.* Boston: Northeastern University Press.

Porter, John. 1965. *The Vertical Mosaic: An Analysis of Social Class and Power in Canada.* Toronto: The University of Toronto Press....

Rapp, Rayna. 1978. "Family and Class in Contemporary America: Notes Toward an Understanding of Ideology," *Science and Society* 42 Fall, pp. 278-301.
Riley, Denis. 1983. *War in the Nursery: Theories of the Child and the Mother.* London: Virago.
Rosenberg, Harriet. 1987. "Motherwork, Stress and Depression: The Costs of Privatized Social Reproduction." In Heather Jon Maroney and Meg Luxton, eds. *Feminism and Political Economy: Women's Work, Women's Struggles.* Toronto: Methuen Publications.
Rubin, Lilian. 1976. *Worlds of Pain.* New York: Basic Books.
Russell, Susan. 1987. "The Hidden Curriculum of Schools: Reproducing Gender and Class Hierarchies." In Heather Jon Maroney and Meg Luxton, eds. *Feminism and Political Economy: Women's Work, Women's Struggles.* Toronto: Methuen Publications.
Seccombe, Wally. 1983. "Marxism and Demography." *New Left Review No. 137.* pp. 22-47.
Segal, Lynn, ed. 1983. *What Is To Be Done About the Family?* Harmondsworth: Penguin.
Spock, Benjamin. 1968. *Baby and Child Care.* Reprint. Markham, Ontario: Simon and Schuster of Canada.
Stack, Carol. 1974. *All Our Kin: Strategies for Survival in a Black Community.* New York: Harper & Row.
Statistics Canada Catalogue 71-529: 71-201.
Strasser, Susan. 1982. *Never Done: A History of American Housework.* New York: Pantheon.
Thorne, Barrie and Marilyn Yalom, eds. 1982. *Rethinking the Family: Some Feminist Questions.* New York: Longmans.
Weber, Max. 1967. *The Protestant Ethic and the Spirit of Capitalism.* London: Allen and Unwin.
Westwood, Sallie. 1984. *All Day Every Day: Factory and Family in the Making of Women's Lives.* London: Pluto.
Wilson, Elizabeth. 1983. *What is to be Done About Violence Against Women?* London: Penguin.
Wilson, Sue. 1986. *Women, the Family and the Economy.* 2nd edition. Toronto: McGraw-Hill Ryerson.
Zigler, Dr. Ed and Edmund Gordon, eds. 1983. *Daycare: Scientific Issues and Social Policy.* Dover, Mass.: Auburn House.

32

The Family

Claude Levi-Strauss

In this article Levi-Strauss explores the universality and origins of the family institution. Drawing on anthropological studies of various marriage and family arrangements around the world, he argues that the origins of the family are not essentially natural, as we generally assume, but social. Levi-Strauss finds that a recognizable structure underlies the diverse family patterns and that it involves a division of labour among the sexes and an incest taboo among members of the family grouping. The morality associated with both of these indicates that, like the family itself, they are not based in nature even though we customarily explain both in naturalistic terms. Levi-Strauss concludes that they both function to establish conditions of reciprocity in which groups are forced to establish relationships of interdependency and exchange, with one another, thereby making human society possible.

The word *family* is so plain, the kind of reality to which it refers is so close to daily experience that one may expect to be confronted in this chapter with a simple situation. Anthropologists, however, are a strange breed; they like to make even the "familiar" look mysterious and complicated. As a matter of fact, the comparative study of the family among many different peoples has given rise to some of the most bitter arguments in the whole history of anthropological thought and probably to its more spectacular reversal.

During the second half of the nineteenth century and the beginning of the twentieth, anthropologists were working under the influence of biological evolutionism. They were trying to organize their data so that the institutions of the simpler people would correspond to an early state of the evolution of mankind, while our own institutions were related to the more advanced or developed

---

From *Man, Culture and Society* by Harry L. Shapiro. Copyright © 1956, 1971 by Oxford University Press, Inc.; renewed 1984 by Harry L. Shapiro. Reprinted by permission of the publisher.

forms. And since, among ourselves, the family founded on monogamic marriage was considered as the most praiseworthy and cherished institution, it was immediately inferred that savage societies—equated for the purpose with the societies of man at the beginning of its existence—could only have something of a different type. Therefore, facts were distorted and misinterpreted; even more, fanciful "early" stages of evolution were invented, such as "group marriage" and "promiscuity" to account for the period when man was still so barbarous that he could not possibly conceive of the niceties of the social life it is the privilege of civilized man to enjoy. Every custom different from our own was carefully selected as a vestige of an older type of social organization.

This way of approaching the problem became obsolete when the accumulation of data made obvious the following fact: the kind of family featured in modern civilization by monogamous marriage, independent establishment of the young couple, warm relationship between parents and offspring, etc., while not always easy to recognize behind the complicated network of strange customs and institutions of savage peoples, is at least conspicuous among those which seem to have remained on—or returned to—the simplest cultural level.

There are two ways of interpreting this preeminence of the family at both ends of the scale of development of human societies. Some writers have claimed that the simpler peoples may be considered as a remnant of what can be looked at as a "golden age," prior to the submission of mankind to the hardships and perversities of civilization; thus, man would have known in that early stage the bliss of monogamic family only to forgo it late until its more recent Christian rediscovery. The general trend, however, except for the so-called Vienna school, has been that more and more anthropologists have become convinced that familial life is present practically everywhere in human societies, even in those with sexual and educational customs very remote from our own. Thus, after they had claimed for about fifty years that the family, as modern societies knew it, could only be a recent development and the outcome of a slow and long-lasting evolution, anthropologists now lean toward the opposite conviction, i.e., that the family, consisting of a more or less durable union, socially approved, of a man, a woman, and their children, is a universal phenomenon, present in each and every type of society.

These extreme positions, however, suffer equally from oversimplification. It is well known that, in very rare cases, family bonds cannot be claimed to exist. A telling example comes from the Nayar, a very large group living on the Malabar coast of India. In former times, the warlike type of life of the Nayar men did not allow them to found a family. Marriage was a purely symbolical ceremony which did not result in a permanent tie between a man and a woman. As a matter of fact, married women were permitted to have as many lovers as they wished. Children belonged exclusively to the mother line, and familial as well as land authority was exercised not by the ephemeral husband but by the wife's brothers. Since land was cultivated; by an inferior caste, subservient to the Nayar, a woman's brothers were as completely free as their sister's temporary husband or lovers to devote themselves to military activities.

There are a large number of human societies which, although they did not go quite as far as the Nayar in denying recognition to the family as a social unit, have nevertheless limited this recognition by their simultaneous admission of patterns of a different type. For instance, the Masai and the Chagga, both of them African tribes, did recognize the family as a social unit. However, and for the same reason as the Nayar, this was not true for the younger class of adult men who were dedicated to warlike activities and consequently were not allowed to marry and found a family. They used to live in regimental organizations and were permitted, during that period, to have promiscuous relations with the younger class of adult girls. Thus, among these peoples, the family did exist side by side with a promiscuous, non-familial type of relations between the sexes.

During recent years anthropologists have taken great pains to show that, even among people who practice wife-lending, either periodically in religious ceremonies or on a statutory basis (as where men are permitted to enter into a kind of institutional friendship entailing wife-lending among members), these customs should not be interpreted as survivals of "group marriage" since they exist side by side with, and even imply, recognition of the family. It is true enough that, in order to be allowed to lend one's wife, one should first get one. However, if we consider the case of some Australian tribes as the Wunambal of the northwestern part of the continent, a man who would not lend his wife to her other potential husbands during ceremonies would be considered as "very greedy," i.e., trying to keep for himself a privilege intended by the social group to be shared between numerous persons equally entitled to it. And since that attitude toward sexual access to a woman existed along with the official dogma that men have no part in physiological procreation (therefore doubly denying any kind of bond between the husband and his wife's children), the family becomes an economic grouping where man brings the products of his hunt and the woman those of her collecting and gathering. Anthropologists, who claim that this economic unit built upon a "give and take" principle is a proof of the existence of the family even among the lowest savages, are certainly on no sounder basis than those who maintain that such a kind of family has little else in common than the word used to designate it with the family as it has been observed elsewhere.

The same relativistic approach is advisable in respect to the polygamous family. The word polygamy, it should be recalled, refers to polygyny, that is, a system where a man is entitled to several wives, as well as to polyandry, which is the complementary system where several husbands share one wife.

Now it is true that in many observed cases, polygamous families are nothing else than a combination of several monogamous families, although the same person plays the part of several spouses. For instance, in some tribes of Bantu

Africa, each wife lives in a separate hut with her children, and the only difference with the monogamous family results from the fact that the same man plays the part of husband to all his wives. There are other instances, however, where the situation is not so clear. Among the Tupi-Kawahib of central Brazil, a chief may marry several women who may be sisters, or even a mother and her daughters by former marriage; the children are raised together by the women, who do not seem to mind very much whether they nurse their own children or not; also, the chief willingly lends his wives to his younger brothers, his court officers, or to visitors. Here we have not only a combination of polygyny and polyandry, but, the mix-up is increased even more by the fact that the co-wives may be united by close consanguineous ties prior to their marrying the same man.

As to polyandry proper, it may sometimes take extreme forms, as among the Toda where several men, usually brothers, share one wife, the legitimate father of the children being the one who has performed a special ceremony and who remains legal father of all the children to be born until another husband decides to assume the right of fathership by the same process. In Tibet and Nepal, polyandry seems to be explained by occupational factors of the same type as those already stated for the Nayar: for men living a semi-nomadic existence as guides and bearers, polyandry provides a good chance that there will be, at all times, at least one husband at hand to take care of the homestead.

Therefore, it becomes apparent why the problem of the family should not be approached in a dogmatic way. As a matter of fact, this is one of the more elusive questions in the whole field of social organization. Of the type of organization which prevailed in the early stages of mankind, we know very little, since the remnants of man during the Upper Palaeolithic Period of about 50,000 years ago consist principally of skeletal fragments and stone implements which provide only a minimum of information on social customs and laws. On the other hand, when we consider the wide diversity of human societies which have been observed since, let us say, Herodotus' time until present days, the only thing which can be said is as follows: monogamic, conjugal family is fairly frequent. Wherever it seems to be superseded by different types of organizations, this generally happens in very specialized and sophisticated societies and not, as was previously expected, in the crudest and simplest types. Moreover, the few instances of non-conjugal family (even in its polygamous form) establish beyond doubt that the high frequency of the conjugal type of social grouping does not derive from a universal necessity. It is at least conceivable that a perfectly stable and durable society could exist without it. Hence, the difficult problem: if there is no natural law making the family universal, how can we explain why it is found practically everywhere?

In order to try to solve the problem, let us try first to define the family, not by integrating the numerous factual observations made in different societies nor even by limiting ourselves to the prevailing situation among us, but by building up an ideal model of what we have in mind when we use the word *family*. It would then seem that this word serves to designate a social group offering at least three characteristics: (1) it finds its origin in marriage; (2) it consists in husband, wife, and children born out of their wedlock, though it can be conceived that other relatives may find their place close to that nuclear group; and (3) the family members are united together by (a) legal bonds, (b) economic, religious, and other kinds of rights and obligations, (c) a precise network of sexual rights and prohibitions, and a varying and diversified amount of psychological feelings such as love, affection, respect, awe, etc. We will now proceed to a close examination of several aspects in the light of the available data.

As we have already noticed, marriage may be monogamous or polygamous. It should be pointed out immediately that the first kind is not only more frequently found than the second, but even much more than a cursory inventory of human societies would lead to believe. Among the so-called polygamous societies, there are undoubtedly a substantial number which are authentically so; but many others make a strong difference between the "first" wife who is the only true one, endowed with the full right attached to the marital status, while the other ones are sometimes little more than official concubines. Besides, in all polygamous societies, the privilege of having several wives is actually enjoyed by a small minority only. This is easily understandable, since the number of men and women in any random grouping is approximately the same with a normal balance of about 110 to 100 to the advantage of either sex.

Therefore, it is not necessary to wonder a great deal about the predominance of monogamic marriage in human societies. That monogamy is not inscribed in the nature of man is sufficiently evidenced by the fact that polygamy exists in widely different forms and in many types of societies; on the other hand, the prevalence of monogamy results from the fact that, unless special conditions are voluntarily or involuntarily brought about, there is, normally, about just one woman available for each man. In modern societies, moral, religious, and economic reasons have officialized monogamous marriage (a rule which is in actual practice breached by such different means as premarital freedom, prostitution, and adultery). But in societies which are on a much lower cultural level and where there is no prejudice against polygamy, and even where polygamy may be actually permitted or desired, the same result can be brought about by the lack of social or economic differentiation, so that each man has neither the means, nor the power, to obtain more than one wife and where, consequently, everybody is obliged to make a virtue of necessity.

If there are many different types of marriage to be observed in human societies—whether monogamous or polygamous, and in the last case, polygynous, polyandrous, or both; and whether by exchange, purchase, free choice or imposed by the family, etc.—the striking fact is that everywhere a distinction exists between marriage, i.e., a legal, group-sanctioned bond between a man and a woman, and the type of permanent or temporary union resulting either from violence or consent alone.

In the first place, nearly all societies grant a very high rating to the married status. Wherever age-grades exist, either in an institutional way or as non-crystallized forms of grouping, some connection is established between the younger adolescent group and bachelorhood, less young and married without children, and adulthood with full rights, the latter going usually on par with the birth of the first child.

What is even more striking is the true feeling of repulsion which most societies have toward bachelorhood. Generally speaking it can be said that, among the so-called primitive tribes, there are no bachelors, simply for the reason that they could not survive. One of the strongest field recollections of this writer was his meeting, among the Bororo of central Brazil, a man about thirty years old: unclean, ill-fed, sad, and lonesome. When asked if the man were seriously ill, the natives' answer came as a shock: what was wrong with him?—nothing at all, he was just a bachelor. And true enough, in a society where labour is systematically shared between man and woman and where only the married status permits the man to benefit from the fruits of woman's work, including delousing, body painting, and hair-plucking as well as vegetable food and cooked food (since the Bororo woman tills the soil and makes pots), a bachelor is really only half a human being.

This is true of the bachelor and also, to a lesser extent, of a couple without children. Indeed they can make a living, but there are many societies where a childless man (or woman) never reaches full status within the group, or else, beyond the group, in this all-important society which is made up of dead relatives, and where one can only expect recognition as ancestor through the cult, rendered to him or her by one's descendants. Conversely, an orphan finds himself in the same dejected condition as a bachelor. As a matter of fact, both terms provide sometimes the strongest insults existing in the native vocabulary. Bachelors and orphans can even be merged together with cripples and witches, as if their conditions were the outcome of some kind of supernatural malediction.

The interest shown by the group in the marriage of its members can be directly expressed, as it is the case among us where prospective spouses, if they are of marriageable age, have first to get a licence and then to secure the services of an acknowledged representative of the group to celebrate their union. Although this direct relationship between the individuals, on the one hand, and the group as a whole, on the other, is known at least sporadically in other societies, it is by no means a frequent case. It is almost a universal feature of marriage that it is originated, not by the individuals but by the groups concerned (families, lineage, clans, etc.), and that it binds the groups before and above the individuals. Two kinds of reasons bring about this result: on the one hand, the paramount importance of being married tends to make parents, even in very simple societies, start early to worry about obtaining a suitable mate for their offspring and this, accordingly, may lead to children being promised to each other from infancy. But above all, we are confronted here with that strange paradox to which we shall have to return later on, namely, that although marriage gives birth to the family, it is the family, or rather families, which produce marriage as the main legal device at their disposal to establish an alliance between themselves. As a New Guinea native put it, the real purpose of getting married is not so much to obtain a wife but to secure brothers-in-law. If marriage takes place between groups rather than individuals, a large number of strange customs become immediately clearer. For instance, we understand why in some parts of Africa, where descent follows the father's line, marriage becomes final only when the woman has given birth to a male child, thus fulfilling its function of maintaining her husband's lineage. The so-called *levirate* and *sororate* should be explained in the light of the same principle: if marriage is binding between two groups to which the spouses belong there can be without contradiction a replacement of one spouse by his brothers or by her sisters. When the husband dies, the levirate provides that his unmarried brothers have a preferential claim on his widow (or, as it is sometimes differently put, share in their deceased brother's duty to support his wife and children), while the sororate permits a man to marry preferentially in polygamous marriage his wife's sisters, or—when marriage is monogamous—to get a sister to replace the wife in case the latter remains childless, has to be divorced on account of bad conduct, or dies. But whatever the way in which the collectivity expresses its interest in the marriage of its members, whether through the authority vested in strong consanguineous groups, or more directly, through the intervention of the State, it remains true that marriage is not, is never, and cannot be a private business.

We have to look for cases as extreme as the Nayar, already described, to find societies where there is not, at least, a temporary de facto union of the husband, wife, and their children. But we should be careful to note that, while such a group among us constitutes the family and is given legal recognition, this is by no means the case in a large number of human societies. Indeed, there is a maternal instinct which compels the mother to care for her children and makes her find a deep satisfaction in exercising those activities, and there are also psychological drives which explain that a man may feel warmly toward the offspring of a woman with whom he is living, and the development of which he witnesses step by step, even if he does not believe (as is the case among the tribes who are said to disclaim physiological paternity) that he had any actual part in their procreation.

The great majority of societies, however, do not show a very active interest in a kind of grouping which, to some of them at least (including our own), appears so important. Here, too, it is the groups which are important, not the temporary aggregate of the individual representatives of the group. For instance, many societies are interested in clearly establishing the relations of the offspring with the father's group on the one hand, and with the mother's group on the other, but they do it by differentiating strongly the two kinds of relationships. Territorial rights may be inherited through one line, and religious privileges and obligations through the other. Or else, status from one side, magical techniques from the other.

In most of contemporary India and in many parts of western and eastern Europe, sometimes as late as the nineteenth century, the basic social unit was constituted by a type of family which should be described as *domestic* rather than *conjugal*: ownership of the land and of the homestead, parental authority and economic leadership were vested in the eldest living ascendant, or in the community of brothers issued from the same ascendant. In the Russian *bratsvo*, the south-Slavic *zadruga*, the French *maisnie*, the family actually consisted of the elder or the surviving brothers, together with their wives, married sons with their wives and unmarried daughters, and so on down to the great-grandchildren. Such large groups, which could sometimes include several dozen persons living and working under a common authority, have been designated as *joint families* or *extended families*. Both terms are useful but misleading, since they imply that these large units are made up of small conjugal families. As we have already seen, while it is true that the conjugal family limited to mother and children is practically universal, since it is based on the physiological and psychological dependency which exists between them at least for a certain time, and that the conjugal family consisting of husband, wife, and children is almost as frequent for psychological and economic reasons which should be added to those previously mentioned, the historical process which has led among ourselves to the legal recognition of the conjugal family is a very complex one: it has been brought about only in part through an increasing awareness of a natural situation. But there is little doubt that, to a very large extent, it has resulted from the narrowing down to a group, as small as can be, the legal standing of which, in the past of our institutions, was vested for centuries in very large groups. In the last instance, one would not be wrong in disallowing the terms joint family and extended family. Indeed, it is rather the conjugal family which deserves the name of *restricted family*.

We have just seen that when the family is given a small functional value, it tends to disappear even below the level of the conjugal type. On the contrary, when the family has a great functional value, it becomes actualized much above that level. Our would-be universal conjugal family, then, corresponds more to an unstable equilibrium between extremes than to a permanent and everlasting need coming from the deepest requirements of human nature.

To complete the picture, we have finally to consider cases where the conjugal family differs from our own, not so much on account of a different amount of functional value, but rather because its functional value is conceived in a way qualitatively different from our own conceptions.

As will be seen later on, there are many peoples for whom the kind of spouse one should marry is much more important than the kind of match they will make together. These people are ready to accept unions which to us would seem not only unbelievable, but in direct contradiction with the aims and purposes of setting up a family. For instance, the Siberian Chukchee were not in the least abhorrent to the marriage of a mature girl of let us say about twenty, with a baby-husband two or three years old. Then, the young woman, herself a mother by an authorized lover, would nurse together her own child and her little husband. Like the North American Mohave, who had the opposite custom of a man marrying a baby girl and caring for her until she became old enough to fulfil her conjugal duties, such marriages were thought of as very strong ones, since the natural feelings between husband and wife would be reinforced by the recollection of the parental care bestowed by one of the spouses on the other. These are by no means exceptional cases to be explained by extraordinary mental abnormalities. Examples could be brought together from other parts of the world: South America, both highland and tropical, New Guinea, etc.

As a matter of fact, the examples just given still respect, to some extent, the duality of sexes which we feel is a requirement of marriage and raising a family. But in several parts of Africa, women of high rank were allowed to marry other women and have them bear children through the services of unacknowledged male lovers, the noble woman being then entitled to become the "father" of her children and to transmit to them, according to the prevalent father's right, her own name, status, and wealth. Finally, there are the cases, certainly less striking, where the conjugal family was considered necessary to procreate the children but not to raise them, since each family did endeavour to retain somebody else's children (if possible of a higher status) to raise them while their own children were similarly retained (sometimes before they were born) by another family. This happened in some parts of Polynesia, while "fosterage," i.e., the custom whereby a son was sent to be raised by his mother's brother, was a common practice on the Northwest Coast of America as well as in European feudal society.

During the course of centuries we have become accustomed to Christian morality, which considers marriage and setting up a family as the only way to prevent sexual gratification from being sinful. That connection has been shown to exist elsewhere in a few scattered instances; but it is by no means frequent. Among most people, marriage has very little to do with the satisfaction of the sexual urge, since the social setup provides for many opportunities which can be not only external to marriage, but even contradictory to it. For instance, among the Muria of Bastar, in central India, when puberty comes, boys and girls are sent to live together in communal huts where they enjoy a great deal of sexual freedom, but after a few years of such leeway they get married according to the rule that no former adolescent lovers should be permitted to unite. Then, in a rather small village, each man is married to a wife whom he has known during his younger years as his present neighbour's (or neighbours') lover.

On the other hand, if sexual considerations are not paramount for marriage purposes, economic necessities are found everywhere in the first place. We have already shown that what makes marriage a fundamental need in tribal societies is the division of labour between the sexes.

Like the form of the family, the division of labour stems more from social and cultural considerations than from natural ones. Truly, in every human group, women give birth to children and take care of them, and men rather have as their specialty hunting and warlike activities. Even there, though, we have ambiguous cases: of course men never give birth to babies, but in many societies, as we have seen with the couvade, they are made to act as if they did. And there is a great deal of difference between the Nambikwara father nursing his baby and cleaning it when it soils itself, and the European nobleman of not long ago to whom his children were formally presented from time to time, being otherwise confined to the women's quarters until the boys were old enough to be taught riding and fencing.

When we turn to activities less basic than child-rearing and war-making, it becomes still more difficult to discern rules governing the division of labour between the sexes. The Bororo women till the soil while among the Zuni this is man's work; according to tribe, hut-building, pot-making, weaving, may be incumbent upon either sex. Therefore, we should be careful to distinguish the fact of the division of labour between the sexes which is practically universal, from the way according to which different tasks are attributed to one or the other sex, where we should recognize the same paramount influence of cultural factors, let us say the same artificiality which presides over the organization of the family itself.

Here, again, we are confronted with the same question we have already met with: if the natural reasons which could explain the division of labour between the sexes do not seem to play a decisive part, as soon as we leave the solid ground of women's biological specialization in the production of children, why does it exist at all? The very fact that it varies endlessly according to the society selected for consideration shows that, as for the family itself, it is the mere fact of its existence which is mysteriously required, the form under which it comes to exist being utterly irrelevant, at least from the point of view of any natural necessity. However, after having considered the different aspects of the problem, we are now in a position to perceive some common features which may bring us nearer to an answer than we were at the beginning of this chapter. Since family appears to us as a positive social reality, perhaps the only positive social reality, we are prone to define it exclusively by its positive characteristics. Now it should be pointed out that whenever we have tried to show what the family is, at the same time we were implying what it is not, and the negative aspects may be as important as the others. To return to the division of labour we were just discussing, when it is stated that one sex must perform certain tasks, this also means that the other sex is forbidden to do them. In that light, the sexual division of labour is nothing else than a device to institute a reciprocal state of dependency between the sexes.

The same thing may be said of the sexual side of the family life. Even if it is not true, as we have shown, that the family can be explained on sexual grounds, since for many tribes, sexual life and the family are by no means as closely connected as our moral norms would make them, there is a negative aspect which is much more important: the structure of the family, always and everywhere, makes certain types of sexual connections impossible, or at least wrong.

Indeed, the limitations may vary to a great extent according to the culture under consideration. In ancient Russia, there was a custom known as *snokatchestvo* whereby a father was entitled to a sexual privilege over his son's young wife; a symmetrical custom has been mentioned in some parts of southeastern Asia where the persons implied are the sister's son and his mother's brother's wife. We ourselves do not object to a man marrying his wife's sister, a practice which English law still considered incestuous in the mid-nineteenth century. What remains true is that every known society, past or present, proclaims that if the husband-wife relationship, to which, as just seen, some others may eventually be added, implies sexual rights, there are other relationships equally derived from the familial structure, which make sexual connections inconceivable, sinful, or legally punishable. The universal prohibition of incest specifies, as a general rule, that people considered as parents and children, or brother or sister, even if only by name, cannot have sexual relations and even less marry each other. In some recorded instances—such as ancient Egypt, pre-Columbian Peru, also some African, southeast Asian, and Polynesian kingdoms—incest was defined far less strictly than elsewhere. Even there, however, the rule existed, since incest was limited to a minority group, the ruling class (with the exception of, perhaps, ancient Egypt where it may have been more common; on the other hand, not every kind of close relatives were permitted as spouse: for instance it was the half-sister, the full-one being excluded; or, if the full-sister was allowed, then it should be the elder sister, the younger one remaining incestuous.

The space at our disposal is too short to demonstrate that, in this case as previously, there is no natural ground for the custom. Geneticists have shown that while consanguineous marriages are likely to bring ill effects in a society which has consistently avoided them in the past, the danger would be much smaller if the prohibition had never existed, since this would have given ample opportunity for the harmful hereditary characteristics to become apparent and be automatically eliminated through selection: as a matter of fact, this is the way breeders improve the quality of their subjects. Therefore, the dangers of consanguineous marriages are the outcome of the incest prohibition rather than actually explaining it. Furthermore, since very many primitive peoples do not share our belief in biological harm resulting from consanguineous marriages, but have entirely different theories, the reason should be sought elsewhere, in a way more consistent with the opinions generally held by mankind as a whole.

The true explanation should be looked for in a completely opposite direction, and what has been said concerning the sexual division of labour may help us to grasp it. This has been explained as a device to make the sexes mutually dependent on social and economic grounds, thus establishing clearly that marriage is better than celibacy. Now, exactly in the same way that the principle of sexual division of labour establishes a mutual dependency between the sexes, compelling them thereby to perpetuate themselves and to found a family, the prohibition of incest establishes a mutual dependency between families, compelling them, in order to perpetuate themselves, to give rise to new families. It is through a strange oversight that the similarity of the two processes is generally overlooked on account of the use of terms as dissimilar as *division*, on the one hand, and *prohibition* on the other. We could easily have emphasized only the negative aspect of the division of labour by calling it a prohibition of tasks; and conversely, outlined the positive aspects of incest-prohibition by calling it the principle of division of marriageable rights between families. For incest-prohibition simply states that families (however they should be defined) can marry between each other and that they cannot marry inside themselves.

We now understand why it is so wrong to try to explain the family on the purely natural grounds of procreation, motherly instinct, and psychological feelings between man and woman and between father and children. None of these would be sufficient to give rise to a family, and for a reason simple enough: for the whole of mankind, the absolute requirement for the creation of a family is the previous existence of two other families, one ready to provide a man, the other one a woman, who will through their marriage start a third one, and so on indefinitely. To put it in other words: what makes man really different from the animal is that, in mankind, a family could not exist if there were no society; i.e., a plurality of families ready to acknowledge that there are other links than consanguineous ones, and that the natural process of filiation can only be carried on through the social process of affinity.

How this interdependency of families has become recognized is another problem which we are in no position to solve because there is no reason to believe that man, since he emerged from his animal state, has not enjoyed a basic form of social organization, which, as regards the fundamental principles, could not be essentially different from our own. Indeed, it will never be sufficiently emphasized that, if social organization had a beginning, this could only have consisted in the incest prohibition since, as we have just shown, the incest prohibition is, in fact, a kind of remodeling of the biological conditions of mating and procreation (which know no rule, as can be seen from observing animal life), compelling them to become perpetuated only in an artificial framework of taboos and obligations. It is there, and only there, that we find a passage from nature to culture, from animal to human life, and that we are in a position to understand the very essence of their articulation.

As Taylor has shown almost a century ago, the ultimate explanation is probably that mankind has understood very early that, in order to free itself from a wild struggle for existence, it was confronted with the very simple choice of "either marrying-out or being killed-out." The alternative was between biological families living in juxtaposition and endeavouring to remain closed, self-perpetuating units, overridden by their fears, hatreds, and ignorances, and the systematic establishment, through the incest prohibition, of links of intermarriage between them, thus succeeding to build, out of the artificial bonds of affinity, a true human society, despite, and even in contradiction with, the isolating influence of consanguinity.

In order to ensure that families will not become closed and that they will not constitute progressively as many self-sufficient units, we satisfy ourselves with forbidding marriage between near relatives. The number of social contacts which any given individual is likely to maintain outside his or her own family is great enough to afford a good probability that, on the average, the hundreds of thousands of families constituting at any given moment a modern society will not be permitted to "freeze," if one may say so. On the contrary, the greatest possible freedom for the choice of a mate (submitted to the only condition that the choice has to be made outside the restricted family) ensures that these families will be kept in a continuous flow and that a satisfactory process of continuous "mix-up" through intermarriage will prevail among them, thus making for a homogeneous and well-blended social fabric.

Conditions are quite different in the so-called primitive societies: there, the global figure of the population is a small one, although it may vary from a few dozen up to several thousands. Besides, social fluidity is low and it is not likely that many people will have a chance to get acquainted with others, during their lifetime, except within the limits of the village, hunting territory, etc., though it is true that many tribes have tried to organize occasions for wider contacts, for instance, during feasts, tribal ceremonies, etc. Even in such cases, however, the chances are limited to the tribal group, since most primitive peoples consider that the tribe is a kind of wide family, and that the frontiers of mankind stop together with the tribal bonds themselves.

Given such conditions, it is still possible to ensure the blending of families into a well-united society by using procedures similar to our own, i.e., a mere prohibition of marriage between relatives without any kind of positive prescriptions as to where and whom one should correctly marry. Experience shows, however, that this is only possible in small societies under the condition that the diminutive size of the group and the lack of social mobility be compensated by widening to a considerable extent the range of prohibited degrees. It is not only one's sister or daughter that, under such circumstances, one should not marry, but any women with whom blood relationship may be traced, even in the remotest possible way. Very small groups with a low cultural level and a loose political and social organization, such as some desert tribes of North and South America, provide us with examples of that solution.

However, the great majority of primitive peoples have devised another method to solve the problem. Instead of confining themselves to a statistical process, relying on the probability that certain interdictions being set up, a satisfactory equilibrium of exchanges between the biological families will spontaneously result, they have preferred to invent rules which every individual and family should follow carefully, and from which a given form of blending, experimentally conceived of as satisfactory, is bound to arise.

Whenever this takes place, the entire field of kinship becomes a kind of complicated game, the kinship terminology being used to distribute all the members of the group into different categories, the rule being that the category of the parents defines either directly or indirectly the category of the children, and that, according to the categories in which they are placed, rules of kinship and marriage have provided modern anthropology with one of its more difficult and complicated chapters. Apparently ignorant and savage peoples have been able to devise fantastically clever codes which sometimes require, in order to understand their workings and effects, some of the best logical and even mathematical minds available in modern civilization. Therefore, we will limit ourselves to explaining the crudest principles which are the more frequently met with.

One of these is, undoubtedly, the so-called rule of cross-cousin marriage, which has been taken up by innumerable tribes all over the world. This is a complex system according to which collateral relatives are divided into two basic categories: "parallel" collaterals, when the relationship can be traced through two siblings of the same sex, and "cross" collaterals, when the relationship is traced through two siblings of opposite sex. For instance, my paternal uncle is a parallel relative and so is my maternal aunt; while the maternal uncle on the one hand, the paternal aunt on the other, are cross-relatives.

Now, the startling fact about this distinction is that practically all the tribes which make it claim that parallel relatives are the same thing as the closest ones on the same generation level: my father's brother is a "father," my mother's sister a "mother," my parallel-cousins are like brothers and sisters to me, and my parallel-nephews like children. Marriage with any of these would be incestuous and is consequently forbidden. On the other hand, cross-relatives are designated by special terms of their own, and it is among them that one should preferably find a mate.

All these distinctions (to which others could be added) are fantastic at first sight because they cannot be explained on biological or psychological grounds. But, if we keep in mind what has been explained in the preceding section, i.e., that all the marriage prohibitions have as their only purpose to establish a mutual dependency between the biological families, or, to put it in stronger terms, that marriage rules express the refusal, on the part of society, to admit the exclusive existence of the biological family, then everything becomes clear. For all these complicated sets of rules and distinctions are nothing but the outcome of the processes according to which, in a given society, families are set up against each other for the purpose of playing the game of matrimony.

The female reader, who may be shocked to see womankind treated as a commodity submitted to transactions between male operators, can easily find comfort in the assurance that the rules of the game would remain unchanged should it be decided to consider the men as being exchanged by women's groups. As a matter of fact, some very few societies, of a highly developed matrilineal type, have to a limited extent attempted to express things that way. And both sexes can be comforted from a still different (but in that case slightly more complicated) formulation of the game whereby it would be said that consanguineous groups consisting of both men and women are engaged in exchanging together bonds of relationships.

The important conclusion to be kept in mind is that the restricted family can neither be said to be the element of the social group, nor can it be claimed to result from it. Rather, the social group can only become established in contradistinction, and to some extent in compliance, with the family.

Society belongs to the realm of culture, while the family is the emanation, on the social level, of those natural requirements without which there could be no society and indeed no mankind. As a philosopher of the sixteenth century has said, man can only overcome nature by complying with its laws. Therefore, society has to give the family some amount of recognition. And it is not so surprising that, as geographers have also noticed with respect to the use of natural land resources, the greatest amount of compliance with the natural laws is likely to be found at both extremes of the cultural scale: among the simpler peoples as well as among the more highly civilized. Indeed, the first ones are not in a position to afford paying the price of too great a departure, while the second have already suffered from enough mistakes to understand that compliance is the best policy. This explains why, as we have already noticed, the small, relatively stable, monogamic restricted family seems to be given greater recognition, both among the more primitive peoples and in modern societies, than in what may be called (for the sake of the argument) the intermediate levels.

Section Nine

Deviance and Social Control

The only universal in deviance is its very existence. There are no actions that are literally condemned everywhere, but the condemnation of some actions does exist everywhere.
　　　　　Erich Goode, *Deviant Behaviour*, Prentice-Hall, 1978: 18.

33

The Criminal Justice System

Laureen Snider

Who breaks the law? Who ends up in prison? What is the role of the police and the courts in enforcement and punishment? In this selection Snider gives a statistical outline of the Canadian criminal justice system and attempts to explain what these facts mean. Her research shows how decisions made by police, judges, lawyers and other participants both reflect and influence the wider political and economic system within which crime is "made."

Introduction

The criminal justice system in Canada has been the subject of much discussion in recent years. The media dwell at great length on crimes of violence, on alleged crime waves and on the deficiencies of "the system." Urban Canadians are apparently restricting their activities and modifying their life styles out of a fear of being victimized (e.g., by refusing to use public transportation at night, buying more and heavier locks, etc.). Reports that the police are being handicapped by concern for the rights of prisoners and that courts are too lenient share space with accounts of the results of Royal Commissions into police brutality and prison conditions.

There are certain more or less accepted facts about each stage of the criminal justice system—who breaks the law, what criminal laws are routinely enforced by police, what the role of prosecution and defence is in the criminal courts, who the judges are, and who ends up in prison. This chapter tries to explain what these facts mean and what they tell us about Canadian society in a broader perspective.

Laureen Snider, "The Criminal Justice System" in Dennis Forcese and Stephen Richer (ed), *Social Issues: Sociological Views of Canada* (2nd edition) Scarborough: Prentice-Hall Canada, 1988: 287-293.

The Giant Funnel

If everyone who committed an illegal act in Canada on a given day was actually charged with that offence and taken to court, we would end up with 95 to 98 percent of the population going through the court system. And if these people all received the most common sanction for the offence they committed, well over half would serve time in a jail or prison. It is well known in criminological circles (if not outside them) that nearly everyone has committed one or more Criminal Code offences (LeBlanc, 1975; McDonald, 1969; Vaz, 1966; Gold, 1977; Christie, 1965; but see Tribble, 1975, for a quasi-dissenting view). This does *not* include all those who have committed petty offences against municipal by-laws by parking at an expired meter or building a new bathroom without a permit. Typical Criminal Code offences which people in routine surveys admit having committed are:

Theft—over and under $200.00
Assault
Breaking and entering
Theft of a motor vehicle
Fraud—relating to credit card usage and phony cheques
Driving while impaired
Possession and/or sale of illegal or prohibited drugs (e.g., marijuana, cocaine) under the Narcotic Control or Food and Drug Act.

While these offences are most often committed by people under 25 years of age, this does not mean that older or middle-class people "mature out" of crime. Rather, it seems that the type of wrongdoing changes, often to so-called occupational crimes—theft from one's employer, the provincial medicare or legal aid plan, theft from employees through violations of minimum wage laws, payoffs and kickbacks, and violations of laws governing occupational safety in mines, factories and business enterprises throughout the nation. (Reiman [1984:63] suggests the people who break these laws in the U.S. are responsible for *five times* as many deaths per year as are murderers. The rate in Canada would probably be higher, simply because our murder rate is so much lower.)

That most people are *not* known to the police, and think of themselves as upright, law-abiding citizens despite this reality, is the result of many factors. In the first place, the vast majority of illegal acts that are committed are never reported to authorities. This is to be expected when we are dealing with white-collar and occupational crimes, for the victims typically do not realize an offence has been committed, as in polluting offences, occupational safety or misleading advertising—and even if they were aware of the offence, and did know to whom to report it, reporting rates would be low because of the wide-spread and well-founded belief that no effective action would be take. However, it is also true of traditional crime. The figures vary somewhat with the time and place the study was done, but generally speaking it appears that only about one-third of burglaries are reported to police; one-quarter or less of rapes and assaults; one-tenth or less of thefts of all kinds; and no more than one in one hundred of "victimless" crimes such as illegal abortion or possession of illegal drugs (Waller and Okihiro, 1978; Courtis, 1975; Biderman and Reiss, 1967; Hood and Sparks, 1970). The most recent Canadian study found that, in the seven cities studied, the percentage of crimes reported to police varied, with average reporting levels of 70 percent for motor vehicle thefts and 64 percent for break and enters, but only 29 percent of personal thefts, 34 percent of assaults and 35 percent of vandalism incidents (Canada, Solicitor General, 1984: 3). Overall, more than half (58 percent) of all incidents of the eight crimes studied (sexual assault, robbery, assault, break and enter, motor vehicle theft, household theft, personal theft and vandalism) never came to police attention. Many of the unreported incidents, however, were trivial or unsuccessful. (Almost half of the unreported incidents in most of the categories were attempts only.) It is reasonable to assume that the vast majority of these "criminals" who have committed date rape, punched someone in a bar or stolen a bicycle think of themselves as decent respectable citizens, far removed from the criminal rabble.

In those cases that are reported, only a small percentage of the offenders are caught and charged by the police. In Canada in 1985, while 84.8 percent of all reported murders and 79 percent of all reported assaults were cleared by charges, only 31.3 percent of all reported robberies and 27.7 percent of all types of theft (motor vehicle theft, theft over and under $200.00, receiving stolen goods, break and enter, and frauds) were cleared (Canada, Statistics Canada, 1986). In the United States in 1965, only 26 percent of all reported Index crimes were cleared by charges (Silberman, 1980: 350). ("Index" crimes are the offences which must be reported to the F.B.I. by all police forces: murder, burglary, rape, larceny theft and auto theft.) In 1985, this meant that, out of 2 283 352 Criminal Code offences reported to the police in Canada,[1] 490 557 or 22.6 percent were cleared by charges (meaning that charges were laid against the presumed perpetrator) and 270 883 or 12.5 percent were cleared otherwise (meaning that the police "solved" the offence, but did not lay charges) (Canada, Statistics Canada, 1986: 2-5, 2-6). The vast majority of these were prosecuted as summary crimes. Summary crimes are either those offences which are not seen by the state as being very serious, such as taking a motor vehicle without permission or being drunk in a public place, *or* offences in which the Crown Attorney in charge of the case has the option of attempting to get a summary conviction with the lighter penalties this carries, or proceeding by indictment. Theoretically, this decision is based on the circumstances of the offence and the characteristics of the defendant. (In crimes where this choice is available, prosecutors typically proceed by summary conviction for first offenders or for "non-criminal" types where losses are small.) Most serious crimes, such as theft or break and enter, *must* be prosecuted as indictable. Because no statistics on sentencing have been gathered since 1973, we must go back to 1970 to obtain information on this aspect of the funnel. This, however, may be less misleading than one would think, since the total number of crimes reported to the police in 1970 was very similar to the number reported in 1985. (In fact, there were 2 757 442 reported in 1970 and 2 724 308 in 1985, making 33 134 *fewer* reported offences in 1985!) Of the 1 878 172 summary charges laid, nearly a third of these (654 001) were dropped, usually because of insufficient evidence. Of the 1 224 169 convictions entered, 1 148 660 or 92 percent were fined, but 18 598 people ended up serving time in a municipal jail (Silberman and Teevan, 1975: 71). (All sentences under two years duration are served in municipal or provincial institutions; all of more than two years are served in federal prisons.) That leaves us with the indictable offences; some 53 318 in 1970. Nearly 87 percent (45 886) of those charged were convicted. A majority of these received non-institutional sentences such as fines and suspended sentences with or without parole, but 16 337 offences led to a prison sentence. In 1973, 53 964 were charged with indictable offences and 40 761 were convicted (Canada Year Book, 1977-78). Of those convicted, 4.2 percent were sentenced to penitentiary terms, 32.2 percent to provincial institutions, 34.3 percent were fined, 23.5 percent received a suspended sentence with probation, and the remaining 5.8 percent received a suspended sentence without probation (Griffiths et al., 1980: 173). Eventually, everyone sentenced to penitentiaries will be released, either on parole (which is granted only to "good risks" anytime after one-third of their sentence is completed), or, at the end of two-thirds of their sentence, on mandatory supervision. The final one-third of a sentence has traditionally not been served inside the prison; it is used as a device to ensure institutional conformity since prisoners who break rules risk losing varying amounts of this "good time." In either case, ex-inmates are subject to strict regulations (curfews, inability to drink in bars or socialize with ex-inmates) which, if violated, lead to a return to the institution.

This, then, is an overview of the Canadian criminal justice system. Over two and a half million offences are reported annually to the police. The most common offences are related to drinking and driving (82 percent of charges laid in 1977 were automobile-related), and the most common Criminal Code offence is the very minor "theft under $200.00" which made up 27.7 percent of all property crimes in 1985 (Canada, Statistics Canada 1986: 2-3, my computation). Fewer than 1 percent of all the charges laid lead to sentences over two years in length, and only, as we saw, 4.2 percent of all indictable offences do. Does this mean that we are excessively "soft" on criminals? That the courts are hamstrung by an exaggerated respect for the civil liberties of the defendant? That judges are too lenient? Or does it mean, on the other hand, that police are laying unnecessary and trivial charges, or that we have too many laws on the books? We will explore the answer to these questions below.

Policing and the Canadian Legal Code

The vast majority of charges laid under the Criminal Code of Canada are laid by the police. There are three types of police force: municipal, provincial and federal. Most cities have their own municipal forces (Toronto, Vancouver, Montreal, etc.), while smaller communities usually have to depend on either the provincial or the federal police. (Arrangements vary from province to province, but most population centres are legally obliged to set up or contract for police services after they reach a certain size.) Since only Ontario and Quebec have provincial forces, small communities and rural townships and counties in the other eight provinces are policed by the federal force, the Royal Canadian Mounted Police. In addition to the Criminal Code, the police are responsible for enforcing many municipal by-laws and provincial statutes (governing everything from parking to securities legislation), as well as being responsible, in the most general sense, for "keeping the peace." In essence, they are supposed to enforce all laws except those which have other enforcers specified in the legislation; for example, fish and game laws, or laws regulating safety standards and working conditions which provide for inspectors to be the normal enforcement agents. Obviously, no police force can actively enforce all the laws it is theoretically responsible for—the Criminal Code alone contains 774 different sections, forbidding everything from assisting deserters and committing acts "intended to alarm Her Majesty" (this indictable offence carries a maximum penalty of 14 years imprisonment!) to interfering with boundary lines, injuring cattle or making counterfeit money. Which laws are actively enforced is a complex matter determined by subjective judgments on what are the most important laws. These judgments are made by the political authorities responsible for the force and communicated down through the organizational hierarchy to the police chiefs and their staff. There they are translated into working procedures, modes of operation, and rules and regulations which are meant to ensure that basic priorities (usually phrased in such terms as "the protection of the community" or "the security of the citizens") will be met. If, for example, a priority is the protection of private property, then ordinary police routines will concentrate on patrolling business areas at night, and police training manuals will focus on how to spot and apprehend potential thieves. If a basic priority is protection of the state, then the spotting and arresting of dissidents will be emphasized, and resources will be allocated accordingly. Priorities such as these, which both underlie and determine procedures, are usually unstated and unrecognized by police personnel and citizens. They are taken for granted in the truest sense, and seldom is their crucial role in shaping the workings of a police force recognized. These priorities are filtered through the top police personnel. Because they mostly reflect the dominant ideology, strands of which are deeply engrained in the fabric of Canadian society and socialized into every child by family, schools and media, no one has to tell the top police officers what kinds of behaviours they must control. However, on a day-to-day basis police chiefs are likely to be kept informed of the immediate concerns of the elite groups in the society (but *not* of the concerns of the poor or the powerless). As Grosman said in his study of police chiefs across Canada,

> His affiliations and sources of information, however, too often relate primarily to service clubs within the community, merchants, and those citizens and groups to whom the Chief accords high status. It is their preferences which quickly become known to him. He then sifts this select external information and utilizes it...(1975: 53).

This is not to suggest, however, that information and power flow only from the top down. We know from a wide variety of sources (Vincent, 1979; Wilson, 1971; Manning, 1977; Reiss, 1971; Bittner, 1970; Skolnick, 1967; Bordua, 1967) that police have a distinctive occupational subculture. This, combined with the fact that the patrol officer on the beat has tremendous freedom and discretion to decide who and what to officially notice, and who and what to ignore, means that the police can in practice modify or even reverse certain types of orders. Moreover, because the police officer never knows when he/she will need his/her peers as back up in a sticky situation—perhaps to save his/her life in a confrontation, or his/her job before a disciplinary board—he/she[2] is highly motivated to respect the values and norms of this subculture. Let us discuss how theses two factors work together to give the average police officer a considerable amount of unofficial power.

The police officer on the beat decides, on his/her own, such things as how to defuse a touchy domestic dispute where the husband is beating the wife, and whether or not to chase that speeding, possibly stolen, car. His/her superior in the station house cannot know the exact circumstances; moreover, an instant decision is often required. But the police officer exercises this discretion within a framework of rules. Some of these rules are imposed "from above" by the bureaucracy of the police force; for example, what activities lead to promotion? What is a "good" arrest? What arrests will "bring down the heat" and get you in trouble? What kinds of initiative are you discouraged from taking? What laws do you have to *justify* invoking to your superiors?

Others are imposed by peers in the police force. Because of the shift work and the strains and tensions associated with being police officers, they tend to associate, both on and off the job, with other police officers. They have their own definitions of a "good cop" and a "bad cop," and they have developed a set of common values and attitudes about the world, the political system, the criminal, human nature, and the job of the police (Vincent, 1979; Bittner, 1970; Silberman, 1980). They view themselves as high-status people doing an essential but unpleasant task, a role calling for deference from the police. Public perception of the police is usually quite at odds with this self-concept. As a result, police tend to feel persecuted, misunderstood, unloved and unappreciated by the general population, the politicians and their spouses.

A recent study of Canadian police (Vincent, 1979) identified a constellation of behaviours and attitudes which police officers share. They tend to favour capital punishment (witness the recent campaign by the 52 000 member Canadian Police Association to get Parliament to restore it); they believe in gun control; as a group they see parole officers and social workers as "bleeding hearts" or "do-gooders"; and they think the court system and everyone connected with it deals too leniently with criminals. In fact, some think the judges and many of the lawyers are "in cahoots" (Vincent, 1979: 90-110). Police work breeds cynicism and suspicion, so it is no surprise that police officers as a group come to think that people, especially those they deal with in their work, are "assholes" (Silberman, 1980: 323). This jaundiced view of human nature, while understandable in terms of the work they are doing and the reactions they arouse as symbols of the authority of the state, often makes it more difficult to form or maintain relationships with those outside the force. Thus, they tend to stick together, and can be a very cohesive unit. This power has been used to defeat policies that the police do not like; in New York City in 1967, police actions nearly sabotaged an attempt to have prostitution changed from a misdemeanour with a one-year prison sentence to a violation with a 15-day maximum sentence. Until recently, the N.Y.C. police were also successful in invalidating the section of the law which made patronizing a prostitute illegal—simply by not charging the customers when they picked up the prostitutes (Roby, 1976).

Generally speaking, the police subculture calls for strict enforcement not so much of particular laws, but for strict control of particular "types of people." As Silberman has pointed out (1980; also Wilson, 1971; Ericson 1981, 1982) police tend to see themselves as playing cops and robbers. Despite the fact that over 80 percent of their time is spent on serving the public (as social workers sorting out domestic crises, finding lost children, taking people to hospitals, directing traffic, etc.) or on paperwork, police typically see their real work, their only important task, as catching criminals. But their picture of criminals is a very narrow one; it does not encompass 98 percent of all the law breakers we discussed earlier. It focuses on a small number of young, usually lower-class males who are seen as "punks" or troublemakers. These are people who show no respect for the authority of the police and often challenge it, who typically come from families or districts which are known to the police as "bad." They have usually become known to the police over several encounters. They are the people most likely to be noticed, booked, charged, eventually put on probation, and then sent to "reform" school. Their activities, however, will not be so much different from their more respectful middle-class peers. (As pointed out earlier, just about all people, as adolescents, commit illegal acts defined by the law as serious, and change to more specific class-related and occupationally influenced crimes once they are older). However, the "punk's" demeanour, social class, family background, and realistically assessed future prospects have made him into a member of a suspect category. Once he is in reformatory and officially labelled, the police will be keeping an eye on him, and he will be much more likely to be picked up again, charged and end up in prison. He has become an automatic suspect to be checked out whenever certain crimes occur. Nor is this perception necessarily wrong. He may be more likely to commit the kinds of crimes that will eventually lead to prison, as the social network therein (i.e., the prison sub-culture) encourages the rejection of "straight" or conventional values, jobs and people. (It is no accident that, while the vast majority of juveniles who go before juvenile court do *not* become adult criminals, the vast majority of those who *do* were sent away as children.)

Thus, certain kinds of people are precast in the role of potential criminals by police, and the characteristics of these people are taught to all new recruits, as are strategies for dealing with them so they cannot "take advantage." New police officers learn that only certain kinds of crimes are seen as serious. Arrests for these crimes constitute "good busts," whereas arrests for many other illegal acts do not. What are these serious acts? They tend to be property crimes such as bank robbery, break and enter, related indictable criminal code offences, as well as certain crimes of violence (murder; serious, stranger or interclass assaults; or rapes perpetrated against "respectable" women, especially by groups/gangs). And, of course, the people most likely to commit these offences, especially the property crimes, are the very same troublemakers we discussed before! Why not? They have learned the attitude favourable to committing these acts (from peers or reform school); they are cut off from legitimate channels of upward mobility and have no realistic future prospects; they are the last hired and first fired if they do manage, against all odds, to land an unskilled or semi-skilled job; and property crimes are often the only way open to them to survive, let alone "make a fast buck!" After all, no one but a young, unskilled person would choose theft as an occupation—the risks are very high (almost all career criminals end up serving time [Silberman, 1980]), the status is negative and the profits are small. But the vast majority of equally serious crimes being committed by people who do not fit the police stereotype are likely to escape all official notice.

In addition to these underlying and ongoing pressures (the political-economic forces forming overall priorities and the police subculture), more immediate factors influence what laws are enforced at a given time. Pressure groups arise from time to time and try to change either the law itself or the customary enforcement practices in a particular area. For example, in Canada today there are groups attempting to change the enforcement of marijuana laws, abortion laws, laws on homosexuality, on breaking and entering, and on drinking and driving (Law Reform Commission, 1974; Waller and Okihiro, 1978). Business people or hotel owners may spearhead a drive against prostitution or pickpockets. A particularly grisly crime (such as the abduction, sexual assault and murder of Alison Parrot in Toronto in 1986), a race riot or a public meeting which gets out of hand may trigger either crack-downs or a hands-off policy. During such periods, laws on massage parlours or licensing which have not been enforced for 20 years will be dusted off, or enforcement will be relaxed and police will ignore, for a while, public drinking or marijuana smoking offences committed by certain ethnic groups in a certain neighbourhood. After a while, normal enforcement patterns will reassert themselves.

This is not to suggest that policing is predominantly proactive; that is, that police initiate the majority of situations, or that they routinely stumble across crimes in process while on patrol which lead to confrontations and arrests. Indeed, the evidence shows (Silberman, 1980; Vincent, 1979; Wilson, 1971; Manning, 1977; Ericson, 1981, 1982) that much, if not most, of the time police officers are reacting to calls of every sort. One study in Los Angeles figured out that, if present trends continued, the average police officer would come across a burglary once every three months and a robbery once every 14 years (Science and Technology Task Force, 1967). But this does not deny the centrality of police discretion and autonomy. For this is exercised on virtually every call that is made. Even though a victim may have reported an assault, the officer who responds must decide whether the caller is serious or using the police to resolve a personal disagreement; whether the caller is indeed the victim or the aggressor; whether the incident is serious enough to warrant an arrest; and what charges, if any, are justified. He may well decide that the interests of neighbourhood peace and social justice (as he perceives it) are best served by doing nothing. Similar decisions are required in virtually every police-citizen contact.

To sum up: police forces in Canada initiate the criminal justice process by laying the vast majority of charges. To a considerable degree, they choose which of the multitude of laws they are responsible for will be enforced; as Ericson says, they "make crime" (1981). Their choices, in turn, are shaped first by the situation itself on the street and their reaction to/and perception of it; secondly, by the police subculture to the degree that they have internalized its values and codes; thirdly, by "middle level" organizational-bureaucratic concerns set forth by superiors in the police hierarchy; and, ultimately, by the basic political and economic forces that shape the intellectual climate (ideology) of the society itself.

Prosecution and Defence

After charges are laid, what is the next step? Most people, basing their knowledge on television shows from the United States, would guess that the accused, still under arrest, proceeds to hire himself a lawyer and eventually repairs to court to appear before a judge and jury. His lawyer conducts a defence while the lawyer for the state (in Canada, the Crown) attempts to prove his guilt. Then 12 carefully chosen members of the jury, after hearing all the evidence, declare his guilt or innocence and the judge passes sentence. This picture is far from the truth. What *is* likely to happen after one is charged with a criminal offence? The scenario goes something like this.

First, much depends on whether one is arrested or summoned. The police make this initial decision, and it varies according to what you are charged with and who you are. General policy is "for the police to charge every person possible with every offence possible...except for the occasional minor charge...not laid in exchange for information." (Ericson and Baranek, 1982: 128). If it is a drug or Criminal Code offence, even a minor or summary one, chances are you will be arrested (67.5 percent of those charged with a summary Criminal Code offence, 79.4 percent of those on indictable charges, and 89.2 percent on drug charges were arrested in a major study of Toronto provincial courts) (Hann, 1973: 196-197). If arrested, your freedom is at least temporarily curtailed; you are taken into custody. You may be kept in a local jail or detention centre until your case is heard, or you may be released after a court date is set, either on bail or on your own recognizance. In either case you must, in law, be brought before a justice of the peace to determine whether you will be subsequently released or kept in custody, no more than 24 hours after the arrest. If you are poor, as the vast majority of those charged with Criminal Code offences are (Ouimet, 1969; Tepperman, 1977), then the hearing must decide whether or not to release you without the posting of bail. Theoretically, a person is released without bail *if* the judge believes that chances are good that he will show up in court when his case is to be heard, will not commit any new offences while free, and will not jeopardized the prosecution's case (by destroying evidence or threatening witnesses, for example). Generally speaking, the first concern is the paramount one, and it works to the advantage of the established citizens since it is considered easier for someone with no fixed address or a room in a rooming house to leave town than for the person with a job and a house.

Prior to 1971[3] when the Bail Reform Act was passed, all people who could not post bail were imprisoned until their case came up. This resulted in many people spending three to eight months in jail on charges of which they were then found innocent! (Friedland, 1965; Canadian Civil Liberties Education, 1974). The aforementioned Hann study found that even after the Bail Reform Act, 56 percent of all defendants studied were arrested, and only 53.4 percent of these were released before their first court appearance (Hann, 1973: 196). In a Montreal study, MacKay (1976: 8) found 53 percent of all the accused still in custody at their initial court appearance. The pre-trial detention rate for those in adult prisons, per 100,000, was 12.4 in 1980 (Canada, 1982: 105). Ericson and Baranek (1982), in their study of accused persons in a large Ontario city, found that 74 of the 101 accused people they interviewed believed they were under arrest. They also argue that the treat of holding the accused for bail hearings instead of releasing them on their own recognizance has proven to be a powerful factor in persuading many defendants to sign statements implicating themselves, or to forbear from requesting lawyers during interrogation (1982: 61). The ability of Canadian police forces to add a "resisting arrest" charge to those already laid is no doubt an additional incentive for many to cooperate in incriminating themselves. Bail reform, then, does not appear to have had quite the effect which was originally envisaged in safe-guarding the (poor) defendant.

Once bail has been posted or the person released, the case is sent to the office of the Crown Attorney who, with his or her staff, is responsible for prosecuting cases. Some must be dealt with in a provincial court by a provincial judge (for example, all summary offences, driving with licence suspended, theft under $200.00, common assault); others must go to a higher court as they cannot be disposed of at the low-level courts (examples would be treason, sedition, murder and manslaughter). The remainder of indictable offences fall into a twilight zone, and the accused chooses the court level in which he wishes to be tried (provincial or county court), and elects trial by judge alone or by judge and jury. (In three Maritime provinces and Ontario there is yet another layer of procedure for those choosing trial by judge and jury—a grand jury must be convened in secret to examine the evidence against the accused and see whether trial is warranted.) However, the reality appears to be that fewer than 3 percent of all criminal cases are decided in upper-level courts (Griffiths et al., 1980: 146). To call all of this a real choice made by the accused is then, accurate only in theory. In fact, he or she is usually too well aware of his/her perilous and powerless position, or too confused and demoralized to exercise any choices not suggested by police or defence counsel (Ericson and Baranek, 1982). Studies have documented the fact that heavier penalties are demanded from those who inconvenience the court by insisting upon certain rights; for example, defendants who opt for jury trials receive heavier penalties if found guilty than those who plead guilty before a judge (Uhlman and Walker, 1980). Perhaps this partially accounts for the fact that there are, it is estimated, fewer than 2000 criminal jury trials per year in all of Canada (Hagan, 1977: 158; Griffiths et al., 1980).

However, chances are nearly one in two that the accuse we have been discussing will have had all charges dropped by this time. In Robert Hann's study, a full third of all charges were dropped or withdrawn before any court appearance was made, and another 10 percent were dismissed by the judge at the first court appearance (Hann, 1973: 461); Helder (1979) found that 37.5 percent of all charges were dropped in his study of 100 criminal incidents in 1978-1979. Before this happens, however, if he/she is one of the 53.3 percent of defendants kept in custody, the accused may well have served one to three months in jail, lost his job, deprived his family and children of emotional and financial support, meanwhile having been forced to live in a tiny, dirty cell. And there is, of course, no real legal recourse against the state which the defendant can take to secure compensation for this.

If the case has not been dismissed, it will probably proceed to trial in the provincial court—only 3 percent of all cases in Hann's study went on to the county or supreme court levels—and will be disposed of by a guilty plea, without a jury, in a trial lasting less than 20 minutes (and probably less than ten). The Canadian Civil Liberties study of all major Canadian cities found that 69.7 percent of all cases are disposed of in less than 20 minutes, 37.9 percent in less than ten minutes. The length of time spent per case was not significantly longer for more serious cases; that is, those in which the accused received a lengthy as opposed to a short prison sentence (Canadian Civil Liberties Education, 1973: 182-183). Moreover, from first to final appearance, the process will take an average of two months—more if the defendant is represented by a defence lawyer, less if she/he is not. While the length of time taken, and the number of delays experienced in Hann's study, varied with the type of case, the median time from first to final court appearance for summary, traffic and indictable Criminal Code offences was 50 to 63 days (Hann, 1973 117). While the majority of defendants will have to make several court appearances, one in four can expect to have to show up from four to eight times (Hann, 1973: 134). This, of course, costs defendants a lot of money—people must take time off work, hire babysitters, pay transportation costs and waste long hours waiting for the case to come up. And if the accused has been kept in custody, the expense to the state, as well as the potential injustice to the accused, is further multiplied.

Conclusion

Contrary to appearances and to rhetoric, the criminal justice system represents one of the easiest and most efficient ways of solving the problem of social control of excess and troublesome populations. Lower-class males, with or without criminal records, have virtually no legitimacy and no power. People, generally speaking, will not listen to, believe, or care about their allegations of police brutality, judicial unfairness, or inhuman prison conditions. They are unlikely to be able to hire lawyers to protest and publicize their cases; they are seen as having engineered their own predicament, through the myth of individual as opposed to social responsibility; and they do not have the resources or the sophistication to organize and protest politically.

Moreover, they themselves usually have bought the dominant ideology, and feel that they really are bad human beings who have no discipline and no real value (Shover, 1977). Thus, they can be processed through the system at virtually no cost, and, more importantly, with no loss of legitimacy and no potentially embarrassing and expensive accusations of oppression. As Tepperman said, when discussing alternatives to punishments in controlling "problem" populations:

> The achievement of control through reward places most of the hardship on the person seeking compliance. Control through punishment may not be as certain in the long run, but in the short run it is...less expensive and less demanding of patience. (1977: 84)

In short, these people are paying the price for the type of society we apparently want; for inciting everyone to consume when they can never consume enough; for forcing everyone to work to be recognized as a contributing human being, when there can never be enough jobs to go around; and for motivating everyone to want to be glamorous and successful, when by definition only a tiny minority can ever be recognized as such. This game may produce a high standard of living (as measured by the quantity of goods turned out), but it also produces far more losers than winners. Most of these losers adjust, compensate and outwardly conform; a few strike out in frustration and anger. It is these few we have been discussing.

In conclusion, it is time that criminologist, criminal justice employees, and the general public stopped denying the obvious. Processing vast numbers of poor people and reserving the most punitive sanctions for them, while simultaneously denying that social class has anything to do with the exercise of "justice" in this country, is too ludicrous a claim to be accepted any longer. Surely it is time the burden of proof was shifted onto those who would argue, in the face of such overwhelming evidence, that the criminal justice system aims to deliver even-handed justice to all who break the law.

Endnotes

1 The total number of Criminal Code offences reported in 1977 and 1981 are, respectively, 1,654,020 and 2,168,226 (Canada, 1982).

2 The masculine pronoun is used for much of this article, for the simple reason that the vast majority of officers in the criminal justice system, from police to judiciary, and of people charged and processed, are males. However, to underline the fact that we are not *necessarily* talking about males only, the he/she form has been used where it is appropriate.

3 The Act was tightened up on April 26, 1976, but the changes affect primarily repeat offenders. For anyone who has previously been charged with an indictable offence, the onus is on him/her to show why he/she should be released before trial rather than, as in the case with other offenders, on the police and Crown to show why she/he should *not* be (Powell, 1976).

References

Biderman, A.D. and A.J. Reiss, Jr. 1967. "On Exploring the 'Dark Figure' of Crime," *Annals of the American Academy of Political and Social Science.* 374: 1-15.

Bittner, E. 1970. *The Functions of the Police in Modern Society.* Rockville, Md.: National Institute of Mental Health Center of Studies of Crime and Delinquency.

Bordua, D., ed. 1967. *The Police: Six Sociological Essays.* New York: John Wiley and Sons.

Canada. 1982. *The Criminal Law in Canadian Society.* Ottawa, August.

Canada, Solicitor General. 1984. *Bulletin on Reported and Unreported Crimes*, Canadian Urban Victimization Survey, No. 1-4.

Canada, Statistics Canada. 1986. *Canadian Crime Statistics 1985*. Ottawa: Statistics Canada, Canadian Centre for Justice Statistics.
Canada Year Book, Annual. 1977-1978. Ottawa: Supply and Services Canada.
Canadian Civil Liberties Education. 1973. "Due Process Safeguards and Canadian Criminal Justice." In C. Boydell, C. Grindstaff and P.C. Whitehead, *The Administration of Criminal Justice in Canada*. Toronto: Holt, Rinehart and Winston, pp. 155-186.
Christie, N. 1965. "A Study of Self-Reported Crime," *Scandinavian Studies in Criminology*, Vol. 1. London: Tavistock Publications.
Courtis, M.C. 1975. "Victimization in Toronto." In R. Silverman and J. Teevan, *Crime in Canadian Society*. Toronto: Butterworths. pp. 119-127.
Ericson, R. 1981. *Making Crime: A Study of Police Detective Work*. Toronto: Butterworths.
Ericson, R. 1982. *Reproducing Order: A Study of Police Patrol Work*. Toronto: University of Toronto Press.
Ericson, R. and P. Baranek. 1982. *The Ordering of Justice*. Toronto: University of Toronto Press.
Friedland, M.L. 1965. *Detention Before Trial: A Study of Criminal Cases Tried in the Toronto Magistrates Courts*. Toronto: University of Toronto Press.
Gold, M. 1977. "Undetected Delinquent Behaviour," *Journal of Research in Crime and Delinquency*, 3(1) (January, 1966): 27-46.
Griffiths, C.T., J.F. Klein and S.N. Verdun-Jones. 1980. *Criminal Justice in Canada*. Toronto: Butterworths.
Grosman, B. 1975. *Police Command: Decisions and Discretion*. Toronto: Macmillan.
Hagan, J. 1977. *Disreputable Pleasures: Crime and Deviance in Canada*. Toronto: McGraw-Hill Ryerson.
Hann, R. 1973. *Decision Making in the Canadian Criminal Court System: A Systems Analysis*. Toronto: Centre of Criminology Research Report, University of Toronto.
Helder, H. 1979. "The Police, Case Negotiations and the Para-Legal System." Unpublished M.A. dissertation, Centre of Criminology, University of Toronto.
Hood, R. and R. Sparks. 1970. *Key Issues in Criminology*. Toronto: McGraw-Hill, World University Library.
Law Reform Commission of Canada. 1974a. *Principles of Sentencing and Dispositions*. Working Paper #3. Ottawa: Information Canada.
Law Reform Commission of Canada. 1974b. *Discovery in Criminal Cases: Report on the Questionnaire Survey*. Ottawa: Queen's Printer.
LeBlanc, M. 1975. "Upper Class vs. Working Class Delinquency." In R. Silverman and J. Teevan, *Crime in Canadian Society*. Toronto: Butterworths, pp. 102-119.
MacKay, E. 1976. *The Paths of Justice: A Study of the Operation of the Criminal Courts in Montreal*. Montreal: Groupe de Recherche en Jurimetrie, University of Montreal.
McDonald, L. 1969. *Social Class and Delinquency*. London: Faber.
Manning, P.K. 1977. *Police Work: The Social Organization of Policing*. Cambridge, Mass.: M.I.T. Press.
Ouimet, R. 1969. *Towards Unity: Criminal Justice and Corrections*. Report of the Canadian Committ on Corrections. Ottawa: Information Canada.
Powell, C.M. 1976. *Arrest and Bail in Canada*, 2nd ed. Toronto: Butterworths.

Reiman, J. 1984. *The Rich Get Richer and the Poor Get Poorer.* 2nd ed. Toronto: J. Wiley and Sons.
Reiss, A.J. 1971. *The Police and the Public.* New Haven: Yale University Press.
Roby, P. 1976. "Politics and Criminal Law: Revision of the New York State Penal Law on Prostitution." In G.F. Cole, ed., *Criminal Justice: Law and Politics,* 2nd ed. North Scituate, Mass.: Duxbury Press, pp. 28-51.
Science and Technology Task Force. 1967. *A Report to the President's Commission on Law Enforcement and Administration of Justice.* Washington, D.C.: U.S. Government Printing Office.
Shover, N. 1977. "Criminal Behaviour as Theoretical Praxis." In J.F. Galliher and J.L. McCartney, eds., *Criminology: Power, Crime, and Criminal Law.* Homewood, Ill.: Dorsey Press, pp. 159-174.
Silberman, C.E. 1980. *Criminal Violence, Criminal Justice.* New York: Vintage Books.
Silberman, R. and J.J. Teevan. 1975. *Crime in Canadian Society.* Toronto: Butterworths.
Skolnick, J. 1967. *Justice Without Trial.* New York: J. Wiley and Sons.
Tepperman, L. 1977. *Crime Control.* Toronto: McGraw-Hill Ryerson.
Tribble, S. 1975. "Socio-Economic Status and Self-Reported Juvenile Delinquency." In R. Silverman and J. Teevan, *Crime in Canadian Society.* Toronto: Butterworths, pp. 95-102.
Uhlman, T.M. and N.D. Walker. 1980. "He Takes Some of My Time, I Take Some of His: An Analysis of Judicial Sentencing Patterns in Jury Cases," *Law and Social Research,* 14:2 (Winter).
Vaz, E. 1966. "Self-Reported Juvenile Delinquency and Socio-Economic Status," *Canadian Journal of Corrections,* 8: 20-27.
Vincent, C.L. 1979. *Policemen.* Toronto: Gage.
Waller, I. and N. Okihiro. 1978. *Burglary: The Victim and the Public.* Toronto: University of Toronto Press.
Wilson, J.Q. 1971. *Varieties of Police Behavior.* New York: Atheneum.

34

Subterranean Processes in the Maintenance of Power: An Examination of the Mechanisms Coordinating Police Action[1]

Clifford D. Shearing

> *How do the daily activities and interactions of individuals interconnect with the broader social structures of a society? Shearing takes up this question by studying an urban Canadian police department and explores how the everyday practices and group culture of the police are related to the pervasive systems of inequality in our society. How, in particular, does police subculture serve to maintain social inequalities of wealth and power?*

...One of the most persistent theoretical questions in sociological theory has been how to relate social structure and interaction (c.f. Berger and Luckmann, 1967). This question remains a major concern. Within the context of the conflict perspective, it has been posed as the problem of identifying the processes that provide for the reproduction of power relations (Turk, 1969; Giddens, 1976). In specifying this problem conflict theorists have identified the role of the state as critical. Quinney, for example, has argued that 'the theoretical problem at this time is that of *linking* the class structure of advanced capitalism to the capitalist state (1977:80). This problem implies questions such as, 'how is it that the state does what it is supposed to do,' or more concretely, 'what are the mechanisms through which it preserves the hegemony of the dominant classes' (Burawoy, 1978:59).

There is considerable research, especially in the area of criminal justice, that is relevant to these questions. One of the conclusions drawn from it is that law is used as a resource, or weapon, in the preservation of power relations (Bittner, 1967; Chambliss and Seidman, 1971; Turk, 1976). In support of this, researchers have argued that the egalitarian safeguards built into the law in liberal democracies (via a formal emphasis on universalistic and behavioural, rather

---

Clifford D. Shearing, "Subterranean Processes in the Maintenance of Power: An Examination of the Mechanisms Coordinating Police Action" *The Canadian Review of Sociology and Anthropology*, Vol. 18(3). Copyright © 1981 The Canadian Sociology and Anthropology Association.

than status, criteria) are systematically undermined in practice by law enforcers who in making decisions emphasize extra-legal criteria that identify persons as members of 'problem populations' (Spitzer, 1975; Quinney, 1977). Criminality, it is argued, is an ascribed status applied disproportionately to the least powerful (Turk, 1969)....

As the 'gatekeepers' of criminal justice (Reiss, 1971), the police have tended to become the focus of much research. However, under the impact of the liberal ideal of 'equal justice,' this research has been inclined to address the problem of inequality produced by patterns of law enforcement. Consequently, the questions most often addressed have been: Are the police biased in their treatment of the public? Do they discriminate? Are they fair?...

The police subculture has long been a topic of research within the sociology of deviance and a substantial body of literature has been developed (Wexler, 1974). Throughout, one encounters the observation that the police view the public from a we/they perspective. They see themselves, it is argued, as a closely knit group set apart from the public. They believe, it is maintained, that the public view them as a hated and distrusted enemy (Manning, 1971), and they, in turn, reciprocate by regarding the public as their enemy (Westley, 1970; Manning, 1971; Harris, 1973; Wexler, 1974). This perceived enemy relationship, it is suggested, operates to encourage police solidarity, secrecy, and a hostile, sometimes violent, response to the public (Westley, 1953, 1956)....

Recent research by Shearing (1977), however, calls into question the applicability of the 'public as enemy' by arguing that it is applicable only to one of the publics which the police recognize as relevant to their work, and that is not used by the police with respect to the public at large. In developing this point, Shearing notes that a fundamental distinction is made by the police between people they serve and the troublemakers they control in the course of providing their services—that is, between the people they do things for and those they do things to (Hughes, 1971). It is because this distinction has been largely ignored in the literature on the police subculture that the relevance of this culture, as a mechanism for coordinating police activity which links it to the larger social structure, has been missed....

The Research

The tendency in so much literature to gloss over distinctions between different police publics seems, in part, to have been a result of the influence of labelling theory which focussed on police response to troublemakers. One consequence of this was the highlighting of this public as the police public. My research, in contrast, took place in a setting in which victims and complaints were as relevant to the police as troublemakers. This setting—the communications centre of a large urban Canadian police department where citizen calls for police assistance were received and responded to—provided an opportunity to examine the police conception of both the people they do thing to and those they serve. Further, as policemen from many other parts of the department were regularly in touch with the centre, it was possible to develop a police view of citizens based on a wide variety of individuals. Research for this study took place over a six-month period in the fall of 1971, and involved the observation of over sixty shifts as well as the tape-recording of several thousand telephone conversations between both policemen in the centre and citizens, and between policemen in the centre and policemen in other parts of the department (see Shearing, 1977 for a detailed description of the research).

Police Involvement in Class Conflict

In contrast to the currently accepted view of the police subculture, my research indicated that the police did not view themselves as enemies of the public at large. In these dealings with citizens, I found that policemen made a fundamental distinction between 'the public' on the one hand, and 'third- and fourth-class citizens,' 'the dregs,' or more expressively, 'the scum,' on the other. This bifurcated concept of citizens related directly to the work of policemen in the centre and those elsewhere in the department. The public consisted of those the police believed they should serve and protect. The scum were very different. They were the people whom the police prosecuted in the course of helping the public. The scum were troublemakers who impelled the public to seek police assistance. In supporting the public, the police controlled the scum.[2]

The scum were viewed by the police as the enemy of the public. Therefore they were, by implication, also the enemy of the police. The scum were supported by the public by public housing subsidies and welfare and by 'ripping them off' through crime.

> That is a pretty run down area as you can hear from old gravel voice. They're at the very bottom of the ladder—third- and fourth-class citizens. When you've worked in that area, you learn that they haven't seen soap for weeks. They and their houses are filthy dirty.

Not only were the scum unclean, but as enemies they threatened the police and the public both physically and morally. They were dangerous.

> In ——, if you get involved in something, you never know whether you'll get out O.K.
> Pick up one garbage can at ——. Imagine getting a station detail to —— you'd be surprised to get out alive.

The scum, the police believed, showed no respect for the authority of the law.

They gave no quarter and deserved none. They enraged the police. 'That's the first clown of the night. I'd like to go down and arrest the bum myself. I can't stand those pigs.'

As an enemy, the scum deserved no help from the police—their job was to help the public, not the scum. Any harm the scum did to each other was all to the better, as it assisted the police and the public in their conflict with the scum.

> First Policeman: There was a murder at —— yesterday, you know.
> Second Policeman: That's not a murder, that's a local improvement, but if you called it that you'd have to pay taxes on it.
> First Policeman: They should close down that division and put a fence around it. Everyone there deserves each other.
> Second Policeman: Yeah, you better believe it.

It is the scum who, in an age less embarrassed by class difference and less committed to the ideal of equality, were referred to as the 'dangerous' or 'criminal' classes (Silver, 1967), a 'bastardized race,' a 'class degraded by misery whose vices stand like an invincible obstacle to the generous intentions that wish to combat it' (Foucault, 1977: 276).

This distinction between two classes of citizens with whom policemen come into contact is, Hughes argues, common to many service occupations.

> To understand (service occupations) one must understand the system, including the clients and their wants. People and organizations have problems; they want things done for them— for their bodies and souls, for their social and financial relations, for their cars, houses, bridges, sewage systems; and they want things done to the people they consider their competitors or their enemies. (Hughes, 1971: 422).

In distinguishing between clients and competitors and/or enemies, Hughes draws attention to the same sort of relationship as Emerson and Messinger do in their identification of the situation roles of complainants and/or victims and troublemakers. However, unlike Emerson and Messinger, who restricted their analysis to situated roles, Hughes' formulation extends to trans-situational identities. This distinction is critical to an understanding of the categories of citizens identified by the police subculture. Neither the scum nor the public refer to the situated roles of troublemaker and victim/complainant that emerge in the definition of, and reaction to, particular troubles. Rather, they refer to two relatively stable populations of persons who become involved in trouble. Either the scum or the public could be troublemakers in a particular situation. What distinguishes the scum from the public is that the scum are structurally in conflict with, and are the enemies of, the public. The scum are, to use Katz's (1972) formulation, 'in essence' troublemakers, while the public are 'in essence' their victims.

In distinguishing between the scum and the police as two classes who oppose each other as enemies, the police culture makes available to the police a social theory that they can use in the context of their work to define situations and to construct a course of action in response to them. This theory enables the police to transcend the situated features of encounters by relating them to a broader social context which identified the 'real troublemakers' and 'real victims'[3] In using this theory as a guide to action, policemen enter, as participants, into the class conflict that the culture describes. As they do, they are able, and encouraged, to use the power of the state, on behalf of the public, to control the scum, thereby preserving not only the dominance of the public vis à vis the scum, but the system of relationships on which the opposition between the two groups depends.[4]

This system of relationships is strikingly similar to that described by Marx in his analysis of capitalism. The scum and the public are categories which are consistent with Marx's notions of the surplus unproductive population and the productive population engaged in capitalistic modes of production. Furthermore, like Marxist theory, the police subculture recognizes that the surplus population, both because it is outside the controls embodied in the economy itself, and because of its parasitic relationship to the productive population, constitutes a threat to the productive classes. The police subculture directs the working policemen to control the surplus population, precisely as Marxist theories argue is the case: 'From arrest to imprisonment...the criminal justice system exists to control the surplus population' (Quinney, 1977: 136).

What this analysis adds to the general discussion provided by Marxist and other conflict theorists, is a more specific analysis of the mechanisms that coordinate the activities of those working within criminal justice. Marxism, it has been argued, 'is still grappling with the problem of how to transform a theory into a concrete historical force' (Stewart, 1978: 20). In the police subculture, we see how, in a small but systematic way, a conflict theory grounded in an analysis of social class relevant to police work is used as 'a concrete historical force' to reproduce a particular set of relations. This suggest that it is wrong to identify the theory appropriate to advanced capitalism as consensus (Chambliss and Seidman, 1971), and that of revolution as social conflict (Stewart, 1978). Although consensus may be the theory that legitimates criminal justice, our findings suggest that the theory which operates to reproduce order is one that takes class conflict as its major premise. It is at the working level that one finds the 'merger of reason and action' (Stewart, 1978:19), of theory and practice, which conflict theorists refer to. Ironically, however, this merger of conflict theory and action works to reproduce, rather than transcend, capitalist relations.

Class Conflict and Egalitarian Ideals

The acknowledgement that capitalist society incorporates two social theories (conflict and consensus) based on opposing premises, each contributing to the maintenance of order, raises the question of the relationship between them. This is particularly relevant in the case of the police who work within a system that is explicitly committed to liberal egalitarian ideals. Within this context the question that arises is: How does the police subculture retain an influence on the motivations of working policemen in an environment in which egalitarian notions are supposed to prevail? In other words: How is it that the conflict theory of the police subculture is able to motivate, and thereby coordinate, individual policemen in the face of the official commitment by the public, political authorities, and the courts to a consensus social theory? How does the police subculture retain its influence over a working policeman given the hierarchical character of the police organization and the frequent attempts by inquiries, commissions, the media, civil liberties groups, and dedicated liberal politicians to bring police practice into line with egalitarian ideals? In order to answer this question, we must examine the beliefs about the police and 'the brass' endorsed by the police subculture.

In contrast to the scum, the public were viewed by the police as allies who they helped and assisted in their conflict with the scum. This alliance, however, was not, in their view, between equals. In fighting the scum and dealing with the trouble they caused, the police viewed themselves as professional, and contrasted their status and expertise with the helplessness and incompetence of the public. They were, they believed, not only more knowledgeable and experienced than the public, but more objective and impartial. This perceived inequality between police and public proved a chronic source of tension, as it seemed that the public did not always respect professionalism of the law enforcers or acknowledge their own incompetence as laymen.[5] This tension was a primary source of meaning for the set of images the police used to describe the public. Each of these images emphasized the professional distance between the police and the public. Together they identified three major themes which defined the police view of the proper relationship between the public and the police.

In emphasizing their own expertise, the police drew attention to the helplessness and stupidity of the public. As one policeman remarked, 'some of them don't have enough brains to pound sand.' The public, they complained, often created problems for themselves that could have been avoided had they had 'an ounce of brains.' The police felt that many of the problems brought to their attention by the public were trivial, and could have been handled by the victims themselves. Noise complaints were frequently used to illustrate this.

> It makes you sick, all you get on weekends are noisy parties. Why don't they go and bang on doors themselves?

> So why did he have to call us? The guy's a neighbour. Why doesn't he go and ask him to shut up his bloody dog himself?

Not only did the public report problems to the police that the police felt they should have been able to resolve themselves, but the police complained they were sometimes so helpless and incompetent that they could not even request police support properly. 'You have to be another Larry Solway sometimes. You have to put words in their mouths just to find out where they live or their phone numbers.'

While the public's stupidity was frequently defined in terms of their inability to prevent and deal with minor problems, it was also seen as arising from naiveté. The police believed that, as a result of the dramatization of the police role in novels, films, and television dramas, the public had developed unreasonable expectations concerning the police capacity to resolve problems. 'Some people think a policeman's uniform will make everything all right. But it only quietens things down for a little while. It really doesn't accomplish anything.'

This naiveté, the police believed, extended beyond a misunderstanding of police resources and even included a definition of 'police trouble.' A principal complaint was that the public simply did not know what an emergency was, and constantly exaggerated trivial incidents by calling them emergencies. For example, they frequently pointed out that what the public defined as an emergency often proved, on closer inspection, to be no more than a noisy party or a minor traffic accident. The conclusion drawn from all this by the police was that you could not rely on the public's judgement about what problems the police should deal with or how this should be done.

While it was the public's helplessness and incompetence that characterized them and their relationship to the police, it was their persistent failure to recognize and accept this that most annoyed the police. This failure was apparent in the public's tendency *to demand help rather than request it*, thus suggesting that the police related to them as servant to master. This failure to recognize the professional status of the police and their ability and authority to respond to trouble angered the police.[6] 'Send out a car immediately. It really bugs me when they say that.' This disrespect was regarded as particularly insulting when the demanding citizen was a low-status person who scarcely qualified as a member of the public.

> The thing that bugs me is getting a call from a person who can barely speak English, but demands a car 'right away'. The two things they know are 'dollar', and 'send police right away,' and they don't even speak the language. The woman had only called ten minutes ago so I said, 'There are two million people in the city and you are only one of them.'

These views about the public's right to demand police service, like the views about the helplessness and ignorance of the public, served to preserve police autonomy by emphasizing that while the police served the public, they were not to be viewed as servants of the public. This theme was taken up in a somewhat different form in the police view that members of the public sometimes used police to *exploit their relationship as allies*. They complained that the public were often not as helpless as they seemed. The public, they believed, sought to use the police to accomplish their own self-serving ends. The police became particularly incensed when persons misused their power and status for these reasons. In police eyes, one of the worst groups of offenders were private alarm companies who 'had the nerve' to ask the police to respond to their alarms for them.

> Alarm companies, they use the police. They get us to do their work for them.
> God damn phoney outfits. They call the owner and he says not to tell the police anything, so our car sits there at the scene waiting and waiting for someone to show.

It was, however, not only the economically powerful who sought to misuse the police—this tendency was seen as much more widespread. Often it was perceived as not more than the result of laziness and a refusal to take responsibility for problems.

> Very often people called about barking dogs because they do not want to get involved themselves. They want to leave it to the police to do something. Complaints about barking dogs just misuse the police. In the vast majority of cases, it is probably quite unnecessary to involve the police, except as a last resort. The thing to do would be to go directly to the dog's owner and ask him to take the dog inside or quiet it down some other way.

In emphasizing their professional status[7] the police culture served to insulate the police from members of the public who might try to influence them, and to encourage the police to rely on their own experience and the collective wisdom of their peers in making their decisions.

Just as the police subculture served to guard against the situated influences arising from the demands of particular complainants and victims, it also served to insulate the police from the more systematic influences directed at them through the chain of command. Interestingly, in this context the autonomy of the working policeman was encouraged by the police culture on the same grounds as it was with respect to the public—by emphasizing the inequality in expertise and 'know-how' between the working policeman and the brass (a term used to refer roughly to all those superiors in the chain of command above the rank of sergeant).

In distinguishing themselves from the brass, police constables recognized that, as policemen, they shared some things with the brass. It is with these similarities that we must begin, because they constitute the backdrop for their differences.

At the most general level, especially when the police were contrasted with the public, the brass were considered to be police. They had shared many of the experiences familiar to ordinary policemen — 'they had been there.' They had at one time been 'front line' policemen. Even now, a major concern of the brass was to protect and enhance the image of the police. Attacks on the police in the press, for example, served to break down the distinction between the brass and working policemen. When newspaper reporters, for example, criticized the brass, policemen would spring vigorously to their defence. 'There's always some nut who want to get the police into trouble and there's always some reporter who will listen to him.'

Yet the brass, although they had been working policemen, were now 'something quite different.' The concerns of the brass, it was argued, were not only different, but were often competing. When the 'chips were down,' the brass would sacrifice the individual policeman in the name of the 'interests of the force.' Policemen were not reluctant to point out that the 'interests of the force' overlapped with, and were often synonymous with, the 'interests of the brass.'...

The brass were accorded an explicitly ideological role and this role was seen as not only different from, but often opposed to, the demands of 'real' police work. This was emphasized by noting that their concern with 'political matters,' resulted in the brass losing touch with 'real police work' and 'real policemen.'

> They don't understand, and they don't care any more. They've been out of it for too long. Most of them have not done real police work for years. They don't know what police work is any more. They spend their time in their offices. You wonder sometimes. That's why they make all these procedures.
> When they get that commission something happens. They don't know you any more. They make new friends when they become officers....

The apparent ignorance of the brass, together with their tacit approval of 'real police work,' identified a role difference between the brass and working policemen. While the brass were concerned with maintaining an egalitarian image of the police within political and judicial arenas, working policemen were to get on with the job of real policing, or controlling the scum. In providing for this distinction, the police subculture at once encouraged police action which served to reproduce existing power structures, while isolating working policemen from influences which tended to mitigate against this. The police subculture, in contrasting 'real police work' with the brass's concern with legitimizing police work, enabled working policemen to move beyond the common sense view of the law as a set of behaviourally grounded instructions for identifying criminality, to a view of the law as a resource for justifying coercive control of the scum. Good police work, the police subculture made clear, meant participating in the class conflict between the public and scum in a way that could be justified retrospectively with reference to legal criteria—that is, to behavioural, universalistic, and egalitarian criteria....

Linkages to Power: Origins of the Police Subculture

This contrast between the conflict theory of the police subculture and the surrounding ideology raises a final query: Where does the social theory of the police subculture come from, and how does it come to reflect so exactly the class structure and class conflict in the face of an ideology that explicitly denies the applicability of status criteria to police work? Although these questions go beyond the scope of this paper, it is possible, from a review of the analysis presented, to suggest the general outline of an answer and the direction to be followed in developing this outline.

The independence of the police subculture, its low visibility, as well as its operation at the 'front line' of policing, is consistent with Foucault's (1977) analysis that social control is no longer imposed from above and outside the fabric of social life by an authority embodied in the person of the sovereign; rather, it is embedded in the very structure of social relations themselves. It is from this structure, rather than from an identifiable political authority, that the social theory of the police as state agents, participate in the social conflict between the productive and unproductive classes. Their position identifies them as allies of the one and enemies of the other. Within this context the police inevitably come face-to-face with the hostility of the scum. In dealing with this hostility, and in participating in the conflict between the scum and the public, they develop a particular view of the scum and an expertise that sets them apart from the public. In short, a guiding authority emerges which is grounded in the collective experience of working policemen. This authority reflects, in conceptual terms, the social differences and relationships in which it is located. In doing so, it provides a mechanism for transforming structural forces into individual motivations.

The embedded nature of this process gives the police subculture an anonymous and ubiquitous character that 'automatizes and disindividualizes' it (Foucault, 1977:202). It is this feature of modern social control that is reflected in the common sense talk of 'the system.' At first glance, as Foucault notes, this system appears to be 'nothing more than an infra-law' that extends 'the general forms defined by law to the infinitesimal level of individual lives' (1977:22). However, he argues, on closer examination these processes prove to be 'a sort of counter law' which effects 'a suspension of the law that is never totalled, but is never annulled either,' that maintains 'insuperable assymetries,' despite the legal definition of 'juridicial subjects according to universal norms,' by means of a 'series of mechanisms for unbalancing power relations definitively and everywhere' (Foucault, 1977: 222-3). On even closer inspection, as we have seen, the subterranean structures maintaining the asymmetries of power are revealed not as a 'counter law,' but as one face of the institutional hypocrisy that characterized liberal social control. These structures provide for a process of control through social conflict that by-pass political and legal processes at a macroscopic level. The independence of the political and legal superstructure from 'the system' of control that this provides permits those persons acting to legitimize social control within legal and political spheres to pursue egalitarian ideals energetically and with personal integrity, without undermining the work necessary to reproduce relations of dominance. Similarly, it allows the police, and others in similar positions, to get on with their work as participants in class conflict without undermining the belief in the egalitarian nature of liberal democracy.

It is the relationship between the superstructure and substructural levels of social control that frustrates Marxists committed to a utopian society without class conflict, because 'conquering or gaining access to the state through electoral means cannot lead to socialism since the working class party, when it takes over the government, becomes a prisoner of the very system it attempts to overthrow' (Burawoy, 1978: 60). For those of use who do not share this commitment, and who view social conflict in more neutral terms (Turk, 1977), the lesson is simply that the process of social conflict and the stability or change it produces cannot be understood by an analysis that focuses exclusively on political processes and ignores subterranean mechanisms.

Endnotes

This chapter was previously published in *The Canadian Review of Sociology and Anthropology*, Vol. 18 (3). Copyright © 1981 *The Canadian Review of Sociology and Anthropology*. Reprinted by permission.

[1] I would like to than my colleagues Richard Ericson, John Hagan, Jeff Leon, Dianne MacFarlane, Austin Turk and Livy Visano for their comments on this paper. I am grateful to Wanda Crause for her assistance with the field work....

[2] It has been argued (Cumming et al. 1967) that 'support' and 'control' constitute latent and manifest aspects of the police role. This view arises out of the tendency to regard citizens as all forming part of a single category. These findings indicate that support and control refer to two different role relationships with two different populations.

[3] See Kahne and Schwartz (1978) who criticize the Emmerson and Messinger formulation for its failure to consider the more general social contexts that affect actors' definitions of particular situated roles. As Emerson and Messinger's (1977) analysis demonstrates, if one remains analytically at a situational micropolitical level which excludes contextual relationships, decisions about statuses and roles must, of necessity, depend exclusively on an analysis of the activities of those involved. This is precisely the analytical difficulty that labelling theorists like Becker (1973) face in accounting for deviance. It leads them to identify deviance with rule-breaking and thus prevents them from examining how the claim of rule-breaking is used as a method (or weapon) in responding to deviance defined as a trans-situational 'essence' (see Katz, 1972).

[4] The account of operation of the police subculture permits us to answer some puzzling questions. For example, why is it that working policemen regard some statistically important parts of their job — for instance, domestic disputes and traffic work—as not 'real police work,' and why do 'crimes' of some—particularly the powerful—'go largely unrecognized and/or unpunished, while the less consequential (for society as a whole) offences of the lower class are given so much punitive attention'

[5] Hughes (1971) has argued that this tension is found in most service occupations.

[6] This time or disrespect for police authority dominates the literature on police subculture. However, this literature, as the criminal distinction between the disrespect of the scum as an enemy and the disrespect of the public as an ally is not made, disrespect is generally only considered in the context of the enemy metaphor.

[7] This denial or servant/employer relationship between the police and the public is related to the legal position the police hold vis a vis the sovereign authority from whom, it is argued, they derive an original authority (Call, 1975-77).

References

Ball, Richard A., 1978. Sociology and General Systems Theory." *The American Sociologist* 12 (1):65-72....

Becker, Howard S., 1973. *Outsiders: Studies in the Sociology of Deviance*. New York: Free Press.

Berger, Peter L. and Thomas Luckmann, 1967. *The Social Construction of Reality*. New York: Anchor Books....

Bittner, Egon, 1967. "The Police on Skid Row: A Study of Peace Keeping." *American Sociological Review* 32 (6): 699-715....

Black, Donald J., 1976. *The Behaviour of Law*. New York: Academic Press....

Buckner, H. Taylor, 1973. "Police Culture." Paper presented at the Canadian Sociological and Anthropological Association Meetings in Toronto (June).

Burawoy, Michael, 1978. "Contemporary Currents in Marxist Theory." *The American Sociologist* 13 (1): 50-64.

Call, Helen N., 1975-7. "The Enigma of a Police Constable's Status." Victoria University of Wellington Law Review 8: 148-69.

Canada, 1976. *The Report of the Commissions of Inquiry Relating to Public Complaints, Internal Discipline and Grievance Procedure with the Royal Canadian Mounted Police*. Ottawa: Department of Supply and Services....

Chambliss, William J. and Robert B. Seidman, 1971. *Law, Order and Power*. Don Mills, Ontario: Addison-Wesley Publishing Co....

Cumming, Elaine, Ian Cumming and Laura Edell, 1965. "Policeman as Philosopher, Guide and Friend." *Social Problems* 12(3): 276-86....

Emerson, Robert M. and Sheldon L. Messinger, 1977. "The Micro-Politics of Trouble." *Social Problems* 25(2): 121-34.

Foucault, Michel, 1977. *Discipline and Punish: The Birth of the Prison*. New York: Pantheon Books.

Giddens, Anthony, 1976. *New Rules of the Sociological Method*. London: Hutchinson....

Harris, R., 1973. *The Police Academy: An Inside View*. New York: John Wiley....

Hughes, Everett C., 1971. *The Sociological Eye: Selected Papers on Work, Self and the Study of Society*. Chicago and New York: Aldine-Atherton.

Kahne, Merton J. and Charlotte Green Schwartz, 1978. "Negotiating Trouble: The Social Construction and Management of Trouble in a College Psychiatric Context." *Social Problems* 25(5): 461-75.

Katz, Jack, 1972. "Deviance, Charisma and Rule-Defined Behaviour." *Social Problems* 20(2): 186-202....

Manning, Peter K., 1971. "The Police: Mandate, Strategies and Appearances." In Jack D. Douglas (ed.), *Crime and Justice in American Society*. New York: The Bobbs-Merrill Company, Inc....

Quinney, Richard, 1977. *Class, State and Crime: On the Theory and Practise of Criminal Justice*. New York: David McKay and Company, Inc....

Reiss, Albert, J. Jr., 1971. *The Police and the Public*. New Haven and London: Yale University Press....

Shearing, Clifford D., 1977. *Real Men, Good Men, Wise Men and Cautious Men*. Ph.D. dissertation, University of Toronto.

Shibutoni, T., 1970. *Human Nature and Collective Behaviour*. Englewood Cliffs: Prentice Hall.

Silver, Allan, 1967. "The Demand for Order in Civil Society: A Review of Some Themes in the History of Urban Crime, Police and Riot." In D.J. Bordua (ed.), *The Police: Six Sociological Essays*. New York: John Wiley and Sons, Inc....

Spitzer, Steven, 1975. "Toward a Marxian Theory of Deviance." *Social Problems* 22(5): 638-51.

Stewart, John J., 1978. "Critical Theory and the Critique of the Conservative Method." *The American Sociologist* 13(1): 15-22....

Turk, Austin T., 1969. *Criminality and Legal Order*. Chicago: Rand McNally.

Turk, Austin T., 1976. "Law as a Weapon in Social Conflict." *Social Problems* 23(3): 276-91.

Turk, Austin T., 1977. "Class, Conflict and Criminalization. *Sociological Focus* 10(3):209-20.

Westley, Wiliam A., 1953. "Violence and the Police." *American Journal of Sociology* 59(1): 34-41.

Westley, Wiliam A., 1956. "Secrecy and the Police." *Social Forces* 34(2): 254-7.

Westley, Wiliam A., 1970. *Violence and the Police: A Sociological Study of Law, Custom and Morality*. Cambridge, Mass: MIT Press.

Wexler, Mark N., 1974. "Police Culture: A Response to Ambiguous Employment." In C.L. Boydell, C.F. Grindstaff and P.C. Whitehead (eds.), *The Administration of Criminal Justice in Canada*. Toronto: Holt, Rinehart and Winston....

35

Wife Battering in Canada

Linda MacLeod

In this excerpt from Battered but not Beaten: Preventing Wife Battering in Canada, *author Linda McLeod begins by describing the two most commonly held theories concerning the origins and perpetuation of domestic violence. But McLeod goes on to demonstrate the theoretical need to take into account subjective experience in order to formulate an effective response to the problem. Specifically, she shows that the problem is rooted not only in the structure of society but also in the experience as defined by the battered woman. She points to the discrepancy between the intentions of service providers and the understanding of women in the situation. Until women's very real hopes about the relationship are taken into account, she suggests, the initiatives to combat this problem will continue to be limited in their effectiveness and frustrating to battered women and those who seek to help.*

Battered women and batterers come from all walks of life. They may be working outside the home or in the home. They may be unemployed or have a steady job. They may be rich or poor, well-educated or illiterate, of any nationality or race, young or old, with or without children.

Despite the difficulty of understanding wife battering, two major types of explanation have been widely used to respond to battered women, their children, and the men who batter them.

Linda McLeod, "Wife Battering in Canada" from *Battered but not Beaten: Preventing Wife Battering in Canada*, Ottwa: The Canadian Advisory Council on the Status of Women, 1987. [as reprinted in L. Tepperman, J. Curtis, S.J. Wilson and A. Wain, *Small World: International Readings in Sociology*, Prentice-Hall Canada, 1994: 219-226.]

Power-based Theories

These theories explain that violence against women is perpetuated by society's power structure which makes men dominant over women through the creation of separate and unequal roles for each gender. This dominance is reinforced through institutional rules and structures based on male supremacy.

As staff members of the Women's Research Centre in Vancouver have stated:

> Wife assault is a reality in our society because men have the socially ascribed authority to make the rules in marriage, and because violence against their wives is accepted in the eyes of society, as an appropriate instrument of control. The social and economic structure of marriage as an institution in which women are dependent on men, requires this assignment of authority to men.[1]

Power-base theories of wife battering emphasizing sex-based inequality and the patriarchal structure of society have gained acceptance by policy-makers and service-providers in this field. This explanation for wife battering appears in most writings on the subject and helps guide intervention services for battered women, their partners, and their children.

Research on the power dynamics in bettering families also asserts that power is more highly valued in battering families than in non-battering families. On the surface, this power may not always overtly rest with the man. However, research findings suggest that, in families where the woman is dominant in terms of decision-making or earning power, or where the woman is perceived to be superior in some other way, violence is often used by the man to shift the balance of power. Many counsellors reported that many men resort to physical violence when they feel their wives are more articulate than they are. These men frequently complain that they can't win an argument with their wives, so they "shut them up" by the use of force.

In power-based theories, the acceptance and social reinforcement of violence in the family is a means to establish and to maintain the male in a dominant relationship over his wife.

Because male roles are socially created as dominant over female roles,

> Wife assault arises out of the socio-cultural belief that women are less important and less valuable than men and so are not entitled to equal status and respect. Thus, central to the task of dealing with the problem of wife assault is the need to recognize that wife assault is a social problem experienced by many Canadian women each year rather than an isolated interpersonal problem between two particular spouses.[2]

Learning Theories

Learning theorists argue that witnessing or suffering violence teaches people to use violence to try to solve problems or deal with stress.[3] This argument is supported by research and by statements from service-providers which reveal that many batterers come from families where their mothers were battered and/or where they themselves were physically, sexually, or psychologically abused as children.[4] These findings are corroborated by the statistics collected for this study. Sixty-one percent of the partners of the women who stayed in transition houses in 1985 had been abused as children. Thirty-nine percent of the battered women reported being physically abused as children, 24 percent reported being sexually abused, and 48 percent reported being emotionally abused as well. Of the women who said they physically abused their own children, 69 percent said they had themselves been physically abused during their childhood.

Learning theorists also argue that the use of violence as a discipline tool can teach violence. In this vein, researchers report a "strong relationship between parental punishment and aggression" and suggest that

> increasing evidence indicates that a high price is paid for maintaining order in the family through violence. The norms that legitimate violence assure a family institution and a society characterized by violence for years to come.[5]

Learning theorists also frequently explain the perpetuation of violence by stating that victims, friends, and society as a whole unintentionally reinforce the violence.

> The victim after the beating, may indeed do as he insists; others may treat him with more respect and often he feels more in control. Even if he feels remorseful or guilty about her injuries he (and sometimes the victim herself) tends to blame the victim for "causing" him to "lose control." He denies responsibility for the negative behaviour. Due to the tacit acceptance of family violence in society and to the lack of clear messages that his violent behaviour must stop, his violence is rarely punished.[6]

Finally, learning theorists suggest that witnessing violence vicariously can teach some men to use violence within or outside the family. This tenet has created concern about pornography as a teaching tool for violence.

These types of explanations, one based on the structure of power in our society, the other on learning theory, have clarified our understanding of wife battering, and have helped to guide intervention efforts. Yet many shelter workers and other service-providers lamented, "These theories that seem so clear to us just don't seem to ring true for too many of the women who come to us."

How do Battered Women Understand the Battering?

Battered women speak of a shifting, ambiguous power. They spoke sometimes of feeling powerless against their partners. They also spoke of their power in the relationship and of the powerlessness of their partners. Many believe women are more powerful than men, as the quote below elucidates:

> I can't quite make sense of what the women here [at the shelter] are saying about the patriarchal structure of society and about power and society making men more powerful and all that. When I was growing up, my mother was for sure stronger than my Dad in every way but physically. She was smarter, could do more, and more people respected her. I think it's the same with my husband and me. There's no way he's stronger than me, except physically, and that's why he hits me, because he feels so low.

Other women elaborated this theme in terms of a mother-son model of relationships between themselves and their partners.

> My husband and all the men I've ever known are like little boys. We're really like their mothers, underneath. Everyone keeps telling me to leave him; they say he'll destroy me. But they don't know how strong I am and how weak he is underneath.

Others spoke of the power they feel in the relationship.

> Sure I feel sorry for him. He says he would have nothing without me and the kids. I know he's pretty rotten sometimes. But he really needs me. I guess that's why I keep going back. He makes me feel important.

Still others spoke of their partners as victims or losers in society.

> You can talk about men being powerful in our society if you want, but you're not talking about my husband. My husband's never had any power in his whole life. He's never had a chance. He was born poor. He was born Indian. He's never felt better than anyone. He's never felt better than me. It's because he's so low that he hits me.

Many battered women do not feel like powerless victims, and will not respond positively to services which treat them like victims instead of survivors.

These experiences remind us of the complexity of the realization of power in individual relationships. They also remind us that power in our society is not just gender-based; it is also class-, race-, and age-based.

Many battered women also understand battering as something that "got out of hand," as an extension of a normal part of a normal relationship. Many battered women feel their relationship started out much like any other relationship and, in fact, some emphasize that they feel they had an unusually loving, intense, and close relationship.

Intimate relationships, by definition, generate a wide range of emotions. The image of romantic love idealized in our society is characterized by highs and lows. Being "in love" is living "on the edge," participating in a kind of emotional aerobics. The socially accepted use of drugs, the preoccupation with "having it all," with creative stress, the fitness craze, and even our social addiction to soap operas and violent television shows emphasize high energy and intense emotional highs and lows.

For these reasons, wife battering at the outset is often difficult to prevent, or even to identify, because some violence (rough sexual play and psychological games intended to elicit jealousy) is intertwined with our ideal of "being in love" (isolation and possessiveness). In different socio-economic groups, this violence may be more or less psychological, or more or less physical, but the romantic desire to be alone together in a private world and the desire to have constant physical contact with your loved one are simply the "positive" faces of the jealousy and isolation which become part of most wife-battering experiences.

Battered women often talk of the intensity of their love for the batterer. Throughout this study, many battered women made the following kinds of statements: "I've never had better sex with anyone," "I just can't believe he'd hit me. I know he really loves me as much as I love him," "No one's ever loved me the way he does." Battered women also speak of the highs and lows of the relationship:

> You know, life was a roller-coaster with Bill. In the end, of course, that became unbearable—all the tension. But in the beginning, it was just so thrilling. I never wanted to come down.

Many battered women are guilty of no greater "weakness" than being in love with being in love. It's their attempt to stay in love, to retain an idealized vision of their partner, that often prevents many battered women from realizing they are being battered until the battering has become a part of life.

Women who are battered do not generally define themselves as battered the first time they are battered. In fact, because wife battering includes emotional, verbal, and financial battering, as well as physical and sexual battering, it may be difficult to define when the first incident actually occurred. This ambivalence is evident in the words battered women use to describe their early experiences with the batterer. It is not uncommon for battered women to say:

> I was flattered by his jealousy at first—I thought it meant he loved me. He said he would rather stay home, just with me, than go out with friends. I loved the attention and closeness at first. I thought he was the most romantic man in the world.

Even the first case of physical abuse is not always clear-cut. In many cases, the woman is "just pushed." While pushing can result in severe injuries, depending on the location of the push—down the stairs, over a chair, into a pot of boiling water on the stove, etc.—the push itself can be easily re-interpreted by the batterer and by the woman who is battered as something minor. The results of the push can be viewed as an accident.

> I was just baffled the first time he hit me. It wasn't really a hit, you know, not like a punch or even a slap; he just pushed me really hard. I broke an arm, but it was from falling backward over a chair, not from his push.

Another woman's statement mirrors these sentiments:

> I couldn't believe my husband had hit me. I just kept asking, is this the same man who loves me so much that he can't stand it if another man talks to me? It was really easy for me to accept his explanation that he'd had a hard day at work and a little too much to drink. I couldn't see anything else without having to ask if he really did love me, and that was just too painful. It wasn't until much later, years of violence later, that I could see that the way he loved me—his jealousy, his possessiveness—were also part of the violence.

Is this "illogic" really so different from the logic which we call compromising, or "forgiving and forgetting," when it does not involve identifiable violence?

While violence almost always escalates, it may not do so for months or years. The result is that women accept the violence as unpleasant but bearable, given the good things about the relationships (and most battering relationships do still provide sporadic periods of closeness during the honeymoon phases of the violence) until they are so enmeshed in the cycle of violence and so demoralized and trapped by it that they can't "just leave."

Many service-providers, and even women who have been battered, counsel that leaving or calling the police "the first time it happens" is the most effective way to ensure it won't happen again. However, given that it may be hard to define "that first incident," especially since definitions of intolerable violence are culturally relative and since most women have a lot of emotional and practical investment in their relationships, this advice frequently has an unreal, hollow ring to it.

American author Susan Schechter points to the "normalcy" of the early reactions of most battered women, at least in terms of the current "rules" of intimate relationships, in her comment: "Most people feel ambivalent when ending a long-term relationship, Major change is always difficult, often slowly and haltingly undertaken.[7]

There is growing evidence that leaving provides no guarantee the battering will stop and may even escalate the violence. In the present study, 12 percent of the women were separated or divorced. Anecdotal information suggests the majority of these women were battered by their ex-husbands, some by new partners. Michael Smith, in his telephone survey of 315 Toronto women, found that, while the rate of abuse for all women interviewed was 18.1 percent, for women who were separated or divorced, the rate jumped to 42.6 percent.[8]

The reactions of most battered women are often strong and logical and must be treated this way if we are to reach out to battered women and provide services for them which "ring true," will be helpful, and will be used by a greater number of battered women. It is easy to scoff at, or be discouraged by, the astonished response of many women to the suggestion that they leave their violent husbands: "But he's my husband, and the father of my children. I can't just abandon him." It's easy from an outside vantage point which assumes the batterer, the battered wife, their relationship, or all three are defective, to dismiss as misguided sentiment the woman's heroic attempts to keep her marriage together, to keep her children from knowing about the violence, to insist that she loves her husband. The woman's actions and statements are easy to dismiss as long as we assume the battered woman, along with her partner and their relationship, are somehow different from us in terms of the basic personality of the man and woman and in terms of the initial quality of the relationship.

However, as this study has established repeatedly, research shows that battered women do not fit one psychological or socio-economic mould. Few common characteristics which are not the direct result of the battering have been cited. In fact, in the one study known to the author where the personality traits of battered women *before* the violence were discussed, Lenore Walker found women who are battered "perceive themselves as more liberal than most" in their relationships with men[9]—a far cry from the stereotype of the battered woman as a traditional women totally oppressed by, and dependent on, her partner.

It is *after* prolonged battering, as a result of the battering, that battered women begin to display certain similar psychological traits. After prolonged battering, women suffer from low self-esteem and isolation. They are emotionally dependent on the batterer, are compliant, feel guilty, and blame themselves for the violence, and yet demonstrate great loyalty to the batterer. Not only do they want the relationship to continue, they state they are staying for the sake of the family. They believe the batterers' promises to change and frequently believe the violence would stop if only their partners would get the one lucky break they've always wanted.[10]

To understand the actions and perceptions of battered women, it is important to think of how we all act in relationships, what we want, and the extent to which many of us will go to preserve a relationship. As one shelter worker poignantly said:

> Relationships are hard to come by. Sure we should help women know that they have worth outside their marriages, but a marriage isn't just status and a piece of paper... it's warmth, belonging, and a future. Battered women don't always get these good things out of their relationships, but most of them did in the beginning, and they just keep hoping it will come back. People will go to any lengths to feel loved, and love is not just waiting around the next corner for every battered woman who leaves her batterer.

Even the majority of women who report the violence do so out of hope that she and her partner will be helped to return to their pre-violent state. Of course, she may also hope she will get attention and be listened to because she is frequently lonely and unnurtured as a result of the isolation most batterers impose on their victims. She may also hope he will be punished or "get his just desserts." But behind it all, she often just wants them to be happy again. The importance of these hopes should not be diminished.

Unfortunately many of the services which have been created for battered women and for their partners have been built on the assumption that the relationship is not worth saving and ignore or belittle the woman's hopes to save and rekindle it. The hope of the service-providers is most often to save or protect the woman as an individual or to help or change the batterer as an individual in some way. This well-intentioned, institutional hope often buries the woman's pleas for a different kind of help. This discrepancy between the battered woman's hopes and the hopes of the service-providers renders many of the initiatives taken inappropriate and frustrating for the women who are battered and contributes to the burnout and despair of the people who try to help the women, their children, and their partners.

Endnotes

[1] Helga Jacobsen, Co-ordinator. *A Study of Protection for Battered Women* (Vancouver: Women's Research Centre, 1982), p. 5.

[2] Marion Boyd, ed. *Handbook for Advocates and Counsellors of Battered Women* (London, Ontario: London Battered Women's Advocacy Clinic Inc., 1985), pp. 12-13.
[3] Anne Ganley, "Causes and Characteristics of Battering Men," in *Wife Assault Information Kit* (Victoria: Ministry of the Attorney General. April 1986), pp. 68-69.
[4] Research supporting this hypothesis is summarized in Straus and Hotaling, *The Social Causes*, pp. 14-15.
[5] *Ibid.*, p. 15.
[6] Ganley, "Causes and Characteristics," p. 70.
[7] Susan Schechter, *Women and Male Violence: The Visions and Struggles of the Battered Women's Movement* (Boston: South End Press, 1982), p. 20.
[8] Michael D. Smith, *Woman Abuse: The Case for Surveys by Telephone*. The LaMarsh Research Programme Reports on Violence and Conflict Resolution. Report #12 (Toronto: York University, November 1985), p. 29.
[9] Walker, "The Battered Woman Syndrome Study," p. 8.
[10] Alberta, Social Services and Community Health, *Breaking the Pattern: How Alberta Communities Can Help Assaulted Women and Their Families* (Edmonton: November 1985), p. 17.

36

The Body of the Condemned

Michel Foucault

The nature of social control in western industrial societies has changed over the last two hundred years. As this excerpt from Foucault's Discipline and Punish *indicates, the change is most poignantly seen in the shift from the spectacle of punishment to the discipline of the prison. Foucault analyses this shift and examines how our ideas of punishment and justice are related to the human body. Are these ideas also reflected in other examples of social control in modern society?*

On 2 March 1757 Damiens the regicide was condemned "to make the *amende honorable* before the main door of the Church of Paris," where he was to be "taken and conveyed in a cart, wearing nothing but a shirt, holding a torch of burning wax weighting two pounds"; then, "in the said cart, to the Place de Grève, where, on a scaffold that will be erected there, the flesh will be torn from his breasts, arms, thighs and calves with red-hot pincers, his right hand, holding the knife with which he committed the said parricide, burnt with sulphur, and, on those places where the flesh will be torn away, poured molten lead, boiling oil, burning resin, wax and sulphur melted together and then his body drawn and quartered by four horses and his limbs and body consumed by fire, reduced to ashes and his ashes thrown to the winds" (*Pièces originales...*, 372-4).

Bouton, an officer of the watch, left us his account:

> The sulphur was lit, but the flame was so poor that only the top skin of the hand was burnt, and that only slightly. Then the executioner, his sleeves rolled up, took the steel pincers, which had been especially made for the occasion, and which were about a foot and a half long, and pulled first at the calf of the

---

Michel Foucault, "The Body of the Condemned" from *Discipline and Punish: The Birth of the Prison*, New York: Vintage/Random House, 1977. Copyright © 1975 by Éditions Gallimard. Reprinted by permission of Georges Borchardt, Inc.

right leg, then at the thigh, and from there at the two fleshy parts of the right arm; then at the breasts. Though a strong, sturdy fellow, this executioner found it so difficult to tear away the pieces of flesh that he set about the same spot two or three times, twisting the pincers as he did so, and what he took away formed at each part a wound about the size of a six-pound crown piece.

After these tearings with the pincers, Damiens, who cried out profusely, though without swearing, raised his head and looked at himself; the same executioner dipped an iron spoon in the pot containing the boiling potion, which he poured liberally over each wound. Then the ropes that were to be harnessed to the horses were attached with cords to the patient's body; the horses were then harnessed and placed alongside the arms and legs, one at each limb.

Eighty years later, Léon Faucher drew up his rules "for the House of young prisoners in Paris":

- Art. 17. The prisoner's day will begin at six in the morning in winter and at five in summer. They will work for nine hours a day throughout the year. Two hours a day will be devoted to instruction. Work and the day will end at nine o'clock in winter and at eight in summer.
- Art. 18. *Rising.* At the first drum-roll, the prisoners must rise and dress in silence, as the supervisor opens the cell doors. At the second drum-roll, they must be dressed and make their beds. At the third they must line up and proceed to the chapel for morning prayer. There is a five minute interval between each drum-roll.
- Art. 19. The prayers are conducted by the chaplain and followed by a moral or religious reading. This exercise must not last more than half an hour.
- Art. 20. *Work.* At a quarter to six in the summer, a quarter to seven in winter, the prisoners go down into the courtyard where they must wash their hands and faces, and receive their first ration of bread. Immediately afterwards, they form into work-teams and go off to work, which must begin at six in summer and seven in winter.
- Art. 21. *Meal.* At ten o'clock the prisoners leave their work and go to the refectory; they wash their hands in their courtyards and assemble in divisions. After the dinner, there is recreation until twenty minutes to eleven.
- Art. 22. *School.* At twenty minutes to eleven, at the drum-roll, the prisoners form into ranks, and proceed in divisions to the school. The class lasts two hours and consists alternately of reading, writing, drawing and arithmetic.

Art. 23. At twenty minutes to one, the prisoners leave the school, in divisions, and return to their courtyards for recreation. At five minutes to one, at the drum-roll, they form into work-teams.

Art. 24. At one o'clock they must be back in the workshops: they work until four o'clock.

Art. 25. At four o'clock the prisoners leave their workshops and go into the courtyards where they wash their hands and form into divisions for the refectory.

Art. 26. Supper and the recreation that follows it last until five o'clock: the prisoners then return to the workshops.

Art. 27. At seven o'clock in the summer, at eight in winter, work stops; bread is distributed for the last time in the workshops. For a quarter of an hour one of the prisoners or supervisors reads a passage from some instructive or uplifting work. This is followed by evening prayer.

Art. 28. At half-past seven in summer, half-past eight in winter, the prisoners must be back in their cells after the washing of hands and the inspection of clothes in the courtyard; at the first drum-roll, they must undress, and at the second get into bed. The cell doors are closed and the supervisors go the rounds in the corridors, to ensure order and silence (Faucher, 274-82).

We have, then, a public execution and a time-table. They do not punish the same crimes or the same type of delinquent. But they each define a certain penal style. Less than a century separates them. It was a time when, in Europe and in the United States, the entire economy of punishment was redistributed. It was a time of great "scandals" for traditional justice, a time of innumerable projects for reform. It was a new theory of law and crime, a new moral or political justification of the right to punish; old laws were abolished, old customs died out.

Among so many changes, I shall consider one: the disappearance of torture as a public spectacle. Today we are rather inclined to ignore it; perhaps, in its time, it gave rise to too much inflated rhetoric; perhaps it has been attributed too readily and too emphatically to a process of "humanization," thus dispensing with the need for further analysis. And, in any case, how important is such a change, when compared with the great institutional transformations, the formulation of explicit, general codes and unified rules of procedure; with the almost universal adoption of the jury system, the definition of the essentially corrective character of the penalty and the tendency, which has become increasingly marked since the nineteenth century, to adapt punishment to the individual offender? Punishment of a less immediately physical kind, a certain discretion in the art of inflicting pain, a combination of more subtle, more subdued sufferings, deprived of their visible display, should not all this be treated as a special case, an incidental effect of deeper changes? And yet the fact remains that a few decades saw the disappearance of the tortured, dismembered, amputated body, symbolically branded on face or shoulder, exposed alive or dead to public view. The body as the major target of penal repression disappeared.

By the end of the eighteenth and the beginning of the nineteenth century, the gloomy festival of punishment was dying out, though here and there it flickered momentarily into life. In this transformation, two processes were at work. They did not have quite the same chronology or the same *raison d'être*. The first was the disappearance of punishment as a spectacle. The ceremonial of punishment tended to decline; it survived only as a new legal or administrative practice. It was as if the punishment was thought to equal, if not to exceed, in savagery the crime itself, to accustom the spectators to a ferocity from which one wished to divert them, to show them the frequency of crime, to make the executioner resemble a criminal, judges murders, to reverse roles at the last moment, to make the tortured criminal an object of pity or admiration. As early as 1764, Beccaria remarked: "The murder that is depicted as a horrible crime is repeated in cold blood, remorselessly" (Beccaria, 101). The public execution is now seen as a hearth in which violence bursts again into flame.

Punishment, then, will tend to become the most hidden part of the penal process. This has several consequences: it leaves the domain of more or less everyday perception and enters that of abstract consciousness; its effectiveness is seen as resulting from its inevitability, not from its visible intensity; it is the certainty of being punished and not the horrifying spectacle of public punishment that must discourage crime; the exemplary mechanics of punishment changes its mechanisms. As a result, justice no longer takes public responsibility for the violence that is bound up with its practice. If it too strikes, if it too kills, it is not as a glorification of its strength, but as an element of itself that it is obliged to tolerate, that it finds difficult to account for. The apportioning of blame is redistributed: in punishment-as-spectacle a confused horror spread from the scaffold; it enveloped both executioner and condemned; and although it was always ready to invert the shame inflicted on the victim into pity or glory, it often turned the legal violence of the executioner into shame. Now the scandal and the light are to be distributed differently; it is the conviction itself that marks the offender with the unequivocally negative sign: the publicity has shifted to the trial, and to the sentence; the execution itself is like an additional shame that justice is ashamed to impose on the condemned man; so it keeps its distance from the act, tending always to entrust it to others, under the seal of secrecy. It is ugly to be punishable, but there is no glory in punishing. Hence that double system of protection that justice has set up between itself and the punishment it imposes. Those who carry out the penalty tend to become an autonomous sector; justice is relieved of responsibility for it by a bureaucratic concealment of the penalty itself. It is typical that in France the administration of the prisons should for so long have been the responsibility of the Ministry of the Interior, while responsibility for the *bagnes*, for penal servitude in the convict ships and penal settlements, lay with the Ministry of the Navy or the Ministry of the Colonies. And beyond this distribution of roles operates a theoretical disavowal: do not imagine that the sentences that we judges pass are activated by a desire to punish; they are intended to correct, reclaim, "cure"; a technique of improvement represses, in the penalty, the strict expiation of evil-doing, and relieves the magistrates of the demeaning task of punishing. In modern justice and on the part of those who dispense it there is a shame in punishing, which does not always preclude zeal. This sense of shame is constantly growing: the psychologists and the minor civil servants of moral orthopaedics proliferate on the wound it leaves.

The disappearance of public executions marks therefore the decline of the spectacle; but it also marks a slackening of the hold on the body. Generally speaking, punitive practices had become more reticent. One no longer touched the body, or at least as little as possible, and then only to reach something other than the body itself. It might be objected that imprisonment, confinement, forced labour, penal servitude, prohibition from entering certain areas, deportation—which have occupied so important a place in modern penal systems—are "physical" penalties: unlike fines, for example, they directly affect the body. But the punishment-body relation is not the same as it was in the torture during public executions. The body now serves as an instrument or intermediary: if one intervenes upon it to imprison it, or to make it work, it is in order to deprive the individual of a liberty that is regarded both as a right and as property. The body, according to this penalty, is caught up in a system of constraints and privations, obligations and prohibitions. Physical pain, the pain of the body itself, is no longer the constituent element of the penalty. From being an art of unbearable sensations punishment has become an economy of suspended rights. If it is still necessary for the law to reach and manipulate the body of the convict, it will be at a distance, in the proper way, according to strict rules, and with a much "higher" aim. As a result of this new restraint, a whole army of technicians took over from the executioner, the immediate anatomist of pain: warders, doctors, chaplains, psychiatrists, psychologists, educationalists; by their very presence near the prisoner, they sing the praises that the law needs: they reassure it that the body and pain are not the ultimate objects of its punitive action. Today a doctor must watch over those condemned to death, right up to the last moment—thus juxtaposing himself as the agent of welfare, as the alleviator of pain, with the official whose task it is to end life. This is worth thinking about. When the moment of execution approaches, the patients are injected with tranquillizers. A utopia of judicial reticence: take away life, but prevent the patient from feeling it; deprive the prisoner of all rights, but do not inflict pain; impose penalties free of all pain. Recourse to psycho-pharmacology and to various physiological "disconnectors," even if it is temporary, is a logical consequence of this "non-corporal" penalty.

The modern rituals of execution attest to this double process: the disappearance of the spectacle and the elimination of pain. The same movement has affected the various European legal systems, each at its own rate: the same death for all—execution no longer bears the specific mark of the crime or the social status of the criminal; a death that lasts only a moment—no torture must be added to it in advance, no further actions performed upon the corpse; an execution that affects life rather than the body. Punishment had no doubt ceased to be centred on torture as a technique of pain; it assumed as its principal object loss of wealth or rights. But a punishment like forced labour or even imprisonment—mere loss of liberty—has never functioned without a certain additional element of punishment that certainly concerns the body itself: rationing of food, sexual deprivation, corporal punishment, solitary confinement. Are these the unintentional, but inevitable, consequence of imprisonment? In fact, in its most explicit practices, imprisonment has always involved a certain degree of physical pain. The criticism that was often levelled at the penitentiary system in the early nineteenth century (imprisonment is not a sufficient punishment: prisoners are less hungry, less cold, less deprived in general than many poor people or even workers) suggests a postulate that was never explicitly denied: it is just that a condemned man should suffer physically more than other men. It is difficult to dissociate punishment from additional physical pain. What would a non-corporal punishment be?

There remains, therefore, a trace of "torture" in the modern mechanisms of criminal justice—a trace that has not been entirely overcome, but which is enveloped, increasingly, by the non-corporal nature of the penal system.

The reduction in penal severity in the last 200 years is a phenomenon with which legal historians are well acquainted. But, for a long time, it has been regarded in an overall way as a quantitative phenomenon: less cruelty, less pain, more kindness, more respect, more "humanity." In fact, these changes are accompanied by a displacement in the very object of the punitive operation. Is there a diminution of intensity? Perhaps. There is certainly a change of objective.

If the penalty in its most severe forms no longer address itself to the body, on what does it lay hold? The answer of the theoreticians—those who, about 1760 opened up a new period that is not yet at an end—is simple, almost obvious. It seems to be contained in the question itself: since it is no longer the body, it must be the soul. The expiation that once rained down upon the body must be replaced by a punishment that acts in depth on the heart, the thoughts, the will, the inclinations. Mably formulated the principle once and for all: "Punishment, if I may so put it, should strike the soul rather than the body" (Mably, 326).

During the 150 or 200 years that Europe has been setting up its new penal systems, the judges have gradually, by means of a process that goes back very far indeed, taken to judging something other than crimes, namely, the "soul" of the criminal.

And, by that very fact, they have begun to do something other than pass judgment. Or, to be more precise, within the very judicial modality of judgment, other types of assessment have slipped in, profoundly altering its rules of elaboration. Ever since the Middle Ages slowly and painfully built up the great procedure of investigation, to judge was to establish the truth of a crime, it was to determine its author and to apply a legal punishment. Knowledge of the offence, knowledge of the offender, knowledge of the law: these three conditions made it possible to ground a judgment in truth. But now a quite different question of truth is inscribed in the course of the penal judgment. The question is no longer simply: "Has the act been established and is it punishable?" But also: "What *is* the act, what *is* this act of violence or this murder? To what level or to what field of reality does it belong? Is it a fantasy, a psychotic reaction, a delusional episode, a perverse action?" It is no longer simply: "Who committed it?" But: "How can we assign the causal process that produced it? Where did it originate in the author himself? Instinct, unconscious, environment, heredity?" It is no longer simply: "What law punishes this offence?" But: "What would be the most appropriate measures to take? How do we see the future development of the offender? What would be the best way of rehabilitating him?" A whole set of assessing, diagnostic, prognostic, normative judgments concerning the criminal have become lodged in the framework of penal judgment. Another truth has penetrated the truth that was required by the legal machinery; a truth which, entangled with the first, has turned the assertion of guilt into a strange scientifico-juridical complex. A significant fact is the way in which the question of madness has evolved in penal practice. Already the reform of 1832, introducing attenuating circumstances, made it possible to modify the sentence according to the supposed degrees of an illness or the forms of a semi-insanity. And the practice of calling on psychiatric expertise, which is widespread in the assize courts and sometimes extended to courts of summary jurisdiction, means that the sentence, even if it always formulated in terms of legal punishment, implies, more or less obscurely, judgments of normality, attributions of causality, assessments of possible changes, anticipations as to the offender's future. And the sentence that condemns or acquits is not simply a judgment of guilt, a legal decision that lays down punishment; it bears within it an assessment of normality and a technical prescription for a possible normalization. Today the judge—magistrate or juror—certainly does more than "judge."

And he is not alone in judging. Throughout the penal procedure and the implementation of the sentence there swarms a whole series of subsidiary authorities. Small-scale legal systems and parallel judges have multiplied around the principal judgment: psychiatric or psychological experts, magistrates concerned with the implementation of sentences, educationalists, members of the prison service, all fragment the legal power to punish; it might be objected that none of them really shares the right to judge; that some, after sentence is passed, have no other right than to implement the punishment laid down by the court and, above all, that others—the experts—intervene before the sentence not to pass judgment, but to assist the judges in their decision.

To sum up, ever since the new penal system—that defined by the great codes of the eighteenth and nineteenth centuries—has been in operation, a general process has led judges to judge something other than crimes; they have been led in their sentences to do something other than judge; and the power of judging has been transferred, in part, to other authorities than the judges of the offence. The whole penal operation has taken on extra-juridical elements and personnel. It will be said that there is nothing extraordinary in this, that it is part of the destiny of the law to absorb little by little elements that are alien to it. But what is odd about modern criminal justice is that, although it has taken on so many extra-juridical elements, it has done so not in order to be able to define them juridically and gradually to integrate them into the actual power to punish: on the contrary, it has done so in order to make them function within the penal operation as non-juridical elements; in order to stop this operation being simply a legal punishment; in order to exculpate the judge from being purely and simply he who punishes.

> Of course, we pass sentence, but this sentence is not in direct relation to the crime. It is quite clear that for us it functions as a way of treating a criminal. We punish, but this is a way of saying that we wish to obtain a cure.

Today, criminal justice functions and justifies itself only by this perpetual reference to something other than itself, by this unceasing reinscription in non-juridical systems.

But we can surely accept the general proposition that, in our societies, the systems of punishment are to be situated in a certain "political economy" of the body: even if they do not make use of violent or bloody punishment, even when they use "lenient" methods involving confinement or correction, it is always the body that is at issue—the body and its forces, their utility and their docility, their distribution and their submission. It is certainly legitimate to write a history of punishment against the background of moral ideas or legal structures. But can one write such a history against the background of a history of bodies, when such systems of punishment claim to have only the secret souls of criminals as their objective?

Historians long ago began to write the history of the body. They have studied the body in the field of historical demography or pathology; they have considered it as the seat of needs and appetites, as the locus of processes and metabolisms, as a target for the attacks of germs or viruses; they have shown to what extent historical processes were involved in what might seem to be the purely biological base of existence; and what place should be given in the history of society to biological "events" such as the circulation of bacilli, or the extension of the life-span (cf. Le Roy-Ladurie 1974). But the body is also directly involved in a political field; power relations have an immediate hold upon it; they invest it, mark it, train it, torture it, force it to carry out tasks, to perform ceremonies, to emit signs. This political investment of the body is bound up, in accordance with complex reciprocal relations, with its economic use; it is largely as a force of production that the body is invested with relations of power and domination; but, on the other hand, its constitution as labour power is possible only if it is caught up in a system of subjection (in which need is also a political instrument meticulously prepared, calculated and used); the body becomes a useful force only if it is both a productive body and subjected body. This subjection is not only obtained by the instruments of violence or ideology; it can also be direct, physical, pitting force against force, bearing on material elements, and yet without involving violence; it may be calculated, organized, technically thought out; it may be subtle, make use neither of weapons nor of terror and yet remain of a physical order. That is to say, there may be a "knowledge" of the body that is not exactly the science of its functioning, and a mastery of its forces that is more than the ability to conquer them: this knowledge and this mastery constitute what might be called the political technology of the body. Of course, this technology is diffuse, rarely formulated in continuous, systematic discourse; it is often made up of bits and pieces; it implements a disparate set of tools or methods. In spite of the coherence of its results, it is generally no more than a multiform instrumentation. Moreover, it cannot be localized in a particular type of institution or state apparatus. For they have recourse to it; they use, select or impose certain of its methods. But, in its mechanisms and its effects, it is situated at a quite different level. What the apparatuses and institutions operate is, in a sense, a micro-physics of power, whose field of validity is situated in a sense between these great functionings and the bodies themselves with their materiality and their forces.

One might imagine a political "anatomy." This would not be the study of a state in terms of a "body" (with its elements, its resources and its forces), nor would it be the study of the body and its surroundings in terms of a small state. One would be concerned with the "body politic," as a set of material elements and techniques that serve as weapons, relays, communication routes and supports for the power and knowledge relations that invest human bodies and subjugate them by turning them into objects of knowledge.

It is a question of situating the techniques of punishment—whether they seize the body in the ritual of public torture and execution or whether they are addressed to the soul—in the history of this body politic; of considering penal practices less as a consequence of legal theories than as a chapter of political anatomy.

It would be wrong to say that the soul is an illusion, or an ideological effect. On the contrary, it exists, it has a reality, it is produced permanently around, on, within the body of the functioning of a power that is exercised on those punished—and, in a more general way, on those one supervises, trains and corrects, over madmen, children at home and at school, the colonized, over those who are stuck at a machine and supervised for the rest of their lives. This is the historical reality of the soul, which, unlike the soul represented by Christian theology, is not born in sin and subject to punishment, but is born rather out of methods of punishment, supervision and constraint. This real, non-corporal soul is not a substance; it is the element in which are articulated the effects of a certain type of power and the reference of a certain type of knowledge, the machinery by which the power relations give rise to a possible corpus of knowledge, and knowledge extends and reinforces the effects of this power. On this reality reference, various concepts have been constructed and domains of analysis carved out: psyche, subjectivity, personality, consciousness, etc.; on it have been built scientific techniques and discourses, and the moral claims of humanism. But let there be no misunderstanding: it is not that a real man, the object of knowledge, philosophical reflection or technical intervention, has been substituted for the soul, the illusion of the theologians. The man described for us, whom we are invited to free, is already in himself the effect of a subjection much more profound than himself. A "soul" inhabits him and brings him to existence, which is itself a factor in the mastery that power exercises over the body. The soul is the effect and instrument of a political anatomy; the soul is the prison of the body.

That punishment in general and the prison in particular belong to a political technology of the body is a lesson that I have learnt not so much from history as from the present. In recent years, prison revolts have occurred throughout the world. There was certainly something paradoxical about their aims, their slogans and the way they took place. They were revolts against an entire state of physical misery that is over a century old: against cold, suffocation and overcrowding, against decrepit walls, hunger, physical maltreatment. But they were also revolts against model prisons, tranquillizers, isolation, the medical or educational services. Were they revolts whose aims were merely material? Or contradictory revolts: against the obsolete, but also against comfort; against the warders, but also against the psychiatrists? In fact, all these movements—and the innumerable discourses that the prison has given rise to since the early nineteenth century—have been about the body and material things. What has sustained these discourses, these memories and invectives are indeed those minute material details. One may, if one is so disposed, see them as no more than blind demands or suspect the existence behind them of alien strategies. In fact, they were revolts, at the level of the body, against the very body of the prison. What was at issue was not whether the prison environment was too harsh or too aseptic, too primitive or too efficient, but its very materiality as an instrument and vector of power; it is this whole technology of power over the body that the technology of the "soul"—that of the educationalist, psychologists and psychiatrists—fails either to conceal or to compensate, for the simple reason that it is one of its tools.

References

Beccaria, C. de, *Traité des délits et des peines.* 1764, ed. 1856.
Faucher, L., *De la réforme des prisons.* 1838.
Le Roy-Ladurie, E., *Contrepoint.* 1973.
Le Roy-Ladurie, E., "L'histoire immobile," *Annales.* May-June, 1974.
Mably, G. de, *De la législation,* Oeuvres complètes, IX, 1789.
Pièces originales et procédures du procès fait à Robert-François Damiens, III, 1757.

Section Ten

Social Change

Globalization is not the same as imperialism, though the two have some shared characteristics. In particular, it is not carried by nation states; indeed, its progress requires the erasure of national borders and the dwindling of nation-state capacities to impose controls on the movement and application of capital. The capital itself often has no single national origin, and its loyalty to any particular country is notoriously shallow. It comes with accountants, engineers—even some social scientists—rather than with military backup, and its chief technology is the computer rather than the gun, but it can be lethal in its penetration of regional economies, control of markets and the restructuring of societies.

Patricia Marchak, "The Social Sciences in a Global Economy and a Single Planet," *Society/Société: Newsletter of the Canadian Sociology and Anthropology Association*, Vol. 20, No. 1 (Feb, 1996): 7.

Tradition is sacred only so long as it is useful.

Everett C. Hughes, as quoted in H. Guindon, *Quebec Society: Tradition, Modernity and Nationhood*, University of Toronto, 1988: 137.

37

English Society Before and After the Coming of Industry

Peter Laslett

Historically, England was the first society in the world to undergo the "industrial revolution," a process which, so far, has been central to the emergence of modern societies. But, as this excerpt from Laslett's larger study indicates, industrialization refers to more than changing the basis of a society's economy from agriculture to industry. What are the principal social and cultural changes that also are involved in industrialization?

In the year 1619 the bakers of London applied to the authorities for an increase in the price of bread. They sent in support of their claim a complete description of a bakery. There were thirteen or fourteen people in such an undertaking: the baker and his wife, four paid employees who were called journeymen, two apprentices, two maidservants and the three or four children of the master baker himself.

A London bakery was undoubtedly what we should call a commercial or even an industrial undertaking, turning out loaves by the thousand. Yet the business was carried on in the house of the baker himself. There was probably a *shop* as part of the house, *shop* as in *workshop* and not as meaning a retail establishment. Most of the house was taken up with the living-quarters of the dozen people who worked there.

It is obvious that all these people ate in the house since the cost of their food helped to determine the production cost of the bread. Except for the journeymen they were all obliged to sleep in the house at night and live together as a family.

Peter Laslett, "English Society Before and After the Coming of Industry" from *The World We Have Lost*, London, Methuen, 1979. [as reprinted in L. Tepperman, J. Curtis, S.J. Wilson and A. Wain, *Small World: International Readings in Sociology*, Prentice-Hall, 1994: 16-20.]

The Family Setting

The only word used at that time to describe such a group was "family." The man at the head of the group, the employer, or the manager, was then known as the master or head of the family. He was father to some of its members and in place of father to the rest. There was no sharp distinction between his domestic and his economic functions. His wife was both his partner and his subordinate, a partner because she ran the family, took charge of the food and managed the women-servants, a subordinate because she was woman and wife, mother and in place of mother to the rest.

The paid servants of both sexes had their specified and familiar position in the family, as much part of it as the children but not quite in the same position. At that time the family was not one society only but three societies fused together; the society of man and wife, of parents and children and of master and servant. But when they were young, and servants were, for the most part, young, unmarried people, they were very close to children in their status and their function. Here is the agreement made between the parents of a boy about to become an apprentice and his future master. The boy covenants to dwell with his master for seven years, to keep his secrets and to obey his commandments.

> Taverns and alehouses he shall not haunt, dice, cards or any other unlawful games he shall not use, fornication with any woman he shall not commit, matrimony with any women he shall not contract. He shall not absent himself by night or by day without his master's leave but be a true and faithful servant.

On his side, the master undertakes to teach his apprentice his "*art, science or occupation with moderate correction.*"

> Finding and allowing unto his said servant meat, drink, apparel, washing, lodging and all other things during the said term of seven years, and to give unto his said apprentice at the end of the said term double apparel, to wit, one suit for holydays and one suit for worken days.

Apprentices, therefore, and many other servants, were workers who were also children, extra sons or extra daughters (for girls could be apprenticed too), clothed and educated as well as fed, obliged to obedience and forbidden to marry, often unpaid and dependent until after the age of twenty-one. If such servants were workers in the position of sons and daughters, the sons and daughters of the house were workers too. John Locke laid it down in 1697 that the children of the poor must work for some part of the day when they reached the age of three. The children of a London baker were not free to go to school for many years of their young lives, or even to play as they wished when they came back home. Soon they would find themselves doing what they could in bolting, that is sieving flour, or in helping the maidservant with her panniers of loaves on the way to the market stall, or in playing their small parts in preparing the never-ending succession of meals for the whole household.

The patriarchal arrangements which we have begun to explore were not new in the England of Shakespeare and Elizabeth. They were as old as the Greeks, as old as European history, and not confined to Europe. And it may well be that they abused and enslaved people quite as remorselessly as the economic arrangements which had replaced them in the England of Blake and Victoria. When people could expect to live for so short a time, how must a man have felt when he realized that so much of his adult life must go in working for his keep and very little more in someone else's family?

But people very seldom recognize facts of this sort, and no one is content to expect to live as long as the majority in fact will live. Every servant in the old social world was probably quite confident that he or she would some day get married and be at the head of a new family, keeping others in subordination.

It will be noticed that the roles we have allotted to all members of the capacious family of the master-baker of London in the year 1619 are, emotionally, all highly symbolic and highly satisfying. We may feel that in a whole society organized like this, in spite of all the subordination, the exploitation and the obliteration of those who were young, or feminine, or in service, everyone belonged in a group, a family group. Everyone had his circle of affection: every relationship could be seen as a love-relationship.

Not so with us. Who could love the name of a limited company or of a government department as an apprentice could love his superbly satisfactory father-figure master, even if he were a bully and a beater, a usurer and a hypocrite? But if a family is a circle of affection, it can also be the scene of hatred. The worst tyrants among human beings, the murderers and the villains, are jealous husbands and resentful wives, possessive parents and deprived children. In the traditional, patriarchal society of Europe, where practically everyone lived out his whole life within the family, though not usually within one family, tension like this must have been incessant and unrelieved, incapable of release except in crisis. Men, women and children have to be very close together for a very long time to generate the emotional power which can give rise to a tragedy of Sophocles, or Shakespeare, or Racine.

The Size of Society

All this is true to history only if the little knot of people making bread in Stuart London was indeed the typical social unit of the old world in its size, composition and scale. There are reasons why a baker's household might have been a little out of the ordinary, for baking was a highly traditional occupation in a society increasingly subject to economic change. A family of thirteen people, which was also a unit of production of thirteen, less the children still incapable of work, was quite large for English society at that time. Only the families of the really important, the nobility and the gentry, the aldermen and the successful merchants, were ordinarily as large as this. In fact, we can take the bakery to represent the upper limit in size and scale of the group in which ordinary people lived and worked. Among the great mass of society which cultivated the land, the family group was smaller than a substantial London craftsman's entourage.

In the baking household sex and age were mingled together. Fortunate children might go out to school, but adults did not usually go out to work. There was nothing to correspond to the thousands of young men on the assembly line, the hundreds of young women in the offices, the lonely lives of housekeeping wives, which we now know only too well. Those who survived to old age in the much less favourable conditions for survival which then were prevalent, were surprisingly often left to live and die alone, in their tiny cottages or sometimes in the almshouses which were being built so widely in the England of the Tudors and the Stuarts. Poor-law establishments, parochial in purpose and in size, had begun their melancholy chapter in the history of the English people. But institutional life was otherwise almost unknown. There were no hotels, hostels, or blocks of flats for single persons, very few hospitals and none of the kind we are familiar with, almost no young men and women living on their own. The family unit where so great a majority lived was what we should undoubtedly call a "balanced" and "healthy" group.

To every farm there was a family, which spread itself over its portion of the village lands as the family of the master-craftsman filled out his manufactory. When a holding was small, and most were small as are the tiny holdings of European peasants today, a man tilled it with the help of his wife and his children. No single man, we must remember, would usually take charge of the land, any more than a single man would often be found at the head of a workshop in the city. The master of a family was expected to be a householder, whether he was a butcher, a baker, a candlestick maker or simply a husbandman, which was the universal name for one whose skill was in working the land. Marriage we must insists, and it is one of the rules which gave its character to the society of our ancestors, was the entry to full membership, in the enfolding countryside, as well as in the scattered urban centres.

Some peasants did well: their crops were heavier and they had more land to till. To provide the extra labour needed then, the farming householder, like the successful craftsman, would extend his working family by taking on young men and women as servants to live with him and work the fields. This he would have to do, even if the land which he was farming was not his own but rented from the great family in the manor house. Sometimes, he would prefer to send out his own children as servants and bring in other children and young men to do the work. This is one of the few glimpses we can get into the quality of the emotional life of the family at this time, for it shows that parents may have been unwilling to submit children of their own to the discipline of work at home. It meant, too, that servants were not simply the perquisites of wealth and position. A quarter, or a third, of all the families in the country contained servants in Stuart times, and this meant that very humble people had them as well as the titled and the wealthy. Most of the servants, moreover, male or female, in the great house and in the small, were engaged in working the land.

A boy, or a girl, born in a cottage, would leave home for service at any time after the age of ten. A servant-in-husbandry, as he might be called if he were a boy, would usually stay in the position of servant, though very rarely in the same household, until he or she got married. Marriage, when and if it came, would quite often take place with another servant. All this while, and it might be twelve, fifteen or even twenty years, the servant would be kept by the succession of employers in whose houses he dwelt. He was in no danger of poverty of hunger, even if the modest husbandman with whom he lived was worse housed than his landlord's horses, and worse clothed than his landlord's servants.

But poverty awaited the husbandman's servant when he got married, and went himself to live in just such a labourer's cottage as the one in which he had been born. Whoever had been his former master, the labourer, late servant in husbandry, would be liable to fall into want directly when his wife began to have children and he lost the earnings of his companion. Once he found himself outside the farming household his living had to come from his wages, and he, with every member of his family, was subject for his labour to the local vagaries in the market.

The Creation of Mass Society

The removal of the economic functions from the patriarchal family at the point of industrialization created a mass society. It turned the people who worked into a mass of undifferentiated equals, working in a factory or scattered between the factories and mines, bereft for ever of the feeling that work was a family affair, done within the family. Marxist historical sociology presents this as the growth of class consciousness amongst the proletariat, and this is an important historical truth. But because it belongs with the large-scale class model for all social change it can also be misleading. Moreover it has tended to divert attention from the structural function of the family in the pre-industrial world, and has impeded a proper, informed contrast between our world and the lost world we have to analyse.

With the "capitalism changed the world" way of thinking goes a division of history into the ancient, feudal and bourgeois era or stages. But the facts of the contrast which has to be drawn between the world we have lost and the world we now inhabit tends to make all such divisions as these into subdivisions. The time has now come to divide our European past in a simpler way with industrialization as the point of critical change.

The word, alienation, is part of the cant of the mid-twentieth century and it began as an attempt to describe the separation of the worker from his world of work. We need not accept all that this expression has come to convey in order to recognize that it does point to something vital to us all in relation to our past. Time was when the whole of life went forward in the family, in a circle of loved, familiar faces, known and fondled objects, all to human size. That time has gone for ever. It makes us very different from our ancestors.

38

Quebec and the Canadian Question

Hubert Guindon

Guindon's study not only examines the Canadian dilemma of two nations existing within the same state, but also provides an analysis of the relatively recent modernization of Quebec society and its connection to current relations between Quebec and the rest of Canada. What is "the Canadian question?" Why does Guindon present the question such that Quebec appears to be both a part of, and apart from, it?

A century and a half ago, after the Rebellion of 1837, Lord Durham observed in his famous report that when he looked for the cause of the unrest, he found, to his astonishment, 'two nations warring in the bosom of the same state.' He proposed a simple remedy: 'I believe that tranquility can only be restored by subjecting the province [of Quebec] to the vigorous rule of an English majority.'

Were he to return today, Lord Durham would no doubt be astonished to learn that, despite the application of his proposed remedy, his initial observation holds true. Quebec and English Canada still seem to be 'two nations warring in the bosom of the same state.' Today the viability of Canada as a political entity remains in question. And for the Québécois it is *the* question, the distinctively *Canadian* question.

How are we to understand Quebec and its place (or lack thereof) in Canada? For most English Canadians, the rise of the separatists in Quebec has been inexplicable. Quebec, that quiescent paragon of rural provincialism, has suddenly been transformed into a seat of rabid nationalists intent on the dismemberment of Canada.

If this change seems inexplicable, it is because it does not fit the political stereotypes and cultural myths that English Canadians long used to interpret Quebec as an archaic, traditional society. Ruled by an autocratic clergy fiercely

---

Hubert Guindon, "Quebec and the Canadian Question" from *Quebec Society: Tradition, Modernity and Nationhood* (ed. by R. Hamilton and J. McMullan), University of Toronto, 1988: 125-146.

possessive of its own powers and opposed to democracy, modernization, or social progress, Quebec, it was said, was a rural backwater of poverty, illiteracy, and political despotism.

This political/cultural vision of the French in Canada did not emanate from bigoted Orangemen. Strangely enough, it was the conceptual framework of the politically liberal anglophone academics of the 1950s, and it was shared and disseminated by the 'progressive' French-Canadian intellectuals in and around *Cité Libre* magazine, who then lived in Montreal and went on in the 1960s and 1970s to work mainly in Ottawa....

Political fairy tales are always with us, and only belatedly do we become aware of them. It is, therefore, easier to spot distortions of social reality in the older ones than in the current ones. How are we to understand what has really been going on in Quebec these past few decades? What processes have made the Canadian question so urgent for the Québécois?

I have argued elsewhere ['The Modernization of Quebec and the Legitimacy of the Canadian State'] that the delegitimation of the Canadian state in the eyes of the Québécois is a consequence of the modernization of Quebec, which took off with the provincial government's massive intervention in the areas of health, education, and welfare. In this chapter I explore this issue at somewhat greater length and disentangle some of the separate threads in the modernization process. This necessitates distinguishing between the processes of government involvement, secularization, and political alienation.

The modernization of Quebec was heralded by the beginnings of large-scale government involvement in the structure of Quebec society in the early 1960s—a process now called the Quiet Revolution—and by the overthrow of the Union Nationale party, which had held provincial power. The secularization process became visible six or seven years later, as a massive dropout rate among priests and nuns became noticeable. Finally, political alienation became clear in the late 1960s, as the independence movement took shape: the Mouvement Souverainté-association, the precursor of the Parti Québécois, was created.

The Quiet Revolution

Antecedents: Social Unrest in the 1950s

The modernization of Quebec is popularly described as beginning with the Quiet Revolution, as if it had sprung full-blown from the traditional society preceding it. That, of course, is nonsense. The Quiet Revolution was preceded by a decade of unrest, during which more and more Québécois came to question their society and its capacity to meet their needs.

Labour Unrest
The designation of a single event as the beginning of any social change is always

arbitrary. Nevertheless, a logical starting point for this history is the strike of the asbestos miners in 1949, a highly symbolic event. Quebec's asbestos mines, largely American-owned, were virtually closed down by this strike involving some 5,000 workers, who were mainly seeking better job conditions. Their unions were affiliated with the Canadian Catholic Confederation of Labour (the predecessor of the Confédération des syndicats nationaux or CNTU), which until this time had stressed cooperation with management; they received backing from many other Quebec unions, which put aside their history of internecine quarrels and came together to support the asbestos workers. The dispute became particularly bloody, partly because of the goon-squad tactics of the police, who were under orders from the ruling Union Nationale party to aid management and break the strike.

The strike rapidly became much more than a labour dispute. It signalled a questioning of the whole internal political and social order of Quebec society. For many years, the institutional Church had backed the political regime of Maurice Duplessis and the Union Nationale. Now two bishops openly broke with the Church, instituting collections in the parish churches of their dioceses in support of the workers. (One of them, Archbishop Charbonneau of Montreal, was eventually forced to resign his see as a consequence). Equally significant, the intelligentsia of Quebec, who normally did not choose sides of labour disputes, mainly supported the workers.

The whole event was deeply revealing of the kinds of changes that were beginning to occur in Quebec. Here was an American corporation (at that time we did not have the word 'multinational' to describe it) with English-speaking managers and French-speaking workers who were contracting asbestosis. In retrospect, it seems amazing that under such circumstances it was Maurice Duplessis, not the Johns-Manville Corporation, and the provincial police, not the anglophone management, who became the scapegoats and villains in the political unrest that grew out of this prolonged strike.

The World of the Arts
This unrest spread during the 1950s, through the social, political, and cultural institutions of Quebec's traditional society. The world of the fine arts was ready for it. In 1948, Paul-Émile Borduas, an influential painter, lost his teaching position for writing a manifesto, *Le Refus Global*, that called for artists to reject the ideological hegemony exercised by the institutional Church, and to demand total freedom of expression. Although Borduas subsequently went into self-imposed exile, his message left its imprint.

Social Welfare
Unrest also developed in the area of what is now called social welfare (it was then still called charity). New professionals, such as social workers, were beginning to emerge and become critical of Church control over the welfare

institutions and the lack of professional qualifications of many who cared for the socially disadvantaged, the economically deprived, and the mentally disturbed. This growing dissatisfaction with the traditional ways of organizing social activities was an echo from the area of labour, where a growing critique of paternalism foreshadowed a push toward unionization and formalized collective bargaining as the normal way of organizing work.

Education
It was in the area of education that the loudest demands for change were heard. During the mid-1950s, a teaching brother anonymously published a series of letters, collected as *Les Insolences du Frère Untel* (in translation, The Impertinences of Brother Anonymous), which satirically decried the education system, at the time almost entirely controlled and run by the Church. The articles, which were very funny, attracted broad attention within the middle class, partly because the author castigated the atrocious distortions of his students' spoken and written French, coining the term *joual* (a colloquial pronunciation of *cheval*) to refer to their language. That lower-class French could be spoofed meant that a middle class had been sufficiently developed to constitute a willing audience for such humour....

By the end of the 1950s, educational concerns had shifted to the universities....

Health care
Health institutions were also an object of social dissatisfaction. The costs of health care, which were rising fast, were borne exclusively by the patients of their kin. A twofold demand was emerging: increased involvement of the state in funding and, as a consequence, secularization of health-care institutions. In the meantime, lay people were increasingly questioning the selflessness of the religious orders that oversaw the administration of these institutions.

The End of the Decade
Toward the end of the decade, two events occurred that foreshadowed two political developments: the impending demise of the Duplessis regime, and the eventual rise of the independence movement.

In the first, two priests, Fathers Dion and O'Neill, castigated the political immorality of the Union Nationale party—Duplessis's political vehicle—in a clerical periodical, *Ad Usum Sacerdotum*.... Thus, the decade that had begun with the toppling of an archbishop from his see for his expression of sympathies for the workers in a strike declared illegal by the Duplessis regime, ended with a formal, direct attack on the political immorality of that regime—an attack that went unchallenged and its authors unpenalized.

The first ripple of the independence movement, like that of the Quiet Revolution, surfaced in a labour dispute. In 1959, producers at Radio-Canada, the French network of the CBC, tried to start a trade union. The management objected that producers were managers and therefore could not be granted certification as a union. The producers went on a strike that lasted more than two months and galvanized public attention. Once again, amazingly, the villains of the tale were not the francophone bureaucrats of Radio-Canada but the Canadian parliament, not the minister responsible for the operation of the CBC, but Confederation itself. The asbestos strike had signalled the questioning of the internal socio-political regime of Quebec society. A decade later, the Radio-Canada strike began the eventual questioning of the external political and economic constraints on the development of Quebec society.

Agents: The Emerging Middle Classes

The evolution of the social unrest of the 1950s in the fields of labour, welfare, education, politics, and communications raises the question of who, sociologically speaking, was politically restive and why. The reception given *Les Insolences du Frère Untel* was one indication among many of the existence of a new middle class; in Quebec's increasingly differentiated society, it was this group that felt, articulated, and progressively disseminated social unrest.

The massive urbanization that had accompanied the Second World War and immediate post-war period in Quebec had put pressure on the traditional institutions that dealt with education, health care, and welfare. The new demographic conditions required a radical and sudden increase in the scale of these institutions, which, in turn, transformed their nature.... In the eyes of this new middle class, Quebec institutions urgently required state money if they were to grow and thus modernize Quebec society. And the Duplessis regime was so slow to respond as to be proclaimed reactionary.

When the priorities of the new middle class became the priorities of the state, the Quiet Revolution was officially under way. This happened after Duplessis's death, when Paul Sauvé became premier in 1950. He had been in office barely three months before sudden death ended his term; it was seen as a terrible and personal loss by the whole of Quebec society. Since he had had no time to implement any changes, the deep sense of bereavement was a consequence of his promise of change (*désormais*—'henceforth'), which had included three solemnly declared intentions:

1. To provide statutory grants to universities.
2. To establish a royal commission to study the feasibility of free hospitalization.
3. To revise the pay scale for the civil service.

All three promises were soon met, if not by Suavé's Union Nationale, then by the Liberals, who won the following election on the slogan 'It's time for a change.'

Certainly, many of the new Québécois middle class had a sincere commitment to the ideology represented by these goals. But simple sociological analysis shows that the modernization of health and education met the requirements of their career interests, as well as the needs of social progress. Statutory per capita grants to universities and per diem subsidies for hospital beds meant that state money now flowed automatically from the public treasury into educational and health institutions. These institutions were therefore able to plan rapid development....[M]oreover, as resources soared, these institutions could attract an increasingly qualified (and increasingly specialized) staff and reward them accordingly. Full-time careers in these institutions, once very scarce for the laity, became plentiful, and soon the introduction of the practice of tenure meant that they also became, in the universities, lifetime careers.

That the Quiet Revolution meant social progress is beyond question. It achieved increased accessibility and democratization of education, as well as improvements in the quality and accessibility of health care. It meant greater financial and bureaucratic participation by the state and rapid growth of public and para-public institutions, as well as the growth of new elites. That is also involved the secularization of Quebec society was neither so clearly foreseen nor, probably, intended. Unanticipated consequences of periods of rapid change are, however, the norm rather than the exception.

The Secularization of Quebec Society

Secularization is frequently associated with modernization in sociological literature. But the links between the two are usually far from clear and far from convincing. At the theoretical level, 'secularization' is generally defined in terms of the shrinking importance of magic and religion, as a result of the expansion of science and the scientific method. The narrowing sphere of the sacred corresponds to the expansions of knowledge, at the expense of faith and myth. Yet to conceive of secularization as a fading of myths rather than an emergence of new ones is to miss the point. Moreover, this idealistic view of secularization fails to take account of how the process takes shape and how it unfolds historically.

If the theoretical perspective on secularization is often rooted in epistemology (theories of knowledge), the popular perspective is usually put more crudely in institutional terms of ignorance and education, as a byproduct of increased (mass) education. People erroneously assume that the world of knowledge and the world of meaning are the same thing. In fact, education has or should have something to do with knowledge, while secularization has to do with the world of meaning, quite another matter indeed.

Secularization is a question of politics, not epistemology. Historically, secularization started with the separation of the Church from the State, with constitutional proclamations in France and the United States, not of a churchless society, but of a churchless state. In the case of France, this proclamation was made at the time of the Revolution to formalize the break with a feudal past. In the United States, the American Revolution needed to distance the state from an official religion (and therefore from all religions), in order to proclaim freedom of religion and accommodate the denominational pluralism of the citizens.

No such political imperatives ever existed in Britain or its dominion of Canada, where a break from feudalism never occurred (although the evolution of capitalism did) and where freedom of religion became politically tolerated and practised, not constitutionally proclaimed. Yet one can argue quite correctly that secularization took place in the 19th and 20th centuries in both Britain and English Canada. The process was the institutional consequence of the break from Roman Catholicism.

The term 'institutional secularization' refers to the process by which institutions initiated, staffed, or managed by clerics came under lay control. In the 16th and 17th centuries, when the Protestant churches broke from Roman Catholicism, whole societies were deprived of the organizational structure of the religious orders whose missions were to aid the poor, to tend the sick, and to provide education (to the extent that it had been developed). Thus new institutions had to be organized on a community basis under the aegis of the Protestant churches, with increased lay participation through voluntary associations....

In contrast, the secularization of social institutions in most Catholic countries did not take place until after the middle of the 20th century.[1] In fact, both the number of religious orders and their membership increased dramatically during the 19th and early 20th centuries in Catholic countries; the Church became progressively more involved in social institutions during that period of transition when the poor, the sick, and the ignorant, as Everett C. Hughes once put it, no longer belonged to their kin and did not yet belong to the state.

This brief historical outline sets the stage for the analysis of the secularization of Quebec, which, it must be remembered, was—and still is—a Catholic society. We will address three issues: the secularization of institutions, the massive dropout from the ranks of the clergy during the mid-1960s, and finally the substantial drop in religious practice.

The Social Institutions

As the Quiet Revolution swept Quebec, the Church had neither the human nor the financial resources necessary to develop the educational and health-care institutions required to meet social needs as defined by the new middle classes. These needs were broadly defined indeed: nothing short of universal access to free education up to the university level, and heavy subsidies thereafter; free hospitalization for all citizens; and (later in the 1960s) free medical care. When the State accepted such a mandate, it sealed the fate of the Church in the whole area of social institutions. Such massive and rapid investment of public money required the development of a public bureaucracy to act on behalf of the public will (at least theoretically). Neither the Church as an institution nor the traditional community elites could be the agents of this institutional development. New elites—trained in everything from accounting to engineering, from personnel to industrial relations, from purchasing to architectural design—would swell the ranks of the new middle classes in the ever-growing public bureaucracies....

Once the state decided to modernize and expand the educational system by the use of incentives, the secularization of the education system was greatly accelerated. This acceleration had nothing to do, as is commonly assumed, with a growing loss of religious belief or decrease in religiosity. Rather, it came from simple economic calculation at the community level. As long as the costs of education were borne locally, through taxes raised from local pockets, it made local economic sense to have clerical teachers, who cost much less than lay teachers because they lived communally and frugally and were low-level consumers. However, once the provincial government bore an overwhelming share of the costs of education, it quickly dawned on local business people (who made up most local school boards) that it made much more sense—if not to the total local community, at least to its merchants—to seek lay people with the highest possible qualifications. Not only were their salaries highly subsidized; they were big spenders with an assured income. In contrast to nuns and priests, lay teachers paid taxes and got married. Everyone—the hairdressers, the car dealer, the real-estate agent, and the insurance salesperson—could expect some share of the action. When principle and self-interest so neatly coincided, no wonder institutional change was both swift and harmonious.

While communities were securing immediate economic advantage, however, their control over local institutions was being sapped. Whether community elites were aware of this erosion or felt it was a fair tradeoff, the fact is that bureaucratic centralization soon eclipsed the importance of the community. Norms as well as subsidies started to come from outside. Since loyalty is most often a function of dependence, the loyalty of the teaching staff belonged no longer to the school board but to the professional association, which bargained with government for working conditions and salary. In the process, school boards came to represent the government more than the community.

Similar analyses could be made in the realm of social welfare. The voluntary agencies that had traditionally been organized, staffed, and managed by the Church in local communities were now to be organized by lay professionals employed by state agencies.

This massive modernization initiated by the growing state bureaucracies was far from the unique to Quebec society. It was common to all industrially developed countries, in fact. What was unique to Quebec (and to similar Catholic societies elsewhere in North America) is that the sudden, rapid secularization of social institutions was mostly conflict-free.

The Exodus of Clergy

During the late 1960s and the early 1970s, Quebec, like English Canada, the United States, and some European countries, quite suddenly saw a new phenomenon: priests and nuns left their vocations in droves. Part of the process may be explained by ideological changes within the Catholic church and part by the fact that the Vatican increasingly facilitated the release of individuals from their clerical vows. Equally facilitating these 'defections' in Quebec was the fact that, contrary to the situation before the Quiet Revolution, priests or nuns who left orders could now quite easily find a place for themselves within the social structure. No longer were former clerics—especially priests—viewed as having committed spiritual treason by leaving the sacred calling; no longer could a defector cope only by either leaving the society or concealing his or her previous occupation. Suddenly, with the change in the social order, ex-priests could (and did) enter the growing ranks of the public and semipublic bureaucracies. The change was so thorough and so pervasive that priests who taught religion at the Université de Montréal, which holds a pontifical charter, were able, because of tenure, to keep their positions after quitting the ranks of the clergy and celibacy. Such a situation would have been inconceivable less than a decade earlier.

Paradoxically, the same reasons that had prompted men and women to enter the clergy in remarkable numbers in the none-too-distant past could also explain the sudden, massive exodus. Without doubting the selflessness and sincere motives of those who became priests, brothers, or nuns, one can argue that, in social terms, joining the clergy of Quebec had certainly not involved downward social mobility. For women, it had meant an assurance of comfortable, if austere, living quarters and an escape from the burden of large families and domestic chores, while gaining access to socially esteemed occupations in teaching and nursing....

For men, joining the clergy, regular or secular,[2] meant entering a career that could lead to important institutional positions. In the secular clergy, the career paths mainly involved pastoral duties in the urban and rural parishes of a geographically circumscribed diocese....

Quebec had long had a relatively high percentage of people who chose to follow these patterns. More or less simultaneously with the Quiet Revolution, decisions to enter the religious life suddenly shrank to a trickle, and defections increased dramatically, especially among younger nuns and priests—those who were beginning, not terminating, their careers. The shrinking role of the Church in the newly emerged social order was certainly a key factor. The Church, which had previously offered both full career patterns and social esteem, could now promise neither....

The Decrease in Religious Practice

'Tradition,' Everett Hughes once pointed out in conversation, 'is sacred only so long as it is useful.' If tradition involves a mix of the sacred and the utilitarian, it follows that the first people to question its sacred character will be those for whom tradition is no longer useful. And indeed in mid-20th century Quebec, it was the intelligentsia and the new middle classes—whose careers and interests were no longer served by the traditional culture, institutions, or leadership—who first challenged the legitimacy of all three.

For traditional Quebec society, including the elites, visible religious practices were interwoven with almost every part of life. Many of these folkways all but disappeared over a very short time. For example, people had been accustomed to locate themselves by referring to the parish in which they resided; this custom rapidly disappeared as the majority of people no longer knew the names or the general locations of parish churches.

It would not be misleading to say that most of the population drifted into secularization through inattention. For the majority, estrangement from religious practice developed as a result of the Church's growing irrelevance in meeting their everyday needs. Schools were no longer linked to the Catholic parish; teachers were more apt to be lay than clerical; hospitals and clinics were professionally administered by specialists who lived far from where they worked, and neither knew nor cared to know about their clients in other than a professional capacity. The secularization of charity in the professionally operated agencies of the state left the Church not only with a shrinking role but also with half-empty buildings whose material upkeep became increasingly dependent on the continuing popularity of bingo....

No longer visible, now basically silent, the Church, once a dominant institution in social and collective life, withdrew to service the spiritual and private needs of those still seeking its counsel. As its political clout faded, the voice of its critics became louder. The political liberals and conservatives maintain that the Church was, in large measure, responsible for the economic underdevelopment of Quebec, because it did not impart to its flock the 'right' values, those that inspire entrepreneurial leadership and economic success. Under its leadership, they argue, Quebec's institutions failed to adapt to the requirements of a modern industrial society. The Marxists, on the other hand, take the Church to task for having collaborated with the anglophone bourgeoisie in exploiting its flock, the working class. Both charges are ideologically inspired distortions. The Church, however, no longer answers its critics. Is this a dignified silence, or the sign of its collapse as an institution?

The Canadian Question

By the late 1970s, a modern and secular social order had indeed emerged in Quebec society. Quebec had put its internal house in order in line with other developed societies. In spite of this—maybe because of this—Quebec remained politically restive. It was readying itself to challenge the legitimacy of another sacred institution: the Canadian state. The internal issue of Church and society having been resolved, the external issue of state and society rose to the top of the political agenda. For Quebec society that was *the* Canadian question.

A Lament for Two Nations

Seldom, if ever, do a conquered people give their consent to a conquering state. Conquered subjects' loyalty to the state is always suspect. This is so true that loyalty oaths are routinely administered to and taken by future civil servants. In times of crisis in national unity, these forgotten oaths become instruments of social control for those who fear for the state's security. The point is raised here not to underscore the vulnerability of those fragile freedoms known as civil liberties, but rather to call attention to the historically enduring price of political domination. Both those who created the state and those who are subject to to are forever condemned to wishful thinking: the first, to the dream of national unity, the latter, to the dream of national independence.

Those who dream of national unity are also forced to lament the absence of a commonly agreed-on history....

Commonly agreed-on history presupposes a common celebration of either a glorious past or a common victory over an undesirable past. France can claim both; Britain can claim the first; the United States, the latter; and Canada neither. The cruelty of this observation is mitigated by the fact that political consensus can also be built on shared visions of the future. Such vision, however, must be based on the correction of history, not its denial. 'Unhyphenated Canadianism' is a mirage based on the confusion of individual biography with group history. All immigrants have a biographical break with a past in which the country of origin somehow, to some degree, became undesirable—often because of denied opportunity or political persecution; the country of adoption, by the mere fact of receiving the immigrants, symbolizes a land of opportunity or a refuge from oppression, both of which are good reasons for thanksgiving. In contrast, the French and the English in Canada are burdened with historical continuity. In both cases, the breaking with the biographical past creates not a new citizen but a marginal one. And while marginal people may invent myths and create new visions, a new political order without group consent remains beyond reach.

A political order is a symbolically mediated structure. In other words, the state, to be legitimate, must rely on the substantial—not just formal—consent of the governed. Formal consent can be engineered by manipulation, trickery, propaganda, publicity, and deception, or it can be claimed on the basis of sufficient numbers alone. Shared consent, however, requires shared meanings, shared myths. The French and the English in Canada may have a common fate, but they share no political myths. The closest they have come was the belief that Canada was a partnership between the French and the English, an idea formalized in the compact theory of Confederation, which presents dualism as central to the nature of the state. John Porter spoke of 'charter groups'—while admitting the junior status of one of them. Stanley Ryerson called Confederation an 'unequal union.' Lester Pearson, in striking the Royal Commission on Bilingualism and Biculturalism, spoke of the 'two founding races.' The commission, sensitive to the connotations that might be evoked by the word 'race,' preferred to speak of 'two societies and two cultures.' Pierre Trudeau watered the concept down still further, referring to two language communities (as though language without culture can be the basis of community) and many cultures. One need say no more to illustrate either the inability to define what Canada is or the incapacity of words to cover up an embarrassing social and political reality.

The last person to speak candidly about the social and political reality of Canada in unambiguous, well-established English words was Lord Durham, in his description of 'two nations warring in the bosom of the same state.' As mentioned at the beginning of this chapter, he recommended the subjugation of the French to the vigorous rule of the British, advice that was heeded but that did not succeed. Before Confederation, following this advice required thwarting democratic principles. With Confederation, those principles ensured political domination of the French nation.

Ever after, the word 'nation' to describe the French fact in Canada was banned from the political vocabulary of Canadian academics and politicians. To make credible this semantic confusion, it became customary to refer not to the Canadian *state* but to the Canadian *nation*—creating unity not politically but semantically.

Such obfuscation obviously requires education. Denying reality rather than assuming it is characteristic of Canadian politicians, not of ordinary Canadian citizens. On leaving or entering Quebec, Québécois and non-Québécois alike quickly perceive the reality of cultural and social differences. Some people are dumbstruck by the differences. Others are paranoid about them. Both types of reaction testify to the reality of social and cultural boundaries. The fact that this dual reality cannot find a political expression in the Canadian political system constitutes its basic vulnerability.

The compact (or dualist) theory of Confederation, the myth that so many French Canadians clung to so that they could symbolically legitimate a dignified commitment to the Canadian state, suffered an ignominious death with the patriation of the Constitution in 1982; one partner, they discovered, could force patriation without the consent of the other. That the death blow was struck by a prime minister who was himself partly French-Canadian made it no less lethal; that in involved political trickery transformed the constitutional process from grand ritual into tragic farce, making the final demise of illusion seem unreal and senseless. Rumour has it that Prime Minister Trudeau's ruthlessness in patriating the Constitution was motivated by his frantic determination to secure a niche for himself in Canadian history. Secure a niche he did indeed: whether it will be an enviable one is quite another matter.

The destruction of dualism as a shared myth through the forcible patriation of the Constitution constitutes a proof by political action, rather than national argument, of a doctrine close to Trudeau's heart: that Quebec is a province *comme les autres*. In other words, Quebec is not the homeland of a people, it is merely a region of the country, one region among ten.

In legal fiction, Quebec has become a province *comme les autres*; in social reality it has not. It also is different economically; only in the province of Quebec is the economy controlled by a minority who differ socially, culturally, and ethnically from the inhabitants. This social and historical fact has arisen partly because of the Canadian state. Therein lies its tainted legitimacy. Therein, too, lies the reason it gave birth to the dream of national independence among its subjects in Quebec.

The Unreachable Dream

The dream of national independence in Quebec society took root when the 'partnership' between French and English in the Canadian state was still a dominant theme in the political rhetoric. In effect, it was the suspicion that English Canadians did not in fact share this political myth that gave rise to the political alienation of the intelligentsia in Quebec society.

While the 1950s were ushered in by the strike in the asbestos mines, the 1960s were opened by the strike at Radio-Canada. Both events heralded basic changes in the sociopolitical order. The asbestos strike led to the Quiet Revolution a decade later. The Radio-Canada strike led, some 15 years later, to the election of the Parti Québécois. With the Quiet Revolution sprang up a modernized and secularized society, founded by the state and managed by bureaucratically employed professionals. With the independence movement was born an enduring, credible challenge to the legitimacy of an externally imposed political order.

As already stated, both strikes at first glance seem paradoxical. The asbestos strike involved a multinational corporation with English-Canadian management and French workers, but it led to a questioning of the Duplessis regime and the social power of the Church. The strike at Radio-Canada involved a conflict between producers and management within the exclusively French network of the CBC but ended by being defined in ethnic terms. Neither interpretation is really paradoxical. The contradiction between objective fact and social response would be real enough in normal times, but in times of social unrest and of heightened tension it is not unusual for an event to be invested with meanings that transcend what actually happens. The discrepancy signals the major redefinitions of historical situations that precede a challenge of political order.

The strike at Radio-Canada, unlike many strikes, directly affected the intelligentsia and initiated their political alienation. Soon they scrutinized the federal government's institutions to ascertain the amount and level of participation of francophones within them. They found this participation appallingly low, giving substance to the emerging conviction that the Canadian state is 'theirs, not ours.' Moreover, as the Royal Commission on Bilingualism and Biculturalism eventually substantiated, the few francophones who did work in these institutions had to check their mother tongue at the door. At the Montreal Harbour Board, for example, bilingual civil servants received a routine memo from their francophone boss: 'Since everybody in the department is bilingual, all reports must be written in English.' It made perfect administrative sense internally. Externally, when leaked to the press, it made no political sense, except as an example of Lord Durham's 'vigorous British rule.'

The memo was quoted in the first of a series of editorials by André Laurendeau, the prestigious editor of *Le Devoir*. Some months later Prime Minister Lester Pearson struck the Royal Commission on Bilingualism and Biculturalism. Noble men filled with good intentions and alarmed by the strains threatening the state, the commissioners came forth with recommendations that perpetuated, rather than eliminated, those strains. By refusing to recommend a language regime based on territory, which would have ensured the francophone majority in Quebec access in their own language to the large corporate sector of Montreal, they proclaimed Quebec the model for the treatment of 'minorities' and urged the rest of Canada to follow suit toward their French minorities. In effect, they recommended leaving Quebec untouched, in terms of language policy, and adopting measures they thought would ensure the viability of French communities outside Quebec.

This viability could not be ensured, however, since postal services and radio and television programming in French were no replacement for a vanishing economic base. Furthermore, they could not convince the politically restive Québécois that Quebec was a model, since within that 'model' they had to choose between a public-sector career in French or a private-sector career in English. If Quebec was to be a province *comme les autres*, as Trudeau insisted, it seemed elementary to correct that strange discrepancy. More skilled in provocation than in integration, Prime Minister Trudeau dismissed the terms of reference of the Royal Commission on Bilingualism and Biculturalism and proclaimed Canada to be bilingual and multicultural. While the proclamation pleased those citizens who were neither French nor English, it certainly did not guarantee any substance to ethnic cultures since they would not be celebrated in their own languages; what it did guarantee was state funds to enable colourful celebrations of official pluralism.

The official bilingualism adopted by the Canadian state was politically irrelevant for the modernizing Québécois majority and politically resented in most of English-speaking Canada. In Western Canada it smacked of privilege, since the few French Canadians living there were fully bilingual but now able to get federally funded French-language radio and television, not to mention bilingual labels on their cornflakes, while the overwhelming majority of neo-Canadians could not receive such services in their cultural languages. The reasons of state clashed with the logic of community, and the reasons of state prevailed, pitting the ethnic Canadians against the French Canadians. The very same result was achieved in Quebec by the failure of the senior government to act, leading, in 1974, the junior government under Robert Bourassa—no wide-eyed separatist but a tame Liberal—to introduce Bill 22, *la loi sur la langue officielle*. Replacing a 1969 act that had the same intent but was less comprehensive, Bill 22 announced that French was the language of the workplace and of government services. It also restricted anglophone education to children who demonstrated a prior knowledge of the English language. Thus, although the new law was loudly denounced by the anglophone media, one of its most immediate effects was to alienate from the Liberal party many of Quebec's new Canadians, who resented having to learn not one but two languages to qualify for effective citizenship....

Only months later, provincial elections brought to power, to the consternation of English Canadians, the Parti Québécois, whose announced goals included the peaceful attainment of independence for Quebec. One of its first actions was to complete the francization of Quebec that Bourassa had begun. It enacted Bill 101, *la charte de la langue française*, which makes French the normal language of work, education, and public life in Quebec. Basically, its authors considered Ontario the model for the treatment of the other official language. But what is normal in Ontario and elsewhere in Canada is considered by those regions to be outrageous in Quebec....

The Parti Québécois had won its electoral victory preaching sovereignty-association—political independence for Quebec within an economic union with Canada—but had promised to seek a specific mandate before attempting to negotiate the change with Ottawa. A referendum was announced for May 1980, and the federal Liberals combined with the provincial party to throw enormous amounts of money and advertising into the campaign. The referendum failed— a joyless victory of national unity. English Canadians stopped holding their breath, even when the PQ unexpectedly won another victory at the polls the next year. What the referendum had done was to make the dream of national independence unreachable.

Then Trudeau delivered on his promise of 'renewed federalism'; in 1982 the Constitution was repatriated without Quebec's consent. The PQ resisted federal blandishments to sign, but in its eagerness to retain power, it loosened some requirements of Bill 101 (which even in its original form was felt by some Québécois to give insufficient protection to the French culture and language), and it announced a new, quasi-federalist platform that drove several well-known *indépendantistes* to leave its ranks. Those moves proved too much for the Quebec electorate. Although they had voted overwhelmingly against the Liberals in the federal election of 1984, sweeping the Conservatives to victory, a few months later they voted almost as decisively *for* the provincial Liberals—the party that, after all, had come to power in 1960 under the slogan *maîtres chez nous*.

The outcome of the referendum and the purge of the *indépendantistes* from the Parti Québécois spells not the end of Québec's 'national' movement, but the end of its embodiment by a specific political party. It also means that the strategy to achieve independence will not follow the route of party politics. A return to less institutionalized forms of political mobilization is not to be excluded.

Conclusion

This essay ends on a melancholy note of disillusionment with statesmanship and party politics in this country. It does not claim to be non-partisan or dispassionate. It is a plea, a public and desperate one, for the youth of this country to distance themselves from the political culture they are exposed to. It is especially a plea to young English Canadians not to accept either the new demonology on Quebec or the idea that all is returning to 'normal' there, but to resolve to help to bring to birth eventually a state that will truly enjoy the consent of the governed.

Endnotes

Originally published in M. Michael Rosenberg, William B. Shaffir, Allan Turowetz, and Morton Weinfeld, eds, *An Introduction to Sociology* (Toronto, 1983)

[1] The exception was France, where after the Revolution the state took over the direct organization of education, producing bitter internal conflict that lasted more than a century.

[2] Catholic priests may be regular or secular clerics. The regular clerics are those who are members of a particular order, such as the Basilians, the Sulpicians, and the Jesuits, and live under its rule (hence 'regular'); they take vows of celibacy, poverty, and obedience (to the hierarchy of the order). Although an order sometimes accepts the responsibility of running a parish, each views itself as having one or more special mandates, which in Quebec before the 1960s was most often education, health, or some form of social service for active orders. (Some orders are strictly contemplative.)

In contrast, secular clerics take a vow of celibacy, but not of poverty or obedience. They work under the local bishop (whose assignment comes from Rome) and run most parishes, as well as other institutions under direct diocesan control.

All nuns and religious brothers are regular clerics.

39

The Dissolution of the Self

Kenneth Gergen

A social scientific understanding of socialization and the development of the self, with its focus on the influence of the social environment, generally implies that the character of the self will change as the character of society changes historically. In this selection Gergen discusses whether or not we are undergoing a radical transformation into a new, post-modern form of society with new cultural sensibilities, and considers what the implications of this form of society will be for the kind of self that develops within it.

...Cultural life in the twentieth century has been dominated by two major vocabularies of the self. Largely from the nineteenth century, we have inherited a romanticist view of the self, one that attributes to each person characteristics of personal depth: passion, soul, creativity, and moral fiber. This vocabulary is essential to the formation of deeply committed relations, dedicated friendships, and life purposes. But since the rise of the *modernist* worldview beginning in the early twentieth century, the romantic vocabulary has been threatened. For modernists, the chef characteristics of the self reside not in the domain of depth, but rather in our ability to reason—in our beliefs, opinions, and conscious intentions. In the modernist idiom, normal persons are predictable, honest, and sincere. Modernists believe in educational systems, a stable family life, moral training, and rational choice of marriage partners.

Yet, as I shall argue, both the romantic and the modern beliefs about the self are falling into disuse, and the social arrangements that they support are eroding. This is largely a result of the forces of social saturation. Emerging technologies saturate us with the voices of humankind—both harmonious and

---

Kenneth Gergen, "The Dissolution of the Self" from *The Saturated Self*, Basic Books, 1991: 6-7, 61-62; 68-71; 73-80; 146; 170. [as reprinted in Spencer E. Cahill, *Inside Social Life: Readings on Psychology and Microsociology*, Los Angeles: Roxbury Publishing, 1995: 146-154.]

alien. As we absorb their varied rhymes and reasons, they become part of us and we of them. Social saturation furnishes us with a multiplicity of incoherent and unrelated languages of the self. For everything we "know to be true" about ourselves, other voices within respond with doubt and even derision. This fragmentation of self-conceptions corresponds to a multiplicity of incoherent and disconnected relationships. These relationships pull us in a myriad directions, inviting us to play such a variety of roles that the very concept of an "authentic self" with knowable characteristics recedes from view. The fully saturated self becomes no self at all....

I...equate the saturating of self with the condition of *postmodernism*. As we enter the postmodern era, all previous beliefs about the self are placed in jeopardy, and with them the patterns of action they sustain. Postmodernism does not bring with it a new vocabulary for understanding ourselves, new traits or characteristics to be discovered or explored. Its impact is more apocalyptic than that: the very concept of personal essences is thrown into doubt. Selves as possessors of real and identifiable characteristics—such as rationality, emotion, inspiration, and will—are dismantled....

The Process of Social Saturation

A century ago, social relationships were largely confined to the distance of an easy walk. Most were conducted in person, within small communities: family, neighbors, townspeople. Yes, the horse and carriage made longer trips possible, but even a trip of thirty miles could take all day. The railroad could speed one away, but the cost and availability limited such travel. If one moved from the community, relationships were likely to end. From birth to death, one could depend on relatively even-textured social surroundings. Words, faces, gestures, and possibilities were relatively consistent, coherent, and slow to change.

For much of the world's population, especially the industrialized West, the small, face-to-face community is vanishing into the pages of history. We go to country inns for weekend outings, we decorate condominium interiors with clapboards and brass beds, and we dream of old age in a rural cottage. But as a result of the technological developments just described, contemporary life is a swirling sea of social relations. Words thunder in by radio, television, newspaper, mail, radio, telephone, fax, wire service, electronic mail, billboards, Federal Express, and more. Waves of new faces are everywhere—in town for a day, visiting for the weekend, at the Rotary lunch, at the church social—and incessantly and incandescently on television. Long weeks in a single community are unusual; a full day within a single neighborhood is becoming rare. We travel casually across town, into the countryside, to neighboring towns, cities, states; one might go thirty miles for coffee and conversation.

Through the technologies of the century, the number and variety of relationships in which we are engaged, potential frequency of contact, expressed intensity of relationship, and endurance through time all are steadily increasing. As this increase becomes extreme, we reach a state of social saturation.

In the face-to-face community, the cast of others remained relatively stable. There were changes by virtue of births and deaths, but moving from one town—much less state or country—to another was difficult. The number of relationships commonly maintained in today's world stands in stark contrast. Counting one's family, the morning television news, the car radio, colleagues on the train, and the local newspaper, the typical commuter may confront as many different persons (in terms of views or images) in the first two hours of a day as the community-based predecessor did in a month. The morning calls in a business office may connect one to a dozen different locales in a given city, often across the continent, and very possibly across national boundaries. A single hour of prime-time melodrama immerses one in the lives of a score of individuals. In an evening of television, hundreds of engaging faces insinuate themselves into our lives. It is not only the immediate community that occupies our thoughts and feelings, but a constantly changing cast of characters spread across the globe....

Populating the Self

Consider the moments:
- Over lunch with friends, you discuss Northern Ireland. Although you have never spoken a word on the subject, you find yourself heatedly defending British policies.
- You work as an executive in the investments department of a bank. In the evenings, you smoke marijuana and listen to the Grateful Dead.
- You sit in a café and wonder what it would be like to have an intimate relationship with various strangers walking past.
- You are a lawyer in a prestigious midtown firm. On the weekends, you work on a novel about romance with a terrorist.
- You go to a Moroccan restaurant and afterward take in the latest show at a country-and-western bar.

In each case, individuals harbor a sense of coherent identify or self-sameness, only to find themselves suddenly propelled by alternative impulses. They seem securely to be one sort of person, but yet another comes bursting to the surface—in a suddenly voiced opinion, a fantasy, a turn of interests, or a private activity. Such experiences with variation and self-contradiction may be viewed as preliminary effects of social saturation. They may signal a *populating of the self*, the acquisition of multiple and disparate potentials for beginning. It is this process of self-population that begins to undermine the traditional commitments to both romanticist and modernist forms of being. It is of pivotal importance in setting the stage for the postmodern turn. Let us explore.

The technologies of social saturation expose us to an enormous range of persons, new forms of relationship, unique circumstances and opportunities, and special intensities of feeling. One can scarcely remain unaffected by such exposure. As child-development specialists now agree, the process of socialization is lifelong. We continue to incorporate information from the environment throughout our lives. When exposed to other persons, we change in two major ways. We increase our capacities for *knowing that* and for knowing how. In the first case, through exposure to others, we learn myriad details about their words, actions, dress, mannerisms, and so on. We ingest enormous amounts of information about patterns of interchange. Thus, for example, from an hour on a city street, we are informed of the clothing styles of blacks, whites, upper class, lower class, and more. We may learn the ways of Japanese businessmen, bag ladies, Sikhs, Hare Krishnas, or flute players from Chile. We see how relationships are carried out between mothers and daughters, business executives, teenage friends, and construction workers. An hour in a business office may expose us to the political views of a Texas oilman, a Chicago lawyer, and a gay activist from San Francisco. Radio commentators espouse views on boxing, pollution, and child abuse; pop music may advocate machoism, racial bigotry, and suicide. Paperback books cause hearts to race over the unjustly treated, those who strive against impossible odds, those who are brave or brilliant. And this is to say nothing of television input. Via television, myriad figures are allowed into the home who would never otherwise trespass. Millions watch as talk-show guests—murders, rapists, women prisoners, child abusers, members of the KKK, mental patients, and others often discredited—attempt to make their lives intelligible. There are few six year olds who cannot furnish at least a rudimentary account of life in an African village, the concerns of divorcing parents, or drug-pushing in the ghetto. Hourly, our storehouse of social knowledge expands in range and sophistication.

This massive increase in knowledge of the social world lays the ground work for a second kind of learning, a *knowing how*. We learn how to place such knowledge into action, to shape it for social consumption, to act so that social life can proceed effectively. And the possibilities for placing this supply of information into effective action are constantly expanding. The Japanese businessman glimpsed on the street today, and on the television tomorrow, may well be confronted in one's office the following week. On these occasions, the rudiments of appropriate behavior are already in place. If a mate announces that he or she is thinking about divorce, the other's reaction is not likely to be dumb dismay. The drama has so often been played out on television and movie screens that one is already prepared with multiple options. If one wins a wonderful prize, suffers a humiliating loss, faces temptation to cheat, or learns of a sudden death in the family, the reactions are hardly random. One more or less knows how it goes, is more or less ready for action. Having seen it all before, one approaches a state of ennui.

In an important sense, as social saturation proceeds we become pastiches, imitative assemblages of each other. In memory, we carry others' patterns of being with us. If the conditions are favorable, we can place these patterns into action. Each of us becomes the other, a representative, or a replacement. To put it more broadly, as the century has progressed, selves become increasingly populated with the character of others....

Multiphrenia

It is sunny Saturday morning, and he finishes breakfast in high spirits. It is a rare day in which he is free to do as he pleases. With relish, he contemplates his options. The back door needs fixing, which calls for a trip to the hardware store. This would allow a much-needed haircut; and, while in town, he could get a birthday card for his brother, leave off his shoes for repair, and pick up shirts at the cleaners. But, he ponders, he really should get some exercise; is there time for jogging in the afternoon? That reminds him of a championship game he wanted to see at the same time. To be taken more seriously was his ex-wife's repeated request for a luncheon talk. And shouldn't he also settle his vacation plans before all the best locations are taken? Slowly, his optimism gives way to a sense of defeat. The free day has become chaos of competing opportunities and necessities.

If such a scene is vaguely familiar, it attests only further to the pervasive effects of social saturation and the populating of the self. More important, one detects amid the hurly-burly of contemporary life a new constellation of feelings or sensibilities, a new pattern of self-consciousness. This syndrome may be termed *multiphrenia*, generally referring to the splitting of the individual into a multiplicity of self-investments. This condition is partly an outcome of self-population, but partly a result of the populated self's efforts to exploit the potentials of the technologies of relationship. In this sense, there is a cyclical spiraling toward a state of multiphrenia. As one's potentials are expanded by the technologies, so one increasingly employs the technologies for self-expression; yet, as the technologies are further utilized, so do they add to the repertoire of potentials. It would be a mistake to view this multiphrenic condition as a form of illness, for it is often suffused with a sense of expansiveness and adventure. Someday, there may indeed be nothing to distinguish multiphrenia from simply "normal living."

However, before we pass into this oceanic state, let us pause to consider some prominent features of the condition. Three of these are especially noteworthy.

Vertigo of the Valued

With the technology of social saturation, two of the major factors traditionally impeding relationships—namely time and space—are both removed. The past can be continuously renewed—via voice, video, and visits, for example—and distance poses no substantial barriers to ongoing interchange. Yet this same freedom ironically leads to a form of enslavement. For each person, passion, or potential incorporated into oneself exacts a penalty—penalty both of *being* and of *being with*. In the former case, as others are incorporated into the self, their tastes, goals, and values also insinuate themselves into one's being. Through continued interchange, one acquires, for example, a yen for Thai cooking, the desire for retirement security, or an investment in wildlife preservation. Through others, one becomes to value wholegrain breads, novels from Chile, or community politics. Yet as Buddhists have long been aware, to desire is simultaneously to become a slave of the desirable. To "want" reduces one's choice to "want not." Thus, as others are incorporated into the self, and their desires become one's own, there is an expansion of goals—of "musts," wants, and needs. Attention is necessitated, effort is exerted, frustrations are encountered. Each new desire places its demands and reduces one's liberties.

There is also the penalty of being with. As relationships develop, their participants acquire local definitions—friend, lover, teacher, supporter, and so on. To sustain the relationship requires an honoring of the definitions—both of self and other. If two persons become close friends, for example, each acquires certain rights, duties, and privileges. Most relationships of any significance carry with them a range of obligations—for communication, joint activities, preparing for the other's pleasure, rendering appropriate congratulations, and so on. Thus, as relationships accumulate and expand over time, there is a steadily increasing range of phone calls to make and answer, greeting cards to address, visits or activities to arrange, meals to prepare, preparations to be made, clothes to buy, makeup to apply....And with each new opportunity—for skiing together in the Alps, touring Australia, camping in the Adironadacks, or snorkling in the Bahamas—there are "opportunity costs." One must unearth information, buy equipment, reserve hotels, arrange travel, work long hours to clear one's desk, locate babysitters, dogsitters, homesitters.... Liberation becomes a swirling vertigo of demands.

In the professional world, this expansion of "musts" is strikingly evident. In the university of the 1950s, for example, one's departmental colleagues were often vital to one's work. One could walk but a short distance for advice, information, support, and so on. Departments were often close-knit and highly interdependent; travels to other departments or professional meetings were notable events. Today, however, the energetic academic will be linked by post, long-distance phone, fax, and electronic mail to like-minded scholars around the globe. The number of interactions possible in a day is limited only by the constraints of time. The technologies have also stimulated the development of hundreds of new organizations, international conferences, and professional meetings. A colleague recently informed me that if funds were available, he could spend his entire sabbatical traveling from one professional gathering to another. A similar condition pervades the business world. One's scope of business opportunities is no longer so limited by geography; the technologies of the age enable projects to be pursued around the world. (Colgate Tartar Control toothpaste is now sold in over forty countries.) In effect, the potential for new connection and new opportunities is practically unlimited. Daily life has become a sea of drowning demands, and there is no shore in sight.

The Expansion of Inadequacy

It is not simply the expansion of self through relationships that hounds one with the continued sense of "ought." There is also the seeping of self-doubt into everyday consciousness, a subtle feeling of inadequacy that smothers one's activities with an uneasy sense of impending emptiness. In important respects, this sense of inadequacy is a by-product of the populating of self and the presence of social ghosts. For as we incorporate others into ourselves, so does the range of properties expand—that is, the range of what we feel a "good," "proper," or "exemplary" person should be. Many of us carry with us the "ghost of a father," reminding us of the values of honesty and hard work, or a mother challenging us to be nurturing and understanding. We may also absorb from a friend the values of maintaining a healthy body, from a lover the goal of self-sacrifice, from a teacher the ideal of worldly knowledge, and so on. Normal development leaves most people with a rich sense of personal well-being by fulfilling these goals.

But now consider the effects of social saturation. The range of one's friends and associates expands exponentially; one's past life continues to be vivid; and the mass media expose one to an enormous array of new criteria for self-evaluation. A friend from California reminds one to relax and enjoy life; in Ohio, an associate is getting ahead by working eleven hours a day. A relative from Boston stresses the importance of cultural sophistication, while a Washington colleague belittles one's lack of political savvy. A relative's return from Paris reminds one to pay more attention to personal appearance, while a ruddy companion from Colorado suggests that one grows soft.

Meanwhile, newspapers, magazines, and television provide a barrage of new criteria of self-evaluation. Is one sufficiently adventurous, clean well-traveled, well read, low in cholesterol, slim, skilled in cooking, friendly, odor free, coiffed, frugal, burglar proof, family oriented? The list is unending. More than once, I have heard the lament of a subscriber to the Sunday *New York Times*. Each page of this weighty tome will be read by millions. Thus, each page remaining undevoured by day's end will leave one precariously disadvantaged—a potential idiot in a thousand unpredictable circumstances.

Yet the threat of inadequacy is hardly limited to the immediate confrontation with mates and media. Because many of these criteria for self-evaluation are incorporated into the self-existing within the cadre of social ghosts—they are free to speak at any moment. The problem with value is that they are sufficient unto themselves. To value justice, for example, is to say nothing of the value of love; investing in duty will blind one to the value of spontaneity. No one value in itself recognizes the importance of any alternative value. And so it is with the chorus of social ghosts. Each voice of value stands to discredit all that does not meet its standard. All the voices at odds with one's current conduct thus stand as internal critics, scolding, ridiculing, and robbing action of its potential for fulfillment. One settles in front of the television for enjoyment, and the chorus begins: "twelve year old, " "couch potato, " "lazy," "irresponsible"....One sits down with a good book, and again: "sedentary," "antisocial," "inefficient," "fantasist".... Join friends for a game of tennis, and "skin cancer," "shirker of household duties," "underexercised," "overly competitive" come up. Work late and it is "workaholic," "heart attack-prone," "overly ambitious," "irresponsible family member." Each moment is enveloped in the guilt born of all that was possible but now foreclosed.

Rationality in Recession

A third dimension of multiphrenia is closely related to the others. The focus here is on the rationality of everyday decision-making instances in which one tries to be a "reasonable person." Why, one asks, is it important for one's children to attend college? The rational reply is that a college education increases one's job opportunities, earnings, and likely sense of personal fulfillment. Why should I stop smoking? One asks, and the answer is clear that smoking causes cancer, so to smoke is simply to invite a short life. Yet these "obvious" lines of reasoning are obvious only so long as one's identity remains fixed within a particular group.

The rationality of these replies depends altogether on the sharing of opinions—of each incorporating the views of others. To achieve identity in other cultural enclaves turns these "good reasons" into "rationalizations," "false consciousness," or "ignorance." Within some subcultures, a college education is a one-way ticket to bourgeois conventionality—a white-collar job, picket fence in the suburbs, and chronic boredom. For many, smoking is an integral part of a risky lifestyle; it furnishes a sense of intensity, offbeatness, rugged individualism. In the same way, saving money for old age is "sensible" in one family, and "oblivious to the erosions of inflation" in another. For most Westerners, marrying for love is the only reasonable (if not conceivable) thing to do. But many Japanese will point to statistics demonstrating greater longevity and happiness in arranged marriages. Rationality is a vital by-product of social participation.

Yet as the range of our relationships is expanded, the validity of each localized rationality is threatened. What is rational in one relationship is questionable or absurd from the standpoint of another. The "obvious choice" while talking with a colleague lapses into absurdity when speaking with a spouse, and into irrelevance when an old friend calls that evening. Further, because each relationship increases one's capacities for discernment, one carries with oneself a multiplicity of competing expectations, values, and beliefs about "the obvious solution." Thus, if the options are carefully evaluated, every decision becomes a leap into gray vapors. Hamlet's bifurcated decision becomes all too simple, for it is no longer being or non-being that is in question, but to which of multifarious beings one can be committed.

Conclusion

So we find a profound sea change taking place in the character of social life during the twentieth century. Through an array of newly emerging technologies, the world of relationships becomes increasingly saturated. We engage in greater numbers of relationships, in a greater variety of forms, and with greater intensities than ever before. With the multiplication of relationships also comes a transformation in the social capacities of the individual—both in knowing how and knowing that. The relatively coherent and unified sense of self inherent in a traditional culture gives way to manifold and competing potentials. A multiphrenic condition emerges in which one swims in ever shifting, concatenating, and contentious currents of being. One bears the burden of an increasing array of oughts, of self-doubts and irrationalities, The possibility for committed romanticism or strong and single-minded modernism recedes, and the way is opened for the postmodern being....

As belief in essential selves erodes, awareness expands of the ways in which personal identity can be created and recreated.... This consciousness of construction does not strike as a thunderbolt; rather, it eats slowly and irregularly away at the edge of consciousness. And as it increasingly colors our understanding of self and relationships, the character of this consciousness undergoes a qualitative change.... [P]ostmodern consciousness [brings] the erasure of the category of self. No longer can one securely determine what it is to be a specific kind of person...or even a person at all. As the category of the individual person fades from view, consciousness of construction becomes focal. We realize increasingly that who and what we are is not so much the result of our "person essence" (real feelings, deep beliefs, and the like), but of how we are constructed in various social groups.... [T]he concept of the individual self ceases to be intelligible....

40

Jihad vs. McWorld

Benjamin R. Barber

Barber argues that underlying many current changes and conflicts in the world are two opposing historical forces—globalism and tribalism—both of which are a threat to democracy. Barber's article raises several questions. First, of the 195 nation-states that made up the international system in 1995 only a few had credible liberal democracies. Is democracy necessarily the best form of political organization for everyone, as Barber assumes?

Second, as a solution Barber recommends "confederal democracy" where powers are divided between a central government with coordinative functions and smaller units like provinces or states which hold major political power. While he suggests we examine America's Articles of Confederation as an early example of such a system, Canada's experiment with Confederation, particularly as it has been unfolding in recent years, offers a more mature example. What lessons does Canada offer to understanding and managing the conflicting forces of globalism and tribalism?

Just beyond the horizon of current events lie two possible political figures—both bleak, neither democratic. The first is a retribalization of large swaths of humankind by war and bloodshed: a threatened Lebanonization of national states in which culture is pitted against culture, people against people, tribe against tribe—a Jihad in the name of a hundred narrowly conceived faiths against every kind of interdependence, every kind of artificial social cooperation and civic mutuality. The second is being borne in on us by the onrush of economic and ecological forces that demand integration and uniformity and that mesmerize the world with fast music, fast computers, and fast food—with MTV, Macintosh,

---

Published originally in the March, 1992 issue of *The Atlantic Monthly*. Revised as the introduction to *Jihad Versus McWorld* (Times Books, 1995), a volume that discusses and extends the themes of the original article.

and McDonald's, pressing nations into one commercially homogenous global network: one McWorld tied together by technology, ecology, communications, and commerce. The planet is falling precipitantly apart and coming reluctantly together at the very same moment.

These two tendencies are sometimes visible in the same countries at the same instant: thus Yugoslavia, clamoring just recently to join the New Europe, is exploding into fragments; India is trying to live up to its reputation as the world's largest integral democracy while powerful new fundmentalist parties like the Hindu nationalist Bharatiya Janata Party, along with nationalist assassins, are imperiling its hard-won unity. States are breaking up or joining up: the Soviet Union has disappeared almost overnight, its parts forming new unions with one another or with like-minded nationalities in neighboring states. The old interwar national state based on territory and political sovereignty looks to be a mere transitional development.

The tendencies of what I am here calling the forces of Jihad and the forces of McWorld operate with equal strength in opposite directions, the one driven by parochial hatreds, the other by universalizing markets, the one re-creating ancient subnational and ethnic borders from within, the other making national borders porous from without. They have one thing in common: neither offers much hope to citizens looking for practical ways to govern themselves democratically. If the global future is to put Jihad's centrifugal whirlwind against McWorld's centripetal black hole, the outcome is unlikely to be democratic—or so I will argue.

McWorld, or the Globalization of Politics

Four imperatives make up the dynamic of McWorld: a market imperative, a resource imperative, an information-technology imperative, and an ecological imperative. By shrinking the world and diminishing the salience of national borders, these imperatives have in combination achieved a considerable victory over factiousness and particularism, and not least of all over their most virulent form—nationalism. It is the realists who are now Europeans, the utopians who dream nostalgically of a resurgent England or Germany, perhaps even a resurgent Wales or Saxony. Yesterday's wishful cry for one world has yielded to the reality of McWorld.

The market imperative. Marxist and Leninist theories of imperialism assumed that the quest for ever-expanding markets would in time compel nation-based capitalist economies to push against national boundaries in search of an international economic imperium. Whatever else has happened to the scientistic predictions of Marxism, in this domain they have proved farsighted. All national economies are now vulnerable to the inroads of larger, transnational markets within which trade is free, currencies are convertible, access to banking is open, and contracts are enforceable under law. In Europe, Asia, Africa, the South Pacific, and the Americas such markets are eroding national sovereignty and giving rise to entities—international banks, trade associations, transnational lobbies like OPEC and Greenpeace, world news services like CNN and the BBC, and multinational corporations that increasingly lack a meaningful national identity—that neither reflect nor respect nationhood as an organizing or regulative principle.

The market imperative has also reinforced the quest for international peace and stability, requisites of an efficient international economy. Markets are enemies of parochialism, isolation, fractiousness, war. Market psychology attenuates the psychology of ideological and religious cleavages and assumes a concord among producers and consumers—categories that ill fit narrowly conceived national or religious cultures. Shopping has little tolerance for blue laws, whether dictated by pub-closing British paternalism, Sabbath-observing Jewish Orthodox fundamentalism, or no-Sunday-liquor-sales Massachusetts puritanism. In the context of common markets, international law ceases to be a vision of justice and becomes a workaday framework for getting things done—enforcing contracts, ensuring that governments abide by deals, regulating trade and currency relations, and so forth.

Common markets demand a common language, as well as a common currency, and they produce common behaviors of the kind bred by cosmopolitan city life everywhere. Commercial pilots, computer programmers, international bankers, media specialists, oil riggers, entertainment celebrities, ecology experts, demographers, accountants, professors, athletes—these compose a new breed of men and women for whom religion, culture, and nationality can seem only marginal elements in a working identity. Although sociologists of everyday life will no doubt continue to distinguish a Japanese from an American mode, shopping has a common signature throughout the world. Cynics might even say that some of the recent revolutions in Eastern Europe have had as their true goal not liberty and the right to vote but well-paying jobs and the right to shop (although the vote is proving easier to acquire than consumer goods). The market imperative is, then, plenty powerful; but, notwithstanding some of the claims made for "democratic capitalism," it is not identical with the democratic imperative.

The resource imperative. Democrats once dreamed of societies whose political autonomy rested firmly on economic independence. The Athenians idealized what they called autarky, and tried for a while to create a way of life simple and austere enough to make the polis genuinely self-sufficient. To be free meant to be independent of any other community or polis. Not even the Athenians were able to achieve autarky, however: human nature, it turns out, is dependency. By the time of Pericles, Athenian politics was inextricably bound up with a flowering empire held together by naval power and commerce—an empire that, even as it appeared to enhance Athenian might, ate away at Athenian independence and autarky. Master and slave, it turned out, were bound together by mutual insufficiency.

The dream of autarky briefly engrossed nineteenth-century America as well, for the underpopulated, endlessly bountiful land, the cornucopia of natural resources, and the natural barriers of a continent walled in by two great seas led many to believe that America could be a world unto itself. Given this past, it has been harder for Americans than for most to accept the inevitability of interdependence. But the rapid depletion of resources even in a country like ours, where they once seemed inexhaustible, and the maldistribution of arable soil and mineral resources on the planet, leave even the wealthiest societies ever more resource-dependent and many other nations in permanently desperate straits.

Every nation, it turns out, needs something another nation has; some nations have almost nothing they need.

The information-technology imperative. Enlightenment science and the technologies derived from it are inherently universalizing. They entail a quest for descriptive principles of general application, a search for universal solutions to particular problems, and an unswerving embrace of objectivity and impartiality.

Scientific progress embodies and depends on open communication, a common discourse rooted in rationality, collaboration, and an easy and regular flow and exchange of information. Such ideals can be hypocritical covers for power-mongering by elites, and they may be shown to be wanting in many other ways, but they are entailed by the very idea of science and they make science and globalization practical allies.

Business, banking, and commerce all depend on information flow and are facilitated by new communication technologies. The hardware of these technologies tends to be systemic and integrated—computer, television, cable, satellite, laser, fiber-optic, and microchip technologies combining to create a vast interactive communications and information network that can potentially give every person on earth access to every other person, and make every datum, every byte, available to every set of eyes. If the automobile was, as George Ball once said (when he gave his blessing to a Fiat factory in the Soviet Union during the Cold War), "an ideology on four wheels," then electronic telecommunication and information systems are an ideology at 186,000 miles per second—which makes for a very small planet in a very big hurry. Individual cultures speak particular languages; commerce and science increasingly speak English; the whole world speaks logarithms and binary mathematics.

Moreover, the pursuit of science and technology asks for, even compels, open societies. Satellite footprints do not respect national borders; telephone wires penetrate the most closed societies. With photocopying and then fax machines having infiltrated Soviet universities and *samizdat* literary circles in the eighties, and computer modems having multiplied like rabbits in communism's bureaucratic warrens thereafter, *glasnost* could not be far behind. In their social requisites, secrecy and science are enemies.

The new technology's software is perhaps even more globalizing than its hardware. The information arm of international commerce's sprawling body reaches out and touches distinct nations and parochial cultures, and gives them a common face chiseled in Hollywood, on Madison Avenue, and in Silicon Valley. Throughout the 1980s one of the most-watched television programs in South Africa was *The Cosby Show*. The demise of apartheid was already in production. Exhibitors at the 1991 Cannes film festival expressed growing anxiety over the "homogenization" and "Americanization" of the global film industry when, for the third year running, American films dominated the awards ceremonies. America has dominated the world's popular culture for much longer, and much more decisively. In November of 1991 Switzerland's once insular culture boasted bestseller lists featuring *Terminator 2* as the No. 1 movie, *Scarlett* as the No. 1 book, and Prince's *Diamonds and Pearls* as the No. 1 record album. No wonder the Japanese are buying Hollywood film studio sets even faster than Americans are buying Japanese television sets. The kind of software supremacy may in the long term be far more important than hardware superiority, because culture has become more potent than armaments. What is the power of the Pentagon compared with Disneyland? Can the Sixth Fleet keep up with CNN? McDonald's in Moscow and Coke in China will do more to create a global culture than military colonization ever could. It is less the goods than the brand names that do the work, for they convey life-style images that alter perception and challenge behavior. They make up the seductive software of McWorld's common (at times much too common) soul.

Yet in all this high-tech commercial world there is nothing that looks particularly democratic. It lends itself to surveillance as well as liberty, to new forms of manipulation and covert control as well as new kinds of participation, to skewed, unjust market outcomes as well as greater productivity. The consumer society and the open society are not quite synonymous. Capitalism and democracy have a relationship, but it is something less than a marriage. An efficient free market after all requires that consumers be free to vote their dollars on competing goods, not that citizens be free to vote their values and beliefs on competing political candidates and programs. The free market flourished in junta-run Chile, in military-governed Taiwan and Korea, and, earlier, in a variety of autocratic European empires as well as their colonial possessions.

The ecological imperative. The impact of globalization on ecology is a cliché even to world leaders who ignore it. We know well enough that the German forests can be destroyed by Swiss and Italians driving gas-guzzlers fueled by leaded gas. We also know that the planet can be asphyxiated by greenhouse gases because Brazilian farmers want to be part of the twentieth century and are burning down tropical rain forests to clear a little land to plough, and because Indonesians make a living out of converting their lush jungle into toothpicks for fastidious Japanese diners, upsetting the delicate oxygen balance and in effect puncturing our global lungs. Yet this ecological consciousness has meant not only greater awareness but also greater inequality, as modernized nations try to slam the door behind them, saying to developing nations, "The world cannot afford *your* modernization; ours has wrung it dry!"

Each of the four imperatives just cited is transnational, transideological, and transcultural. Each applies impartially to Catholics, Jews, Muslims, Hindus, and Buddhists; to democrats and totalitarians; to capitalists and socialists. The Enlightenment dream of a universal rational society has to a remarkable degree been realized—but in a form that is commercialized, homogenized, depoliticized, bureaucratized, and, of course, radically incomplete, for the movement toward McWorld is in competition with forces of global breakdown, national dissolution, and centrifugal corruption. These forces, working in the opposite direction, are the essence of what I call Jihad.

Jihad, or the Lebanonization of the World

OPEC, the World Bank, the United Nations, the International Red Cross, the multinational corporation...there are scores of institutions that reflect globalization. But they often appear as ineffective reactors to the world's real actors: national states and, to an ever greater degree, subnational factions in permanent rebellion against uniformity and integration—even the kind represented by universal law and justice. The headlines feature these players regularly: they are cultures, not countries; parts, not wholes; sects, not religions; rebellious factions and dissenting minorities at war not just with globalism but with the traditional nation-state. Kurds, Basques, Puerto Ricans, Ossetians, East Timoreans, Quebecois, the Catholics of Northern Ireland, Abkhasians, Kurile Islander Japanese, the Zulus of Inkatha, Catalonians, Tamils, and, of course, Palestinians—people without countries, inhabiting nations not their own, seeking smaller worlds within borders that will seal them off from modernity.

A powerful irony is at work here. Nationalism was once a force of integration and unification, a movement aimed at bringing together disparate clans, tribes, and cultural fragments under new, assimilationist flags. But as Ortega y Gasset noted more than sixty years ago, having won its victories, nationalism changed its strategy. In the 1920s, and again today, it is more often a reactionary and divisive force, pulverizing the very nations it once helped cement together. The force that creates nations is "inclusive," Ortega wrote in *The Revolt of the Masses*. "In periods of consolidation, nationalism has a positive value, and is a lofty standard. But in Europe everything is more than consolidated, and nationalism is nothing but a mania...."

This mania has left the post-Cold War world smoldering with hot wars; the international scene is little more unified than it was at the end of the Great War, in Ortega's own time. There were more than thirty wars in progress last year, most of them ethnic, racial, tribal, or religious in character, and the list of unsafe regions doesn't seem to be getting any shorter. Some new world order!

The aim of many of these small-scale wars is to redraw boundaries, to implode states and resecure parochial identities: to escape McWorld's dully insistent imperatives. The mood is that of Jihad: war not as an instrument of policy but as an emblem of identity, an expression of community, an end in itself. Even where there is no shooting war, there is fractiousness, secession, and the quest for ever smaller communities. Add to the list of dangerous countries those at risk: In Switzerland and Spain, Jurassian and Basque separatists still argue the virtues of ancient identities, sometimes in the language of bombs. Hyperdisintegration in the former Soviet Union may well continue unabated—not just a Ukraine independent from the Soviet Union but a Bessarabian Ukraine independent from the Ukrainian republic; not just Russia severed from the defunct union but Tatarstan severed from Russia. Yugoslavia makes even the disunited, ex-Soviet, nonsocialist republics that were once the Soviet Union look integrated, its sectarian fatherlands springing up within factional motherlands like weeds within weeds within weeds. Kurdish independence would threaten the territorial integrity of four Middle Eastern nations. Well before the current cataclysm Soviet Georgia made a claim for autonomy from the Soviet Union, only to be faced with its Ossetians (164,000 in a republic of 5.5 million) demanding their own self-determination within Georgia. The Abkhasian minority in Georgia has followed suit. Even the good will established by Canada's once promising Meech Lake protocols is in danger, with francophone Quebec again threatening the dissolution of the federation. In South Africa the emergence from apartheid was hardly achieved when friction between Inkatha's Zulus and the African National Congress's tribally identified members threatened to replace Europeans' racism with an indigenous tribal war after thirty years of attempted integration using the colonial language (English) as a unifier, Nigeria is now playing with the idea of linguistic multiculturalism—which could mean the cultural breakup of the nation into hundreds of tribal fragments. Even Saddam Hussein has benefited from the threat of internal Jihad, having used renewed tribal and religious warfare to turn last season's mortal enemies into reluctant allies of an Iraqi nationhood that he nearly destroyed.

The passing of communism has torn away the thin veneer of internationalism (workers of the world unite!) to reveal ethnic prejudices that are not only ugly and deep-seated but increasingly murderous. Europe's old scourge, anti-Semitism, is back with a vengeance, but it is only one of many antagonisms. It appears all too easy to throw the historical gears into reverse and pass from a Communist dictatorship back into a tribal state.

Among the tribes, religion is also a battlefield. ("Jihad" is a rich word whose generic meaning is "struggle"—usually the struggle of the soul to avert evil. Strictly applied to religious war, it is used only in reference to battles where the faith is under assault, or battles against a government that denies the practice of Islam. My use here is rhetorical, but does follow both journalistic practice and history.) Remember the Thirty Years War? Whatever forms of Enlightenment universalism might once have come to grace such historically related forms of monotheism as Judaism, Christianity, and Islam, in many of their modern incarnations they are parochial rather than cosmopolitan, angry rather than loving, proselytizing rather than ecumenical, zealous rather than rationalist, sectarian rather than deistic, ethnocentric rather than universalizing. As a result, like the new forms of hypernationalism, the new expressions of religious fundamentalism are fractious and pulverizing, never integrating. This is religion as the Crusaders knew it: a battle to the death for souls that if not saved will be forever lost.

The atmospherics of Jihad have resulted in a breakdown of civility in the name of identity, of comity in the name of community. International relations have sometimes taken on the aspect of gang war—cultural turf battles featuring tribal factions that were supposed to be sublimated as integral parts of large national, economic, postcolonial, and constitutional entities.

The Darkening Future of Democracy

These rather melodramatic tableaux vivants do not tell the whole story, however. For all their defects, Jihad and McWorld have their attractions. Yet, to repeat and insist, the attractions are unrelated to democracy. Neither McWorld nor Jihad is remotely democratic in impulse. Neither needs democracy; neither promotes democracy.

McWorld does manage to look pretty seductive in a world obsessed with Jihad. It delivers peace, prosperity, and relative unity—if at the cost of independence, community, and identity (which is generally based on difference). The primary political values required by the global market are order and tranquillity, and freedom—as in the phrases "free trade," "free press," and "free love." Human rights are needed to a degree, but not citizenship or participation—and no more social justice and equality than are necessary to promote efficient economic production and consumption. Multinational corporations sometimes seem to prefer doing business with local oligarchs, inasmuch as they can take confidence from dealing with the boss on all crucial matters. Despots who slaughter their own populations are no problem, so long as they leave markets in place and refrain from making war on their neighbors (Saddam Hussein's fatal mistake). In trading partners, predictability is of more value than justice.

The Eastern European revolutions that seemed to arise out of concern for global democratic values quickly deteriorated into a stampede in the general direction of free markets and their ubiquitous, television-promoted shopping malls. East Germany's Neues Forum, that courageous gathering of intellectuals, students, and workers which overturned the Stalinist regime in Berlin in 1989, lasted only six months in Germany's mini-version of McWorld. Then it gave way to money and markets and monopolies from the West. By the time of the first all-German elections, it could scarcely manage to secure three percent of the vote. Elsewhere there is growing evidence that *glasnost* will go and *perestroika*—defined as privatization and an opening of markets to Western bidders—will stay. So understandably anxious are the new rulers of Eastern

Europe and whatever entities are forged from the residues of the Soviet Union to gain access to credit and markets and technology—McWorld's flourishing new currencies—that they have shown themselves willing to trade away democratic prospects in pursuit of them: not just old totalitarian ideologies and command-economy production models but some possible indigenous experiments with a third way between capitalism and socialism, such as economic cooperatives and employee stock-ownership plans, both of which have their ardent supporters in the East.

Jihad delivers a different set of virtues: a vibrant local identity, a sense of community, solidarity among kinsmen, neighbors, and countrymen, narrowly conceived. But it also guarantees parochialism and is grounded in exclusion. Solidarity is secured through war against outsiders. And solidarity often means obedience to a hierarchy in governance, fanaticism in beliefs, and the obliteration of individual selves in the name of the group. Deference to leaders and intolerance toward outsiders (and toward "enemies within") are hallmarks of tribalism—hardly the attitudes required for the cultivation of new democratic women and men capable of governing themselves. Where new democratic experiments have been conducted in retribalizing societies, in both Europe and the Third World, the result has often been anarchy, repression, persecution, and the coming of new, non-communist forms of very old kinds of despotism. During the past year, Havel's velvet revolution in Czechoslovakia was imperiled by partisans of "Czechland" and of Slovakia as independent entities. India seemed little less rent by Sikh, Hindu, Muslim, and Tamil infighting than it was immediately after the British pulled out, more than forty years ago.

To the extent that either McWorld or Jihad has a *natural* politics, it has turned out to be more of an antipolitics. For McWorld, it is the antipolitics of globalism: bureaucratic, technocratic, and meritocratic, focused (as Marx predicted it would be) on the administration of things—with people, however, among the chief things to be administered. In its politico-economic imperatives McWorld has been guided by laissez-faire market principles that privilege efficiency, productivity, and beneficence at the expense of civic liberty and self-government.

For Jihad, the antipolitics of tribalization has been explicitly antidemocratic: one-party dictatorship, government by military junta, theocratic fundamentalism—often associated with a version of the *Führerprinzip* that empowers an individual to rule on behalf of a people. Even the government of India, struggling for decades to model democracy for a people who will soon number a billion, longs for great leaders; and for every Mahatma Gandhi, Indira Gandhi, or Ranjiv Gandhi taken from them by zealous assassins, the Indians appear to seek a replacement who will deliver them from the lengthy travail of their freedom.

The Confederal Option

How can democracy be secured and spread in a world whose primary tendencies are at best indifferent to it (McWorld) and at worst deeply antithetical to it (Jihad)? My guess is that globalization will eventually vanquish retribalization. The ethos of material "civilization" has not yet encountered an obstacle it has been unable to thrust aside. Ortega may have grasped in the 1920s a clue to our own future in the coming millennium.

> Everyone sees the need of a new principle of life. But as always happens in similar crises—some people attempt to save the situation by an artificial intensification of the very principle which has led to decay. This is the meaning of the "nationalist" outburst of recent years...things have always gone that way. The last flare, the longest; the last sigh, the deepest. On the very eve of their disappearance there is an intensification of frontiers—military and economic.

Jihad may be a last deep sigh before the eternal yawn of McWorld. On the other hand, Ortega was not exactly prescient; his prophecy of peace and internationalism came just before blitzkrieg, world war, and the Holocaust tore the old order to bits. Yet democracy is how we remonstrate with reality, the rebuke our aspirations offer to history. And if retribalization is inhospitable to democracy, there is nonetheless a form of democratic government that can accommodate parochialism and communitarianism, one that can even save them from their defects and make them more tolerant and participatory: decentralized participatory democracy. And if McWorld is indifferent to democracy, there is nonetheless a form of democratic government that suits global markets passably well—representative government in its federal or, better still, confederal variation.

With its concern for accountability, the protection of minorities, and the universal rule of law, a confederalized representative system would serve the political needs of McWorld as well as oligarchic bureaucratism or meritocratic elitism is currently doing. As we are already beginning to see, many nations may survive in the long term only as confederations that afford local regions smaller than "nations" extensive jurisdiction. Recommended reading for democrats of the twenty-first century is not the U.S. Constitution or the French Declaration of Rights of Man and Citizen but the Articles of Confederation, that suddenly pertinent document that stitched together the thirteen American colonies into what then seemed a too loose confederation of independent states but now appears a new form of political realism, as veterans of Yeltsin's new Russia and the new Europe created at Maastricht will attest.

By the same token, the participatory and direct form of democracy that engages citizens in civic activity and civic judgment and goes well beyond just voting and accountability—the system I have called "strong democracy"—suits the political needs of decentralized communities as well as theocratic and nationalist party dictatorships have done. Local neighborhoods need not be democratic, but they can be. Real democracy has flourished in diminutive settings: the spirit of liberty, Tocqueville said, is local. Participatory democracy, if not naturally apposite to tribalism, has an undeniable attractiveness under conditions of parochialism.

Democracy in any of these variations will, however, continue to be obstructed by the undemocratic and antidemocratic trends toward uniformitarian globalism and intolerant retribalization which I have portrayed here. For democracy to persist in our brave new McWorld, we will have to commit acts of conscious political will—a possibility, but hardly a probability, under these conditions. Political will requires much more than the quick fix of the transfer of institutions. Like technology transfer, institution transfer rests on foolish assumptions about a uniform world of the kind that once fired the imagination of colonial administrators. Spread English justice to the colonies by exporting wigs. Let an East Indian trading company act as the vanguard to Britain's free parliamentary institutions. Today's well-intentioned quick-fixers in the National Endowment for Democracy and the Kennedy School of Government, in the unions and foundations and universities zealously nurturing contacts in Eastern Europe and the Third World, are hoping to democratize by long distance. Post Bulgaria a parliament by first-class mail. Fed Ex the Bill of Rights to Sri Lanka. Cable Cambodia some common law.

Yet Eastern Europe has already demonstrated that importing free political parties, parliaments, and presses cannot establish a democratic civil society; imposing a free market may even have the opposite effect. Democracy grows from the bottom up and cannot be imposed from the top down. Civil society has to be built from the inside out. The institutional superstructure comes last. Poland may become democratic, but then again it may heed the Pope, and prefer to found its politics on its Catholicism, with uncertain consequences for democracy. Bulgaria may become democratic, but it may prefer tribal war. The former Soviet Union may become a democratic confederation, or it may just grow into an anarchic and weak conglomeration of markets for other nations' goods and services.

Democrats need to seek out indigenous democratic impulses. There is always a desire for self-government, always some expression of participation, accountability, consent, and representation, even in traditional hierarchical societies. These need to be identified, tapped, modified, and incorporated into new democratic practices with an indigenous flavor. The tortoises among the democratizers may ultimately outlive or outpace the hares, for they will have the time and patience to explore conditions along the way, and to adapt their gait to changing circumstances. Tragically, democracy in a hurry often looks something like France in 1794 or China in 1989.

It certainly seems possible that the most attractive democratic ideal in the face of the brutal realities of Jihad and the dull realities of McWorld will be a confederal union of semi-autonomous communities smaller than nation-states, tied together into regional economic associations and markets larger than nation-states—participatory and self-determining in local matters at the bottom, representative and accountable at the top. The nation-state would play a diminished role, and sovereignty would lose some of its political potency. The Green movement adage "Think globally, act locally" would actually come to describe the conduct of politics.

This vision reflects only an ideal, however—one that is not terribly likely to be realized. Freedom, Jean-Jacques Rousseau once wrote, is a food easy to eat but hard to digest. Still, democracy has always played itself out against the odds. And democracy remains both a form of coherence as binding as McWorld and a secular faith potentially as inspiring as Jihad.

Benjamin R. Barber is Whitman Professor of Political Science and Director of the Whitman Centre at Rutgers University and the author of many books including Strong Democracy *(1984),* An Aristrocracy for Everyone *(1992) and* Jihad Versus McWorld *(Times Books, 1995).*

Appendix

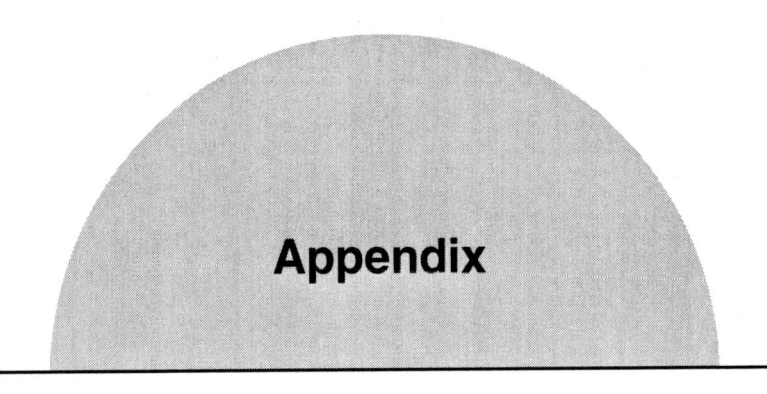

Field Projects

Before inquiring into the method suited to the study of social facts, it is important to know which facts are commonly called "social".... [I]n reality there is in every society a certain group of phenomena which may be differentiated from those studied by the other natural sciences. When I fulfil my obligations as brother, husband, or citizen, when I execute my contracts, I perform duties which are defined, externally to myself and my acts, in law and in custom.... Here, then, is a category of facts with very distinctive characteristics: it consists of ways of acting, thinking and feeling, external to the individual, and endowed with a power of coercion, by reason of which they control him.
Emile Durkheim, *The Rules of Sociological Method*,
New York: Free Press, 1966; 1,3.

Sociology...is a science which attempts the interpretive understanding of social action in order thereby to arrive at a causal explanation of its course and effects.
Max Weber, *The Theory of Social and Economic Organization*
(Trans. by A.M. Anderson and T. Parsons)
New York: Free Press, 1947: 88).

1

Observation

Jacqueline Aaron and Marcia Wiseman

Although sociology may be generally described as a field of study with society as its object of inquiry, it is perhaps more accurately a practice, a distinctive way of inquiring into human conduct and collective life. It is our contention that only as a practice of inquiry does the student discover the excitement, the discipline and the power of sociology, and that this should be the focus of any introduction to sociology.

In the following selections, Aaron and Wiseman outline some basic sociology projects which the introductory student can undertake. Each project centres on a qualitative research method, and can stand as an exercise in its own right. However, they also can be used as part of larger projects that encourage students to analyze and account for their findings in terms of a group's culture and/or social organization. Enjoy!

Observation as a Research Tool

Observation as a means of increasing one's knowledge is basic to the investigation of almost any phenomenon. Some types of social action can only be truly understood and appreciated when they are actually witnessed—seen "in the flesh." The pomp and ceremony of rituals, the life conditions of men in prison, and the subtle nuances of flirting are but a few aspects of social life best grasped through firsthand observation. Many of the most memorable sociological studies have been conducted by investigators who used observation techniques. That such studies are often of interest far beyond the immediate application of their findings bears witness to the vitality of observation as a research tool.

Jacqueline Aaron and Marcia Wiseman, "Observation," "Participant Observation," "The Depth Interview," "Role Analysis" and "Content Analysis" from *Field Projects for Sociology Students*, Canfield-Haper and Row, 1970: 15-18; 20-23; 27-34; 49-56; 83-91; 113-125. Reprinted by permission of the authors.

Observation of social phenomena is obviously not restricted to the sociologist. All people observe social situations to which they are privy or about which they would like greater understanding. Moreover, they offer amateur reports of such scenes by describing and interpreting them to friends or relatives who were not present, in order to increase these persons' understanding of what happened. There is an important difference between the observations of the sociologist and those of the lay observer, however. Because the sociologist must organize and analyse his data in terms of sociological theories and concepts, he is sensitized to attending to human group life in a far more systematic fashion than the average person is. The layman relies primarily on his memory, but the researcher attempts to keep written descriptions of what he sees, for he is interested in more detail than his memory can retain. For this reason the sociologist is forced to think of systematic ways to conduct his observations and record what happens as it a happens, or soon after, without upsetting his subjects or missing significant actions. Such planning is a part of the observation technique for which laymen seldom have patience or need.

How to Do Observation Research

Observation research is part craft and part art. Anyone can observe, but it takes practice and careful planning to observe and record a scene accurately and then to analyse perceptively what happened of sociological significance. Such skills improve with experience.

An early decision the observer must make is the setting. He must choose this with the goals of the study in mind. For instance, if the observer is studying strategies of flirting, he must select a setting in which this interaction is likely to occur both openly and frequently. Furthermore, he must think of an unobtrusive way to record his observations in an organized manner. Sometimes it is helpful to set up tally sheets before going into the field.

Professional observers try to blend with others in the settings they are observing. They may dress and act as if they belong to the groups so as not to influence the interactions by their presence. Sometimes an observer also participates in the activities to get a feel for the meaning they have to the persons he is studying. Blending into the scene can make the recording of data a problem. Of course, if the subjects of the research are very young, or if writing is expected in a particular setting, the problem is eliminated. But if writing might seem out of place, the observer must find a private area where he can record events and descriptions of them from time to time, because he cannot rely on memory alone.

Once on the scene the observer must remain alert and flexible. Keeping track of the interactions of even a few persons can be very demanding. An observer must be able to adjust his tally sheets and focus of attention as the situation dictates, because the true gold mined through observation is the unexpected.

At frequent intervals the sociologist observing human group life in action should stop and ponder (usually in private) what he has seen and recorded. What is its sociological significance? What sorts of interactions seem to bring on what kinds of counter moves? What sociological concepts seem to be in play? (The investigator may also discuss his findings with other sociologists to get their insights.) Once he has made some preliminary decisions about these and other questions, the investigator will try to think of ways to confirm his hunches about what is going on in the scene he is watching. Thus sensitized by his introspection, he returns to continue his observations.

Not least among the talents of an observer of human group life is the ability to organize the findings and relay them to a reader via well-written description. Deciding on the central theme of the data often aids its organization. Descriptive passages should aim at reproducing, as closely as subtleties of language will permit, the situations observed. The sociological import of descriptions should be included in order to relate the particular findings to the broader spectrum of theory about human group life.

Advantages and Disadvantages

Observation is particularly useful for gaining insight into a respondent's habitual round of activities. The average person seldom sees these activities as sociologically significant and rarely reports them to the researcher during an interview. The routines and rituals that families develop in the course of living together, for example, can so recede into the background of daily events that they do not seem sufficiently important to the people involved to mention to an investigator. Interactions that are difficult to describe or that people are reluctant to talk about are often amenable to observation, provided they are accessible to an outsider. Techniques of parental discipline, times of personal embarrassment, riots, strikes, and other collective behaviour are but a few such situations.

Of course, observation research can have drawbacks. It is time-consuming and, somewhat like police stake-outs, it is not always rewarding in the type of data desired. Observations cannot be scheduled solely at the convenience of the investigator; instead he must be on the scene when the scene is on! Perhaps the most troublesome problem in observation is researcher bias that can contaminate findings. If the investigator is aware of the following sources of bias, he should be able to neutralize their effects—to some extent, at least.
1. Unlimited selectivity in perception, recording or reporting.
2. Imputation of meaning that the actors themselves do not intend or experience.
3. Mistaking an idiosyncratic event for a recurrent one.
4. Affecting the action by his presence.

It is obvious, of course, that the lay observer also runs afoul of these biasing factors. We are often aware of flaws in the descriptions that other people offer us concerning an event at which we were not present. We know, for instance, that in reporting, some of our friends tend to select only certain features of a situation, or to emphasize certain aspects in a way that distorts it. Then, too, people frequently misinterpret the actions they witness. And we have all experienced the occasion when a person tells us that so and so is always engaged in a certain activity, when we know the speaker has viewed such action by the person in question only once or twice.

Some Applications of This Method

Observation techniques have been used to gather data on the means people employ to ease embarrassing moments—for example, a male doctor's examinations of female patients (Emerson, 1963). Observation has also been used to watch intake procedures at a drug and alcoholism clinic in order to detect unwritten screening principles (Wiseman, 1970); to look at the police in action (Sudnow, 1965); to see how children act and interact in a small town in various natural habitats such as the library and drugstore (Barker and Wright, 1955); and to observe men living on Skid Row to discover what their typical day is like (Wiseman, 1970). These are but a few studies based on observation.

Although many investigators use natural settings and look at whatever develops in the normal course of events, psychologists and social psychologists often use observation techniques to watch people in experimental laboratory situations. In such cases the observers often remain behind mirror-windows, unseen by the subjects—who are often aware, however, that they are taking part in a controlled experiment of some kind (Asch, 1956; Garfinkel, 1963; Lippitt, 1940; Milgram, 1965, and Bales, 1950, 1970).

Before Going into the Field

1. Gain access to the setting. Some settings, like bus depots, are open to everyone. Others are closed and present problems of access. If you do observation research in an educational institution (for example, a classroom), you are likely to need permission. Often you need the recommendation of someone whose name carries some weight. If such is the case, perhaps your instructor can make arrangements for you. Where negotiations fail and the researcher still wishes to pursue the subject, he must locate alternative areas.
2. Narrow your topic of inquiry. Do not be afraid to do something that seems "too simple." Better a simple project elegantly handled than a complex one that is botched.
3. Decide what you want to know about the topic you select. This is actually an additional narrowing of your inquiry.
4. Select a setting that offers an opportunity for the type of social activity you wish to study.

5. Organize your observation and note-taking in advance. Do some preliminary planning on how you will keep track of your data. Set up some sort of tally sheet for the structured portion of the observations that will allow you to keep track of the acts you are interested in, the specific persons acting, and the responses to them. You will undoubtedly have to revise this after being in the field a short time, but this planning will force you to think of the types of activity to watch for and how you can organize their collection.
6. For the unstructured portions of the observation project, plan to write the details of pertinent social interactions and your interpretation of them at the time. This should include verbatim records of conversations (or as close to verbatim as possible) and descriptions of specific situations.

In the Field

1. Find a location where you can watch without disturbing the interaction.
2. Test your tally and revise as necessary to accommodate what is occurring.
3. If at all convenient, jot down descriptions and sociological interpretations as they occur to you. You may be unpleasantly surprised at the good ideas you will be unable to recall later when you are writing the report unless you note important items while in the field.
4. If you get some special, unexpected insight into your sociological problem, be flexible enough to follow it up in your systematic and descriptive observations even though you did not originally plan for it.

References

Asch, S.E. (1956). "Studies of Independence and Conformity." *Psychological Monographs* 70:9.

Bales, Robert F. (1950). *Interaction Process Analysis: A Method for the Study of Small Groups.* Reading, Mass.: Addison-Wesley.

Bales, Robert F. (1970). *Personality and Interpersonal Behaviour.* New York: Holt, Rinehart and Winston.

Barker, Roger and H.F. Wright. (1955). *The Midwest and Its Children.* Evanston, Ill.: Row, Peterson.

Emerson, Joan (1963). "Social Functions of Humour in a Hospital Setting." Unpublished Ph.D. dissertation, University of California. Berkeley.

Garfinkel, H. (1963). "A Conception of, and Experiments with, 'Trust' as a Condition of Stable, Concerted Actions." pp.187-238 in O.J. Harvey (ed.), *Motivation and Social Interaction.* New York: Ronald.

Lippitt, Ronald (1940). "An Experimental Study of the Effect of Democratic and Authoritarian Group Atmospheres." *University of Iowa Studies in Child Welfare* 16 February: 43-195.

Milgram, Stanley (1965). "Some Conditions of Obedience and Disobedience to Authority." pp. 243-262 in Ivan D. Steiner and Martin Fishbein (eds.), *Current Studies in Social Psychology.* New York: Holt, Rinehart and Winston.

Sudnow, David (1965). "Normal Crimes: Sociological Features of the Penal Code in A Public Defender's Office." *Social Problems* 12 (Winter): 255-276.

Wiseman, Jaqueline P. (1970). *Stations of the Lost.* Englewood Cliffs, N.J.: Prentice Hall.

2
Participant Observation

Jacqueline Aaron and Marcia Wiseman

Participant Observation, a Definition

Now that you are acquainted with the field technique of observation you should be ready to take a turn with its research cousin, participant observation. Both of these techniques are important sociological tools. It is only by observing what people do when they interact with one another, as well as by recording what they say they do, that we can begin to get an understanding of the dynamics of social processes.

The method of research known as participant observation differs from the previous structured and unstructured observations in several important ways. As the name implies, the participant observer is a researcher who becomes a member of the group he is observing, while the non-participant observer tries to remain aloof from it. This distinction is not clear cut since there is a wide range in the level of participation—from the sociologist who stays out of the group and just watches the action to the researcher who is actually a member. Usually a researcher participates to a degree somewhere between these two extremes by either posing as a member or announcing himself as a scientific investigator and hoping to be accepted by the group in that role. Inevitably, a time continuum parallels the degree of participation. The longer an observer stays on the scene, the more likely he is to be drawn into participating in the group's way of life. As a general rule, the participant observer commits himself to a group for a considerable period of time, ranging from several weeks or months to many years.

A second characteristic of the participant observer is that he tries to understand the frame of reference of the group he is investigating. He does this primarily by joining the members in their daily activities in order to experience things as they do. The autobiographies of those who have lived for many years in institutions such as prisons (Black, 1927) or convents (Baldwin, 1959) are particularly insightful studies of these "closed" societies. Though these individuals were not trained sociologists, they were participant observers par excellence.

There is a certain similarity between this approach and espionage. The observer must exist mentally on two levels. Instead of being socialized to the new way of life almost unknowingly, as are most individuals after they join a group, the scientific investigator must learn to be simultaneously "inside" and "outside" the group life he is studying. He must learn the meanings that behaviour has for the members of the group, and he has to become sufficiently involved with the group to be able to understand what makes it tick. At the same time, he cannot be so involved that he is unable to report accurately what is happening and why. He cannot be so far "inside" that everything seems so "normal" as to be not worth reporting. And to top it all off, he must be able to report patterns of behaviour and interrelationships objectively, without moral judgment or bias. The reason for this double frame of reference is that the participant observer wants to understand the group and its actions not only in its own terms—that is, how the members themselves live and feel the culture—but also in terms of a larger and more general set of sociological hypotheses or theories about the nature of human interaction.

Do these sound like impossible tasks? They are difficult, but with practice they can be handled fairly well. Anthropologists occasionally find some of the attitudes, beliefs, and behaviours of the societies they study repugnant or immoral. However, they are trained not to judge, but rather to try to faithfully record and to determine what meaning these behaviour patterns have for the people who practice them.[1] Perhaps an even more common outcome of close contact with a new group over a prolonged period of time is the observer's identification with the group. He starts to accept their behaviour patterns as his own and may find it hard to re-enter his old way of life when he has finished his study. Many Peace Corps volunteers have had this problem after living for a year or two in a foreign culture with a way of life dissimilar from their own. These twin dangers—aversion and over-identification—can be partially neutralized if the researcher is aware that he is not merely a recording machine—and that he is going to have personal reactions to any new group he enters.

How to Do Participant Observation

Traditionally, participant observation requires access to a group or community over a long time period since it is essentially a research technique to learn about and describe a group's total culture or way of life. How long should an investigator stay with a group or community to obtain the information he seeks? Certainly he must remain long enough to observe recurring behavioural patterns. This may mean attendance at all the weekly activities of a small club for two or three months, or living in a community (small town or primitive society) for several years. In the first case, he may be interested in learning how the leadership of the club maintains its power; in the second, whether there is a relationship between child-rearing techniques and achievement motivation.

What should the participant observer notice and record? This depends on the purpose of the study. If it is exploratory, presumably the researcher does not know the culture of the group. Thus he must be careful to keep comprehensive and detailed notes on all that occurs around him. Even behaviour that seems trivial or unimportant should be recorded in his researcher's "diary." The good investigator will record observations as often as possible and not rely on his memory, which more often than not is untrustworthy when it comes to detail. Sometimes it is necessary to record as often as five or six times a day if the observer is living with the group. No matter how difficult the circumstances, he should keep his diary current.

If the researcher is only interested in one particular aspect of a group—for example, the leadership pattern—then it would seem permissible for him to limit his observations and note-taking to those actions of the participants that exhibit "leadership" qualities. Even here, however, seemingly unimportant behaviour patterns (speech, facial expressions, gestures) may offer clues that aid in giving insight into the research problem.

Because the participant observer attempts to understand how the people he is studying feel about their situation, he is trying to do more than simply describe the distinctive behaviour patterns of the individuals interacting in a particular group. He is also trying to explain why they, as individuals, are behaving as they are.

Whether the researcher is aware of it or not, whenever he enters a group as a newcomer he is assigned a role by the old members. He may be accepted as an "observer" or as a "member," but in whatever role he is cast, he has altered the previous structure of role-relationships. Thus he is a potential, if not an actual, disturbance in existing schizoid patterns. It is only when the observer has been "placed" by the other members and is interacting with them in a "normal" way that his is able to start collecting information without arousing fear and hostility (Blau, 1967). After this normalizing has occurred will members of the group feel comfortable and act naturally.[2]

The degree to which a participant observer can bias his results by his mere presence can probably never be fully known. The effect of his presence varies with the size of the group (the smaller the group, the greater the effect), how deeply entrenched previous patterns of interaction were, and whether the group knows it is being studied. Because you already have a place in the group and a role to play, your research efforts will probably not change previously established patterns of behaviour and the biasing effect of your presence presumably will not be a problem.

Advantages and Disadvantages

A major advantage of participant observation is that the investigator need not rely totally on "empathetic insight" or intuition to understand the perspective of his research subject, as he might from observation alone. He sees the world, at least part of the time, in the same way other members of the group see it because he is living their kind of life with them. Therefore, personal introspection will provide him with clues for understanding his data. Also, as with non-participant observation, he watches human group life as it is lived, not as it is reported to an interviewer. All the contradictions between what people say they believe in doing and what they actually do, their consistencies and inconsistencies, are played out before the observer. Also, as a participant he can often casually ask for the types of explanations that an interviewer arriving "cold" on the scene cannot. He can ask, "Hey, what's so funny?" or "Why did everyone look so glum just then?" and it will not sound inappropriate. The method offers great flexibility in the field. If the observer notes some activity that seems significant to the problem he is investigating and that he knew nothing about before he began his study, he can arrange his observation efforts to encompass this behaviour.

Participation has one other major advantage—a built-in validity test. If the participant who is trying to "pass" as a member in the group he is studying misinterprets some bit of interaction and then acts on the basis of his misinterpretation, the group will soon show him the error of his ways!

Participant observation has its disadvantages too. It is time-consuming. Also, the investigator is not usually able to control the action (although this depends to a large extent on his role in the group), so that he must wait for events that are of interest to him to occur. Sometimes he will have to spend hours watching interaction he has already seen while waiting for some new data. Because of the "ongoing" nature of the happenings in the group, a participant observation project cannot be planned so completely in advance as can a survey research project.

Being a participant in some groups can be very demanding. Sociologists have performed in dance bands (Becker, 1963), successfully faked the symptoms and problems of mental illness (Caudill, 1958), and worked with the police on stake-outs (Skolnick, 1966). Often those who participated with some deviant groups found themselves faced with the choice of either joining what they considered to be immoral or illegal actions or severing their ties with the group.

Finally, one of participant observation's greatest virtues can also be one of its most troublesome areas (we mentioned this before, but it deserves repeating). The deeper the participant investigator immerses himself in the group's culture, the more difficult he finds it to study it "objectively," and the more likely he is to miss the sociological significance of action that becomes increasingly "normal" to him.

Some Applications

Participation in the normal life of a community or group to understand its social processes better has a long and interesting history in social investigation. One of the first important studies using this technique was conducted by Frederic LePlay (1808-1882), who studied the family life of European workers by actually living in their homes. His major interest was the interrelationships between geographical location, type of work, and a family's way of life.

Anthropologists have found this method of investigation particularly useful in studying primitive communities, and it is often associated with this branch of the social sciences. Most of what we know today of non-literate societies has been because of excellent anthropological field studies. Sociologists have found participant observation particularly valuable for the study of groups that the average American—including the investigator himself, usually—does not understand. It has been used to study mental hospitals (Goffman, 1961), delinquent gangs, and gamblers (Scott, 1968), to name but a few. Sociologists have also used the technique to study small towns (Withers, 1945; Lowry, 1965), industrial plants (Warner and Lew, 1947), and other more conventional settings.

Before You Go into the Field

1. Determine what particular aspect of the group you want to study. Since you have limited time available to complete this assignment, it is essential that you determine the kinds of group interaction you want to know more about. Here are a few suggestions:
   a. Focus on the communication patterns of the group. All groups develop a "secret language" by using both vocal and non-vocal gestures.
   b. Examine the leadership patterns. Who are the leaders, and how do they maintain their position?
   c. Look at this group's problems. How does it solve them?
   d. Discover the modes of cooperation, or the exchange processes. Who does what for whom?
   e. Identify the sanctions or punishments of members who violate the rules or norms or who try to change their expected role-behaviour. (You as a member could deliberately change your accustomed behaviour in order to test whether other members attempt to bring you back into line. If this tack is taken, it would first be necessary to observe the group in your "normal" role so that you could make a comparison.)
2. Specify more clearly the dimensions of your topic. Think out the kinds of social phenomena you will use as real-life examples of problems. For example, if you are interested in how the group solves problems, what will you regard as a problem? Will it be the necessity to make a decision—such as to charge non-members for tickets to a play? Or will it be the necessity to ease tensions arising from arguments? Or would both of these different kinds of interactions be considered as problems you want to study? What will you consider as "solutions" to these problems?

3. Go into the field only after giving considerable time and thought to 1 and 2 above.

In the Field

It is essential that your retire to privacy from time to time or as soon as possible after your observation to write up your description. Keep a diary of events, separating your observations from your interpretations.

Endnotes

1. The diary of Bronislaw Malinowski, the famous English anthropologist, was published recently and a great many people, including social scientists, were shocked at the disclosures he made of his personal feelings about the Trobriand Islanders (Malinowski, 1967).
2. Anything that is out of the ordinary can affect the status quo of a group, and there may be less danger that a single observer will contaminate (or bias) the group's identity and integrity than would the artificiality of a laboratory experiment.

References

Baldwin, Monica (1959). *The Called and the Chosen*. New York: New American Library.
Becker, Howard S. (1963). *The Outsiders: Studies in the Sociology of Deviance*. New York: The Free Press.
Black, Jack (1927). *You Can't Win*. New York: Macmillan.
Blau, Peter (1967). "The Research Process in the Study of The Dynamics of Bureaucracy." pp. 18-57 in Philip E. Hammond (ed.), *Sociologists at Work: The Craft of Social Research*. Garden City, N.Y.: Doubleday.
Caudill, William (1958). *A Psychiatric Hospital as a Small Society*. Cambridge, Mass.: Harvard University Press.
Goffman, Erving (1961). *Asylums: Essays on the Social Situation of Mental Patients and Other Inmates*. Garden City, N.Y.: Doubleday.
LePlay, Frederic (1879). *Les Ouvriers Europeans*. Paris: Alfred Mame et Fils.
Lowry, Ritchie P. (1965). *Who's Running This Town?* New York: Harper and Row.
Malinowski, Bronislaw (1967). *A Diary in the Strict Sense of the Word*. New York: Harcourt, Brace and World.
Scott, Marvin B. (1968). *The Racing Game*. Chicago: Aldine.
Skolnick, Jerome H. (1966). *Justice Without Trial*. New York: Wiley.
Warner, William Lloyd, and J.O. Lew (1947). *The Social System of the Modern Factory*. New Haven, Conn.: Yale University Press.
Withers, Carl [James West, pseud.] (1945). *Plainville, U.S.A.* New York: Columbia University Press.

3

The Depth Interview

Jacqueline Aaron and Marcia Wiseman

The Depth Interview, a Definition

One of the major tools of the social scientist—the depth interview—is also a favourite of the average citizen. Everyone at one time or another has used this technique to learn more about a subject of interest. A person will start by asking someone general questions. As he receives answers, he follows up on certain points with increasingly specific questions until he has acquired "an understanding" of the topic.

Depth interviewing, as generally conducted by sociologists, has the same pattern as that used by a curious non-professional. The major difference is that the answers social researchers receive are usually carefully recorded and reviewed in terms of concepts and theories of concern to the discipline. As an exploratory tool, depth interviewing is a way to locate important information for further study. It can also become an end in itself—that is, a way to get detailed descriptions or even explanations of certain types of social behaviour.

The depth interview enables the investigator to probe the intensity of an individual's feelings about a given social phenomenon, the intricacies of his definition of it, and how he relates it to other areas of his social life.

Respondents will often give their judgments of what the attitudes of others are and how these affect their own attitudes and behaviour. Memories of past events (technically called retrospective longitudinal data) can be obtained through depth interviews, especially when respondents are allowed adequate time to recall past events and place them in proper order or perspective.

Depth interviewing can be viewed as a fishing expedition, because the sociologist does it to get information when he has so little knowledge on a subject that he cannot ask structured questions. He also uses it to obtain more detail than a formal questionnaire normally makes available. The depth interview is a major tool in the social sciences, one that every competent researcher should be able to handle.

How to Do Depth Interviewing

The researcher attempting a depth interview is initially faced with the problem of creating and maintaining personal rapport with the respondent. This is essential if the interviewee is to be able to express in detail his deepest thoughts and feelings. To obtain the rapport he needs, the depth interviewer must assure the respondent that his identity will be kept confidential, and that he is collecting the information as part of a legitimate research project. Throughout the interview, the social investigator must take pains to be as neutral as possible. He must resist the temptation to moralize, to give advice, or to otherwise indicate how he feels about the information given. Above all, he must encourage his respondent to keep talking. A nod of the head once in a while, to indicate understanding, is sufficient after a relationship has been established and answers are forthcoming. More reaction might interrupt the respondent's train of thought and elaboration of various points.

Because a depth interview will often last for over an hour, recording detailed answers can present problems. The tape recorder is often used, but it is by no means necessary. In fact many researchers avoid using it because of the time involved in typing tapes—approximately two to three times the length of the interview. There is also the fear that respondents may feel inhibited if they know they are being recorded, though most people forget the machine is there. Seasoned depth interviewers learn to write rapidly (using abbreviations and bits of shorthand) during an interview. They also find that respondents, far from being annoyed at the time it takes to write down their comments, are flattered that the investigator is taking pains to get what they say correctly.

Because depth interviewing is used to develop categories and hypotheses, the interviewer usually asks very general questions. "What's going on?" or some variation of this question was a favourite query of Howard Becker and his associates when they interviewed respondents for their study of the medical student world (Becker and Geer, 1960). Other examples of general questions (depending on the subject) are:

> Would you describe a typical day here to me?
> Tell me about the thoughts and reasons you had before doing _____.
> In general, how do you feel about _____?

The investigator may gradually focus a depth interview on those portions of the material about which he would like further information. To do this, he must be alert at all times for clues that could be pertinent to his problem. He may then ask more non-directive questions about these specific areas; for example:

> You say that a typical day here always includes _____ activity?
> Why is that? Do you participate? Why or why not?

A spot analysis of previous interviews will often reveal clues about the subject matter under investigation that can be followed up in greater detail in subsequent interviews. The more rechecking the interviewer does of past responses, the more he is able to determine areas that he has not covered or where he has only scratched the surface. Thus as the research progresses, the questions tend to become increasingly focused (Merton and Kendall, 1946).

Eventually the investigator returns to the field with a short list of topics to cover. For instance, a typical list of focused topics for a depth interview concerning the respondent's job might include:

> Describe a typical day here. (This is always a good opening question.)
> What is your job here? What do you do? How do you feel about your job?
> Why?
> Describe various supervisors (or top ranking employees) you see during the day. What are they like?
> What are the other employees like? What do you think of them? Why?

Note that even when the questions are concentrated on a special topic, the *tone* of the questions is as neutral and open as possible so as not to suggest answers. A questions like, "What do you think of it here?" is preferable to "Do you like it here?" The same principle applies to "probing"—that is, pursuing the answer to a question to be certain you have a complete understanding of it. The best probes do not suggest answers:

> Can you think of anything else to tell me about that?
> What are your reasons for feeling this way?
> Why do you think others do that?

The interviewer usually inserts a hash-mark "/" where he probed for more detail. A short excerpt from his verbatim notes of the respondent's answers might look like this:

> Well, this job pays well, but that's about all I can say for it. It's just a job, that's all./ Well, I can support my family, keep up on my bills. We aren't wanting for anything./ Well, what I mean about that's all that's good about the job is that it is

boring. It's the same thing day after day and there is not real hope for advancement to something more challenging./ Oh, you know, challenging to the mind, something that really interests me and makes me think about it and makes me feel proud of what I do. It doesn't offer that.

Advantages and Disadvantages

A researcher uses depth interviews rather than observation techniques when he decides that the only way to know what is on the subject's mind is to ask him. As we mentioned earlier, the researcher uses depth interviewing rather than the standard structured survey interview (especially those with fixed-choice answers) when he wants detail on social interactions and interrelated attitudes that he does not have and therefore cannot "build into" his questionnaire.

A major advantage of depth interviewing is its flexibility. Instead of going into the field with a narrow and specific hypothesis that he assumes to be the best approach to the study area, the researcher goes in with the idea of developing hypotheses and categories in the course of the investigation. He can, of course, narrow the topical scope of his inquiry to the subject of his interest; but the interview framework must not be so rigid as to prohibit consideration of all material a respondent offers on this subject. The goal, then, of this unstructured approach is to obtain information that cannot be anticipated.

Obviously depth interviewing, like observation, is time consuming. Often, in order to establish or maintain rapport, the investigator must allow the respondent to tell him many things he already knows about a given phenomenon before he can work his way to new material.

As with observation, the major disadvantage of depth interviewing is the difficulty of quantifying—or even organizing—data that was collected in semi-haphazard ways. There comes a time, however, when the mass of material must be put into some kind of logical order so that the investigator can present what he has learned in an understandable fashion. Usually this is accomplished by analysing the respondents' remarks for content that will become the focus of the report. The goal of the study offers some guidance here, but many of these decisions depend on the insight of the researcher.

Among the other arguments used against depth interviewing is the presumed inability of the average person to verbalize the "true" reasons for his decisions and actions. Researchers who believe people act for reasons they are not consciously aware of will use depth interviews—if they approve use of them at all—only to get at what they call "rationalizations." On the other hand, researchers who advocate depth interviews as a tool to study motivation are convinced that people do know why they act in certain ways. Therefore, they say, it would be less than professional to ignore a viable, worthwhile avenue to a respondent's thought processes.

Some Applications

A person in a social grouping will ordinarily have complex feelings of satisfaction and dissatisfaction about his role there. He is also usually concerned about the judgment of his "performance" by others, and about the possibilities of gaining friends and making enemies. Depth interviewing is applicable to topics where the actor's point of view and inner feelings are important to the research goals.

The depth approach has been used as a means of interviewing deviants such as prostitutes (Bryan, 1965), alcoholics (Wiseman, 1970), homosexuals (Hoffman, 1968), and felons (Irwin, 1970; Sykes, 1965). In the area of family interaction, where attitudes and emotions are crucial, the depth interview has also proved valuable (Hess and Handel, 1959). On an institutional level, students' feelings about their curricula, their instructors, and their classmates (Werthman, 1963) have been probed through the depth interview, as have the attitudes of employees toward their jobs and bosses (Roethlisberger and Dickson, 1939).

Depth interviews are also used in combination with observation techniques as an approach to data collection. Often the information obtained through these two methods will stimulate the researcher to conduct a broader survey on a larger sample of respondents using a structured questionnaire.

Before You Go into the Field

1. Select your specific topic of inquiry.
2. Think out a small number of neutral questions—six at most—that will lead your subject to talk about your topic. Jot these down in your interviewing notebook.
3. Decide whom you will need as respondents.

In the Field

1. As usual, you must gain access to subjects who have had experience with the topic of your interest. Tell a prospective respondent you are doing research on a given subject (make your description very general) and that you would appreciate interviewing him.
2. Once you have gained permission to interview a subject, it is important to gain rapport so that he will talk freely and comfortably with you. The best way to do this is to be courteous, interested in what he says, and non-judgmental regardless of your own feelings or beliefs.
3. Get repondent's answers as nearly verbatim as possible. This means in his own words, not in a summary composed by you. If you try to summarize his thoughts, there is a danger that you will give them meaning they did not actually possess.
4. If you feel you are holding up the interview by writing the answers, it often helps to say, "I hope you don't mind the delay. I want to be certain

to get all of your answer." An alternative is to write up the interview as soon as you are alone, counting on your memory for details, but this has definite liabilities.

Where you probe for more detail, insert a hash-mark to indicate that you interjected a "Why?" or "What are your reasons for feeling this way?" at that point in the interview.

5. Read over each interview before embarking on the next. Watch for points that you will want to follow up in this and subsequent interviews.

References

Becker, Howard S., and Blanche Geer (1960). "Participant Observation: The Analysis of Qualitative Field Data." pp. 267-289 in Richard H. Adams and Jack J. Preiss (eds.), *Human Organization Research*. Homewood, Ill.: Dorsey.

Bryan, James H. (1965). "Apprenticeship in Prostitution." *Social Problems* 12 (Winter): 287-297.

Hess, Robert D., and Gerald Handel (1959). *Family Worlds*. Chicago: University of Chicago Press.

Hoffman, Martin (1968). *The Gay World: Male Homosexuality and Social Creation of Evil*. New York: Basic Books.

Irwin, John (1970). *The Felon*. Englewood Cliffs, NJ.: Prentice Hall.

Merton, Robert K., and Patricia L. Kendall (1946). "The Focused Interview." *American Journal of Sociology* 51 (May): 541-557.

Roethlisberger, F.J., and W.J. Dickson (1939). *Management and the Worker*. Cambridge, MA: Harvard University Press.

Sykes, Gresham M. (1965). *The Society of Captives*. New York: Atheneum.

Werthman, Carl (1963). "Delinquents in Schools: A Test for the Legitimacy of Authority." *Berkeley Journal of Sociology* 8:39-60.

Wiseman, Jaqueline P. (1970). *Stations of the Lost*. Englewood Cliffs, N.J.: Prentice Hall.

4

Role Analysis

Jacqueline Aaron and Marcia Wiseman

Role Analysis, a Definition

Role analysis is concerned with the effects of fairly well-established social structures and their concomitant role relationships on the behaviour of participants. Just as social life is not carried out in a vacuum but reflects the characteristics of its physical settings, so it is also affected by the expectations that people have developed concerning the proper role behaviour for themselves and others. Thus, if a researcher can draw a map of socially important ecological elements such as barriers, pathways, hiding places, and conversation areas in a setting, he can also chart the role and counter-role relationships in society.

Sociologists have borrowed the term "role" from the theatre. It refers to a cluster of behaviour norms (rules) that apply to a given position in the social structure. These norms consist of a set of expectations by others that include not only how one should perform the role itself, but also how one should act toward others while performing it, and even how one should feel at the time. The term also includes the role occupant's expectations about how others should act toward him. These reciprocal norms usually remain consistent over time. Such interrelationships of role activities and the expectations it created mean that a noticeable deviation in behaviour is upsetting. Such complaints as "He doesn't act at all as a minister (or teacher, father, etc.) should act toward a parishioner (student, son)" reflect this disappointment in role enactment. The speaker is essentially arguing that the cluster of behaviours toward others by a minister and from others to a minister form a coherent whole that has social-psychological boundaries, so far as the expectations of others are concerned. This includes a minister's mode of dress, his behaviour and demeanour toward others, and his status vis-à-vis them.

Society is possible, in part, because people go about quietly fulfilling the role expectations of the different positions they occupy. Often we become consciously aware of what those role expectations are only when someone transgresses them. When a child "smarts off" to an adult, for instance, or a professor arrives at class "inappropriately" dressed, or a low-ranking employee gets "too friendly" with the boss at a company picnic, the discomfiture signals a digression from role expectations.

Role analysts believe the concept of "internalization" of role obligations can explain much of people's behaviour, and the motivations for this behaviour. We have all witnessed the socializing effect of roles on their occupants: the flighty young girl who marries and slowly takes on the role of "matron" because she believes it is expected of her; the vice president who is suddenly catapulted to power by the death of the president and begins to show qualities of statesmanship no one knew he possessed; the contestant who bravely acts the role of the gracious loser, because this is part of playing the game. Some of the most dramatic illustrations of the socializing effect of acquiring a social position with accompanying role expectations are to be found in literature and the theatre. In *Pygmalion*, and its musical counterpart, *My Fair Lady*, a lower-class woman is socialized to the role of "lady" and surprises everyone by feeling like one as well as acting the part. *Becket* is the story of a medieval playboy whose appointment to the position of Archbishop of Canterbury gradually socializes him to the point where he acts as is expected of a man in this position. Thus we often act to fulfil the expectations we believe others have of us.

How to Do Role Research and Analysis

Role analysis is not a method of data-gathering per se, but a conceptual and analytic tool. In action, it is an excellent illustration of the interplay between theory and method in research, because its concepts circumscribe the data to be gathered and direct the analysis.

The concept "role" is only one in a constellation of related terms used in role analysis to study the behaviour of individuals. These terms are:

Position: One's "situation" in the social structure.

Role: The dynamic or behavioural aspect of position.

Status: The evaluative aspect of position—whether others see it as "high" or "low."

Counter role: A role that is complementary to the role (that is, "completes" the dyadic interaction), allowing, by its existence, the enactment of the role. Teacher-pupil, parent-child, and clerk-customer are three pairs of counter roles that reinforce and make possible each other's performance.

Rights and obligations: Every role carries with it certain actions owed by others and to others. These are the shared expectations or ideal patterns of our own and counter role enactments that we carry in our heads.

Role perception: How one thinks of his social role, what he thinks he should be doing.

Role behaviour: Actual performance in a role. (Sometimes we fall below our own role expectations, or those of others. Sometimes we are gloriously successful—we "carry it off.")

Figure 1

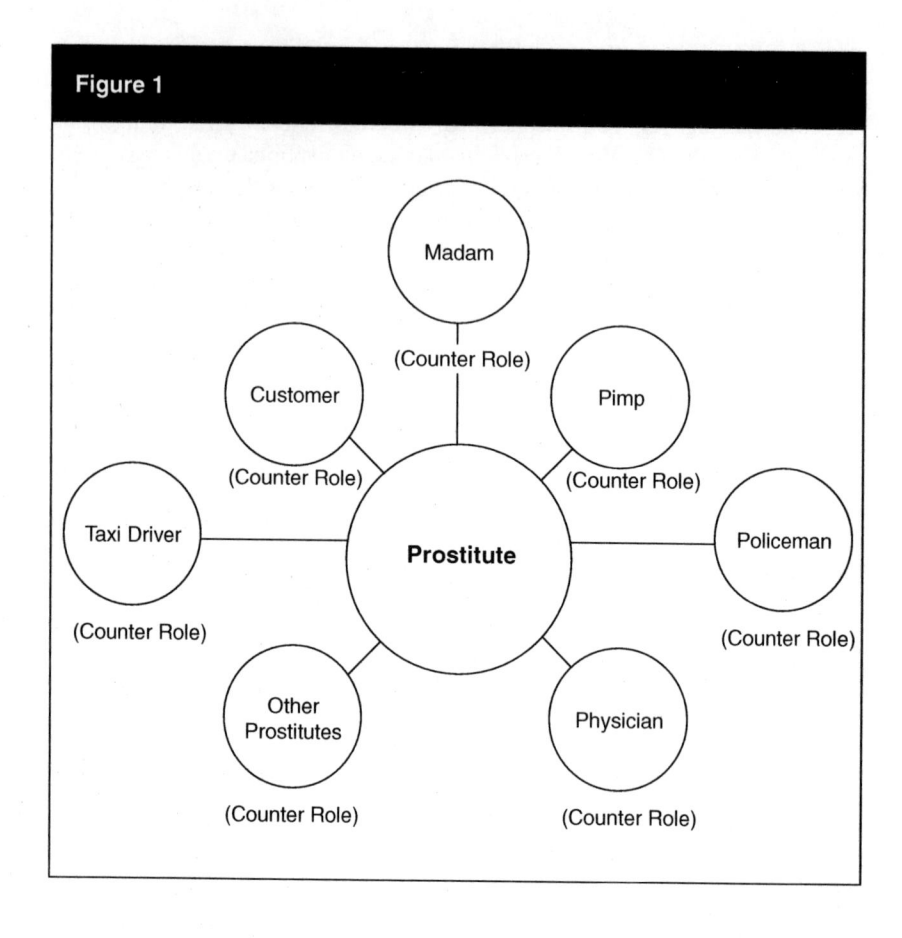

[Diagram: Central circle labeled "Prostitute" connected via (Counter Role) links to surrounding circles: Madam, Pimp, Policeman, Physician, Other Prostitutes, Taxi Driver, Customer.]

Role conflict: A situation in which a person finds that his proper enactment of one role results in falling below expectations in another. Thus, no matter what he does, he has some guilt feelings. (Women who are trying to be good mothers and good students too often experience such role conflict.)

Using these concepts as guides for data-gathering, the social scientist is able to take the information he obtains and map out a "role system" that can in turn be a useful device to alert the researcher to other areas of interaction that might be fruitfully investigated. For instance, Gross et al. (1958) suggested that one way to understand the pressures experienced by a school superintendent was first to map out the counter roles of positions relative to his, such as principles, teachers, school-board members, and students. In an analogous discussion of role and counter role, Merton (1957) uses as his illustration the student physician and focuses on persons who share the same small world—what he refers to as a "status set." In Merton's status set of the student physician, one finds physicians, nurses, social workers, medical technologists, and so on. Each of these, though fundamentally in the same "world" as the student physician (the "medical world"), looks at him from a different perspective and thus interacts with him in somewhat different ways and has somewhat different expectations of him as well.

Following Gross's or Merton's lead, in Figure 1 we have charted the counter roles of a prostitute. (It should be clear that the designations "central role" and "counter role" depend upon the researcher's interests. One man's counter role could be another's central role; thus the pimp could be in the focal position and the prostitute in a counter role if the pimp were the major research interest. Furthermore, counter-role occupants also interact with each other. These interactions may be included in or excluded from a research efforts, depending upon the goal of the study.)

Once the researcher has mapped out (literally and figuratively) the significant counter roles that are a part of the social situation under study, he can examine the behaviour of persons occupying these roles with the following questions in mind:

1. How do individuals in a counter-role relationship interact with each other? (Specific emphasis would be placed on interaction with the designated "central role.")
2. What unspoken expectations do they seem to have of each other? (As mentioned, moments of obviously violated expectations—noted because of the outrage expressed by one person in a role dyad—are very revealing in this area.) For instance, what is expected of a school superintendent? What happens if he falls below expectations?
3. How does each person in the role apparently see himself? How does he see others? For instance, how does a pimp see himself? How do others view him?
4. What expectations must be fulfilled for a role to be properly played? How much leeway in performance is permitted? For instance, how must a student physician act toward others in his set?
5. Is there any difference in the status of the roles under study? (Here look for signs of deference shown by one role occupant for another.) For instance, does one call the other "Sir?"
6. What sorts of sanctions, positive or negative, do role players use on each other? What does this reveal about variations in power of the roles (and status as well)? For instance, what threats can a superintendent use to keep teachers in line? And vice versa?
7. Are some roles more insulated from observation than others? How can such private areas be penetrated? Where, for instance, can interns relax together?
8. What sorts of "props"—clothing, language, demeanour, general appearance—do persons use to maintain themselves in their roles? How does a prostitute dress, for example?

9. What sorts of conflicts does a person with multiple role expectations experience? What, for example, happens when a school superintendent is torn between the expectations of the teachers and those of the school board?

How Can the Researcher Obtain Such Information?
1. *Observation* of persons enacting a role. This would include noting how persons in counter roles talk and act toward each other and attempting to catch their mutual expectations.
2. *Participant observation* in a role set. Here the investigator notes role players' reactions to him and other persons in roles, and from these experiences (and his reactions to others in the situation) he draws some descriptions of role enactment and expectations.
3. *Depth interview* with some persons in roles pertinent to the study. How do they see the role? What kinds of behaviour would they include in a proper enactment of it? The same sort of questions can be asked of pertinent counter-role occupants. This gives the investigator a feeling for the cluster of *normative expectations and counter expectations* found in constellations of role sets.

Advantages and Disadvantages

Perhaps the major advantage of role analysis is that a search for roles, counter roles, and the normative expectations incumbent upon each imposes an order on social life. Such organization aids the investigator to pull into a meaningful whole data about human group life that might otherwise appear to be bits and pieces of unrelated social behaviour. The very act of mapping roles and counter roles helps to locate explanations for such phenomena as patterns of deference and manipulation and brings possible areas of social conflict and other problems of interaction to the investigator's attention.

Role analysis furnishes clues to motivation that may not be physically evident to the sociologist in an interactional situation; yet he know these motives should be considered because people mentally refer to the expectations of others before acting. For instance, a person may think, "If I do something to satisfy Person A (in the counter role), what will Person B (in another counter role) think of me?" In other words, role analysis expands the boundaries of the investigation into the social-psychological histories of the actors involved.

As with all approaches to the understanding of social life, role analysis has its limitations. It can lull the investigator into perceiving a rather static social structure in which persons fulfil one role at a time for the continued successful existence of the social system. Some role theorists forget that social life is actually in a constant flux and that people may be able to play several roles simultaneously (an age role, a sex role, an occupational role, in addition to unique interpersonal roles with people). A single counter role may also have several, often contradictory, aspects rather than being the simple unity some researcher depicts.

Conceptually, the term "role" has become so popularized in sociology that almost any cluster of normative expectations has been called a role. These roles are not always tied in the same way to an actual position in the social structure, nor are their behavioural expectations equally formalized. For example, there are conventional occupational roles generally associated with employment that are well demarcated in the social structure and have rather well-defined behavioural expectations. On the other hand, age and sex roles have more nebulous behavioural boundaries, and the positions associated with them are quite loosely defined. Interpersonal roles (Shibutani, 1961: 323-366) established by the idiosyncratic relationships of people—such as the "fool" (Klapp, 1962) or the "tension manager" (Bales, 1950)—are so unusual that they have no formalized place in most social structures, but they still develop behavioural expectations among significant others.

The role analyst's most dangerous pitfall is to assume that all behaviour is role behaviour. People do act for other reasons than role expectations, and other types of theoretical approaches are often better for capturing these activities.

Some Applications

Role analysis is a useful approach to the study of how an individual is incorporated into any social structure, from the family and informal peer groups to such highly bureaucratized organizations as educational institutions and businesses. Social dilemmas can often be pinpointed through attention to problems of role conflict or role discontinuities. For instance, Komarovsky (1957) noted that college girls are expected to show an interest both in a career and in marriage, and that these two demands often cause problems and indecision about proper action, especially since it is considered impossible for a girl to be feminine and intelligent simultaneously. Role analyses of "middle-management" positions reveal the conflicting pressures exerted on their occupants. The foreman in a factory, for instance, deals simultaneously with executives and assembly-line workers. In attempting to cope with the problems of each, he often finds his loyalties torn, because he is in the difficult position of trying to fulfil the often conflicting demands of groups whose interests and perspectives frequently do not coincide (Roethlisberger, 1957).

Because a role can be viewed as a conceptual link between personality structure and social structure, a number of sociologists and social psychologists have been interested in the "fit" or "congruence" (or lack of it) between role demands and the personality of the individual in the role. Are bureaucratic personalities or organization men recruited, or are they created by the roles available to them? Are such roles eventually "internalized" to become the fulcrum of the person's outlook on life—the centre of his self-concept? Are people pushed into roles incompatible with their self-images? Erving Goffman (1961) has suggested that in such cases the social actor will display "role distance"—that is, public disdain for the role he is forced to play.

Some sociologists (called functionalists) are interested in what each role does to help maintain the social system, and how roles in a given system support each other. The roles in small social systems such as the family or some other primary group are often analysed—especially when there is a deviant member. Such analyses (Dentler and Erikson, 1959) may indicate that the deviant person is actually functional to the system, because his bad behaviour is the one thing other members can agree upon and rally against! Occupational roles in bureaucracies can also function to reduce strain for people who must work together despite personal animosity. This is because the occupant of a position in the social system can fill a role requirement without putting his total "self" into the performance.

Social psychologists are interested in how people apprehend what their actual behaviour in a role should be, and how they adjust and readjust their behaviour to the expectations and counter roles of others when the standards of acceptable role behaviour are nebulous. In pursuit of answers to these questions, researchers have looked at how people emulate role models (other people already in the role). Such studies often focus on mass media—movies, television, popular magazines, and newspapers—as the sources of models for individuals who wish to become something other than what they are.

Some psychologists feel that the measure of a person's successful socialization is his ability to stay in a role—that is, to act appropriately—regardless of inner tension (Sarbin, 1954). Children gradually develop this ability, a fact to which any parent who has given birthday parties over a period of years can testify. It has also been suggested (Brim, 1960) that the measure of a mature person is his ability to shift roles as the occasion demands—from boss at the office to loving husband at home, etc.

Before You Go into the Field

1. Decide on the role and counter-role interaction you wish to study.
2. Decide on the best setting for this study in terms of the role sets usually found there.
3. Decide on your method of gathering data. You may use more than one method if you wish. (Interviewing and observation complement each other nicely, for instance.) Remember, in asking questions the sociologist does not use technical terms, but devises laymen's substitutes. Therefore, you should not ask, "How do you see the role of mother as properly handled?" but rather, "What do you think makes for a good mother? A bad mother?" and so on.

References

Bales, Robert F. (1950). *Interaction Process Analysis.* Reading, MA: Addison-Wesley.
Brim, O.G. (1960). "Personality Development as Role Learning." pp. 127-159 in Ira Iscoe and Harold Stevenson (eds.), *Personality Development in Children.* Austin, Texas: University of Texas Press.
Dentler, Robert A., and Kai T. Erikson (1959). "The Functions of Deviance in Groups." *Social Problems* 7 (Fall): 98-107.
Goffman, Erving (1961). *Encounters.* Indianapolis, Ind.: Bobbs-Merrill.
Gross, Neal, W.L. Mason, and A.W. McEachern (1958). *Explorations in Role Analysis.* New York: Wiley.
Klapp, Orrin E. (1962). *Heroes, Villains, and Fools.* Englewood Cliffs, N.J.: Prentice Hall.
Komarovsky, Mirra (1957). "Cultural Contradictions and Sex Role." pp. 230-234 in R.W. O'Brien, C.C. Schrag, and W.T. Martin (eds.), *Readings in General Sociology.* Boston: Houghton Mifflin.
Merton, Robert K. (1957). "Role Sets." *British Journal of Sociology* 8 (June): 106-120.
Roethlisberger, F.J. (1957). "The Foreman." pp. 243-249 in R.W. O'Brien, C.C. Schrag, and W.T. Martin (eds.), *Readings in General Sociology.* Boston: Houghton Mifflin.
Sarbin, Theodore R. (1954). "Role Theory." pp. 223-258 in Gardner Lindzey (ed.), *Handbook of Social Psychology.* Reading, MA: Addison-Wesley.
Shibutani, Tamotsu (1961). *Society and Personality.* Englewood Cliffs. NJ: Prentice-Hall. pp. 323-366.

5
Content Analysis

Jacqueline Aaron and Marcia Wiseman

Content analysis is a technique that enables the sociologist to observe men's behavior in an indirect way, through an analysis of the things they write (their verbal symbols). The social researcher who uses content analysis as a method for gathering data is usually concerned with the manifest content of the written document—with that which is openly stated. It should be noted that a group's conscious and unconscious beliefs attitudes, values, and behavior patterns are revealed not only in newspapers, magazines, literature, drama, advertisements, and so on, but that such nonverbal symbols as architecture and art can also contain clues of society's life styles (Spengler, 1950).*

The sociologist assumes that communication both affects and is affected by the social environment. It follows, therefore, that an analysis of communication messages could reflect a great deal about human group life at any given point in time. To analyze these messages, the sociologist needs to order the vast amount of material available to him. So he develops pertinent categories that allow him to count or compare what he thinks is important. For example, what was the role of women in America in the mid-1800's? This is so far in the past that persons who could tell us about attitudes toward women in those days are no longer living. But the researcher could examine short stories in magazines of the decade 1850—1860 and, by using categories of the "types" of women portrayed—traditional housewife, mother, career girl, glamour girl, pal, and so on—he could tell us about the roles that women played or were supposed to play and the incidence of each.

It is apparent that by using this technique the investigator can observe, indirectly, anything from trends in child-rearing practices (comparison over time) to type of heroes preferred by people of different cultures (cross-cultural comparison). Material can be analyzed for propaganda content; differences can be revealed in the handling of the same event by mass media in different countries—or by different media in the same country. Or, through the analysis of literature and popular magazines, comic strips, cartoons, and movies, the researcher can reveal how countries differ in their emphasis on sex, crime, religion, ethnic groups, expressions of affection and love, or violence and hatred.

The rise and fall of fads can be noted. From these data, a researcher can make comparisons about the attitudes and beliefs of various groups of people separated by time, geographic locale, or culture.

How to do Content Analysis

Content analysis, like other techniques of collecting data by sociologists, is a refinement of ways used by the layman to describe and explain social phenomena and changes in the social world. For example, the parents of an unruly and aggressive boy may say the cause of his behavior is that there is "too much violence on television these days." Parents may blame the promiscuous behavior of their teen-age daughter on "all that sex in the magazines and movies." They may emphasize that "it wasn't this way when I was your age," much to their children's anger, disdain, or amusement. What the layman is saying is that—based on his impressions of the contents of television, movies, magazines, and other mass media—there is a greater emphasis on violence and sex now than in his own formative years. He is also saying that the contents of mass media influence the behavior of his children.

The social researcher also looks at mass media (as well as other types of symbols) to try to describe their contents. He too makes some assumptions about change over time and the impact the material could be having on the audience it reaches. The major difference between a layman's intuitive impressions and the sociologist's approach is that the sociologist tries to describe the messages contained in these communications in an objective and systematic way. The sociologist tries to define as precisely as possible what aspects of the content he is going to investigate and then to formulate categories that are relevant to his investigation—categories that are so explicit that another analyst could use them to examine the same material and obtain substantially the same results—that is, find the same proportion of topics emphasized or ignored. This introduces a second characteristic of content analysis—*quantification*. Each time a unit in a pertinent category is found it is "counted."

Counting certain words, for instance, may be an important way to analyze content if he is interested in determining the prevalence of terms that convey group stereotypes or that have loaded emotional overtones.... For example, the words "black" and "Negro" in a magazine (or magazines, depending on the sample) could be tallied to see if there had been a significant shift in the preference of one word over the other in a specified period of time.

It may be that the researcher wants to determine certain characteristics of a specific group. For example, he might want to compare short stories in women's magazines to see what kinds of heroes are presented to the readers. He would first select his sample—that is, which magazines he would read, over what time period, and which issues (for instance, 25 issues of each magazine between 1945 and 1965, selected by a set of random numbers). He could then formulate tentative categories representing characteristics of heroes, which might include physical, emotional, social and personality characteristics. These in turn he would break down into even smaller coding units such as:

Physical Characteristics	Emotional Characteristics	Social Characteristics
Color of hair	Warm	Race
Color of eyes	Aloof	Religion
Height	Stable, secure	Occupation
Weight	Anxious, insecure	Income
Age	Hostile	Housing
Scars	etc.	etc.
etc.		

A third possibility for category creation might be to attempt to isolate the major ideas, values, attitudes, or behavior patterns expressed in some communication. The sociologist could want to see if there are different attitudes expressed toward intimate human relationships described in the mass media of the United States, England, France, and Sweden. Films would be an excellent and accessible source for this analysis, though obviously the categories and coding units within each category would be much more difficult to formulate (not to mention the problem of taking notes in the dark), but it could be done. For instance, three general categories could be formed using Karen Horney's typology (1945) of relationships: "going toward," "going away from," and "going against." The researcher would then look for instances of these concepts expressed in the movies. Such units of behavior as hitting or slapping someone, sarcasm, aloof behavior, and holding hands or kissing are illustrations of possible categories.

A final way to analyze the content of mass media is to use "space" or "time" units. For example, in the past few years, how many inches or newsprint have been devoted to student demonstrations on campuses? How many minutes have television news programs devoted to the riots in Watts or Chicago?

Advantages and Disadvantages

As we have indicated, much of what we know is obtained, not through direct interaction with others, but through books, newspapers, and other symbolic products of man. One of the major advantages of content analysis is that the researcher can delve into past records and documents in order to get some feeling for the social life of an earlier day. He is not limited by time and space to the study of present events.

Content analysis is also useful because it is an unobtrusive measure (Webb et al., 1966); the investigator can "observe" without being observed, since mass media are not influenced by the investigator's presence. Information that might be difficult or impossible to obtain through direct observation or interview techniques can be gained through available communication material without the producer's awareness of its being examined. Finally, since the data is always available (except for television and movies, and even these media offer reruns), the method allows replication of a study by other researchers.

There are major disadvantages to content analysis too. Foremost is its limited nature. If we are studying the past, we normally have records only of what has survived or what was though to be sufficient importance to write down. Since each generation has a somewhat different perspective, what may be considered important today might not be available from years past. Parallel to this disadvantage is the possibility that what mass media present are often an ideal nature, in the sense that media reflect cultural ideals rather than actual activities. To offset this kind of bias, an investigator might wish to check his analysis of mass media against a content analysis of letters and diaries of the times (if they are available), on the assumption that personal documents are more forthright about what human group life was really like in those days than materials produced for public consumption. (This assumption may not always be warranted, however.)

Finally, there is sometimes a temptation among social scientists to consider that the data gleaned from a content analysis were *causes* of social phenomena rather than reflections of them. For example, violence in the mass media may be pointed to as a cause of violence in the streets (Wertham, 1954), but a more reasonable conclusion is that mass media both reflect and change the social world around us. Certainly much work has to be done to determine the relationship between mass media and human behavior. For example, some people think that reading pornographic books and magazines causes decay in the moral fiber of all individuals who read them. It is up to the sociologists, however, to check out such assumptions by finding out who the targets of the message-makers are, whether these targets are reached, and what effect, if any, the message has.* Pornography may (and probably does) affect groups differently because of such factors as selective perception, group affiliation, and past experience.

Some Applications

Content analysis is a technique that has almost unlimited applicability in social research. It can be used as the primary method to:
1. Describe trends in science, leisure, politics, and human relationships (Bronfenbrenner, 1958; Lowenthal, 1950; Rosen, 1964).
2. Reveal propaganda themes (Evans, 1967; Stewart, 1964; Berelson, 1964).
3. Show how different levels of communication media handle the same material (Winick, 196).
4. Infer attitudes, values, and cultural patterns of historical and foreign

peoples (McClelland, 1961; Sebald, 1962).
5. Compare the myths people hold of their cultural past with historical records and documents (Lowry, 1965; Lantz et al., 1968).

Content analysis can also be used to supplement other, more direct methods of research. Attitudes toward women who are working in so-called men's occupations can be investigated in a variety of ways: by questionnaire, depth interview, participant observation, and content analysis of magazines, television, newspapers, films, and autobiographies that touch on this subject. The "boss lady" stereotype may be more a creation of the media than a case of spontaneous social typing. Once established, however, it creates expectations in others about women in executive positions.

Content analysis can also be used to give the researcher insight into problems or hypotheses he can test by a more direct method. A sociologist might analyze the content of an underground newspaper to obtain information for use in devising questionnaires or formulating questions for depth interviews with youth.

Finally, content analysis can be used to make practical decisions. For example, a recent study by the Federal communications Commission determined the percentage of television time the major networks throughout the United States gave to cigarette commercials, as compared to the time allowed for warnings against the use of cigarettes for health reasons. The results led to the threat of loss of license for several television stations because of unequal time allotment.

Project Assignment

You are to do a content analysis of some aspect of collective behavior as described by the mass media. For your data you may select one topic below and do a comparative analysis as described:
1. The major themes in the fiction of two different kinds of popular magazines. For example: Playboy and Ladies' Home Journal, McCall's and True Confessions, etc. (One issue of each magazine you select is sufficient.)
2. The types of news emphasized in two daily newspapers—one issue each, a current issue and an issue of fifty years ago.
3. The general subject matter of a foreign film (Swedish, French, Italian) and an American film.
4. The cartoons in two issues of the New Yorker (one a current issue and the other a ten-year-old issue), or of an issue of Punch and an issue of the New Yorker for the same year.
5. Three thirty-minute television news broadcasts, two during the week and one on a weekend.
6. The fads or fashions being created—aside from the product advertised—on television commercials; i.e., the fashions worn by models, male and female; the way mothers speak to children, and so on.

Steps for the Content Analysis

A. Before You Go into the Field

1. Choose one of the topics in the project assignment.
2. Formulate a problem or hypothesis that will allow a comparison between two groups or two types of activities. For example: a comparison between television time devoted to demonstrations versus time devoted to sports.
3. Decide on the content you want to describe. What categories are you going to use? Do you want to study riots? Fashions? Fads?
4. Decide on your unit of analysis. What will you "count"? All advertisements in the magazine that pertain to clothing styles or only the color ads? All news dealing with collective behavior, or only that mentioning demonstrations and protests?

Endnote

* The identification of the message-makers and their targets and a determination of their degree of influence are also integral parts of content analysis, but these topics will not be dealt with here.

Selected Bibliography

A. Methodology

Berelson, Bernard. 1952. *Content Analysis in Communication Research*. New York: Free Press

Cartwright, Dorwin P. 1953. "Analysis of qualitative material." Pp. 421-470 in Leon Festinger and Daniel Katz (eds.), *Research Methods in the Behavioral Sciences*. New York: Dryden.

Holsti, Ole R., with the collaboration of Joanne K. Loomba and Robert C. North. 1968. "Content analysis." Pp. 596-692 in Gardner Lindzey and Elliot Aronson (eds.), *The Handbook of Social Psychology 2*. Reading, Mass.: Addison-Wesley.

Lasswell, Harold D., and Nathan Leites (eds.). 1949. *Language of Politics*. New York: George W. Stewart.

McGranahan, Donald V. 1951. "Content analysis of the mass media of communication." Pp. 539-560 in Marie Jahoda, Morton Deutsch and Stuart W. Cook (eds.), *Research Methods in Social Relations*. New York: Dryden.

Webb, Eugene, and Donald T. Campbell, Richard D. Schwartz, and Lee Sechrest. 1966. *Unobtrusive measures; Nonreactive Research in Social Science*, Chicago: Rand McNally

B. References and Studies

Albrecht, Milton C. 1956. "Does literature reflect common values?" *American Sociological Review* 21 (December): 722-729

Berelson, Bernard, and Patricia J. Salter. 1946. "Majority and minority Americans: an analysis of magazine fiction." *Public Opinion Quarterly* 10 (Summer): 108-190.

Berkman, Dave. 1963. "Advertising in Ebony and Life: Negro aspirations vs. reality." *Journalism Quarterly* 40 (Winter): 53-64.

Bronfenbrenner, Urie. 1958. "Socialization through time and space." Pp. 400-425 in Eleanor E. Maccoby, Theodore M. Newcomb, and Eugene O. Hartz (eds.), *Readings in Social Psychology*. New York: Holt, Rinehart & Winston.

DeCharms, Richard, and Gerald H. Moeller. 1962. "Values expressed in American children's readers: 1900-1950." *Journal of Abnormal and Social Psychology* 64 (February): 136-142.

DeFleur, Melvin L. 1964. "Occupational roles as portrayed on television." *Public Opinion Quarterly* 28 (Spring): 57-74

Evans, James F. 1967. "What the church tells children in story and song." *Journalism Quarterly* 44 (Autumn): 513-519.

Hoopes, Paul R. 1966. "Content analysis of news in three Argentine dailies." *Journalism Quarterly* 43 (Autumn): 534-537

Horney, Karen. 1945. *Our Inner Conflicts*. New York: Norton.

Lantz, Herman R., Eloise C. Snyder, Margaret Britton, and Raymond Schmitt. 1968. "Pre-industrial patterns in the colonial family in America: a content analysis of colonial magazines." *American Sociological Review* 33 (June): 413-426.

Lowenthal, Leo. 1950. "Biographies in popular magazines." Pp. 289-298 in Bernard Berelson and Morris Janowitz (eds.), *Reader in Public Opinion and Communication*. Glencoe, Ill.: Free Press.

Lowry, Ritchie P. 1965. *Who's Running this Town?* New York: Harper & Row.

McClelland, David C. 1961. *The Achieving Society*. Princeton, N.J.: Van Nostrand.

Rosen, Bernard. 1964. "Attitude changes within the Negro press toward segregation and discrimination." *Journal of Social Psychology* 62 (February): 77-83

Sebald, H. 1962. "Studying national character through comparative content analysis." *Social Forces* 40 (May): 318-322.

Spengler, Oswald. 1926. *The Decline of the West*. Authorized translation with notes by Charles Frances Atkinson. New York: Knopf.

Stewart, James S. 1964. "Content and readership of teen magazines." *Journalism Quarterly* 41 (Autumn): 580-583

Wertham, Frederic. 1954. *Seduction of the Innocent*. New York: Holt, Rinehart & Winston.

Winick, Charles. 1963. "Trends in the occupations of celebrities—a study of news profiles and television interviews." *Journal of Social Psychology* 60 (August): 301-310.